ANDROID SECURITY INTERNALS

ANDROID SECURITY INTERNALS

An In-Depth Guide to Android's Security Architecture

by Nikolay Elenkov

no starch press

San Francisco

Printed in USA

First printing

18 17 16 15 14   1 2 3 4 5 6 7 8 9

Text stock is SFI certified

ISBN-10: 1-59327-581-1
ISBN-13: 978-1-59327-581-5

Publisher: William Pollock
Production Editor: Alison Law
Cover Illustration: Garry Booth
Interior Design: Octopod Studios
Developmental Editor: William Pollock
Technical Reviewer: Kenny Root
Copyeditor: Gillian McGarvey
Compositor: Susan Glinert Stevens
Proofreader: James Fraleigh
Indexer: BIM Proofreading & Indexing Services

For information on distribution, translations, or bulk sales, please contact No Starch Press, Inc. directly:

No Starch Press, Inc.
245 8th Street, San Francisco, CA 94103
phone: 415.863.9900; info@nostarch.com
www.nostarch.com

Library of Congress Control Number: 2014952666

About the Author

Nikolay Elenkov has been working on enterprise security projects for the past 10 years. He has developed security software on various platforms, ranging from smart cards and HSMs to Windows and Linux servers. He became interested in Android shortly after the initial public release and has been developing applications for it since version 1.5. Nikolay's interest in Android internals intensified after the release of Android 4.0 (Ice Cream Sandwich), and for the past three years he's been documenting his findings and writing about Android security on his blog, *http://nelenkov.blogspot.com/*.

About the Technical Reviewer

Kenny Root has been a core contributor to the Android platform at Google since 2009, where his focus has been primarily on security and cryptography. He is the author of ConnectBot, the first SSH app for Android, and is an avid open source contributor. When he's not hacking on software, he's spending time with his wife and two boys. He is an alumnus of Stanford University, Columbia University, Chinese University of Hong Kong, and Baker College, but he's originally from Kansas City, which has the best barbecue.

BRIEF CONTENTS

CONTENTS IN DETAIL

3 PACKAGE MANAGEMENT 51

4 USER MANAGEMENT 87

6
NETWORK SECURITY AND PKI 145

7
CREDENTIAL STORAGE 171

8
ONLINE ACCOUNT MANAGEMENT 191

9
ENTERPRISE SECURITY 215

10
DEVICE SECURITY 251

FOREWORD

I first became aware of the quality of Nikolay's work in Android security with the release of Android 4.0, Ice Cream Sandwich. I needed a better explanation of the new Android backup format; I was struggling to exploit a vulnerability I had found, because I didn't have a full grasp of the new feature and format. His clear, in-depth explanation helped me understand the issue, exploit the vulnerability, and get a patch into production devices quickly. I have since been a frequent visitor to his blog, often referring to it when I need a refresher.

While I was honored to be asked to write this foreword, I honestly didn't believe I'd learn much from the book because I've been working on Android security for many years. This belief could not have been more wrong. As I read and digested new information regarding subjects I thought I knew thoroughly, my mind whirled with thoughts of what I had missed and what I could have done better. Why wasn't a reference like this available when I first engrossed myself in Android?

This book exposes the reader to a wide range of security topics, from Android permissions and sandboxing to the Android SELinux implementation, SEAndroid. It provides excellent explanations of minute details and rarely seen features such as dm-verify. Like me, you'll walk away from this book with a better understanding of Android security features.

Android Security Internals has earned a permanent spot on my office bookshelf.

Jon "jcase" Sawyer
CTO, Applied Cybersecurity LLC
Port Angeles, WA

ACKNOWLEDGMENTS

I would like to thank everyone at No Starch Press who worked on this book. Special thanks to Bill Pollock for making my ramblings readable and to Alison Law for her patience in turning them into an actual book.

A big thanks to Kenny Root for reviewing all chapters and sharing the backstories behind some of Android's security features.

Thanks to Jorrit "Chainfire" Jongma for maintaining SuperSU, which has been an invaluable tool for poking at Android's internals, and for reviewing my coverage of it in Chapter 13.

Thanks to Jon "jcase" Sawyer for continuing to challenge our assumptions about Android security and for contributing a foreword to my book.

INTRODUCTION

In a relatively short period of time, Android has become the world's most popular mobile platform. Although originally designed for smartphones, it now powers tablets, TVs, and wearable devices, and will soon even be found in cars. Android is being developed at a breathtaking pace, with an average of two major releases per year. Each new release brings a better UI, performance improvements, and a host of new user-facing features which are typically blogged about and dissected in excruciating detail by Android enthusiasts.

One aspect of the Android platform that has seen major improvements over the last few years, but which has received little public attention, is security. Over the years, Android has become more resistant to common exploit techniques (such as buffer overflows), its application isolation (sandboxing) has been reinforced, and its attack surface has been considerably reduced by aggressively decreasing the number of system processes that run as root. In addition to these exploit mitigations, recent versions of Android have introduced major new security features such as restricted user support, full-disk encryption, hardware-backed credential storage, and support for centralized device management and provisioning. Even more enterprise-oriented features and security improvements such as managed profile support, improved full-disk encryption, and support for biometric authentication have been announced for the next Android release (referred to as *Android L* as I write this).

As with any new platform feature, discussing cutting-edge security improvements is exciting, but it's arguably more important to understand Android's security architecture from the bottom up because each new security feature builds upon and integrates with the platform's core security model. Android's sandboxing model (in which each application runs as a separate Linux user and has a dedicated data directory) and permission system (which requires each application to explicitly declare the platform features it requires) are fairly well understood and documented. However, the internals of other fundamental platform features that have an impact on device security, such as package management and code signing, are largely treated as a black box beyond the security research community.

One of the reasons for Android's popularity is the relative ease with which a device can be "flashed" with a custom build of Android, "rooted" by applying a third-party update package, or otherwise customized. Android enthusiast forums and blogs feature many practical "How to" guides that take users through the steps necessary to unlock a device and apply various customization packages, but they offer very little structured information about how such system updates operate under the hood and what risks they carry.

This books aims to fill these gaps by providing an exploration of how Android works by describing its security architecture from the bottom up and delving deep into the implementation of major Android subsystems and components that relate to device and data security. The coverage includes broad topics that affect all applications, such as package and user management, permissions and device policy, as well as more specific ones such as cryptographic providers, credential storage, and support for secure elements.

It's not uncommon for entire Android subsystems to be replaced or rewritten between releases, but security-related development is conservative by nature, and while the described behavior might be changed or augmented across releases, Android's core security architecture should remain fairly stable in future releases.

Who This Book Is For

This book should be useful to anyone interested in learning more about Android's security architecture. Both security researchers looking to evaluate the security level of Android as a whole or of a specific subsystem and platform developers working on customizing and extending Android will find the high-level description of each security feature and the provided implementation details to be a useful starting point for understanding the underlying platform source code. Application developers can gain a deeper understanding of how the platform works, which will enable them to write more secure applications and take better advantage of the security-related APIs that the platform provides. While some parts of the book are accessible to a non-technical audience, the bulk of the discussion is closely tied to Android source code or system files, so familiarity with the core concepts of software development in a Unix environment is useful.

Prerequisites

The book assumes basic familiarity with Unix-style operating systems, preferably Linux, and does not explain common concepts such as processes, user groups, file permissions, and so on. Linux-specific or recently added OS features (such as capability and mount namespaces) are generally introduced briefly before discussing Android subsystems that use them. Most of the presented platform code comes from core Android daemons (usually implemented in C or C++) and system services (usually implemented in Java), so basic familiarity with at least one of these languages is also required. Some code examples feature sequences of Linux system calls, so familiarity with Linux system programming can be helpful in understanding the code, but is not absolutely required. Finally, while the basic structure and core components (such as activities and services) of Android apps are briefly described in the initial chapters, basic understanding of Android development is assumed.

Android Versions

The description of Android's architecture and implementation in this book (except for several proprietary Google features) is based on source code publicly released as part of the Android Open Source Project (AOSP). Most of the discussion and code excerpts reference Android 4.4, which is the latest publicly available version released with source code at the time of this writing. The master branch of AOSP is also referenced a few times, because commits to master are generally a good indicator of the direction future Android releases will take. However, not all changes to the master branch are incorporated in public releases as is, so it's quite possible that future releases will change and even remove some of the presented functionality.

A developer preview version of the next Android release (Android L, mentioned earlier) was announced shortly after the draft of this book was completed. However, as of this writing, the full source code of Android L is not available and its exact public release date is unknown. While the preview release does include some new security features, such as improvements to device encryption, managed profiles, and device management, none of these features are final and so are subject to change. That is why this book does not discuss any of these new features. Although we could introduce some of Android L's security improvements based on their observed behavior, without the underlying source code, any discussion about their implementation would be incomplete and speculative.

How Is This Book Organized?

This book consists of 13 chapters that are designed to be read in sequence. Each chapter discusses a different aspect or feature of Android security, and subsequent chapters build on the concepts introduced by their predecessors. Even if you're already familiar with Android's architecture and security model and are looking for details about a specific topic, you should at least skim Chapters 1 through 3 because the topics they cover form the foundation for the rest of the book.

- **Chapter 1: Android's Security Model** gives a high-level overview of Android's architecture and security model.
- **Chapter 2: Permissions** describes how Android permissions are declared, used, and enforced by the system.
- **Chapter 3: Package Management** discusses code signing and details how Android's application installation and management process works.
- **Chapter 4: User Management** explores Android's multi-user support and describes how data isolation is implemented on multi-user devices.
- **Chapter 5: Cryptographic Providers** gives an overview of the Java Cryptography Architecture (JCA) framework and describes Android's JCA cryptographic providers.
- **Chapter 6: Network Security and PKI** introduces the architecture of the Java Secure Socket Extension (JSSE) framework and delves into its Android implementation.
- **Chapter 7: Credential Storage** explores Android's credential store and introduces the APIs it provides to applications that need to store cryptographic keys securely.
- **Chapter 8: Online Account Management** discusses Android's online account management framework and shows how support for Google accounts is integrated into Android.
- **Chapter 9: Enterprise Security** presents Android's device management framework, details how VPN support is implemented, and delves into Android's support for the Extensible Authentication Protocol (EAP).
- **Chapter 10: Device Security** introduces verified boot, disk encryption, and Android's lockscreen implementation, and shows how secure USB debugging and encrypted device backups are implemented.
- **Chapter 11: NFC and Secure Elements** gives an overview of Android's NFC stack, delves into secure element (SE) integration and APIs, and introduces host-based card emulation (HCE).
- **Chapter 12: SELinux** starts with a brief introduction to SELinux's architecture and policy language, details the changes made to SELinux in order to integrate it in Android, and gives an overview of Android's base SELinux policy.

- **Chapter 13: System Updates and Root Access** discusses how Android's bootloader and recovery OS are used to perform full system updates, and details how root access can be obtained on both engineering and production Android builds.

Conventions

Because the main topic of this book is Android's architecture and implementation, it contains multiple code excerpts and file listings, which are extensively referenced in the sections that follow each listing or code example. A few format conventions are used to set those references (which typically include multiple OS or programming language constructs) apart from the rest of the text.

Commands; function and variable names; XML attributes; and SQL object names are set in `monospace` (for example: "the `id` command," "the `getCallingUid()` method," "the `name` attribute," and so on). The names of files and directories, Linux users and groups, processes, and other OS objects are set in *italic* (for example: "the *packages.xml* file," "the *system* user," "the *vold* daemon," and so on). String literals are also set in *italic* (for example: "the *AndroidOpenSSL* provider"). If you use such string literals in a program, you typically need to enclose them in double or single quotes (for example: `Signature.getInstance("SHA1withRSA", "AndroidOpenSSL")`).

Java class names are typically in their unqualified format without the package name (for example: "the `Binder` class"); fully qualified names are only used when multiple classes with the same name exist in the discussed API or package, or when specifying the containing package is otherwise important (for example: "the `javax.net.ssl.SSLSocketFactory` class"). When referenced in the text, function and method names are shown with parentheses, but their parameters are typically omitted for brevity (for example: "the `getInstance()` factory method"). See the relevant reference documentation for the full function or method signature.

Most chapters include diagrams that illustrate the architecture or structure of the discussed security subsystem or component. All diagrams follow an informal "boxes and arrows" style and do not conform strictly to a particular format. That said, most diagrams borrow ideas from UML class and deployment diagrams, and boxes typically represent classes or objects, while arrows represent dependency or communication paths.

1

ANDROID'S SECURITY MODEL

This chapter will first briefly introduce Android's architecture, inter-process communication (IPC) mechanism, and main components. We then describe Android's security model and how it relates to the underlying Linux security infrastructure and code signing. We conclude with a brief overview of some newer additions to Android's security model, namely multi-user support, mandatory access control (MAC) based on SELinux, and verified boot. Android's architecture and security model are built on top of the traditional Unix process, user, and file paradigm, but this paradigm is not described from scratch here. We assume a basic familiarity with Unix-like systems, particularly Linux.

Android's Architecture

Let's briefly examine Android's architecture from the bottom up. Figure 1-1 shows a simplified representation of the Android stack.

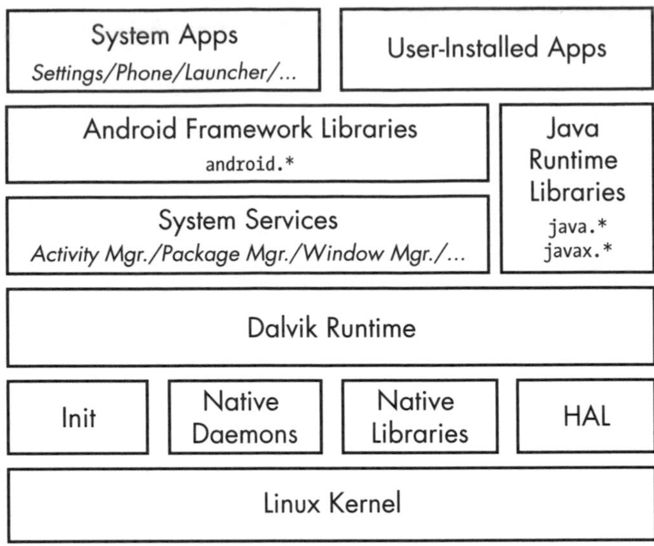

Figure 1-1: The Android architecture

Linux Kernel

As you can see in Figure 1-1, Android is built on top of the Linux kernel. As in any Unix system, the kernel provides drivers for hardware, networking, file-system access, and process management. Thanks to the Android Mainlining Project,[1] you can now run Android with a recent vanilla kernel (with some effort), but an Android kernel is slightly different from a "regular" Linux kernel that you might find on a desktop machine or a non-Android embedded device. The differences are due to a set of new features (sometimes called *Androidisms*[2]) that were originally added to support Android. Some of the main Androidisms are the low memory killer, wakelocks (integrated as part of wakeup sources support in the mainline Linux kernel), anonymous shared memory (ashmem), alarms, paranoid networking, and Binder.

The most important Androidisms for our discussion are Binder and paranoid networking. Binder implements IPC and an associated security mechanism, which we discuss in more detail on page 5. Paranoid networking restricts access to network sockets to applications that hold specific permissions. We delve deeper into this topic in Chapter 2.

Native Userspace

On top of the kernel is the native userspace layer, consisting of the *init* binary (the first process started, which starts all other processes), several native daemons, and a few hundred native libraries that are used throughout the system. While the presence of an *init* binary and daemons is reminiscent

1. *Android Mainlining Project, http://elinux.org/Android_Mainlining_Project*

2. For a more detailed discussion of Androidisms, see Karim Yaghmour's *Embedded Android*, O'Reilly, 2013, pp. 29–38.

of a traditional Linux system, note that both *init* and the associated startup scripts have been developed from scratch and are quite different from their mainline Linux counterparts.

Dalvik VM

The bulk of Android is implemented in Java and as such is executed by a Java Virtual Machine (JVM). Android's current Java VM implementation is called *Dalvik* and it is the next layer in our stack. Dalvik was designed with mobile devices in mind and cannot run Java bytecode (*.class* files) directly: its native input format is called *Dalvik Executable (DEX)* and is packaged in *.dex* files. In turn, *.dex* files are packaged either inside system Java libraries (JAR files), or inside Android applications (APK files, discussed in Chapter 3).

Dalvik and Oracle's JVM have different architectures—register-based in Dalvik versus stack-based in the JVM—and different instruction sets. Let's look at a simple example to illustrate the differences between the two VMs (see Listing 1-1).

```
public static int add(int i, int j) {
    return i + j;
}
```

Listing 1-1: Static Java method that adds two integers

When compiled for each VM, the `add()` static method, which simply adds two integers and returns the result, would generate the bytecode shown in Figure 1-2.

JVM Bytecode

```
public static int add(int, int);
  Code:
     0: iload_0❶
     1: iload_1❷
     2: iadd❸
     3: ireturn❹
```

Dalvik Bytecode

```
.method public static add(II)I

    add-int v0, p0, p1❺


    return v0❻
.end method
```

Figure 1-2: JVM and Dalvik bytecode

Here, the JVM uses two instructions to load the parameters onto the stack (❶ and ❷), then executes the addition ❸, and finally returns the result ❹. In contrast, Dalvik uses a single instruction to add parameters (in registers *p0* and *p1*) and puts the result in the *v0* register ❺. Finally, it returns the contents of the *v0* register ❻. As you can see, Dalvik uses fewer instructions to achieve the same result. Generally speaking, register-based VMs use fewer instructions, but the resulting code is larger than the corresponding code in a stack-based VM. However, on most architectures, loading code is less expensive than instruction dispatch, so register-based VMs can be interpreted more efficiently.[3]

In most production devices, system libraries and preinstalled applications do not contain device-independent DEX code directly. As a performance optimization, DEX code is converted to a device-dependent format and stored in an Optimized DEX (*.odex*) file, which typically resides in the same directory as its parent JAR or APK file. A similar optimization process is performed for user-installed applications at install time.

Java Runtime Libraries

A Java language implementation requires a set of runtime libraries, defined mostly in the `java.*` and `javax.*` packages. Android's core Java libraries are originally derived from the Apache Harmony project[4] and are the next layer on our stack. As Android has evolved, the original Harmony code has changed significantly. In the process, some features have been replaced entirely (such as internationalization support, the cryptographic provider, and some related classes), while others have been extended and improved. The core libraries are developed mostly in Java, but they have some native code dependencies as well. Native code is linked into Android's Java libraries using the standard *Java Native Interface (JNI)*,[5] which allows Java code to call native code and vice versa. The Java runtime libraries layer is directly accessed both from system services and applications.

System Services

The layers introduced up until now make up the plumbing necessary to implement the core of Android—system services. *System services* (79 as of version 4.4) implement most of the fundamental Android features, including display and touch screen support, telephony, and network connectivity. Most system services are implemented in Java; some fundamental ones are written in native code.

With a few exceptions, each system service defines a remote interface that can be called from other services and applications. Coupled with the service discovery, mediation, and IPC provided by Binder, system services effectively implement an object-oriented OS on top of Linux.

Let's look at how Binder enables IPC on Android in detail, as this is one of the cornerstones of Android's security model.

Inter-Process Communication

As mentioned previously, Binder is an inter-process communication (IPC) mechanism. Before getting into detail about how Binder works, let's briefly review IPC.

---

3. Yunhe Shi et al., *Virtual Machine Showdown: Stack Versus Registers, https://www.usenix.org/legacy/events/vee05/full_papers/p153-yunhe.pdf*

4. The Apache Software Foundation, *Apache Harmony, http://harmony.apache.org/*

5. Oracle, *Java™ Native Interface, http://docs.oracle.com/javase/7/docs/technotes/guides/jni/*

As in any Unix-like system, processes in Android have separate address spaces and a process cannot directly access another process's memory (this is called *process isolation*). This is usually a good thing, both for stability and security reasons: multiple processes modifying the same memory can be catastrophic, and you don't want a potentially rogue process that was started by another user to dump your email by accessing your mail client's memory. However, if a process wants to offer some useful service(s) to other processes, it needs to provide some mechanism that allows other processes to discover and interact with those services. That mechanism is referred to as *IPC*.

The need for a standard IPC mechanism is not new, so several options predate Android. These include files, signals, sockets, pipes, semaphores, shared memory, message queues, and so on. While Android uses some of these (such as local sockets), it does not support others (namely System V IPCs like semaphores, shared memory segments, and message queues).

Binder

Because the standard IPC mechanisms weren't flexible or reliable enough, a new IPC mechanism called *Binder* was developed for Android. While Android's Binder is a new implementation, it's based on the architecture and ideas of OpenBinder.[6]

Binder implements a distributed component architecture based on abstract interfaces. It is similar to Windows Common Object Model (COM) and Common Object Broker Request Architectures (CORBA) on Unix, but unlike those frameworks, it runs on a single device and does not support remote procedure calls (RPC) across the network (although RPC support could be implemented on top of Binder). A full description of the Binder framework is outside the scope of this book, but we introduce its main components briefly in the following sections.

Binder Implementation

As mentioned earlier, on a Unix-like system, a process cannot access another process's memory. However, the kernel has control over all processes and therefore can expose an interface that enables IPC. In Binder, this interface is the */dev/binder* device, which is implemented by the Binder kernel driver. The *Binder driver* is the central object of the framework, and all IPC calls go through it. Inter-process communication is implemented with a single `ioctl()` call that both sends and receives data through the `binder_write_read` structure, which consists of a `write_buffer` containing commands for the driver, and a `read_buffer` containing commands that the userspace needs to perform.

But how is data actually passed between processes? The Binder driver manages part of the address space of each process. The Binder driver-managed chunk of memory is read-only to the process, and all writing

6. PalmSource, Inc., *OpenBinder*, *http://www.angryredplanet.com/~hackbod/openbinder/docs/html/*

is performed by the kernel module. When a process sends a message to another process, the kernel allocates some space in the destination process's memory, and copies the message data directly from the sending process. It then queues a short message to the receiving process telling it where the received message is. The recipient can then access that message directly (because it is in its own memory space). When a process is finished with the message, it notifies the Binder driver to mark the memory as free. Figure 1-3 shows a simplified illustration of the Binder IPC architecture.

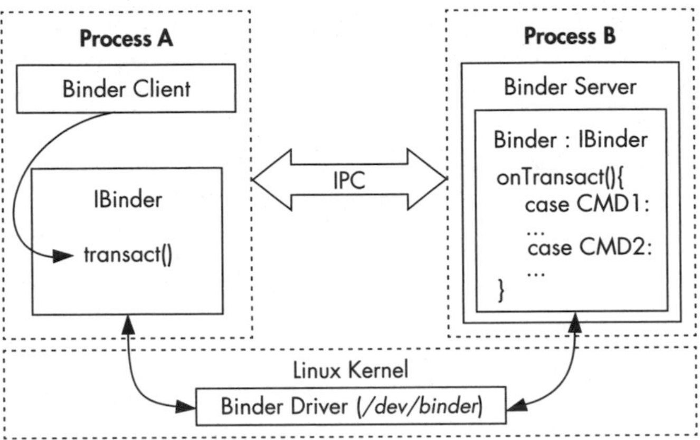

Figure 1-3: Binder IPC

Higher-level IPC abstractions in Android such as *Intents* (commands with associated data that are delivered to components across processes), *Messengers* (objects that enable message-based communication across processes), and *ContentProviders* (components that expose a cross-process data management interface) are built on top of Binder. Additionally, service interfaces that need to be exposed to other processes can be defined using the *Android Interface Definition Language (AIDL)*, which enables clients to call remote services as if they were local Java objects. The associated `aidl` tool automatically generates *stubs* (client-side representations of the remote object) and *proxies* that map interface methods to the lower-level `transact()` Binder method and take care of converting parameters to a format that Binder can transmit (this is called *parameter marshalling/unmarshalling*). Because Binder is inherently typeless, AIDL-generated stubs and proxies also provide type safety by including the target interface name in each Binder transaction (in the proxy) and validating it in the stub.

Binder Security

On a higher level, each object that can be accessed through the Binder framework implements the `IBinder` interface and is called a *Binder object*. Calls to a Binder object are performed inside a *Binder transaction*, which contains a reference to the target object, the ID of the method to execute, and a data buffer. The Binder driver automatically adds the process ID (PID) and effective user ID (EUID) of the calling process to the transaction data. The called process (*callee*) can inspect the PID and EUID and decide whether it should execute the requested method based on its internal logic or system-wide metadata about the calling application.

Since the PID and EUID are filled in by the kernel, caller processes cannot fake their identity to get more privileges than allowed by the system (that is, Binder prevents *privilege escalation*). This is one of the central pieces of Android's security model, and all higher-level abstractions, such as permissions, build upon it. The EUID and PID of the caller are accessible via the `getCallingPid()` and `getCallingUid()` methods of the `android.os.Binder` class, which is part of Android's public API.

NOTE *The calling process's EUID may not map to a single application if more than one application is executing under the same UID (see Chapter 2 for details). However, this does not affect security decisions, as processes running under the same UID are typically granted the same set of permissions and privileges (unless process-specific SELinux rules have been defined).*

Binder Identity

One of the most important properties of Binder objects is that they maintain a unique identity across processes. Thus if process A creates a Binder object and passes it to process B, which in turn passes it to process C, calls from all three processes will be processed by the same Binder object. In practice, process A will reference the Binder object directly by its memory address (because it is in process A's memory space), while process B and C will receive only a handle to the Binder object.

The kernel maintains the mapping between "live" Binder objects and their handles in other processes. Because a Binder object's identity is unique and maintained by the kernel, it is impossible for userspace processes to create a copy of a Binder object or obtain a reference to one unless they have been handed one through IPC. Thus a Binder object is a unique, unforgeable, and communicable object that can act as a security *token*. This enables the use of capability-based security in Android.

Capability-Based Security

In a *capability-based security model*, programs are granted access to a particular resource by giving them an unforgeable *capability* that both references the target object and encapsulates a set of access rights to it. Because capabilities are unforgeable, the mere fact that a program possesses a capability is sufficient to give it access to the target resource; there is no need to maintain access control lists (ACLs) or similar structures associated with actual resources.

Binder Tokens

In Android, Binder objects can act as capabilities and are called *Binder tokens* when used in this fashion. A Binder token can be both a capability and a target resource. The possession of a Binder token grants the owning process full access to a Binder object, enabling it to perform Binder transactions on the target object. If the Binder object implements multiple actions (by selecting the action to perform based on the `code` parameter of the Binder transaction), the caller can perform any action when it has a reference to that Binder object. If more granular access control is required, the implementation of each action needs to implement the necessary permission checks, typically by utilizing the PID and EUID of the caller process.

A common pattern in Android is to allow all actions to callers running as *system* (UID 1000) or *root* (UID 0), but perform additional permission checks for all other processes. Thus access to important Binder objects such as system services is controlled in two ways: by limiting who can get a reference to that Binder object and by checking the caller identity before performing an action on the Binder object. (This check is optional and implemented by the Binder object itself, if required.)

Alternatively, a Binder object can be used only as a capability without implementing any other functionality. In this usage pattern, the same Binder object is held by two (or more) cooperating processes, and the one acting as a server (processing some kind of client requests) uses the Binder token to authenticate its clients, much like web servers use session cookies.

This usage pattern is used internally by the Android framework and is mostly invisible to applications. One notable use case of Binder tokens that is visible in the public API is *window tokens*. The top-level window of each activity is associated with a Binder token (called a window token), which Android's window manager (the system service responsible for managing application windows) keeps track of. Applications can obtain their own window token but cannot get access to the window tokens of other applications. Typically you don't want other applications adding or removing windows on top of your own; each request to do so must provide the window token associated with the application, thus guaranteeing that window requests are coming from your own application or from the system.

Accessing Binder Objects

Although Android controls access to Binder objects for security purposes, and the only way to communicate with a Binder object is to be given a reference to it, some Binder objects (most notably system services) need to be universally accessible. It is, however, impractical to hand out references to all system services to each and every process, so we need some mechanism that allows processes to discover and obtain references to system services as needed.

In order to enable service discovery, the Binder framework has a single *context manager*, which maintains references to Binder objects. Android's context manager implementation is the *servicemanager* native daemon. It is started very early in the boot process so that system services can register with it as they start up. Services are registered by passing a service name and a Binder reference to the service manager. Once a service is registered, any client can obtain its Binder reference by using its name. However, most system services implement additional permission checks, so obtaining a reference does not automatically guarantee access to all of its functionality. Because anyone can access a Binder reference when it is registered with the service manager, only a small set of whitelisted system processes can register system services. For example, only a process executing as UID 1002 (`AID_BLUETOOTH`) can register the *bluetooth* system service.

You can view a list of registered services by using the `service list` command, which returns the name of each registered service and the implemented `IBinder` interface. Sample output from running the command on an Android 4.4 device is shown in Listing 1-2.

```
$ service list
service list
Found 79 services:
0       sip: [android.net.sip.ISipService]
1       phone: [com.android.internal.telephony.ITelephony]
2       iphonesubinfo: [com.android.internal.telephony.IPhoneSubInfo]
3       simphonebook: [com.android.internal.telephony.IIccPhoneBook]
4       isms: [com.android.internal.telephony.ISms]
5       nfc: [android.nfc.INfcAdapter]
6       media_router: [android.media.IMediaRouterService]
7       print: [android.print.IPrintManager]
8       assetatlas: [android.view.IAssetAtlas]
9       dreams: [android.service.dreams.IdreamManager]
--snip--
```

Listing 1-2: Obtaining a list of registered system services with the `service list` command

Other Binder Features

While not directly related to Android's security model, two other notable Binder features are reference counting and death notification (also known as link to death). *Reference counting* guarantees that Binder objects are automatically freed when no one references them and is implemented in the kernel driver with the `BC_INCREFS`, `BC_ACQUIRE`, `BC_RELEASE`, and `BC_DECREFS` commands. Reference counting is integrated at various levels of the Android framework but is not directly visible to applications.

Death notification allows applications that use Binder objects that are hosted by other processes to be notified when those processes are killed by the kernel and to perform any necessary cleanup. Death notification is implemented with the `BC_REQUEST_DEATH_NOTIFICATION` and `BC_CLEAR_DEATH_NOTIFICATION` commands in the kernel driver and the `linkToDeath()` and `unlinkToDeath()` methods of the `IBinder` interface[7] in the framework. (Death notifications for local binders are not sent, because local binders cannot die without the hosting process dying as well.)

7. Google, *Android APIs Reference*, "IBinder," *http://developer.android.com/reference/android/os/IBinder.html*

Android Framework Libraries

Next on the stack are the Android framework libraries, sometimes called just "the framework." The framework includes all Java libraries that are not part of the standard Java runtime (`java.*`, `javax.*`, and so on) and is for the most part hosted under the `android` top-level package. The framework includes the basic blocks for building Android applications, such as the base classes for activities, services, and content providers (in the `android.app.*` packages); GUI widgets (in the `android.view.*` and `android.widget` packages); and classes for file and database access (mostly in the `android.database.*` and `android.content.*` packages). It also includes classes that let you interact with device hardware, as well as classes that take advantage of higher-level services offered by the system.

Even though almost all Android OS functionality above the kernel level is implemented as system services, it is not exposed directly in the framework but is accessed via facade classes called *managers*. Typically, each manager is backed by a corresponding system service; for example, the `BluetoothManager` is a facade for the `BluetoothManagerService`.

Applications

On the highest level of the stack are *applications* (or *apps*), which are the programs that users directly interact with. While all apps have the same structure and are built on top of the Android framework, we distinguish between system apps and user-installed apps.

System Apps

System apps are included in the OS image, which is read-only on production devices (typically mounted as */system*), and cannot be uninstalled or changed by users. Therefore, these apps are considered secure and are given many more privileges than user-installed apps. System apps can be part of the core Android OS or can simply be preinstalled user applications, such as email clients or browsers. While all apps installed under */system* were treated equally in earlier versions of Android (except by OS features that check the app signing certificate), Android 4.4 and higher treat apps installed in */system/priv-app/* as privileged applications and will only grant permissions with protection level *signatureOrSystem* to privileged apps, not to all apps installed under */system*. Apps that are signed with the platform signing key can be granted system permissions with the *signature* protection level, and thus can get OS-level privileges even if they are not preinstalled under */system*. (See Chapter 2 for details on permissions and code signing.)

While system apps cannot be uninstalled or changed, they can be updated by users as long as the updates are signed with the same private key, and some can be overridden by user-installed apps. For example, a user can choose to replace the preinstalled application launcher or input method with a third-party application.

User-Installed Apps

User-installed apps are installed on a dedicated read-write partition (typically mounted as */data*) that hosts user data and can be uninstalled at will. Each application lives in a dedicated security sandbox and typically cannot affect other applications or access their data. Additionally, apps can only access resources that they have explicitly been granted a permission to use. Privilege separation and the principle of least privilege are central to Android's security model, and we will explore how they are implemented in the next section.

Android App Components

Android applications are a combination of loosely coupled *components* and, unlike traditional applications, can have more than one entry point. Each component can offer multiple entry points that can be reached based on user actions in the same or another application, or triggered by a system event that the application has registered to be notified about.

Components and their entry points, as well as additional metadata, are defined in the application's manifest file, called *AndroidManifest.xml*. Like most Android resource files, this file is compiled into a binary XML format (similar to ASN.1) before bundling it in the application package (APK) file in order to decrease size and speed up parsing. The most important application property defined in the manifest file is the application package name, which uniquely identifies each application in the system. The package name is in the same format as Java package names (reverse domain name notation; for example, *com.google.email*).

The *AndroidManifest.xml* file is parsed at application install time, and the package and components it defines are registered with the system. Android requires each application to be signed using a key controlled by its developer. This guarantees that an installed application cannot be replaced by another application that claims to have the same package name (unless it is signed with the same key, in which case the existing application is updated). We'll discuss code signing and application packages in Chapter 3.

The main components of Android apps are listed below.

Activities

An *activity* is a single screen with a user interface. Activities are the main building blocks of Android GUI applications. An application can have multiple activities and while they are usually designed to be displayed in a particular order, each activity can be started independently, potentially by a different app (if allowed).

Services

A *service* is a component that runs in the background and has no user interface. Services are typically used to perform some long-running operation, such as downloading a file or playing music, without blocking the user interface. Services can also define a remote interface using

AIDL and provide some functionality to other apps. However, unlike system services, which are part of the OS and are always running, application services are started and stopped on demand.

Content providers
Content providers provide an interface to app data, which is typically stored in a database or files. Content providers can be accessed via IPC and are mainly used to share an app's data with other apps. Content providers offer fine-grained control over what parts of data are accessible, allowing an application to share only a subset of its data.

Broadcast receivers
A *broadcast receiver* is a component that responds to systemwide events, called *broadcasts*. Broadcasts can originate from the system (for example, announcing changes in network connectivity), or from a user application (for example, announcing that background data update has completed).

Android's Security Model

Like the rest of the system, Android's security model also takes advantage of the security features offered by the Linux kernel. Linux is a multiuser operating system and the kernel can isolate user resources from one another, just as it isolates processes. In a Linux system, one user cannot access another user's files (unless explicitly granted permission) and each process runs with the identity (*user* and *group ID*, usually referred to as *UID* and *GID*) of the user that started it, unless the set-user-ID or set-group-ID (SUID and SGID) bits are set on the corresponding executable file.

Android takes advantage of this user isolation, but treats users differently than a traditional Linux system (desktop or server) does. In a traditional system, a UID is given either to a physical user that can log into the system and execute commands via the shell, or to a system service (daemon) that executes in the background (because system daemons are often accessible over the network, running each daemon with a dedicated UID can limit the damage if one is compromised). Android was originally designed for smartphones, and because mobile phones are personal devices, there was no need to register different physical users with the system. The physical user is implicit, and UIDs are used to distinguish applications instead. This forms the basis of Android's application sandboxing.

Application Sandboxing

Android automatically assigns a unique UID, often called an *app ID*, to each application at installation and executes that application in a dedicated process running as that UID. Additionally, each application is given a dedicated data directory which only it has permission to read and write to. Thus, applications are isolated, or *sandboxed*, both at the process level (by having each run in a dedicated process) and at the file level (by having a private data directory). This creates a kernel-level application sandbox, which applies to all applications, regardless of whether they are executed in a native or virtual machine process.

System daemons and applications run under well-defined and constant UIDs, and very few daemons run as the root user (UID 0). Android does not have the traditional */etc/password* file and its system UIDs are statically defined in the *android_filesystem_config.h* header file. UIDs for system services start from 1000, with 1000 being the *system* (`AID_SYSTEM`) user, which has special (but still limited) privileges. Automatically generated UIDs for applications start at 10000 (`AID_APP`), and the corresponding usernames are in the form *app_XXX* or *uY_aXXX* (on Android versions that support multiple physical users), where *XXX* is the offset from *AID_APP* and *Y* is the Android user ID (not the same as UID). For example, the 10037 UID corresponds to the *u0_a37* username and may be assigned to the Google email client application (*com.google.android.email* package). Listing 1-3 shows that the email application process executes as the *u0_a37* user ❶, while other application processes execute as different users.

```
$ ps
--snip--
u0_a37    16973 182   941052  60800 ffffffff 400d073c S com.google.android.email❶
u0_a8     18788 182   925864  50236 ffffffff 400d073c S com.google.android.dialer
u0_a29    23128 182   875972  35120 ffffffff 400d073c S com.google.android.calendar
u0_a34    23264 182   868424  31980 ffffffff 400d073c S com.google.android.deskclock
--snip--
```

Listing 1-3: Each application process executes as a dedicated user on Android

The data directory of the email application is named after its package name and is created under */data/data/* on single-user devices. (Multi-user devices use a different naming scheme as discussed in Chapter 4.) All files inside the data directory are owned by the dedicated Linux user, *u0_a37*, as shown in Listing 1-4 (with timestamps omitted). Applications can optionally create files using the `MODE_WORLD_READABLE` and `MODE_WORLD_WRITEABLE` flags to allow direct access to files by other applications, which effectively sets the `S_IROTH` and `S_IWOTH` access bits on the file, respectively. However, the direct sharing of files is discouraged, and those flags are deprecated in Android versions 4.2 and higher.

```
# ls -l /data/data/com.google.android.email
drwxrwx--x u0_a37   u0_a37            app_webview
drwxrwx--x u0_a37   u0_a37            cache
drwxrwx--x u0_a37   u0_a37            databases
drwxrwx--x u0_a37   u0_a37            files
--snip--
```

Listing 1-4: Application directories are owned by the dedicated Linux user

Application UIDs are managed alongside other package metadata in the */data/system/packages.xml* file (the canonical source) and also written to the */data/system/packages.list* file. (We discuss package management and the *packages.xml* file in Chapter 3.) Listing 1-5 shows the UID assigned to the *com.google.android.email* package as it appears in *packages.list*.

```
# grep 'com.google.android.email' /data/system/packages.list
com.google.android.email 10037 0 /data/data/com.google.android.email default 3003,1028,1015
```

Listing 1-5: The UID corresponding to each application is stored in /data/system/packages.list

Here, the first field is the package name, the second is the UID assigned to the application, the third is the debuggable flag (`1` if debuggable), the fourth is the application's data directory path, and the fifth is the *seinfo* label (used by SELinux). The last field is a list of the supplementary GIDs that the app launches with. Each GID is typically associated with an Android permission (discussed next) and the GID list is generated based on the permissions granted to the application.

Applications can be installed using the same UID, called a *shared user ID*, in which case they can share files and even run in the same process. Shared user IDs are used extensively by system applications, which often need to use the same resources across different packages for modularity. For example, in Android 4.4 the system UI and keyguard (lockscreen implementation) share UID 10012 (see Listing 1-6).

```
# grep ' 10012 ' /data/system/packages.list
com.android.keyguard 10012 0 /data/data/com.android.keyguard platform 1028,1015,1035,3002,3001
com.android.systemui 10012 0 /data/data/com.android.systemui platform 1028,1015,1035,3002,3001
```

Listing 1-6: System packages sharing the same UID

While the shared user ID facility is not recommended for non-system apps, it's available to third-party applications as well. In order to share the same UID, applications need to be signed by the same code signing key. Additionally, because adding a shared user ID to a new version of an installed app causes it to change its UID, the system disallows this (see Chapter 2). Therefore, a shared user ID cannot be added retroactively, and apps need to be designed to work with a shared ID from the start.

Permissions

Because Android applications are sandboxed, they can access only their own files and any world-accessible resources on the device. Such a limited application wouldn't be very interesting though, and Android can grant additional, fine-grained access rights to applications in order to allow for richer functionality. Those access rights are called *permissions*, and they can control access to hardware devices, Internet connectivity, data, or OS services.

Applications can request permissions by defining them in the *AndroidManifest.xml* file. At application install time, Android inspects the list of requested permissions and decides whether to grant them or not. Once granted, permissions cannot be revoked and they are available to the application without any additional confirmation. Additionally, for features such as private key or user account access, explicit user confirmation is required for each accessed object, even if the requesting application has been granted the corresponding permission (see Chapters 7 and 8). Some permission can only be granted to applications that are part of the Android OS, either because they're preinstalled or signed with the same key as the OS. Third-party applications can define custom permissions and define similar restrictions known as permission *protection levels*, thus restricting access to an app's services and resources to apps created by the same author.

Permission can be enforced at different levels. Requests to lower-level system resources, such as device files, are enforced by the Linux kernel by checking the UID or GID of the calling process against the resource's owner and access bits. When accessing higher-level Android components, enforcement is performed either by the Android OS or by each component (or both). We discuss permissions in Chapter 2.

IPC

Android uses a combination of a kernel driver and userspace libraries to implement IPC. As discussed in "Binder" on page 5, the Binder kernel driver guarantees that the UID and PID of callers cannot be forged, and many system services rely on the UID and PID provided by Binder to dynamically control access to sensitive APIs exposed via IPC. For example, the system Bluetooth manager service only allows system applications to enable Bluetooth silently if the caller is running with the *system* UID (1000) by using the code shown in Listing 1-7. Similar code is found in other system services.

```
public boolean enable() {
    if ((Binder.getCallingUid() != Process.SYSTEM_UID) &&
        (!checkIfCallerIsForegroundUser())) {
        Log.w(TAG,"enable(): not allowed for non-active and non-system user");
        return false;
     }
--snip--
}
```

Listing 1-7: Checking that the caller is running with the system *UID*

More coarse-grained permissions that affect all methods of a service exposed via IPC can be automatically enforced by the system by specifying a permission in the service declaration. As with requested permissions, required permissions are declared in the *AndroidManifest.xml* file. Like the dynamic permission check in the example above, per-component permissions are also implemented by consulting the caller UID obtained from Binder under the hood. The system uses the package database to determine the permission required by the callee component, and then maps the caller UID to a package name and retrieves the set of permissions granted to the caller. If the required permission is in that set, the call succeeds. If not, it fails and the system throws a `SecurityException`.

Code Signing and Platform Keys

All Android applications must be signed by their developer, including system applications. Because Android APK files are an extension of the Java JAR package format,[8] the code signing method used is also based on JAR signing. Android uses the APK signature to make sure updates for an app are coming from the same author (this is called the *same origin policy*) and to establish trust relationships between applications. Both of these security features are implemented by comparing the signing certificate of the currently installed target app with the certificate of the update or related application.

System applications are signed by a number of *platform keys*. Different system components can share resources and run inside the same process when they are signed with the same platform key. Platform keys are generated and controlled by whoever maintains the Android version installed on a particular device: device manufacturers, carriers, Google for Nexus devices, or users for self-built open source Android versions. (We'll discuss code signing and the APK format in Chapter 3.)

Multi-User Support

Because Android was originally designed for handset (smartphone) devices that have a single physical user, it assigns a distinct Linux UID to each installed application and traditionally does not have a notion of a physical user. Android gained support for multiple physical users in version 4.2, but multi-user support is only enabled on tablets, which are more likely to be shared. Multi-user support on handset devices is disabled by setting the maximum number of users to 1.

Each user is assigned a unique user ID, starting with 0, and users are given their own dedicated data directory under */data/system/users/<user ID>/*, which is called the user's *system directory*. This directory hosts user-specific settings such as homescreen parameters, account data, and a list of currently installed applications. While application binaries are shared between users, each user gets a copy of an application's data directory.

To distinguish applications installed for each user, Android assigns a new effective UID to each application when it is installed for a particular user. This effective UID is based on the target physical user's user ID and the app's UID in a single-user system (the *app ID*). This composite structure of the granted UID guarantees that even if the same application is installed by two different users, both application instances get their own sandbox. Additionally, Android guarantees dedicated shared storage (hosted on an SD card for older devices), which is world-readable, to each physical user.

---

8. Oracle, *JAR File Specification*, *http://docs.oracle.com/javase/7/docs/technotes/guides/jar/jar.html*

The user to first initialize the device is called the *device owner*, and only they can manage other users or perform administrative tasks that influence the whole device (such as factory reset). (We discuss multi-user support in greater detail in Chapter 4.)

SELinux

The traditional Android security model relies heavily on the UIDs and GIDs granted to applications. While those are guaranteed by the kernel, and by default each application's files are private, nothing prevents an application from granting world access to its files (whether intentionally or due to a programming error).

Similarly, nothing prevents malicious applications from taking advantage of the overly permissive access bits of system files or local sockets. In fact, inappropriate permissions assigned to application or system files have been the source of a number of Android vulnerabilities. Those vulnerabilities are unavoidable in the default access control model employed by Linux, known as *discretionary access control (DAC)*. *Discretionary* here means that once a user gets access to a particular resource, they can pass it on to another user at their discretion, such as by setting the access mode of one of their files to world-readable. In contrast, *mandatory access control (MAC)* ensures that access to resources conforms to a system-wide set of *authorization rules* called a *policy*. The policy can only be changed by an administrator, and users cannot override or bypass it in order to, for example, grant everyone access to their own files.

Security Enhanced Linux (SELinux) is a MAC implementation for the Linux kernel and has been integrated in the mainline kernel for more than 10 years. As of version 4.3, Android integrates a modified SELinux version from the Security Enhancements for Android (SEAndroid) project[9] that has been augmented to support Android-specific features such as Binder. In Android, SELinux is used to isolate core system daemons and user applications in different security *domains* and to define different access policies for each domain. As of version 4.4, SELinux is deployed in *enforcing mode* (violations to the system policy generate runtime errors), but policy enforcement is only applied to core system daemons. Applications still run in *permissive mode* and violations are logged but do not cause runtime errors. (We give more details about Android's SELinux implementation in Chapter 12.)

System Updates

Android devices can be updated over-the-air (OTA) or by connecting the device to a PC and pushing the update image using the standard Android debug bridge (ADB) client or some vendor-provided application with similar functionality. Because in addition to system files, an Android update might need to modify the baseband (modem) firmware, bootloader, and

9. SELinux Project, *SE for Android*, *http://seandroid.bitbucket.org/*

other parts of the device that are not directly accessible from Android, the update process typically uses a special-purpose, minimal OS with exclusive access to all device hardware. This is called a *recovery OS* or simply *recovery*.

OTA updates are performed by downloading an OTA package file (typically a ZIP file with an added code signature), which contains a small script file to be interpreted by the recovery, and rebooting the device in *recovery mode*. Alternatively, the user can enter recovery mode by using a device-specific key combination when booting the device, and apply the update manually by using the menu interface of the recovery, which is usually navigated using the hardware buttons (Volume up/down, Power, and so on) of the device.

On production devices, the recovery accepts only updates signed by the device manufacturer. Update files are signed by extending the ZIP file format to include a signature over the whole file in the comment section (see Chapter 3), which the recovery extracts and verifies before installing the update. On some devices (including all Nexus devices, dedicated developer devices, and some vendor devices), device owners can replace the recovery OS and disable system update signature verification, allowing them to install updates by third parties. Switching the device bootloader to a mode that allows replacing the recovery and system images is called *bootloader unlocking* (not to be confused with SIM-unlocking, which allows a device to be used on any mobile network) and typically requires wiping all user data (factory reset) in order to make sure that a potentially malicious third-party system image does not get access to existing user data. On most consumer devices, unlocking the bootloader has the side effect of voiding the device's warranty. (We discuss system updates and recovery images in Chapter 13.)

Verified Boot

As of version 4.4, Android supports verified boot using the *verity* target[10] of Linux's Device-Mapper. Verity provides transparent integrity checking of block devices using a cryptographic hash tree. Each node in the tree is a cryptographic hash, with leaf nodes containing the hash value of a physical data block and intermediary nodes containing hash values of their child nodes. Because the hash in the root node is based on the values of all other nodes, only the root hash needs to be trusted in order to verify the rest of the tree.

Verification is performed with an RSA public key included in the boot partition. Device blocks are checked at runtime by calculating the hash value of the block as it is read and comparing it to the recorded value in the hash tree. If the values do not match, the read operation results in an I/O error indicating that the filesystem is corrupted. Because all checks are performed by the kernel, the boot process needs to verify the integrity of the kernel in order for verified boot to work. This process is device-specific and is typically implemented by using an unchangeable, hardware-specific key that

10. Linux kernel source tree, *dm-verity*, *http://git.kernel.org/cgit/linux/kernel/git/torvalds/linux.git/tree/Documentation/device-mapper/verity.txt*

is "burned" (written to write-only memory) into the device. That key is used to verify the integrity of each bootloader level and eventually the kernel. (We discuss verified boot in Chapter 10.)

Summary

Android is a privilege-separated operating system based on the Linux kernel. Higher-level system functions are implemented as a set of cooperating system services that communicate using an IPC mechanism called Binder. Android isolates applications from each other by running each with a distinct system identity (Linux UID). By default, applications are given very few privileges and have to request fine-grained permission in order to interact with system services, hardware devices, or other applications. Permissions are defined in each application's manifest file and are granted at install time. The system uses the UID of each application to find out what permissions it has been granted and to enforce them at runtime. In recent versions, system processes isolation takes advantage of SELinux to further constrain the privileges given to each process.

2

PERMISSIONS

In the previous chapter, we gave an overview of Android's security model and briefly introduced permissions. In this chapter we'll provide more details about permissions, focusing on their implementation and enforcement. We will then discuss how to define custom permissions and apply them to each of Android's components. Finally, we'll say a few words about *pending intents*, which are tokens that allow an application to start an intent with the identity and privileges of another application.

The Nature of Permissions

As we learned in Chapter 1, Android applications are sandboxed and by default can access only their own files and a very limited set of system services. In order to interact with the system and other applications, Android applications can request a set of additional permissions that are granted at install time and cannot be changed (with some exceptions, as we'll discuss later in this chapter).

In Android, a *permission* is simply a string denoting the ability to perform a particular operation. The target operation can be anything from accessing a physical resource (such as the device's SD card) or shared data (such as the list of registered contacts) to the ability to start or access a component in a third-party application. Android comes with a built-in set of predefined permissions. New permissions that correspond to new features are added in each version.

NOTE *New built-in permissions, which lock down functionality that previously didn't require a permission, are applied conditionally, depending on the* targetSdkVersion *specified in an app's manifest: applications targeting Android versions that were released before the new permission was introduced cannot be expected to know about it, and therefore the permission is usually granted implicitly (without being requested). However, implicitly granted permissions are still shown in the list of permissions on the app installer screen so that users can be aware of them. Apps targeting later versions need to explicitly request the new permission.*

Built-in permissions are documented in the platform API reference.[1] Additional permissions, called *custom permissions,* can be defined by both system and user-installed applications.

To view a list of the permissions currently known to the system, use the `pm list permissions` command (see Listing 2-1). To display additional information about permissions, including the defining package, label, description, and protection level, add the `-f` parameter to the command.

```
$ pm list permissions
All Permissions:

permission:android.permission.REBOOT❶
permission:android.permission.BIND_VPN_SERVICE❷
permission:com.google.android.gallery3d.permission.GALLERY_PROVIDER❸
permission:com.android.launcher3.permission.RECEIVE_LAUNCH_BROADCASTS❹
--snip--
```

Listing 2-1: Getting a list of all permissions

Permission names are typically prefixed with their defining package concatenated with the string *.permission*. Because built-in permissions are defined in the `android` package, their names start with *android.permission.* For example, in Listing 2-1, the `REBOOT` ❶ and `BIND_VPN_SERVICE` ❷ are built-in permissions, while `GALLERY_PROVIDER` ❸ is defined by the Gallery application (package `com.google.android.gallery3d`) and `RECEIVE_LAUNCH_BROADCASTS` ❹ is defined by the default launcher application (package `com.android.launcher3`).

1. Google, *Android API Reference,* "Manifest.permission class," *http://developer.android.com/reference/android/Manifest.permission.html*

Requesting Permissions

Applications request permissions by adding one or more `<uses-permission>` tags to their *AndroidManifest.xml* file and can define new permissions with the `<permission>` tag. Listing 2-2 shows an example manifest file that requests the `INTERNET` and `WRITE_EXTERNAL_STORAGE` permissions. (We show how to define custom permission in "Custom Permissions" on page 42.)

```
<?xml version="1.0" encoding="utf-8"?>
<manifest xmlns:android="http://schemas.android.com/apk/res/android"
    xmlns:tools="http://schemas.android.com/tools"
    package="com.example.app"
    android:versionCode="1"
    android:versionName="1.0" >

    <uses-permission android:name="android.permission.INTERNET" />
    <uses-permission android:name="android.permission.WRITE_EXTERNAL_STORAGE" />
    --snip--
    <application android:name="SampleApp" ...>
    --snip--
    </application>
</manifest>
```

Listing 2-2: Requesting permissions using the application manifest file

Permission Management

Permissions are assigned to each application (as identified by a unique *package name*) at install time by the system *package manager* service. The package manager maintains a central database of installed packages, both preinstalled and user-installed, with information about the install path, version, signing certificate, and assigned permissions of each package, as well as a list of all permissions defined on a device. (The `pm list permissions` command introduced in the previous section obtains this list by querying the package manager.) This package database is stored in the XML file */data/system/packages.xml*, which is updated each time an application is installed, updated, or uninstalled. Listing 2-3 shows a typical application entry from *packages.xml*.

```
<package name="com.google.android.apps.translate"
        codePath="/data/app/com.google.android.apps.translate-2.apk"
        nativeLibraryPath="/data/app-lib/com.google.android.apps.translate-2"
        flags="4767300" ft="1430dfab9e0" it="142cdf04d67" ut="1430dfabd8d"
        version="30000028"
        userId="10204"❶
        installer="com.android.vending">

    <sigs count="1">
        <cert index="7" />❷
    </sigs>
```

```
    <perms>❸
        <item name="android.permission.READ_EXTERNAL_STORAGE" />
        <item name="android.permission.USE_CREDENTIALS" />
        <item name="android.permission.READ_SMS" />
        <item name="android.permission.CAMERA" />
        <item name="android.permission.WRITE_EXTERNAL_STORAGE" />
        <item name="android.permission.INTERNET" />
        <item name="android.permission.MANAGE_ACCOUNTS" />
        <item name="android.permission.GET_ACCOUNTS" />
        <item name="android.permission.ACCESS_NETWORK_STATE" />
        <item name="android.permission.RECORD_AUDIO" />
    </perms>

    <signing-keyset identifier="17" />
    <signing-keyset identifier="6" />
</package>
```

Listing 2-3: Application entry in packages.xml

We discuss the meaning of most tags and attributes in Chapter 3, but for now let's focus on the ones that are related to permissions. Each package is represented by a `<package>` element, which contains information about the assigned UID (in the `userId` attribute ❶), signing certificate (in the `<cert>` tag ❷), and assigned permissions (listed as children of the `<perms>` tag ❸). To get information about an installed package programmatically, use the `getPackageInfo()` method of the `android.content.pm.PackageManager` class, which returns a `PackageInfo` instance that encapsulates the information contained in the `<package>` tag.

If all permissions are assigned at install time and cannot be changed or revoked without uninstalling the application, how does the package manager decide whether it should grant the requested permissions? To understand this, we need to discuss permission protection levels.

Permission Protection Levels

According to the official documentation,[2] a permission's *protection level* "characterizes the potential risk implied in the permission and indicates the procedure that the system should follow when determining whether or not to grant the permission." In practice, this means that whether a permission is granted or not depends on its protection level. The following sections discuss the four protection levels defined in Android and how the system handles each.

normal

This is the default value. It defines a permission with low risk to the system or other applications. Permissions with protection level *normal* are

2. Google, *Android API Guides*, "App Manifest: <permission> tag," *http://developer.android.com/guide/topics/manifest/permission-element.html#plevel*

automatically granted without requiring user confirmation. Examples are ACCESS_NETWORK_STATE (allows applications to access information about networks) and GET_ACCOUNTS (allows access to the list of accounts in the Accounts Service).

dangerous

Permissions with the *dangerous* protection level give access to user data or some form of control over the device. Examples are READ_SMS (allows an application to read SMS messages) and CAMERA (gives applications access to the camera device). Before granting dangerous permissions, Android shows a confirmation dialog that displays information about the requested permissions. Because Android requires that all requested permission be granted at install time, the user can either agree to install the app, thus granting the requested *dangerous* permission(s), or cancel the application install. For example, for the application shown in Listing 2-3 (Google Translate), the system confirmation dialog will look like the one shown in Figure 2-1.

Google Play and other application market clients display their own dialog, which is typically styled differently. For the same application, the Google Play Store client displays the dialog shown in Figure 2-2. Here, all *dangerous* permissions are organized by permission group (see "System Permissions" on page 37) and normal permissions are not displayed.

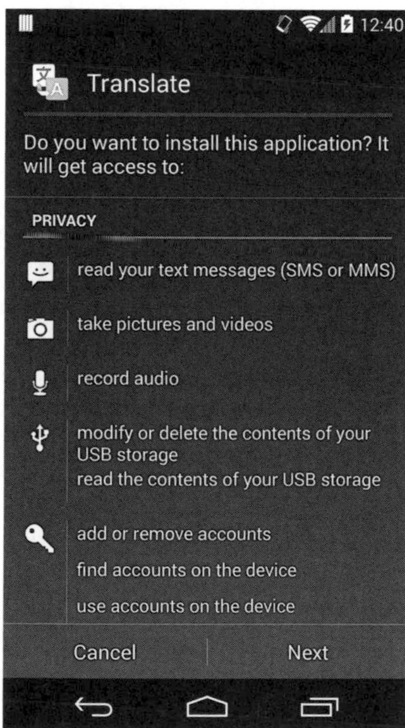

Figure 2-1: Default Android application install confirmation dialog

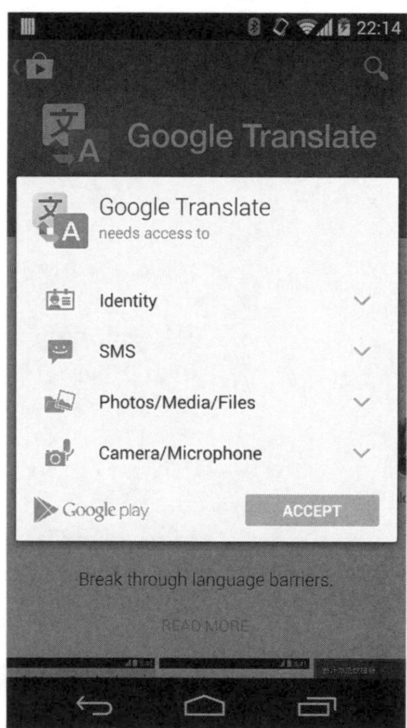

Figure 2-2: Google Play Store client application install confirmation dialog

signature

A *signature* permission is only granted to applications that are signed with the same key as the application that declared the permission. This is the "strongest" permission level because it requires the possession of a cryptographic key, which only the app (or platform) owner controls. Thus, applications using *signature* permissions are typically controlled by the same author. Built-in signature permissions are typically used by system applications that perform device management tasks. Examples are `NET_ADMIN` (configure network interfaces, IPSec, and so on) and `ACCESS_ALL_EXTERNAL_STORAGE` (access all multi-user external storage). We'll discuss *signature* permissions in more detail in "Signature Permissions" on page 39.

signatureOrSystem

Permissions with this protection level are somewhat of a compromise: they are granted to applications that are either part of the system image, or that are signed with the same key as the app that declared the permission. This allows vendors that have their applications preinstalled on an Android device to share specific features that require a permission without having to share signing keys. Until Android 4.3, any application installed on the *system* partition was granted *signatureOrSystem* permissions automatically. Since Android 4.4, applications need to be installed in the */system/priv-app/* directory in order to be granted permissions with this protection level.

Permission Assignment

Permissions are enforced at various layers in Android. Higher-level components such as applications and system services query the package manager to determine which permissions have been assigned to an application and decide whether to grant access. Lower-level components like native daemons typically do not have access to the package manager and rely on the UID, GID, and supplementary GIDs assigned to a process in order to determine which privileges to grant it. Access to system resources like device files, Unix domain sockets (local sockets), and network sockets is regulated by the kernel based on the owner and access mode of the target resource and the UID and GIDs of the accessing process.

We'll look into framework-level permission enforcement in "Permission Enforcement" on page 30. Let's first discuss how permissions are mapped to OS-level constructs such as UID and GIDs and how these process IDs are used for permission enforcement.

Permissions and Process Attributes

As in any Linux system, Android processes have a number of associated process attributes, most importantly real and effective UID and GID, and a set of supplementary GIDs.

As discussed in Chapter 1, each Android application is assigned a unique UID at install time and executes in a dedicated process. When the application is started, the process's UID and GID are set to the application UID assigned by the installer (the package manager service). If additional permissions have been assigned to the application, they are mapped to GIDs and assigned as supplementary GIDs to the process. Permission to GID mappings for built-in permissions are defined in the */etc/permission/platform.xml* file. Listing 2-4 shows an excerpt from the *platform.xml* file found on an Android 4.4 device.

```
<?xml version="1.0" encoding="utf-8"?>
<permissions>
    --snip--
    <permission name="android.permission.INTERNET" >❶
        <group gid="inet" />
    </permission>

    <permission name="android.permission.WRITE_EXTERNAL_STORAGE" >❷
        <group gid="sdcard_r" />
        <group gid="sdcard_rw" />
    </permission>

    <assign-permission name="android.permission.MODIFY_AUDIO_SETTINGS"
                                                 uid="media" />❸
    <assign-permission name="android.permission.ACCESS_SURFACE_FLINGER"
                                                 uid="media" />❹
    --snip--
</permissions>
```

Listing 2-4: Permission to GID mapping in platform.xml

Here, the `INTERNET` permission is associated with the *inet* GID ❶, and the `WRITE_EXTERNAL_STORAGE` permission is associated with the *sdcard_r* and *sdcard_rw* GIDs ❷. Thus any process for an app that has been granted the `INTERNET` permission is associated with the supplementary GID corresponding to the *inet* group, and processes with the `WRITE_EXTERNAL_STORAGE` permission have the GIDs of *sdcard_r* and *sdcard_rw* added to the list of associated supplementary GIDs.

The `<assign-permission>` tag serves the opposite purpose: it is used to assign higher-level permissions to system processes running under a specific UID that do not have a corresponding package. Listing 2-4 shows that processes running with the *media* UID (in practice, this is the *mediaserver* daemon) are assigned the `MODIFY_AUDIO_SETTINGS` ❸ and `ACCESS_SURFACE_FLINGER` ❹ permissions.

Android does not have an */etc/group* file, so the mapping from group names to GIDs is static and defined in the *android_filesystem_config.h* header file. Listing 2-5 shows an excerpt containing the *sdcard_rw* ❶, *sdcard_r* ❷, and *inet* ❸ groups.

```
--snip--
#define AID_ROOT             0  /* traditional unix root user */
#define AID_SYSTEM        1000  /* system server */
--snip--
```

```
#define AID_SDCARD_RW       1015  /* external storage write access */
#define AID_SDCARD_R        1028  /* external storage read access */
#define AID_SDCARD_ALL      1035  /* access all users external storage */
--snip--
#define AID_INET            3003  /* can create AF_INET and AF_INET6 sockets */
--snip--

struct android_id_info {
    const char *name;
    unsigned aid;
};

static const struct android_id_info android_ids[] = {
    { "root",           AID_ROOT, },
    { "system",         AID_SYSTEM, },
    --snip--
    { "sdcard_rw",      AID_SDCARD_RW, },❶
    { "sdcard_r",       AID_SDCARD_R, },❷
    { "sdcard_all",     AID_SDCARD_ALL, },
    --snip--
    { "inet",           AID_INET, },❸
};
```

Listing 2-5: Static user and group name to UID/GID mapping in android_filesystem_config.h

The *android_filesystem_config.h* file also defines the owner, access mode, and associated capabilities (for executables) of core Android system directories and files.

The package manager reads *platform.xml* at startup and maintains a list of permissions and associated GIDs. When it grants permissions to a package during installation, the package manager checks whether each permission has an associated GID(s). If so, the GID(s) is added to the list of supplementary GIDs associated with the application. The supplementary GID list is written as the last field of the *packages.list* file (see Listing 1-5 on page 14).

Process Attribute Assignment

Before we see how the kernel and lower-level system services check and enforce permissions, we need to examine how Android application processes are started and assigned process attributes.

As discussed in Chapter 1, Android applications are implemented in Java and are executed by the Dalvik VM. Thus each application process is in fact a Dalvik VM process executing the application's bytecode. In order to reduce the application memory footprint and improve startup time, Android does not start a new Dalvik VM process for each application. Instead, it uses a partially initialized process called *zygote* and forks it (using the `fork()` system call[3]) when it needs to start a new application. However,

3. For detailed information about process management functions like `fork()`, `setuid()`, and so on, see the respective man pages or a Unix programming text, such as W. Richard Stevens and Stephen A. Rago's *Advanced Programming in the UNIX Environment (3rd edition)*, Addison-Wesley Professional, 2013.

instead of calling one of the exec() functions like it does when starting a native process, it merely executes the main() function of the specified Java class. This process is called *specialization*, because the generic *zygote* process is turned into a specific application process, much like cells originating from the zygote cell specialize into cells that perform different functions. Thus the forked process inherits the memory image of the *zygote* process, which has preloaded most core and application framework Java classes. Because those classes never change and Linux uses a copy-on-write mechanism when forking processes, all child processes of *zygote* (that is, all Android applications) share the same copy of framework Java classes.

The *zygote* process is started by the *init.rc* initialization script and receives commands on a Unix-domain socket, also named *zygote*. When *zygote* receives a request to start a new application process, it forks itself, and the child process executes roughly the following code (abbreviated from forkAndSpecializeCommon() in *dalvik_system_Zygote.cpp*) in order to specialize itself as shown in Listing 2-6.

```
pid = fork();

if (pid == 0) {
    int err;
    /* The child process */
    err = setgroupsIntarray(gids);❶
    err = setrlimitsFromArray(rlimits);❷
    err = setresgid(gid, gid, gid);❸
    err = setresuid(uid, uid, uid);❹
    err = setCapabilities(permittedCapabilities, effectiveCapabilities);❺
    err = set_sched_policy(0, SP_DEFAULT);❻
    err = setSELinuxContext(uid, isSystemServer, seInfo, niceName);❼
    enableDebugFeatures(debugFlags);❽
}
```

Listing 2-6: Application process specialization in zygote

As shown here, the child process first sets its supplementary GIDs (corresponding to permissions) using setgroups(), called by setgroupsIntarray() at ❶. Next, it sets resource limits using setrlimit(), called by setrlimitsFromArray() at ❷, then sets the real, effective, and saved user and group IDs using setresgid() ❸ and setresuid() ❹.

The child process is able to change its resource limits and all process attributes because it initially executes as root, just like its parent process, *zygote*. After the new process attributes are set, the child process executes with the assigned UIDs and GIDs and cannot go back to executing as root because the saved user ID is not 0.

After setting the UIDs and GIDs, the process sets its capabilities[4] using capset(), called from setCapabilities() ❺. Then, it sets its scheduling policy

4. For a discussion of Linux capabilities, see Chapter 39 of Michael Kerrisk's *The Linux Programming Interface: A Linux and UNIX System Programming Handbook*, No Starch Press, 2010.

by adding itself to one of the predefined control groups ❻.[5] At ❼, the process sets its nice name (displayed in the process list, typically the application's package name) and *seinfo* tag (used by SELinux, which we discuss in Chapter 12). Finally, it enables debugging if requested ❽.

NOTE *Android 4.4 introduces a new, experimental runtime called Android RunTime (ART), which is expected to replace Dalvik in a future version. While ART brings many changes to the current execution environment, most importantly ahead-of-time (AOT) compilation, it uses the same zygote-based app process execution model as Dalvik.*

The process relationship between *zygote* and application process is evident in the process list obtained with the ps command, as shown in Listing 2-7.

```
$ ps
USER     PID   PPID  VSIZE  RSS     WCHAN    PC         NAME
root      1     0     680    540   ffffffff 00000000 S /init❶
--snip--
root     181    1     858808 38280 ffffffff 00000000 S zygote❷
--snip--
radio    1139  181    926888 46512 ffffffff 00000000 S com.android.phone
nfc      1154  181    888516 36976 ffffffff 00000000 S com.android.nfc
u0_a7    1219  181    956836 48012 ffffffff 00000000 S com.google.android.gms
```

Listing 2-7: zygote and application process relationship

Here, the PID column denotes the process ID, the PPID column denotes the parent process ID, and the NAME column denotes the process name. As you can see, *zygote* (PID 181 ❷) is started by the *init* process (PID 1 ❶) and all application processes have *zygote* as their parent (PPID 181). Each process executes under a dedicated user, either built-in (*radio*, *nfc*), or automatically assigned (*u0_a7*) at install time. The process names are set to the package name of each application (com.android.phone, com.android.nfc, and com.google.android.gms).

Permission Enforcement

As discussed in the previous section, each application process is assigned a UID, GID, and supplementary GIDs when it is forked from *zygote*. The kernel and system daemons use these process identifiers to decide whether to grant access to a particular system resource or function.

Kernel-Level Enforcement

Access to regular files, device nodes, and local sockets is regulated just as it is in any Linux system. One Android-specific addition is requiring processes that want to create network sockets to belong to the group *inet*. This Android kernel addition is known as "paranoid network security" and is implemented as an additional check in the Android kernel, as shown in Listing 2-8.

5. Linux Kernel Archives, *CGROUPS*, *https://www.kernel.org/doc/Documentation/cgroups/cgroups.txt*

```
#ifdef CONFIG_ANDROID_PARANOID_NETWORK
#include <linux/android_aid.h>

static inline int current_has_network(void)
{       return in_egroup_p(AID_INET) || capable(CAP_NET_RAW);❶}
#else
static inline int current_has_network(void)
{       return 1;❷
}
#endif
--snip--
static int inet_create(struct net *net, struct socket *sock, int protocol,
                                                         int kern)
{
        --snip--
        if (!current_has_network())
                return -EACCES;❸
        --snip--
}
```

Listing 2-8: Paranoid network security implementation in the Android kernel

Caller processes that do not belong to the `AID_INET` (GID 3003, name *inet*) group and do not have the `CAP_NET_RAW` capability (allowing the use of RAW and PACKET sockets) receive an access denied error (❶ and ❸). Non-Android kernels do not define `CONFIG_ANDROID_PARANOID_NETWORK` and thus no special group membership is required to create a socket ❷. In order for the *inet* group to be assigned to an application process, it needs to be granted the `INTERNET` permission. As a result, only applications with the `INTERNET` permission can create network sockets. In addition to checking process credentials when creating sockets, Android kernels also grant certain capabilities to processes executing with specific GIDs: processes that execute with the `AID_NET_RAW` (GID 3004) are given the `CAP_NET_RAW` capability, and those executing with `AID_NET_ADMIN` (GID 3005) are given the `CAP_NET_ADMIN` capability.

Paranoid network security is also used to control access to Bluetooth sockets and the kernel tunneling driver (used for VPN). A full list of Android GIDs that the kernel treats in a special way can be found in the *include/linux/android_aid.h* file in the kernel source tree.

Native Daemon-Level Enforcement

While Binder is the preferred IPC mechanism in Android, lower-level native daemons often use Unix domain sockets (local sockets) for IPC. Because Unix domain sockets are represented as nodes on the filesystem, standard filesystem permission can be used to control access.

As most sockets are created with an access mode that only allows access to their owner and group, clients running under a different UID and GID cannot connect to the socket. Local sockets for system daemons are defined in *init.rc* and created by *init* on startup with the specified access mode. For example, Listing 2-9 shows how the volume management daemon (*vold*) is defined in *init.rc*:

```
service vold /system/bin/vold
    class core
    socket vold stream 0660 root mount❶
    ioprio be 2
```

Listing 2-9: vold daemon entry in init.rc

vold declares a socket called *vold* with the 0660 access mode, owned by *root* and with group set to *mount* ❶. The *vold* daemon needs to run as root in order to mount or unmount volumes, but members of the *mount* group (AID_MOUNT, GID 1009) can send it commands via the local socket without needing to run as the superuser. Local sockets for Android daemons are created in the */dev/socket/* directory. Listing 2-10 shows that the *vold* socket ❶ has the owner and permission specified in *init.rc*.

```
$ ls -l /dev/socket

srw-rw---- system   system           1970-01-18 14:26 adbd
srw------- system   system           1970-01-18 14:26 installd
srw-rw---- root     system           1970-01-18 14:26 netd
--snip--
srw-rw-rw- root     root             1970-01-18 14:26 property_service
srw-rw---- root     radio            1970-01-18 14:26 rild
srw-rw---- root     mount            1970-01-18 14:26 vold❶
srw-rw---- root     system           1970-01-18 14:26 zygote
```

Listing 2-10: Local sockets for core system daemons in /dev/socket/

Unix domain sockets allow the passing and querying of client credentials using the SCM_CREDENTIALS control message and the SO_PEERCRED socket option. Like the effective UID and effective GUID that are part of a Binder transaction, the peer credentials associated with a local socket are checked by the kernel and cannot be forged by user-level processes. This allows native daemons to implement additional, fine-grained control over the operations that they allow for a particular client, as shown in Listing 2-11 using the *vold* daemon as an example.

```
int CommandListener::CryptfsCmd::runCommand(SocketClient *cli,
                                                    int argc, char **argv) {
    if ((cli->getUid() != 0) && (cli->getUid() != AID_SYSTEM)) {❶
        cli->sendMsg(ResponseCode::CommandNoPermission,
               "No permission to run cryptfs commands", false);
        return 0;
    }
    --snip--
}
```

Listing 2-11: Fine-grained access control based on socket client credentials in vold

The *vold* daemon only allows encrypted container management commands to clients running as the *root* (UID 0) or *system* (`AID_SYSTEM`, UID 1000) users. Here, the UID returned by `SocketClient->getUid()` ❶ is initialized with the client UID obtained using `getsockopt(SO_PEERCRED)` as shown in Listing 2-12 at ❶.

```
void SocketClient::init(int socket, bool owned, bool useCmdNum) {
    --snip--
    struct ucred creds;
    socklen_t szCreds = sizeof(creds);
    memset(&creds, 0, szCreds);

    int err = getsockopt(socket, SOL_SOCKET, SO_PEERCRED, &creds, &szCreds);❶
    if (err == 0) {
        mPid = creds.pid;
        mUid = creds.uid;
        mGid = creds.gid;
    }
}
```

Listing 2-12: Obtaining local socket client credentials using `getsockopt()`

Local socket connection functionality is encapsulated in the `android.net.LocalSocket` class and is available to Java applications as well, allowing higher-level system services to communicate with native daemons without using JNI code. For example, the `MountService` framework class uses `LocalSocket` to send commands to the *vold* daemon.

Framework-Level Enforcement

As discussed in the introduction to Android permissions, access to Android components can be controlled using permissions by declaring the required permissions in the manifest of the enclosing application. The system keeps track of the permissions associated with each component and checks to see whether callers have been granted the required permissions before allowing access. Because components cannot change the permissions they require at runtime, enforcement by the system is *static*. Static permissions are an example of declarative security. When using declarative security, security attributes such as roles and permissions are placed in the metadata of a component (the *AndroidManifest.xml* file in Android), rather than in the component itself, and are enforced by the container or runtime environment. This has the advantage of isolating security decisions from business logic but can be less flexible than implementing securing checks within the component.

Android components can also check to see whether a calling process has been granted a certain permission without declaring the permissions in the manifest. This *dynamic permission enforcement* requires more work but allows for more fine-grained access control. Dynamic permission enforcement is an example of imperative security, because security decisions are made by each component rather than being enforced by the runtime environment.

Let's look at how dynamic and static permission enforcement are implemented in more detail.

Dynamic Enforcement

As discussed in Chapter 1, the core of Android is implemented as a set of cooperating system services that can be called from other processes using the Binder IPC mechanism. Core services register with the service manager and any application that knows their registration name can obtain a Binder reference. Because Binder does not have a built-in access control mechanism, when clients have a reference they can call any method of the underlying system service by passing the appropriate parameters to `Binder.transact()`. Therefore, access control needs to be implemented by each system service.

In Chapter 1, we showed that system services can regulate access to exported operations by directly checking the UID of the caller obtained from `Binder.getCallingUid()` (see Listing 1-7 on page 15). However, this method requires that the service knows the list of allowed UIDs in advance, which only works for well-known fixed UIDs such as those of *root* (UID 0) and *system* (UID 1000). Also, most services do not care about the actual UID of the caller; they simply want to check if it has been granted a certain permission.

Because each application UID in Android is associated with a unique package (unless it is part of a shared user ID), and the package manager keeps track of the permissions granted to each package, this is made possible by querying the package manager service. Checking to see whether the caller has a certain permission is a very common operation, and Android provides a number of helper methods in the `android.content.Context` class that can perform this check.

Let's first examine how the `int Context.checkPermission(String permission, int pid, int uid)` method works. This method returns `PERMISSION_GRANTED` if the passed UID has the permission, and returns `PERMISSION_DENIED` otherwise. If the caller is *root* or *system*, the permission is automatically granted. As a performance optimization, if the requested permission has been declared by the calling app, it is granted without examining the actual permission. If that is not the case, the method checks to see whether the target component is public (exported) or private, and denies access to all private components. (We'll discuss component export in "Public and Private Components" on page 43.) Finally, the code queries the package manager service to see if the caller has been granted the requested permission. The relevant code from the `PackageManagerService` class is shown in Listing 2-13.

```
public int checkUidPermission(String permName, int uid) {
    synchronized (mPackages) {
        Object obj = mSettings.getUserIdLPr(❶UserHandle.getAppId(uid));
        if (obj != null) {
            GrantedPermissions gp = (GrantedPermissions)obj;❷
            if (gp.grantedPermissions.contains(permName)) {
                return PackageManager.PERMISSION_GRANTED;
            }
```

```
        } else {
            HashSet<String> perms = mSystemPermissions.get(uid);❸
            if (perms != null && perms.contains(permName)) {
                return PackageManager.PERMISSION_GRANTED;
            }
        }
    }
    return PackageManager.PERMISSION_DENIED;
}
```

Listing 2-13: UID-based permission check in `PackageManagerService`

Here the `PackageManagerService` first determines the *app ID* of the application based on the passed UID ❶ (the same application can be assigned multiple UIDs when installed for different users, which we discuss in detail in Chapter 4) and then obtains the set of granted permissions. If the `GrantedPermission` class (which holds the actual `java.util.Set<String>` of permission names) contains the target permission, the method returns `PERMISSION_GRANTED` ❷. If not, it checks whether the target permission should be automatically assigned to the passed-in UID ❸ (based on the `<assign-permission>` tags in `platform.xml`, as shown in Listing 2-4). If this check fails as well, it finally returns `PERMISSION_DENIED`.

The other permission-check helper methods in the `Context` class follow the same procedure. The `int checkCallingOrSelfPermission(String permission)` method calls `Binder.getCallingUid()` and `Binder.getCallingPid()` for us, and then calls `checkPermission(String permission, int pid, int uid)` using the obtained values. The `enforcePermission(String permission, int pid, int uid, String message)` method does not return a result but instead throws a `SecurityException` with the specified message if the permission is not granted. For example, the `BatterStatsService` class guarantees that only apps that have the `BATTERY_STATS` permission can obtain battery statistics by calling `enforceCallingPermission()` before executing any other code, as shown in Listing 2-14. Callers that have not been granted the permission receive a `SecurityException`.

```
public byte[] getStatistics() {
    mContext.enforceCallingPermission(
                android.Manifest.permission.BATTERY_STATS, null);
    Parcel out = Parcel.obtain();
    mStats.writeToParcel(out, 0);
    byte[] data = out.marshall();
    out.recycle();
    return data;
}
```

Listing 2-14: Dynamic permission check in `BatteryStatsService`

Static Enforcement

Static permission enforcement comes into play when an application tries to interact with a component declared by another application. The enforcement process takes into account the permissions declared for each target component (if any) and allows the interaction if the caller process has been granted the required permission.

Android uses intents to describe an operation it needs to perform, and intents that fully specify the target component (by package and class name) are called *explicit*. On the other hand, *implicit* intents contain some data (often only an abstract action such as `ACTION_SEND`) that allows the system to find a matching component, but they do not fully specify a target component.

When the system receives an implicit intent, it first resolves it by searching for matching components. If more than one matching component is found, the user is presented with a selection dialog. When a target component has been selected, Android checks to see whether it has any associated permissions, and if it does, checks whether they have been granted to the caller.

The general process is similar to dynamic enforcement: the UID and PID of the caller are obtained using `Binder.getCallingUid()` and `Binder.getCallingPid()`, the caller UID is mapped to a package name, and the associated permissions are retrieved. If the set of caller permissions contains the ones required by the target component, the component is started; otherwise, a `SecurityException` is thrown.

Permission checks are performed by the `ActivityManagerService`, which resolves the specified intent and checks to see whether the target component has an associated permission attribute. If so, it delegates the permission check to the package manager. The timing and concrete sequence of permission checks is slightly different depending on the target component. (Next, we'll examine how checks are performed for each component.)

Activity and Service Permission Enforcement

Permission checks for activities are performed if the intent passed to `Context.startActivity()` or `startActivityForResult()` resolves to an activity that declares a permission. A `SecurityException` is thrown if the caller does not have the required permission. Because Android services can be started, stopped, and bound to, calls to `Context.startService()`, `stopService()`, and `bindService()` are all subject to permission checks if the target service declares a permission.

Content Provider Permission Enforcement

Content provider permissions can either protect the whole component or a particular exported URI, and different permissions can be specified for reading and writing. (You'll learn more about permission declaration in "Content Provider Permissions" on page 46.) If different permissions for reading and writing have been specified, the read permission controls who can call `ContentResolver.query()` on the target provider or URI, and the write permission controls who can call `ContentResolver.insert()`, `ContentResolver.update()`, and `ContentResolver.delete()` on the provider or one of its exported URIs. The checks are performed synchronously when one of these methods is called.

Broadcast Permission Enforcement

When sending a broadcast, applications can require that receivers hold a particular permission by using the `Context.sendBroadcast (Intent intent, String receiverPermission)` method. Because broadcasts are asynchronous, no permission check is performed when calling this method. The check is performed when delivering the intent to registered receivers. If a target receiver does not hold the required permission, it is skipped and does not receive the broadcast, but no exception is thrown. In turn, broadcast receivers can require that broadcasters hold a specific permission in order to be able to target them.

The required permission is specified in the manifest or when registering a broadcast dynamically. This permission check is also performed when delivering the broadcast and does not result in a `SecurityException`. Thus delivering a broadcast might require two permission checks: one for the broadcast sender (if the receiver specified a permission) and one for the broadcast receiver (if the sender specified a permission).

Protected and Sticky Broadcasts

Some system broadcasts are declared as *protected* (for example, `BOOT_COMPLETED` and `PACKAGE_INSTALLED`) and can only be sent by a system process running as one of `SYSTEM_UID`, `PHONE_UID`, `SHELL_UID`, `BLUETOOTH_UID`, or *root*. If a process running under a different UID tries to send a protected broadcast, it receives a `SecurityException` when calling one of the `sendBroadcast()` methods. Sending "sticky" broadcasts (if marked as sticky, the system preserves the sent `Intent` object after the broadcast is complete) requires that the sender holds `BROADCAST_STICKY` permission; otherwise, a `SecurityException` is thrown and the broadcast is not sent.

System Permissions

Android's built-in permissions are defined in the `android` package, sometimes also referred to as "the framework" or "the platform." As we learned in Chapter 1, the core Android framework is the set of classes shared by system services, with some exposed via the public SDK as well. Framework classes are packaged in JAR files found in */system/framework/* (about 40 in latest releases).

Besides JAR libraries, the framework contains a single APK file, *framework-res.apk*. As the name implies, it packages framework resources (animation, drawables, layouts, and so on), but no actual code. Most importantly, it defines the `android` package and system permissions. As *framework-res.apk* is an APK file, it contains an *AndroidManifest.xml* file where permission groups and permissions are declared (see Listing 2-15).

```
<?xml version="1.0" encoding="utf-8"?>
<manifest xmlns:android="http://schemas.android.com/apk/res/android"
    package="android" coreApp="true" android:sharedUserId="android.uid.system"
    android:sharedUserLabel="@string/android_system_label">
```

```
    --snip--
    <protected-broadcast android:name="android.intent.action.BOOT_COMPLETED" />❶
    <protected-broadcast android:name="android.intent.action.PACKAGE_INSTALL" />
    --snip--
    <permission-group android:name="android.permission-group.MESSAGES"
        android:label="@string/permgrouplab_messages"
        android:icon="@drawable/perm_group_messages"
        android:description="@string/permgroupdesc_messages"
        android:permissionGroupFlags="personalInfo"
        android:priority="360"/>❷
    <permission android:name="android.permission.SEND_SMS"
        android:permissionGroup="android.permission-group.MESSAGES"❸
        android:protectionLevel="dangerous"
        android:permissionFlags="costsMoney"
        android:label="@string/permlab_sendSms"
        android:description="@string/permdesc_sendSms" />
    --snip--
    <permission android:name="android.permission.NET_ADMIN"
        android:permissionGroup="android.permission-group.SYSTEM_TOOLS"
        android:protectionLevel="signature" />❹
    --snip--
    <permission android:name="android.permission.MANAGE_USB"
        android:permissionGroup="android.permission-group.HARDWARE_CONTROLS"
        android:protectionLevel="signature|system"❺
        android:label="@string/permlab_manageUsb"
        android:description="@string/permdesc_manageUsb" />
    --snip--
    <permission android:name="android.permission.WRITE_SECURE_SETTINGS"
        android:permissionGroup="android.permission-group.DEVELOPMENT_TOOLS"
        android:protectionLevel="signature|system|development"❻
        android:label="@string/permlab_writeSecureSettings"
        android:description="@string/permdesc_writeSecureSettings" />
    --snip--
</manifest>
```

Listing 2-15: System permission definitions in the manifest of framework-res.apk

As shown in this listing, the *AndroidManifest.xml* file also declares the system's protected broadcasts ❶. A *permission group* ❷ specifies a name for a set of related permissions. Individual permission can be added to a group by specifying the group name in their `permissionGroup` attribute ❸.

Permission groups are used to display related permissions in the system UI, but each permission still needs to be requested individually. That is, applications cannot request that they be granted all the permissions in a group.

Recall that each permission has an associated protection level declared using the `protectionLevel` attribute, as shown at ❹.

Protection levels can be combined with *protection flags* to further constrain how permissions are granted. The currently defined flags are `system` (0x10) and `development` (0x20). The `system` flag requires that applications be part of the system image (that is, installed on the read-only *system* partition) in order to be granted a permission. For example, the `MANAGE_USB` permission, which allows applications to manage preferences and permissions for

USB devices, is only granted to applications that are both signed with the platform signing key and installed on the *system* partition ❺. The `development` flag marks development permissions ❻, which we'll discuss after presenting signature permissions.

Signature Permissions

As discussed in Chapter 1, all Android applications are required to be code signed with a signature key controlled by the developer. This applies to system applications and the framework resource package as well. We discuss package signing in detail in Chapter 3, but for now let's say a few words about how system applications are signed.

System applications are signed by a *platform key*. By default, there are four different keys in the current Android source tree: *platform*, *shared*, *media*, and *testkey* (*releasekey* for release builds). All packages considered part of the core platform (System UI, Settings, Phone, Bluetooth, and so on) are signed with the *platform* key; the search- and contacts-related packages with the *shared* key; the gallery app and media related providers with the *media* key; and everything else (including packages that don't explicitly specify the signing key in their makefile) with the *testkey* (or *releasekey*). The *framework-res.apk* APK that defines system permissions is signed with the *platform* key. Thus any app trying to request a system permission with *signature* protection level needs to be signed with the same key as the framework resource package.

For example, the `NET_ADMIN` permission shown in Listing 2-15 (which allows a granted application to control network interfaces), is declared with the *signature* protection level ❹ and can only be granted to applications signed with the *platform* key.

NOTE *The Android open source repository (AOSP) includes pregenerated test keys that are used by default when signing compiled packages. They should never be used for production builds because they are public and available to anyone who downloads Android source code. Release builds should be signed with newly generated private keys that belong only to the build owner. Keys can be generated using the* make_key *script, which is included in the* development/tools/ *AOSP directory. See the* build/target/product/security/README *file for details on platform key generation.*

Development Permissions

Traditionally, the Android permission model does not allow for dynamically granting and revoking permissions, and the set of granted permission for an application is fixed at install time. However, since Android 4.2, this rule has been relaxed a little by adding a number of *development permissions* (such as `READ_LOGS` and `WRITE_SECURE_SETTINGS`). Development permission can be granted or revoked on demand using the *pm grant* and *pm revoke* commands on the Android shell.

NOTE *Of course, this operation is not available to everyone and is protected by the* `GRANT_REVOKE_PERMISSIONS` *signature permission. It is granted to the* android .uid.shell *shared user ID (UID 2000), and to all processes started from the Android shell (which also runs as UID 2000).*

Shared User ID

Android applications signed with the same key can request the ability to run as the same UID, and optionally in the same process. This feature is referred to as *shared user ID* and is extensively used by core framework services and system applications. Because it can have subtle effects on process accounting and application management, the Android team does not recommend that third-party applications use it, but it is available to user-installed applications as well. Additionally, switching an existing applications that does not use a shared user ID to a shared user ID is not supported, so cooperating applications that need to use shared user ID should be designed and released as such from the start.

Shared user ID is enabled by adding the `sharedUserId` attribute to *AndroidManifest.xml*'s root element. The user ID specified in the manifest needs to be in Java package format (containing at least one dot [`.`]) and is used as an identifier, much like package names for applications. If the specified shared UID does not exist, it is created. If another package with the same shared UID is already installed, the signing certificate is compared to that of the existing package, and if they do not match, an `INSTALL_FAILED_SHARED_USER_INCOMPATIBLE` error is returned and installation fails.

Adding the `sharedUserId` attribute to a new version of an installed app will cause it to change its UID, which would result in losing access to its own files (that was the case in some early Android versions). Therefore, this is disallowed by the system, which will reject the update with the `INSTALL_FAILED_UID_CHANGED` error. In short, if you plan to use shared UID for your apps, you have to design for it from the start, and must have used it since the very first release.

The shared UID itself is a first class object in the system's package database and is treated much like applications: it has an associated signing certificate(s) and permissions. Android has five built-in shared UIDs, which are automatically added when the system is bootstrapped:

- *android.uid.system* (SYSTEM_UID, 1000)
- *android.uid.phone* (PHONE_UID, 1001)
- *android.uid.bluetooth* (BLUETOOH_UID, 1002)
- *android.uid.log* (LOG_UID, 1007)
- *android.uid.nfc* (NFC_UID, 1027)

Listing 2-16 shows how the *android.uid.system* shared user is defined:

```
<shared-user name="android.uid.system" userId="1000">
<sigs count="1">
```

```
<cert index="4" />
</sigs>
<perms>
<item name="android.permission.MASTER_CLEAR" />
<item name="android.permission.CLEAR_APP_USER_DATA" />
<item name="android.permission.MODIFY_NETWORK_ACCOUNTING" />
--snip--
<shared-user/>
```

Listing 2-16: Definition of the android.uid.system *shared user*

As you can see, apart from having a bunch of scary permissions (about 66 on a 4.4 device), the definition is very similar to the package declarations shown earlier. Conversely, packages that are part of a shared user do not have an associated granted permission list. Instead, they inherit the permissions of the shared user, which are a union of the permissions requested by all currently installed packages with the same shared user ID. One side effect of this is that if a package is part of a shared user, it can access APIs that it hasn't explicitly requested permissions for, as long as some package with the same shared user ID has already requested them. Permissions are dynamically removed from the `<shared-user>` definition as packages are installed or uninstalled though, so the set of available permissions is neither guaranteed nor constant.

Listing 2-17 shows how the declaration of the `KeyChain` system app that runs under a shared user ID looks like. As you can see, it references the shared user with the `sharedUserId` attribute and lacks explicit permission declarations:

```
<package name="com.android.keychain"
        codePath="/system/app/KeyChain.apk"
        nativeLibraryPath="/data/app-lib/KeyChain"
        flags="540229" ft="13cd65721a0"
        it="13c2d4721f0" ut="13cd65721a0"
        version="19"
        sharedUserId="1000">
       <sigs count="1">
           <cert index="4" />
       </sigs>
       <signing-keyset identifier="1" />
    </package>
```

Listing 2-17: Package declaration of an application that runs under a shared user ID

The shared UID is not just a package management construct; it actually maps to a shared Linux UID at runtime as well. Listing 2-18 shows an example of two system apps running as the *system* user (UID 1000):

```
system    5901  9852  845708 40972 ffffffff 00000000 S com.android.settings
system    6201  9852  824756 22256 ffffffff 00000000 S com.android.keychain
```

Listing 2-18: Applications running under a shared UID (system)

Applications that are part of a shared user can run in the same process, and because they already have the same Linux UID and can access the same system resources, this typically does not require any additional modifications. A common process can be requested by specifying the same process name in the process attribute of the <application> tag in the manifests of all apps that need to run in one process. While the obvious result of this is that the apps can share memory and communicate directly instead of using IPC, some system services allow special access to components running in the same process (for example, direct access to cached passwords or getting authentication tokens without showing UI prompts). Google applications (such as Play Services and the Google location service) take advantage of this by requesting to run in the same process as the Google login service in order to be able to sync data in the background without user interaction. Naturally, they are signed with the same certificate and are part of the *com.google.uid.shared* shared user.

Custom Permissions

Custom permissions are simply permissions declared by third-party applications. When declared, they can be added to application components for static enforcement by the system, or the application can dynamically check to see if callers have been granted the permission using the checkPermission() or enforcePermission() methods of the Context class. As with built-in permissions, applications can define permission groups that their custom permissions are added to. For example, Listing 2-19 shows the declaration of a permission group ❷ and the permission belonging to that group ❸.

```
<?xml version="1.0" encoding="utf-8"?>
<manifest xmlns:android="http://schemas.android.com/apk/res/android"
    package="com.example.app"
    android:versionCode="1"
    android:versionName="1.0" >
    --snip--
    <permission-tree
        android:name="com.example.app.permission"
        android:label="@string/example_permission_tree_label" />❶

    <permission-group
        android:name="com.example.app.permission-group.TEST_GROUP"
        android:label="@string/test_permission_group_label"
        android:description="@string/test_permission_group_desc"/>❷

    <permission
        android:name="jcom.example.app.permission.PERMISSION1"
        android:label="@string/permission1_label"
        android:description="@string/permission1_desc"
        android:permissionGroup="com.example.app.permission-group.TEST_GROUP"
        android:protectionLevel="signature" />❸
```

```
    --snip--
</manifest>
```

Listing 2-19: Custom permission tree, permission group, and permission declaration

As with system permissions, if the protection level is *normal* or *dangerous*, custom permission will be granted automatically when the user okays the confirmation dialog. In order to be able to control which applications are granted a custom permission, you need to declare it with the *signature* protection level to guarantee that it will only be granted to applications signed with the same key.

NOTE *The system can only grant a permission that it knows about, which means that applications that define custom permissions need to be installed before the applications that make use of those permissions are installed. If an application requests a permission unknown to the system, it is ignored and not granted.*

Applications can also add new permissions dynamically using the `android.content.pm.PackageManager.addPermission()` API and remove them with the matching `removePermision()` API. Such dynamically added permissions must belong to a *permission tree* defined by the application. Applications can only add or remove permissions from a permission tree in their own package or another package running as the same shared user ID.

Permission tree names are in reverse domain notation and a permission is considered to be in a permission tree if its name is prefixed with the permission tree name plus a dot (.). For example, the `com.example.app.permission.PERMISSION2` permission is a member of the `com.example.app.permission` tree defined in Listing 2-19 at ❶. Listing 2-20 shows how to add a dynamic permission programmatically.

```
PackageManager pm = getPackageManager();
PermissionInfo permission = new PermissionInfo();
permission.name = "com.example.app.permission.PERMISSION2";
permission.labelRes = R.string.permission_label;
permission.protectionLevel = PermissionInfo.PROTECTION_SIGNATURE;
boolean added = pm.addPermission(permission);
Log.d(TAG, "permission added: " + added);
```

Listing 2-20: Adding a dynamic permission programmatically

Dynamically added permissions are added to the package database (*/data/system/packages.xml*). They persist across reboots, just like permissions defined in the manifest, but they have an additional `type` attribute set to *dynamic*.

Public and Private Components

Components defined in the *AndroidManifest.xml* file can be public or private. Private components can be called only by the declaring application, while public ones are available to other applications as well.

With the exception of content providers, all components are private by default. Because the purpose of content providers is to share data with other applications, content providers were initially public by default, but this behavior changed in Android 4.2 (API Level 17). Applications that target API Level 17 or later now get private content providers by default, but they are kept public for backward compatibility when targeting a lower API level.

Components can be made public by explicitly setting the `exported` attribute to `true`, or implicitly by declaring an intent filter. Components that have an intent filter but that do not need to be public can be made private by setting the `exported` attribute to `false`. If a component is not exported, calls from external applications are blocked by the activity manager, regardless of the permissions the calling process has been granted (unless it is running as *root* or *system*). Listing 2-21 shows how to keep a component private by setting the `exported` attribute to `false`.

```
<service android:name=".MyService" android:exported="false" >
    <intent-filter>
        <action android:name="com.example.FETCH_DATA" />
    </intent-filter>
</service>
```

Listing 2-21: Keeping a component private by setting `exported="false"`

Unless explicitly intended for public consumption, all public components should be protected by a custom permission.

Activity and Service Permissions

Activities and services can each be protected by a single permission set with the `permission` attribute of the target component. The activity permission is checked when other applications call `Context.startActivity()` or `Context.startActivityForResult()` with an intent that resolves to that activity. For services, the permission is checked when other applications call one of `Context.startService()`, `stopService()`, or `bindService()` with an intent that resolves to the service.

For example, Listing 2-22 shows two custom permissions, `START_MY_ACTIVITY` and `USE_MY_SERVICE`, set to an activity ❶ and service ❷, respectively. Applications that want to use these components need to request the respective permissions using the `<uses-permission>` tag in their manifest.

```
<?xml version="1.0" encoding="utf-8"?>
<manifest xmlns:android="http://schemas.android.com/apk/res/android"
    package="com.example.myapp"
    ... >
    <permission android:name="com.example.permission.START_MY_ACTIVITY"
        android:protectionLevel="signature"
        android:label="@string/start_my_activity_perm_label"
        android:description="@string/start_my_activity_perm_desc" />
    <permission android:name="com.example.permission.USE_MY_SERVICE"
```

```
        android:protectionLevel="signature"
        android:label="@string/use_my_service_perm_label"
        android:description="@string/use_my_service_perm_desc" />

    --snip--
    <activity android:name=".MyActivity"
        android:label="@string/my_activity"
        android:permission="com.example.permission.START_MY_ACTIVITY">❶
        <intent-filter>
        --snip--
       </intent-filter>
    </activity>
    <service android:name=".MyService"
        android:permission="com.example.permission.USE_MY_SERVICE">❷
        <intent-filter>
        --snip--
        </intent-filter>
    </service>
    --snip--
</manifest>
```

Listing 2-22: Protecting activities and services with custom permissions

Broadcast Permissions

Unlike activities and services, permissions for broadcast receivers can be specified both by the receiver itself and by the application sending the broadcast. When sending a broadcast, applications can either use the `Context.sendBroadcast(Intent intent)` method to send a broadcast to be delivered to all registered receives, or limit the scope of components that receive the broadcast by using the `Context.sendBroadcast(Intent intent, String receiverPermission)`. The `receiverPermission` parameter specifies the permission that interested receivers need to hold in order to receive the broadcast. Alternatively, starting with Android 4.0, senders can use the `Intent.setPackage(String packageName)` to limit the scope of receivers to those defined in the specified package. On multi-user devices, system applications that hold the `INTERACT_ACROSS_USERS` permission can send a broadcast that is delivered only to a specific user by the using the `sendBroadcastAsUser(Intent intent, UserHandle user)` and `sendBroadcastAsUser(Intent intent, UserHandle user, String receiverPermission)` methods.

Receivers can limit who can send them broadcasts by specifying a permission using the `permission` attribute of the <receiver> tag in the manifest for statically registered receivers, or by passing the required permission to the `Context.registerReceiver(BroadcastReceiver receiver, IntentFilter filter, String broadcastPermission, Handler scheduler)` method for dynamically registered receivers.

Only broadcasters that have been granted the required permission will be able to send a broadcast to that receiver. For example, device administration applications that enforce systemwide security policies (we discuss device administration in Chapter 9) require the `BIND_DEVICE_ADMIN` permission in order to receive the DEVICE_ADMIN_ENABLED broadcast. Because this is a system permission with protection level *signature*, requiring the permission guarantees that only the system can activate device administration applications. For example, Listing 2-23 shows how the default Android Email application specifies the BIND_DEVICE_ADMIN ❶ permission for its PolicyAdmin receiver.

```
<?xml version="1.0" encoding="utf-8"?>
<manifest xmlns:android="http://schemas.android.com/apk/res/android"
    package="com.android.email"
    android:versionCode="500060" >
        --snip--
        <receiver
            android:name=".SecurityPolicy$PolicyAdmin"
            android:label="@string/device_admin_label"
            android:description="@string/device_admin_description"
            android:permission="android.permission.BIND_DEVICE_ADMIN" >❶
            <meta-data
                android:name="android.app.device_admin"
                android:resource="@xml/device_admin" />
            <intent-filter>
                <action
                    android:name="android.app.action.DEVICE_ADMIN_ENABLED" />
            </intent-filter>
        </receiver>
        --snip--
</manifest>
```

Listing 2-23: Specifying a permission for a statically registered broadcast receiver

As with other components, private broadcast receivers can only receive broadcasts originating from the same application.

Content Provider Permissions

As mentioned in "The Nature of Permissions" on page 21, content providers have a more complex permission model than other components, as we'll describe in detail in this section.

Static Provider Permissions

While a single permissions that controls access to the whole provider can be specified using the permission attribute, most providers employ different permission for reading and writing, and can also specify per-URI permissions. One example of a provider that uses different permissions for reading and writing is the built-in ContactsProvider. Listing 2-24 shows the declaration of its ContactsProvider2 class.

```
<manifest xmlns:android="http://schemas.android.com/apk/res/android"
        package="com.android.providers.contacts"
        android:sharedUserId="android.uid.shared"
        android:sharedUserLabel="@string/sharedUserLabel">
```

```
        --snip--
        <provider android:name="ContactsProvider2"
            android:authorities="contacts;com.android.contacts"
            android:label="@string/provider_label"
            android:multiprocess="false"
            android:exported="true"
            android:readPermission="android.permission.READ_CONTACTS"❶
            android:writePermission="android.permission.WRITE_CONTACTS">❷
            --snip--
            <path-permission
                    android:pathPattern="/contacts/.*/photo"
                    android:readPermission="android.permission.GLOBAL_SEARCH" />❸
            <grant-uri-permission android:pathPattern=".*" />
        </provider>
        --snip--
</manifest>
```

Listing 2-24: `ContactsProvider` *permission declarations*

The provider uses the `readPermission` attribute to specify one permission for reading data (`READ_CONTACTS` ❶), and a separate permission for writing data using the `writePermission` attribute (`WRITE_CONTACTS` ❷). Thus, applications that only hold the `READ_CONTACTS` permission can only call the `query()` method of the provider, and calls to `insert()`, `update()`, or `delete()` require the caller to hold the `WRITE_CONTACTS` permission. Applications that need to both read and write to the contacts provider need to hold both permissions.

When the global read and write permission are not sufficiently flexible, providers can specify per-URI permissions to protect a certain subset of their data. Per-URI permissions have higher priority than the component-level permission (or read and write permissions, if specified separately). Thus if an application wants to access a content provider URI that has an associated permission, it needs to hold only the target URI's permission, and not the component-level permission. In Listing 2-24, the `ContactsProvider2` uses the `<path-permission>` tag to require that applications trying to read photos of contacts hold the `GLOBAL_SEARCH` permission ❸. As per-URI permissions override the global read permission, interested applications do not need to hold the `READ_CONTACTS` permission. In practice, the `GLOBAL_SEARCH` permission is used to grant read-only access to some of the system providers' data to Android's search system, which cannot be expected to hold read permissions to all providers.

Dynamic Provider Permissions

While statically defined per-URI permissions can be quite powerful, applications sometimes need to grant temporary access to a particular piece of data (referred to by its URI) to other apps, without requiring that they hold a particular permission. For example, an email or messaging application may need to cooperate with an image viewer app in order to display an attachment. Because the app cannot know the URIs of attachments in advance, if it used static per-URI permissions, it would need to grant read access to all attachments to the image viewer app, which is undesirable.

To avoid this situation and potential security concern, applications can dynamically grant temporary per-URI access using the `Context.grantUriPermission(String toPackage, Uri uri, int modeFlags)` method and revoke access using the matching `revokeUriPermission(Uri uri, int modeFlags)` method. Temporary per-URI access is enabled by setting the global `grantUriPermissions` attribute to `true` or by adding a `<grant-uri-permission>` tag in order to enable it for a specific URI. For example, Listing 2-25 shows how the Email application uses the `grantUriPermissions` attribute ❶ to allow temporary access to attachments without requiring the `READ_ATTACHMENT` permission.

```
<?xml version="1.0" encoding="utf-8"?>
<manifest xmlns:android="http://schemas.android.com/apk/res/android"
    package="com.android.email"
    android:versionCode="500060" >
        <provider
           android:name=".provider.AttachmentProvider"
           android:authorities="com.android.email.attachmentprovider"
           android:grantUriPermissions="true"❶
           android:exported="true"
           android:readPermission="com.android.email.permission.READ_ATTACHMENT"/>
        --snip--
</manifest>
```

Listing 2-25: `AttachmentProvider` *declaration from the Email app*

In practice, applications rarely use the `Context.grantPermission()` and `revokePermission()` methods directly to allow per-URI access. Instead, they set the `FLAG_GRANT_READ_URI_PERMISSION` or `FLAG_GRANT_WRITE_URI_PERMISSION` flags to the intent used to start the cooperating application (image viewer in our example). When those flags are set, the recipient of the intent is granted permission to perform read or write operations on the URI in the intent's data.

Beginning with Android 4.4 (API Level 19), per-URI access grants can be persisted across device reboots with the `ContentResolver.takePersistableUriPermission()` method, if the received intent has the `FLAG_GRANT_PERSISTABLE_URI_PERMISSION` flag set. Grants are persisted to the */data/system/urigrants.xml* file and can be revoked by calling the `releasePersistableUriPermission()` method. Both transient and persistent per-URI access grants are managed by the system `ActivityManagerService`, which APIs related to per-URI access call internally.

Beginning with Android 4.1 (API level 16), applications can use the `ClipData` facility[6] of intents to add more than one content URI to temporarily be granted access to.

Per-URI access is granted using one of the `FLAG_GRANT_*` intent flags, and automatically revoked when the task of the called application finishes, so there is no need to call `revokePermission()`. Listing 2-26 shows how the Email application creates an intent that launches an attachment viewer application.

6. Google, *Android API Reference*, "ClipData," *http://developer.android.com/reference/android/content/ClipData.html*

```
public Intent getAttachmentIntent(Context context, long accountId) {
    Uri contentUri = getUriForIntent(context, accountId);
    Intent intent = new Intent(Intent.ACTION_VIEW);
    intent.setDataAndType(contentUri, mContentType);
    intent.addFlags(Intent.FLAG_GRANT_READ_URI_PERMISSION |
                    Intent.FLAG_ACTIVITY_CLEAR_WHEN_TASK_RESET);
    return intent;
}
```

Listing 2-26: Using the `FLAG_GRANT_READ_URI_PERMISSION` flag to start a viewer application

Pending Intents

Pending intents are neither an Android component nor a permission, but because they allow an application to grant its own permissions to another application, we discuss them here.

Pending intents encapsulate an intent and a target action to perform with it (start an activity, send a broadcast, and so on). The main difference from "regular" intents is that pending intents also include the identity of the applications that created them. This allows pending intents to be handed to other applications, which can use them to perform the specified action using the identity and permissions of the original application. The identity stored in pending intents is guaranteed by the system `ActivityManagerService`, which keeps track of the currently active pending intents.

Pending intents are used to implement alarms and notifications in Android. Alarms and notifications allow any application to specify an action that needs to be performed on its behalf, either at a specified time for alarms, or when the user interacts with a system notification. Alarms and notifications can be triggered when the application that created them is no longer running, and the system uses the information in the pending intent to start it and perform the intent action on its behalf. Listing 2-27 shows how the Email application uses a pending intent created with the `PendingIntent.getBroadcast()` ❶ to schedule broadcasts that trigger email synchronization.

```
private void setAlarm(long id, long millis) {
    --snip--
    Intent i = new Intent(this, MailboxAlarmReceiver.class);
    i.putExtra("mailbox", id);
    i.setData(Uri.parse("Box" + id));
    pi = PendingIntent.getBroadcast(this, 0, i, 0);❶
    mPendingIntents.put(id, pi);
    AlarmManager am =
            (AlarmManager)getSystemService(Context.ALARM_SERVICE);
    m.set(AlarmManager.RTC_WAKEUP,
          System.currentTimeMillis() + millis, pi);
    --snip--
}
```

Listing 2-27: Using a pending intent to schedule an alarm

Pending intents can be handed to non-system applications as well. The same rules apply: applications that receive a `PendingIntent` instance can perform the specified operation with the same permissions and identity as creator applications. Therefore, care should be taken when building the base intent, and base intents should generally be as specific as possible (with component name explicitly specified) to ensure that the intent is received by the intended components.

The implementation of pending intents is rather complex, but it is based on the same IPC and sandboxing principles that other Android components are built upon. When an application creates a pending intent, the system retrieves its UID and PID using `Binder.getCallingUid()` and `Binder.getCallingPid()`. Based on those, the system retrieves the package name and user ID (on multi-user devices) of the creator and stores them in a `PendingIntentRecord` along with the base intent and any additional metadata. The activity manager keeps a list of active pending intents by storing the corresponding `PendingIntentRecords`, and when triggered, retrieves the necessary record. It then uses the information in the record to assume the identity of the pending intent creator and execute the specified action. From there, the process is the same as when starting any Android component and the same permission checks are performed.

Summary

Android runs each application in a restricted sandbox and requires that applications request specific permissions in order to interact with other apps or the system. Permissions are strings that denote the ability to perform a particular action. They are granted at application install time and (with the exception of development permissions) remain fixed during an application's lifetime. Permissions can be mapped to Linux supplementary group IDs, which the kernel checks before granting access to system resources.

Higher-level system services enforce permissions by obtaining the UID of the calling application using Binder and looking up the permissions it holds in the package manager database. Permissions associated with a component declared in an application's manifest file are automatically enforced by the system, but applications can also choose to perform additional permission checks dynamically. In addition to using built-in permissions, applications can also define custom permissions and associate them with their components in order to control access.

Each Android component can require a permission, and content providers can additionally specify read and write permissions on a per-URI basis. Pending intents encapsulate the identity of the application that created them as well as an intent and an action to perform, which allows the system or third-party applications to perform actions on behalf of the original applications with the same identity and permissions.

3

PACKAGE MANAGEMENT

In this chapter, we take an in-depth look at Android package management. We begin with a description of Android's package format and code signing implementation, and then detail the APK install process. Next, we explore Android's support for encrypted APKs and secure application containers, which are used to implement a form of DRM for paid applications. Finally, we describe Android's package verification mechanism and its most widely used implementation: the Google Play application verification service.

Android Application Package Format

Android applications are distributed and installed in the form of application package (APK) files, which are usually referred to as *APK files*. APK files are container files that include both application code and resources, as well as the application manifest file. They can also include a code signature. The

APK format is an extension of the Java JAR format,[1] which in turn is an extension of the popular ZIP file format. APK files typically have the *.apk* extension and are associated with the *application/vnd.android.package-archive* MIME type.

Because APK files are simply ZIP files, you can easily examine their contents by extracting them with any compression utility that supports the ZIP format. Listing 3-1 shows the contents of a typical APK file after it has been extracted.

```
apk/
|-- AndroidManifest.xml❶
|-- classes.dex❷
|-- resources.arsc❸
|-- assets/❹
|-- lib/❺
|   |-- armeabi/
|   |   `-- libapp.so
|   `-- armeabi-v7a/
|       `-- libapp.so
|-- META-INF/❻
|   |-- CERT.RSA
|   |-- CERT.SF
|   `-- MANIFEST.MF
`-- res/❼
    |-- anim/
    |-- color/
    |-- drawable/
    |-- layout/
    |-- menu/
    |-- raw/
    `-- xml/
```

Listing 3-1: Contents of a typical APK file

Every APK file includes an *AndroidManifest.xml* file ❶ which declares the application's package name, version, components, and other metadata. The *classes.dex* file ❷ contains the executable code of the application and is in the native DEX format of the Dalvik VM. The *resources.arsc* ❸ packages all of the application's compiled resources such as strings and styles. The *assets* directory ❹ is used to bundle raw asset files with the application, such as fonts or music files.

Applications that take advantage of native libraries via JNI contain a *lib* directory ❺, with subdirectories for each supported platform architecture. Resources that are directly referenced from Android code, either directly using the `android.content.res.Resources` class or indirectly via higher-level APIs, are stored in the *res* directory ❼, with separate directories for each resource type (animations, images, menu definitions, and so on). Like JAR files, APK files also contain a *META-INF* directory ❻, which hosts the package manifest file and code signatures. We'll describe the contents of this directory in the next section.

1. Oracle, *JAR File Specification*, *http://docs.oracle.com/javase/7/docs/technotes/guides/jar/jar.html*

Code Signing

As we learned in Chapter 2, Android uses APK code signing, in particular the APK signing certificate, in order to control which applications can be granted permission with the *signature* protection level. The APK signing certificate is also used for various checks during the application installation process, so before we get into details about APK installation, we should become more familiar with code signing in Android. This section provides some details about Java code signing in general and highlights the differences with Android's implementation.

Let's start with a few words about code signing in general. Why would anyone want to sign code? For the usual reasons: integrity and authenticity. Before executing any third-party program, you want to make sure that it hasn't been tampered with (integrity) and that it was actually created by the entity that it claims to come from (authenticity). These features are usually implemented by a digital signature scheme, which guarantees that only the entity owning the signing key can produce a valid code signature.

The signature verification process verifies both that the code has not been tampered with and that the signature was produced with the expected key. But one problem that code signing doesn't solve directly is whether the code signer (software publisher) can be trusted. The usual way to establish trust is to require that the code signer holds a digital certificate and attaches it to the signed code. Verifiers decide whether to trust the certificate based on a trust model (such as PKI or web of trust) or on a case-by-case basis.

Another problem that code signing does not even attempt to solve is whether the signed code is safe to run. As Flame[2] and other code-signed malware have demonstrated, even code that appears to have been signed by a trusted third party might not be safe.

Java Code Signing

Java code signing is performed at the JAR file level. It reuses and extends JAR manifest files in order to add a code signature to the JAR archive. The main JAR manifest file (*MANIFEST.MF*) has entries with the filename and digest value of each file in the archive. For example, Listing 3-2 shows the start of the JAR manifest file of a typical APK file. (We'll use APKs instead of regular JARs for all examples in this section.)

```
Manifest-Version: 1.0
Created-By: 1.0 (Android)

Name: res/drawable-xhdpi/ic_launcher.png
SHA1-Digest: K/0Rd/lt0qSlgDD/9DY7aCNlBvU=
```

2. Microsoft Corporation, *Flame malware collision attack explained, http://blogs.technet.com/b/srd/archive/2012/06/06/more-information-about-the-digital-certificates-used-to-sign-the-flame-malware.aspx*

```
Name: res/menu/main.xml
SHA1-Digest: kG8WDil9ur0f+F2AxgcSSKDhjn0=

Name: ...
```

Listing 3-2: JAR manifest file excerpt

Implementation

Java code signing is implemented by adding another manifest file called a *signature file* (with extension *.SF*), which contains the data to be signed, and a digital signature over it. The digital signature is called a *signature block file* and is stored in the archive as a binary file with one of the *.RSA*, *.DSA*, or *.EC* extensions, depending on the signature algorithm used. As shown in Listing 3-3, the signature file is very similar to the manifest.

```
Signature-Version: 1.0
SHA1-Digest-Manifest-Main-Attributes: ZKXxNW/3Rg7JA1r0+RlbJIP6IMA=
Created-By: 1.7.0_51 (Sun Microsystems Inc.)
SHA1-Digest-Manifest: zb0XjEhVBxE0z2ZC+B4OW25WBxo=❶

Name: res/drawable-xhdpi/ic_launcher.png
SHA1-Digest: jTeE2Y5L3uBdQ2g40PB2n72L3dE=❷

Name: res/menu/main.xml
SHA1-Digest: kSQDLtTE07cLhTH/cY54UjbbNBo=❸

Name: ...
```

Listing 3-3: JAR signature file excerpt

The signature file contains the digest of the whole manifest file (*SHA1-Digest-Manifest* ❶), as well as digests for each entry in *MANIFEST.MF* (❷ and ❸). SHA-1 was the default digest algorithm until Java 6, but Java 7 and later can generate file and manifest digests using the SHA-256 and SHA-512 hash algorithms, in which case the digest attributes become *SHA-256-Digest* and *SHA-512-Digest*, respectively. Since version 4.3, Android supports SHA-256 and SHA-512 digests.

The digests in the signature file can easily be verified by using the following OpenSSL commands, as shown in Listing 3-4.

```
$ openssl sha1 -binary MANIFEST.MF |openssl base64❶
zb0XjEhVBxE0z2ZC+B4OW25WBxo=
$ echo -en "Name: res/drawable-xhdpi/ic_launcher.png\r\nSHA1-Digest: \
K/0Rd/lt0qSlgDD/9DY7aCNlBvU=\r\n\r\n"|openssl sha1 -binary |openssl base64❷
jTeE2Y5L3uBdQ2g40PB2n72L3dE=
```

Listing 3-4: Verifying JAR signature file digests using OpenSSL

The first command ❶ takes the SHA-1 digest of the entire manifest file and encodes it to Base64 to produce the *SHA1-Digest-Manifest* value. The second command ❷ simulates the way the digest of a single manifest entry is calculated. It also demonstrates the attribute canonicalization format required by the JAR specification.

The actual digital signature is in binary PKCS#7[3] (or more generally, CMS[4]) format and includes the signature value and signing certificate. Signature block files produced using the RSA algorithm are saved with the extension *.RSA*, and those generated with DSA or EC keys are saved with *.DSA* or *.EC* extensions. Multiple signatures can also be performed, resulting in multiple *.SF* and *.RSA/DSA/EC* files in the JAR file's *META-INF* directory.

The CMS format is rather involved, allowing for signing *and* encryption, both with different algorithms and parameters. It's also extensible via custom signed or unsigned attributes. A thorough discussion is beyond the scope of this chapter (see RFC 5652 for details about CMS), but as used for JAR signing, a CMS structure basically contains the digest algorithm, signing certificate, and signature value. The CMS specifications allows for including signed data in the `SignedData` CMS structure (a format variation called *attached signature*), but JAR signatures don't include it. When the signed data is not included in the CMS structure, the signature is called a *detached signature* and verifiers need to have a copy of the original signed data in order to verify it. Listing 3-5 shows an RSA signature block file parsed into *ASN.1*,[5] with the certificate details trimmed:

```
$ openssl asn1parse -i -inform DER -in CERT.RSA
    0:d=0  hl=4 l= 888 cons: SEQUENCE
    4:d=1  hl=2 l=   9 prim:  OBJECT            :pkcs7-signedData❶
   15:d=1  hl=4 l= 873 cons:  cont [ 0 ]
   19:d=2  hl=4 l= 869 cons:   SEQUENCE
   23:d=3  hl=2 l=   1 prim:    INTEGER           :01❷
   26:d=3  hl=2 l=  11 cons:    SET
   28:d=4  hl=2 l=   9 cons:     SEQUENCE
   30:d=5  hl=2 l=   5 prim:      OBJECT            :sha1❸
   37:d=5  hl=2 l=   0 prim:      NULL
   39:d=3  hl=2 l=  11 cons:    SEQUENCE
   41:d=4  hl=2 l=   9 prim:     OBJECT            :pkcs7-data❹
   52:d=3  hl=4 l= 607 cons:    cont [ 0 ]❺
   56:d=4  hl=4 l= 603 cons:     SEQUENCE
   60:d=5  hl=4 l= 452 cons:      SEQUENCE
   64:d=6  hl=2 l=   3 cons:       cont [ 0 ]
   66:d=7  hl=2 l=   1 prim:        INTEGER           :02
   69:d=6  hl=2 l=   1 prim:       INTEGER           :04
   72:d=6  hl=2 l=  13 cons:       SEQUENCE
   74:d=7  hl=2 l=   9 prim:        OBJECT            :sha1WithRSAEncryption
   85:d=7  hl=2 l=   0 prim:        NULL
   87:d=6  hl=2 l=  56 cons:       SEQUENCE
```

3. EMC RSA Laboratories, *PKCS #7: Cryptographic Message Syntax Standard, http://www.emc.com/emc-plus/rsa-labs/standards-initiatives/pkcs-7-cryptographic-message-syntax-standar.htm*

4. Housley, *RFC 5652 – Cryptographic Message Syntax (CMS), http://tools.ietf.org/html/rfc5652*

5. *Abstract Syntax Notation One (ASN.1)* is a standard notation that describes rules and structures for encoding data in telecommunications and computer networking. It's used extensively in cryptography standards to define the structure of cryptographic objects.

```
 89:d=7  hl=2 l=  11 cons:          SET
 91:d=8  hl=2 l=   9 cons:           SEQUENCE
 93:d=9  hl=2 l=   3 prim:            OBJECT            :countryName
 98:d=9  hl=2 l=   2 prim:            PRINTABLESTRING   :JP
--snip--
735:d=5  hl=2 l=   9 cons:        SEQUENCE
737:d=6  hl=2 l=   5 prim:         OBJECT            :sha1❻
744:d=6  hl=2 l=   0 prim:         NULL
746:d=5  hl=2 l=  13 cons:        SEQUENCE
748:d=6  hl=2 l=   9 prim:         OBJECT            :rsaEncryption❼
759:d=6  hl=2 l=   0 prim:         NULL
761:d=5  hl=3 l= 128 prim:        OCTET STRING      [HEX DUMP]:892744D30DCEDF74933007...❽
```

Listing 3-5: Contents of a JAR file signature block

The signature block contains an object identifier ❶ that describes the type of data (ASN.1 object) that follows: `SignedData`, and the data itself. The included `SignedData` object contains a version ❷ (1); a set of hash algorithm identifiers used ❸ (only one for a single signer, SHA-1 in this example); the type of data that was signed ❹ (*pkcs7-data*, which simply means "arbitrary binary data"); the set of signing certificates ❺; and one or more (one for each signer) `SignerInfo` structures that encapsulates the signature value (not shown in full in Listing 3-5). `SignerInfo` contains a version; a `SignerIdentifier` object, which typically contains the DN of the certificate issuer and the certificate serial number (not shown); the digest algorithm used ❻ (SHA-1, included in ❸); the digest encryption algorithm used to generate the signature value ❼; and the encrypted digest (signature value) itself ❽.

The most important elements of the `SignedData` structure, with regard to JAR and APK signatures, are the set of signing certificates ❺ and the signature value ❽ (or values, when signed by multiple signers).

If we extract the contents of a JAR file, we can use the OpenSSL `smime` command to verify its signature by specifying the signature file as the content or signed data. The `smime` command prints the signed data and the verification result as shown in Listing 3-6:

```
$ openssl smime -verify -in CERT.RSA -inform DER -content CERT.SF signing-cert.pem
Signature-Version: 1.0
SHA1-Digest-Manifest-Main-Attributes: ZKXxNW/3Rg7JA1r0+RlbJIP6IMA=
Created-By: 1.7.0_51 (Sun Microsystems Inc.)
SHA1-Digest-Manifest: zb0XjEhVBxE0z2ZC+B4OW25WBxo=

Name: res/drawable-xhdpi/ic_launcher.png
SHA1-Digest: jTeE2Y5L3uBdQ2g40PB2n72L3dE=

--snip--
Verification successful
```

Listing 3-6: Verifying a JAR file signature block

JAR File Signing

The official JDK tools for JAR signing and verification are the jarsigner and keytool commands. Since Java 5.0 jarsigner also supports timestamping the signature by a Timestamping Authority (TSA), which can be quite useful when you need to ascertain whether a signature was produced before or after the signing certificate expired. However, this feature is not widely used and is not supported on Android.

A JAR file is signed using the jarsigner command by specifying a keystore file (see Chapter 5) together with the alias of the key to use for signing (the first eight characters of the alias become the base name for the signature block file, unless the -sigfile option is specified) and optionally a signature algorithm. See ❶ in Listing 3-7 for an example invocation of jarsigner.

NOTE *Since Java 7, the default algorithm has changed to* SHA256withRSA, *so you need to specify it explicitly if you want to use SHA-1 for backward compatibility. SHA-256- and SHA-512-based signatures have been supported since Android 4.3.*

```
$ jarsigner -keystore debug.keystore -sigalg SHA1withRSA test.apk androiddebugkey❶
$ jarsigner -keystore debug.keystore -verify -verbose -certs test.apk❷
--snip--

smk       965 Sat Mar 08 23:55:34 JST 2014 res/drawable-xxhdpi/ic_launcher.png

      X.509, CN=Android Debug, O=Android, C=US (androiddebugkey)❸
      [certificate is valid from 6/18/11 7:31 PM to 6/10/41 7:31 PM]

smk    458072 Sun Mar 09 01:16:18 JST 2013 classes.dex

      X.509, CN=Android Debug, O=Android, C=US (androiddebugkey)❹
      [certificate is valid from 6/18/11 7:31 PM to 6/10/41 7:31 PM]

         903 Sun Mar 09 01:16:18 JST 2014 META-INF/MANIFEST.MF
         956 Sun Mar 09 01:16:18 JST 2014 META-INF/CERT.SF
         776 Sun Mar 09 01:16:18 JST 2014 META-INF/CERT.RSA

  s = signature was verified
  m = entry is listed in manifest
  k = at least one certificate was found in keystore
  i = at least one certificate was found in identity scope

jar verified.
```

Listing 3-7: Signing an APK file and verifying the signature using the jarsigner command

The jarsigner tool can use all keystore types supported by the platform, as well as keystores that are not natively supported and that require a dedicated JCA provider, such as those backed by a smart card, HSM, or another hardware device. The type of store to be used for signing is specified with the -storetype option, and the provider name and class with the -providerName and -providerClass options. Newer versions of the Android-specific signapk tool (discussed in "Android Code Signing Tools" on page 60), also support the -providerClass option.

JAR File Verification

JAR file verification is performed using the jarsigner command by specifying the -verify option. The second jarsigner command at ❷ in Listing 3-7 first verifies the signature block and signing certificate, ensuring that the signature file has not been tampered with. Next it verifies that each digest in the signature file (*CERT.SF*) matches its corresponding section in the manifest file (*MANIFEST.MF*). (The number of entries in the signature file does not have to match those in the manifest file. Files can be added to a signed JAR without invalidating its signature: as long as none of the original files have been changed, verification succeeds.)

Finally, jarsigner reads each manifest entry and checks that the file digest matches the actual file contents. If a keystore has been specified with the -keystore option (as in our example), jarsigner also checks to see whether the signing certificate is present in the specified keystore. As of Java 7, there is a new -strict option that enables additional certificate validations, including a time validity check and certificate chain verification. Validation errors are treated as warnings and are reflected in the exit code of the jarsigner command.

Viewing or Extracting Signer Information

As you can see in Listing 3-7, by default, jarsigner prints certificate details for each entry (❸ and ❹) even though they are the same for all entries. A slightly better way to view signer info when using Java 7 is to specify the -verbose:summary or -verbose:grouped options, or alternatively use the keytool command, as shown in Listing 3-8.

```
$ keytool -list -printcert -jarfile test.apk
Signer #1:
Signature:
Owner: CN=Android Debug, O=Android, C=US
Issuer: CN=Android Debug, O=Android, C=US
Serial number: 4dfc7e9a
Valid from: Sat Jun 18 19:31:54 JST 2011 until: Mon Jun 10 19:31:54 JST 2041
Certificate fingerprints:
         MD5:  E8:93:6E:43:99:61:C8:37:E1:30:36:14:CF:71:C2:32
         SHA1: 08:53:74:41:50:26:07:E7:8F:A5:5F:56:4B:11:62:52:06:54:83:BE
         Signature algorithm name: SHA1withRSA
         Version: 3
```

Listing 3-8: Viewing APK signer information using the keytool command

Once you have found the signature block filename (by listing the archive contents for example), you can use OpenSSL with the unzip command to easily extract the signing certificate to a file, as shown in Listing 3-9. (If the

SignedData structure includes more than one certificate, all certificates will be extracted. In that case, you will need to parse the SignedInfo structure to find the identifier of the actual signing certificate.)

```
$ unzip -q -c test.apk META-INF/CERT.RSA|openssl pkcs7 -inform DER -print_certs -out cert.pem
```

Listing 3-9: Extracting the APK signing certificate using the unzip *and OpenSSL* pkcs7 *commands*

Android Code Signing

Because Android code signing is based on Java JAR signing, it uses public key cryptography and X.509 certificates like many code signing schemes, but that's where the similarities end.

In practically all other platforms that use code signing (such as Java ME and Windows Phone), code signing certificates must be issued by a CA that the platform trusts. While there are many CAs that issue code signing certificates, it can prove quite difficult to obtain a certificate that is trusted by all targeted devices. Android solves this problem quite simply: it doesn't care about the contents or signer of the signing certificate. Thus you do not need to have it issued by a CA, and virtually all code signing certificates used in Android are self-signed. Additionally, you don't need to assert your identity in any way: you can use pretty much anything as the subject name. (The Google Play Store does have a few checks to weed out some common names, but not the Android OS itself.) Android treats signing certificates as binary blobs, and the fact that they are in X.509 format is merely a consequence of using the JAR format.

Android doesn't validate certificates in the PKI sense (see Chapter 6). In fact, if a certificate is not self-signed, the signing CA's certificate does not have to be present or trusted; Android will even happily install apps with an expired signing certificate. If you are coming from a traditional PKI background, this may sound like heresy, but keep in mind that Android does not use PKI for code signing, it only uses the same certificate and signature formats.

Another difference between Android and "standard" JAR signing is that all APK entries must be signed by the same set of certificates. The JAR file format allows each file to be signed by a different signer and permits unsigned entries. This makes sense in the Java sandboxing and access control mechanism, which was originally designed for applets, because that model defines a *code source* as a combination of a signer certificate and code origin URL. However, Android assigns signers per-APK (usually only one, but multiple signers are supported) and does not allow different signers for different APK file entries.

Android's code signing model, coupled with the poor interface of the java.util.jar.JarFile class, which is not a good abstraction for the complexities of the underlying CMS signature format, makes it rather difficult to properly verify the signature of APK files. While Android manages to both verify APK integrity and ensure that all APK file entries have been signed by the same set of certificates by adding additional signing certificate checks to its package parsing routines, it is evident that the JAR file format was not the best choice for Android code signing.

Android Code Signing Tools

As the examples in the "Java Code Signing" section showed, you can use the regular JDK code signing tools to sign or verify APKs. In addition to these tools, the AOSP *build/* directory contains an Android-specific tool called `signapk`. This tool performs pretty much the same task as `jarsigner` in signing mode, with a few notable differences. For one, while `jarsigner` requires that keys be stored in a compatible keystore file, `signapk` takes a separate signing key (in DER-encoded *PKCS#8* format[6]) and certificate file (in DER-encoded X.509 format) as input. The advantage of the PKCS#8 format, which is the standard key encoding format in Java, is that it includes an explicit algorithm identifier that describes the type of the encoded private key. The encoded private key might include key material, possibly encrypted, or it might contain only a reference, such as a key ID, to a key stored in a hardware device.

As of Android 4.4, the `signapk` can only produce signatures with the *SHA1withRSA* or *SHA256withRSA* (added to the platform in Android 4.3) mechanisms. As of this writing, the version of `signapk` found in AOSP's master branch has been extended to support ECDSA signatures.

While raw private keys in PKCS#8 format are somewhat hard to come by, you can easily generate a test key pair and a self-signed certificate using the `make_key` script found in *development/tools/*. If you have existing OpenSSL keys, you'll have to convert them to PKCS#8 format first, using something like OpenSSL's `pkcs8` command as shown in Listing 3-10:

```
$ echo "keypwd"|openssl pkcs8 -in mykey.pem -topk8 -outform DER -out mykey.pk8 -passout stdin
```

Listing 3-10: Converting an OpenSSL key to PKCS#8 format

Once you have the needed keys, you can sign an APK using `signapk` as shown in Listing 3-11.

```
$ java -jar signapk.jar cert.cer key.pk8 test.apk test-signed.apk
```

Listing 3-11: Signing an APK using the `signapk` tool

OTA File Code Signing

Besides its default APK signing mode, the `signapk` tool also has a "sign whole file" mode that can be enabled with the `-w` option. When in this mode, in addition to signing each individual JAR entry, the tool generates a signature over the whole archive as well. This mode is not supported by `jarsigner` and is specific to Android.

6. EMC RSA Laboratories, *PKCS #8: Private-Key Information Syntax Standard, http://www.emc.com/emc-plus/rsa-labs/standards-initiatives/pkcs-8-private-key-information-syntax-stand.htm*

Why sign the whole archive when each file is already signed? In order to support over-the-air (OTA) updates. OTA packages are ZIP files in a format similar to JAR files that contain updated files and the scripts to apply them. The packages include a *META-INF/* directory, manifests, a signature block, and a few extra files, including *META-INF/com/android/otacert*, which contains the update signing certificate (in PEM format). Before booting into recovery to apply updates, Android verifies the package signature and then checks to see if the signing certificate is trusted to sign updates. OTA-trusted certificates are separate from the "regular" system trust store (see Chapter 6), and reside in a ZIP file that is usually stored as */system/etc/security/otacerts.zip*. On a production device, this file typically contains a single file usually named *releasekey.x509.pem*. After the device reboots, the recovery OS verifies the OTA package signature once again before applying it in order to make sure that the OTA file has not been tampered with in the meantime.

If OTA files are like JAR files, and JAR files don't support whole-file signatures, where does the signature go? The Android `signapk` tool slightly abuses the ZIP format by adding a null-terminated string comment in the ZIP comment section, followed by the binary signature block and a 6-byte final record containing the signature offset and the size of the entire comment section. Adding the offset record to the end of the file makes it easy to verify the package by first reading and verifying the signature block from the end of the file, and only reading the rest of the file (which could be in the hundreds of megabytes) if the signature checks out.

APK Install Process

There are a few ways to install Android applications:

- Via an application store client (such as the Google Play Store). This is how most users install applications.
- Directly on the device by opening downloaded app files (if the "Unknown sources" option in system settings is enabled). This method is commonly referred to as *sideloading* an app.
- From a USB-connected computer with the `adb install` Android SDK command which, in turn invokes the `pm` command line utility with the `install` parameter. This method is used mostly by application developers.
- By directly copying an APK file to one of the system application directories using the Android shell. Because application directories are not accessible on production builds, this method can only be used on devices running an engineering (development) build.

When an APK file is copied directly to one of the application directories it is automatically detected and installed by the package manager, which watches these directories for changes. In the case of all other install methods, the installer application (whether Google Play Store client, default system package install activity, `pm` command, or other) invokes one of the `installPackage()` methods of the system package manager, which then copies the APK to one of the application directories and installs it. In the following sections, we'll explore the main steps of the Android package install process, and discuss some of the more complex installation steps like encrypted container creation and package verification.

Android's package management functionality is distributed across several system components that interact with each other during package installation, as shown in Figure 3-1. Solid arrows in the figure represent dependencies between components, as well as function calls. Dashed arrows point to files or directories that are monitored for changes by a component, but which are not directly modified by that component.

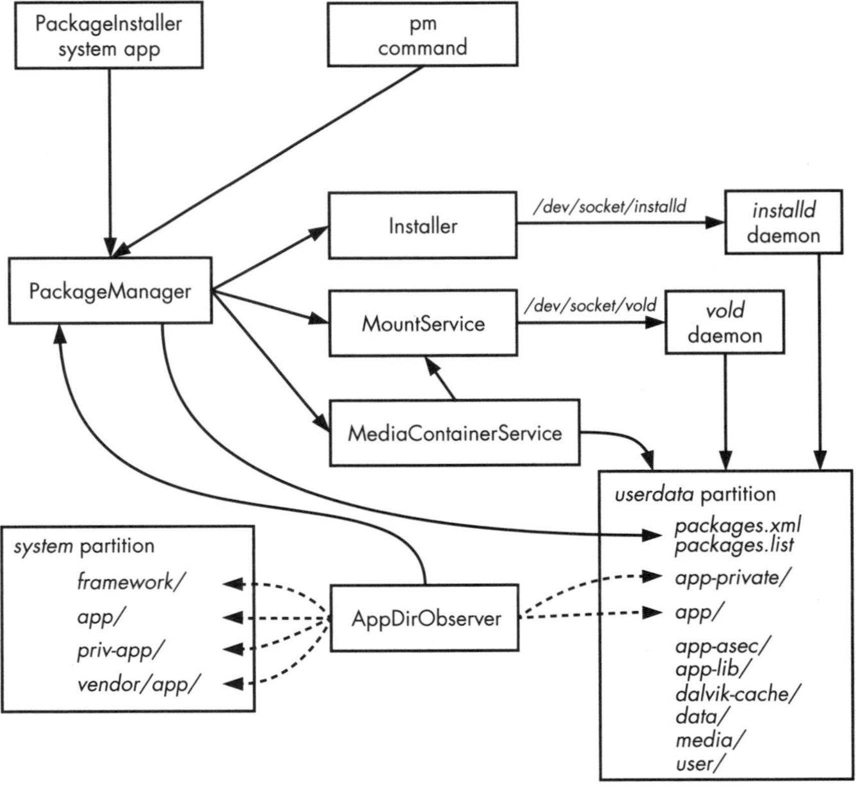

Figure 3-1: Package management components

Location of Application Packages and Data

Recall from Chapter 1 that Android distinguishes between system- and user-installed applications. System applications are found on the read-only *system* partition (bottom left in Figure 3-1) and cannot be changed or uninstalled on production devices. System applications are therefore considered trusted and are given more privileges, and have some signature checks relaxed. Most system applications are found in the */system/app/* directory, while */system/priv-app/* holds privileged apps that can be granted permission with the *signatureOrSystem* protection level (as discussed in Chapter 2). The */system/vendor/app/* directory hosts vendor-specific applications. User-installed applications live on the read-write *userdata* partition (shown at the bottom right in Figure 3-1) and can be uninstalled or replaced at any time. Most user-installed applications are installed in the */data/app/* directory.

Data directories for both system and user-installed applications are created on the *userdata* partition under the */data/data/* directory. The *userdata* partition also hosts the optimized DEX files for user-installed applications (in */data/dalvik-cache/*), the system package database (in */data/system/packages.xml*), and other system databases and settings files. (We'll discuss the rest of the *userdata* partition directories shown in Figure 3-1 when we cover the APK install process.)

Active Components

Having established the roles of the *userdata* and *system* partitions, let's introduce the active components that play a role during package installation.

PackageInstaller System Application

This is the default APK file handler. It provides a basic GUI for package management and when passed an APK file URI with the `VIEW` or `INSTALL_ACTION` intent action, it parses the package and displays an install confirmation screen showing the permissions the application requires (see Figure 2-1 on page 25). Installation using the `PackageInstaller` application is only possible if the user has enabled the Unknown Sources option in the device's security settings (see Figure 3-2). If Unknown Sources is not enabled, `PackageInstaller` will show a dialog informing the user that installation of apps obtained from unknown sources is blocked.

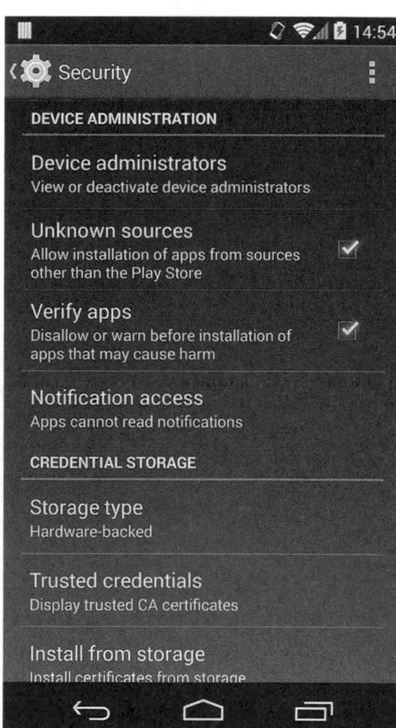

Figure 3-2: Application install security settings

What is considered an "unknown source"? While the on-screen hint defines it as "apps from sources other than the Play Store," the actual definition is a bit more broad. When started, `PackageInstaller` retrieves the UID and package of the app that requested APK installation and checks to see if it is a privileged app (installed in

/system/priv-app/). If the requesting app is unprivileged, it is considered an unknown source. If the Unknown Sources option is selected and the user okays the install dialog, `PackageInstaller` calls the `PackageManagerService`, which performs the actual installation. The `PackageInstaller` GUI is also shown when upgrading side-loaded packages or uninstalling apps from the Apps screen of System Settings.

pm command

The `pm` command (introduced in Chapter 2) provides a command-line interface to some of the functions of the system package manager. It can be used to install or uninstall packages when invoked as `pm install` or `pm uninstall` from the Android shell, respectively. Additionally, the *Android Debug Bridge (ADB)* client provides the `adb install/uninstall` shortcuts.

Unlike the `PackageInstaller`, `pm install` does not depend on the Unknown Sources system option and does not display a GUI, and it provides various useful options for testing package installation that cannot be specified via the `PackageInstaller` GUI. To start the install process, it calls the same `PackageManager` API as the GUI installer.

PackageManagerService

The `PackageManagerService` (`PackageManager` in Figure 3-1) is the central object in Android's package management infrastructure. It is responsible for parsing APK files, starting the application install, upgrading and uninstalling packages, maintaining the package database, and managing permissions.

The `PackageManagerService` also provides a number of `installPackage()` methods that can perform package installation with various options. The most general of these is the `installPackageWithVerificationAndEncryption()`, which allows for the installation of an encrypted APK file, and package verification by a verification agent. (We'll discuss app encryption and verification later in "Installing Encrypted APKs" on page 76 and "Package Verification" on page 83.)

The `android.content.pm.PackageManager` Android SDK facade class exposes a subset of the functionality of the `PackageManagerService` to third-party applications.

Installer class

While the `PackageManagerService` is one of the most privileged Android system services, it still runs inside the system server process (with the *system* UID) and lacks root privileges. However, because creating, deleting, and changing the ownership of application directories requires superuser capabilities, the `PackageManagerService` delegates those operations to the *installd* daemon (discussed next). The `Installer` class connects to the *installd* daemon through the */dev/socket/installd* Unix domain socket and encapsulates the *installd* command-oriented protocol.

installd Daemon

The *installd* daemon is a native daemon with elevated privileges that provides application and user directory management functionality (for multi-user devices) to the system package manager. It is also used to start the `dexopt` command, which generates optimized DEX files for newly installed packages.

The *installd* daemon is accessed via the *installd* local socket, which is only accessible to processes running as the *system* UID. The *installd* daemon does not execute as root (although it used to do so in earlier Android versions), but instead takes advantage of the `CAP_DAC_OVERRIDE` and `CAP_CHOWN` Linux capabilities[7] in order to be able to set the owner and group UID of the application directories and files it creates to those of the owning application.

MountService

The `MountService` is responsible for mounting detachable external storage such as SD cards, as well as *opaque binary blob (OBB) files*, which are used as expansion files for applications. It is also used to kick off device encryption (see Chapter 10) and to change the encryption password.

`MountService` also manages *secure containers*, which hold applications files that should not be accessible to non-system applications. Secure containers are encrypted and used to implement a form of DRM called *forward locking* (discussed in "Forward Locking" on page 79 and "Android 4.1 Forward Locking Implementation" on page 80). Forward locking is used primarily when installing paid applications in order to ensure that their APK files cannot be easily copied off the device and redistributed.

vold daemon

vold is Android's volume management daemon. While the `MountService` contains most system APIs that deal with volume management, because it runs as the *system* user it lacks the privileges required to actually mount and unmount disk volumes. Those privileged operations are implemented in the *vold* daemon, which runs as root.

vold has a local socket interface which is exposed via the */dev/socket/vold* Unix domain socket that is only accessible to root and members of the *mount* group. Because the list of supplementary GIDs of the *system_server* process (which hosts `MountService`) includes *mount* (GID 1009), `MountService` is allowed to access *vold*'s command socket. Besides mounting and unmounting volumes, *vold* can also create and format filesystems and manage secure containers.

MediaContainerService

The `MediaContainerService` copies APK files to their final install location or to an encrypted container, and allows the `PackageManagerService` to access files on removable storage. APK files obtained from a remote location (either

---

7. For a discussion of Linux capabilities, see Chapter 39 of Michael Kerrisk's *The Linux Programming Interface: A Linux and UNIX System Programming Handbook*, No Starch Press, 2010.

directly or through an application market) are downloaded using Android's DownloadManager service and the downloaded files are accessed through DownloadManager's content provider interface. The PackageManager grants temporary access to each downloaded APK to the MediaContainerService process. If the APK file is encrypted, MediaContainerService decrypts the file first (as discussed in "Installing an Encrypted APK with Integrity Check" on page 79). If an encrypted container was requested, MediaContainerService delegates encrypted container creation to the MountService and copies the protected part of the APK (both code and assets) into the newly created container. Files that do not need to be protected by a container are copied directly to the filesystem.

AppDirObserver

An AppDirObserver is a component that monitors an application directory for APK file changes[8] and calls the appropriate PackageManagerService method based on the event type. When an APK file is added to the system, AppDirObserver kicks off a package scan which either installs or updates the application. When an APK file is removed, AppDirObserver starts the uninstall process, which removes app directories and the app entry in the system package database.

Figure 3-1 shows a single AppDirObserver instance due to space constraints, but there is a dedicated instance for each watched directory. The directories monitored on the *system* partition are */system/framework/* (which holds the framework resource package *framework-res.apk*); */system/app/* and */system/priv-app/* (system packages); and the vendor package directory */system/vendor/app/*. The directories monitored on the *userdata* partition are */data/app/* and */data/app-private/* which hosts "old style" (pre-Android 4.1) forward locked APKs and temporary files produced during APK decryption.

Installing a Local Package

Now that we know what Android components are involved in package installation, we'll cover the install process, beginning with the simplest case: installing an unencrypted local package without verification and forward locking.

Parsing and Verifying the Package

Opening a local APK file starts the *application/vnd.android.package-archive* handler, typically the PackageInstallerActivity from the PackageInstaller system application. PackageInstallerActivity first checks to see if the application that requested the install is trusted (that is, not considered from an "unknown source"). If it is not, and the Settings.Global.INSTALL_NON_MARKET_APPS is false (it

8. File monitoring is implemented using Linux's *inotify* facility. For more details about *inotify*, see Chapter 19 of Michael Kerrisk's *The Linux Programming Interface: A Linux and UNIX System Programming Handbook*, No Starch Press, 2010.

is set to true when the Unknown sources checkbox in Figure 3-2 is checked), PackageInstaller shows a warning dialog and ends the install process.

If the installation is allowed, the PackageInstallerActivity parses the APK file and collects information from the *AndroidManifest.xml* file and package signature. The integrity of the APK file is verified automatically while extracting the signing certificates for each of its entries using the java.util.jar.JarFile and related classes. This implementation is necessary because the API of the JarFile class lacks any explicit methods to verify the signature of the whole file or of a particular entry. (System applications are implicitly trusted and only the integrity of the *AndroidManifest.xml* file is verified when parsing their APK files. However, all APK entries are verified for packages that are not part of the system image, such as user-installed applications or updates for system applications.) The hash value of the *AndroidManifest.xml* file is also calculated as part of APK parsing and passed to subsequent install steps, which use it to verify that the APK file was not replaced between the time when the user pressed OK in the install dialog and the APK copy process was started.

NOTE *Another noteworthy detail is that while at install time, APK file integrity is verified using standard Java library classes, at runtime, the Dalvik virtual machine loads APK files using its own native implementation of a ZIP/JAR file parser. Subtle differences in their implementations have been the source of several Android bugs, most notably bug #8219321 (commonly known as the* Android Master Key*) which allows a signed APK file to be modified and still considered valid without resigning. A* StrictJarFile *class, which uses the same ZIP file parsing implementation as Dalvik, has been added in AOSP's master branch in order to address this.* StrictJarFile *is used by the system package manager when parsing APK files, ensuring that both Dalvik and the package manager parse APK files in the same way. This new unified implementation should be incorporated in future Android versions.*

Accepting Permissions and Starting the Install Process

Once the APK has been parsed, PackageInstallerActivity displays information about the application and the permissions it requires in a dialog similar to the one shown in Figure 2-1 (see page 25). If the user OK's the install, PackageInstallerActivity forwards the APK file and its manifest digest, along with install metadata such as the referrer URL, the installer package name, and originating UID to the InstallAppProgress activity, which starts the actual package install process. InstallAppProgress then passes the APK URI and install metadata to the installPackageWithVerificationAndEncryption() method of the PackageManagerService, starting the install process. It then waits for the process to complete and handles any errors.

The install method first verifies that the caller has the INSTALL_PACKAGES permission, which has a protection-level *signature* and is reserved for system applications. On multi-user devices, the method also verifies whether the calling user is allowed to install applications. Next, it determines the preferred install location, which is either internal or external storage.

Copying to the Application Directory

If the APK file is not encrypted and no verification is required, the next step is to copy it to the application directory (*/data/app/*). To copy the file, the `PackageManagerService` first creates a temporary file in the application directory (with the *vmdl* prefix and *.tmp* extension) and then delegates copying to the `MediaContainerService`. The file is not copied directly because it might need to be decrypted, or an encrypted container created for it if it will be forward locked. Because the `MediaContainerServices` encapsulates these tasks, the `PackageManagerService` does not need to be concerned with the underlying implementation.

When the APK file is successfully copied, any native libraries it contains are extracted to a dedicated app directory under the system's native library directory (*/data/app-lib/*). Next, the temporary APK file and the library directory are renamed to their final names, which are based on the package name, such as *com.example.app-1.apk* for the APK and */data/app-lib/com.example.app-1* for the library directory. Finally, the APK file permissions are set to *0644* and its SELinux context is set (see Chapter 12).

NOTE *By default, APK files are world-readable and any other application can access them. This facilitates sharing public app resources and allows the development of third-party launchers and other applications that need to show a list of all installed packages. However, those default permissions also allow anyone to extract APK files from a device, which is problematic for paid applications distributed via an application market. APK file forward locking provides a way for APK resources to remain public, while limiting access to code and assets.*

The Package Scan

The next step in the install process is to trigger a package scan by calling the `scanPackageLI()` method of `PackageManagerService`. (If the install process stops before scanning the new APK file, it will eventually be picked up by the `AppDirObserver` instance which monitors the */data/app/* directory and also triggers a package scan.)

In the case of a new install, the package manager first creates a new `PackageSettings` structure that contains the package name, code path, a separate resource path if the package is forward-locked, and a native library path. It then assigns a UID to the new package and stores it in the settings structure. Once the new app has a UID, its data directory can be created.

Creating Data Directories

Because the `PackageManagerService` does not have enough privileges to create and set ownership of app directories, it delegates directory creation to the *installd* daemon by sending it the `install` command which takes the package name, UID, GID, and *seinfo* tag (used by SELinux) as parameters. The *installd* daemon creates the package data directory (for example,

/data/data/com.example.app/ when installing the *com.example.app* package), shared native library directory (*/data/app-lib/com.example.app/*), and local library directory (*/data/data/com.example.app/lib/*). It then sets the package directory permissions to *0751* and creates symbolic links for the app's native libraries (if any) in the local library directory. Finally, it sets the SELinux context of the package directory and changes its owner to the UID and GID assigned to the app.

If the system has more than one user, the next step is to create data directories for each user by sending the `mkuserdata` command to *installd* (see Chapter 4). When all the necessary directories are created, control returns to the `PackageManagerService`, which extracts any native libraries to the application's native library directory and creates symbolic links in */data/data/com.example.app/lib/*.

Generating Optimized DEX

The next step is to generate optimized DEX for the application's code. This operation is also delegated to *installd* by sending it the `dexopt` command. The *installd* daemon forks a *dexopt* process, which creates the optimized DEX file in the */data/dalivk-cache/* directory. (The optimization process is also referred to as "sharpening.")

NOTE *If the device is using the experimental Android Runtime (ART) introduced in version 4.4 instead of generating optimized DEX,* installd *generates native code using the* `dex2oat` *command.*

File and Directory Structure

When all of the above processes have completed, the application's files and directories might look something like Listing 3-12. (Timestamps and file sizes have been omitted.)

```
-rw-r--r-- system   system   ... /data/app/com.example.app-1.apk❶
-rwxr-xr-x system   system   ... /data/app-lib/com.example.app-1/libapp.so❷
-rw-r--r-- system   all_a215 ... /data/dalvik-cache/data@app@com.example.app-1.apk@classes.dex❸
drwxr-x--x u0_a215  u0_a215  ... /data/data/com.example.app❹
drwxrwx--x u0_a215  u0_a215  ... /data/data/com.example.app/databases❺
drwxrwx--x u0_a215  u0_a215  ... /data/data/com.example.app/files
lrwxrwxrwx install  install  ... /data/data/com.example.app/lib -> /data/app-lib/com.example.app-1❻
drwxrwx--x u0_a215  u0_a215  ... /data/data/com.example.app/shared_prefs
```

Listing 3-12: Files and directories created after installing an application

Here, ❶ is the APK file and ❷ is the extracted native library file. Both files are owned by *system* and are world readable. The file at ❸ is the optimized DEX file for the application's code. Its owner is set to *system* and its group is set to the special *all_a215* group, which includes all device users that have installed the app. This allows all users to share the same optimized DEX file, thus avoiding the need to create a copy for each user, which could take up too much disk space on a multi-user device. The application's data directory ❹ and its subdirectories (such as *databases/* ❺) are owned by the dedicated Linux user created by combining the ID of the device user that installed the application (*u0*, the sole user on single-user devices) and the app ID (*a215*) to produce *u0_a215*. (App data directories are not readable or writable by other users in accordance with Android's sandboxing security model. The *lib/* directory ❻ is merely a symbolic link to the app's shared library directory in */data/app-lib/*.)

Adding the New Package to packages.xml

The next step is to add the package to the system package database. A new package entry that looks like Listing 3-13 is generated and added to *packages.xml*.

```
<package name="com.google.android.apps.chrometophone"
        codePath="/data/app/com.google.android.apps.chrometophone-2.apk"
        nativeLibraryPath="/data/app-lib/com.google.android.apps.chrometophone-2"
        flags="572996"
        ft="142dfa0e588"
        it="142cbeac305"
        ut="142dfa0e8d7"
        version="16"
        userId="10088"
        installer="com.android.vending">❶
    <sigs count="1">
        <cert index="7" key="30820252..." />
    </sigs>❷
    <perms>
        <item name="android.permission.USE_CREDENTIALS" />
        <item name="com.google.android.apps.chrometophone.permission.C2D_MESSAGE" />
        <item name="android.permission.GET_ACCOUNTS" />
        <item name="android.permission.INTERNET" />
        <item name="android.permission.WAKE_LOCK" />
        <item name="com.google.android.c2dm.permission.RECEIVE" />
    </perms>❸
    <signing-keyset identifier="2" />❹
</package>
```

Listing 3-13: Package database entry for a newly installed application

Here, the `<sigs>` ❷ element holds the DER-encoded values of the package signing certificates (typically only one) in hexadecimal string format, or a reference to the first occurrence of the certificate in the case of multiple apps signed by the same key and certificate. The `<perms>` ❸ elements holds the permissions granted to the application, as described in Chapter 2.

The `<signing-keyset>` ❹ element is new in Android 4.4 and holds a reference to the signing key set of the application, which contains all public keys (but *not* certificates) that have signed files inside the APK. The

PackageManagerService collects and stores signing keys for all applications in a global <keyset-settings> element, but key sets are not checked or otherwise used as of Android 4.4.

Package Attributes

The root element <package> ❶ (shown in Listing 3-13) holds the core attributes of each package, such as install location and version. The main package attributes are listed in Table 3-1. The information in each package entry can be obtained via the getPackageInfo(String packageName, int flags) method of the android.content.pm.PackageManager SDK class, which should return a PackageInfo instance that encapsulates the attributes available in each *packages.xml* entry, as well as information about components, permissions, and features defined in the application's manifest.

Table 3-1: Package Attributes

Attribute Name	Description
name	The package name.
codePath	Full path to the location of the package.
resourcePath	Full path to the location of the publicly available parts of the package (primary resource package and manifest). Only set on forward-locked apps.
nativeLibraryPath	Full path to the directory where native libraries are stored.
flags	Flags associated with the application.
ft	APK file timestamp (Unix time in milliseconds, as per System.currentTimeMillis()).
it	The time at which the app was first installed (Unix time in milliseconds).
ut	The time the app was last updated (Unix time in milliseconds).
version	The version number of the package, as specified by the versionCode attribute in the app manifest.
userId	The kernel UID assigned to the application.
installer	The package name of the application that installed the app.
sharedUserId	The shared user ID name of the package, as specified by the sharedUserId attribute in the manifest.

Updating Components and Permissions

After creating the *packages.xml* entry, the PackageManagerService scans all Android components defined in the new application's manifests and adds them to its internal on-memory component registry. Next, any permission groups and permissions the app declares are scanned and added to the permission registry.

NOTE *Custom permissions defined by applications are registered using a "first one wins" strategy: if both app A and B define permission P, and A is installed first, A's permission definition is registered and B's permission definition is ignored (because P is already registered). This is possible because permission names are not bound to the defining app package in any way, and thus any app can define any permission. This "first one wins" strategy can result in permission protection level downgrade: if A's permission definition has a lower protection level (for example,* normal*) than B's definition (for example,* signature*), and A is installed first, access to B's components protected by P will not require callers to be signed with the same key as B. Therefore, when using custom permissions to protect components, be sure to check whether the currently registered permission has the protection level your app expects.*[9]

Finally, changes to the package database (the package entry and any new permissions) are saved to disk and the `PackageManagerService` sends the `ACTION_PACKAGE_ADDED` to notify other components about the newly added application.

Updating a Package

The process of updating a package follows most of the same steps as installing a package, so we'll highlight only the differences here.

Signature Verification

The first step is to check whether the new package has been signed by the same set of signers as the existing one. This rule is referred to as *same origin policy*, or *Trust On First Use (TOFU)*. This signature check guarantees that the update is produced by the same entity as the original application (assuming that the signing key has not been compromised) and establishes a trust relationship between the update and the existing application. As we shall see in "Updating Non-System Apps" on page 75, the update inherits the data of the original application.

NOTE *When signing certificates are compared for equality, the certificates are not validated in the PKI sense of the word (time validity, trusted issuer, revocation, and so on are not checked).*

The certificate equality check is performed by the `PackageManagerService.compareSignatrues()` method as shown in Listing 3-14.

```
static int compareSignatures(Signature[] s1, Signature[] s2) {
    if (s1 == null) {
        return s2 == null
            ? PackageManager.SIGNATURE_NEITHER_SIGNED
            : PackageManager.SIGNATURE_FIRST_NOT_SIGNED;
    }
```

9. See CommonsWare, *CWAC-Security*, *https://github.com/commonsguy/cwac-security*, for further discussion and a sample project that shows how to perform the check.

```
    if (s2 == null) {
        return PackageManager.SIGNATURE_SECOND_NOT_SIGNED;
    }
    HashSet<Signature> set1 = new HashSet<Signature>();
    for (Signature sig : s1) {
        set1.add(sig);
    }
    HashSet<Signature> set2 = new HashSet<Signature>();
    for (Signature sig : s2) {
        set2.add(sig);
    }
    // Make sure s2 contains all signatures in s1.
    if (set1.equals(set2)) {❶
        return PackageManager.SIGNATURE_MATCH;
    }
    return PackageManager.SIGNATURE_NO_MATCH;
}
```

Listing 3-14: Package signature comparison method

Here, the Signature class serves as an "opaque, immutable representation of a signature associated with an application package."[10] In practice, it is a wrapper for the DER-encoded signing certificate associated with an APK file. Listing 3-15 shows an excerpt, focusing on its equals() and hashCode() methods.

```
public class Signature implements Parcelable {
    private final byte[] mSignature;
    private int mHashCode;
    private boolean mHaveHashCode;
    --snip--
    public Signature(byte[] signature) {
        mSignature = signature.clone();
    }

    public PublicKey getPublicKey() throws CertificateException {
        final CertificateFactory certFactory =
                CertificateFactory.getInstance("X.509");
        final ByteArrayInputStream bais = new ByteArrayInputStream(mSignature);
        final Certificate cert = certFactory.generateCertificate(bais);
        return cert.getPublicKey();
    }

    @Override
    public boolean equals(Object obj) {
        try {
            if (obj != null) {
                Signature other = (Signature)obj;
                return this == other
                    || Arrays.equals(mSignature, other.mSignature);❶
            }
```

10. Google, *Android API Reference,* "Signature," *https://developer.android.com/reference/android/content/pm/Signature.html*

```
        } catch (ClassCastException e) {
        }
        return false;
    }

    @Override
    public int hashCode() {
        if (mHaveHashCode) {
            return mHashCode;
        }
        mHashCode = Arrays.hashCode(mSignature);❷
        mHaveHashCode = true;
        return mHashCode;
    }
--snip--
}
```

Listing 3-15: Package signature representation

As you can see at ❶, two signature classes are considered equal if the DER-encoding of the underlying X.509 certificates match exactly, and the `Signature` class hash code is calculated solely based on the encoded certificate ❷. If the signing certificates do not match, the `compareSignatures()` methods returns the `INSTALL_PARSE_FAILED_INCONSISTENT_CERTIFICATES` error code.

This binary certificate comparison naturally knows nothing about CAs or expiration dates. One consequence of this is that after an app (identified by a unique package name) is installed, updates need to use the same signing certificates (with the exception of system app updates, as discussed in "Updating System Apps" on page 75).

While multiple signatures on Android apps are rare, they do occur. If the original application was signed by more than one signer, any updates need to be signed by the same signers, each using its original signing certificate (enforced by ❶ in Listing 3-14). This means that if a developer's signing certificate(s) expires or he loses access to his signing key, he cannot update the app and must release a new one instead. This would result in not only losing any existing user base or ratings, but more importantly losing access to the legacy app's data and settings.

The solution to this problem is straightforward, if not ideal: back up your signing key and don't let your certificate expire. The currently recommended validity period is at least 25 years, and the Google Play Store requires validity until at least October 2033. While technically this only amounts to putting off the problem, proper certificate migration support might eventually be added to the platform.

When the package manager establishes that the update has been signed with the same certificate, it proceeds with updating the package. The process is different for system and user-installed apps, as described next.

Updating Non-System Apps

Non-system apps are updated by essentially reinstalling the app while retaining its data directory. The first step is to kill any process of the package being updated. Next, the package is removed from internal structures and the package database, which removes all components that the app has registered as well. Next, the PackageManagerService triggers a package scan by calling the scanPackageLI() method. The scan proceeds as it would with new installs, except that it updates the package's code, resource path, version, and timestamp. The package manifest is scanned and any defined components are registered with the system. Next, permissions for all packages are re-granted to ensure that they match any definitions in the updated package. Finally, the updated packaged database is written to disk and a PACKAGE_REPLACED system broadcast is sent.

Updating System Apps

As with user-installed apps, preinstalled apps (usually found in */system/app/*) can be updated without a full-blown system update, usually via the Google Play Store or a similar app distribution service. Though because the *system* partition is mounted read-only, updates are installed in */data/app/*, while the original app is left intact. In addition to a <package> entry, the updated app will also have an <updated-package> entry that might look like the example in Listing 3-16.

```
<package name="com.google.android.keep"
        codePath="/data/app/com.google.android.keep-1.apk"❶
        nativeLibraryPath="/data/app-lib/com.google.android.keep-1"
        flags="4767461"❷
        ft="142ee64d980"
        it="14206f3e320"
        ut="142ee64dfcb"
        version="2101"
        userId="10053"❸
        installer="com.android.vending">
    <sigs count="1">
        <cert index="2" />
    </sigs>
    <signing-keyset identifier="3" />
    <signing-keyset identifier="34" />
</package>
--snip--
<updated-package name="com.google.android.keep"
                codePath="/system/app/Keep.apk"
                nativeLibraryPath="/data/app-lib/Keep"
                ft="ddc8dee8"
                it="14206f3e320"
                ut="ddc8dee8"
                version="2051"
                userId="10053">❹
```

```
    <perms>
        <item name="android.permission.READ_EXTERNAL_STORAGE" />
        <item name="android.permission.USE_CREDENTIALS" />
        <item name="android.permission.WRITE_EXTERNAL_STORAGE" />
        --snip--
    </perms>
</updated-package>
```

Listing 3-16: Package database entries for an updated system package

The update's codePath attribute is set to the path of the new APK in */data/app/* ❶. It inherits the original app's permissions and UID (❸ and ❹) and is marked as an update to a system app by adding the FLAG_UPDATED_SYSTEM_APP (0x80) to its flags attribute ❷.

System apps can be updated directly in the *system* partition as well, usually as the result of an OTA system update, and in such case the updated system APK is allowed to be signed with a different certificate. The rationale behind this is that if the installer has enough privileges to write to the *system* partition, it can be trusted to change the signing certificate as well. The UID, and any files and permissions, are retained. The exception is that if the package is part of a shared user (discussed in Chapter 2), the signature cannot be updated, because doing so would affect other apps. In the reverse case, when a new system app is signed by a different certificate than that of the currently installed non-system app (with the same package name), the non-system app will be deleted first.

Installing Encrypted APKs

Support for installing encrypted APKs was added in Android 4.1 along with support for forward locking using ASEC containers. Both features were announced as *app encryption*, but we'll discuss them separately, beginning with support for encrypted APK files. But first let's see how to install encrypted APKs.

Encrypted APKs can be installed using the Google Play Store client, or with the pm command from the Android shell, but the system PackageInstaller does not support encrypted APKs. Because we can't control the Google Play Store installation flow, in order to install an encrypted APK we need to either use the pm command or write our own installer app. We'll take the easy route and use the pm command.

Creating and Installing an Encrypted APK

The adb install command both copies the APK file to a temporary file on the device and starts the install process. The command provides a convenient wrapper to the adb push and pm install commands. adb install gained three new parameters in Android 4.1 in order to support encrypted APKs (see Listing 3-17).

```
adb install [-l] [-r] [-s] [--algo <algorithm name> --key <hex-encoded key>
--iv <hex-encoded iv>] <file>
```

Listing 3-17: `adb install` command options

The `--algo`, `--key`, and `--iv` parameters let you specify the encryption algorithm, key, and initialization vector (IV), respectively. But in order to use those new parameters, we need to create an encrypted APK first.

An APK file can be encrypted using the `enc` OpenSSL commands as shown in Listing 3-18. Here we use AES in CBC mode with a 128-bit key, and specify an IV that is the same as the key in order to make things simpler.

```
$ openssl enc -aes-128-cbc -K 000102030405060708090A0B0C0D0E0F
-iv 000102030405060708090A0B0C0D0E0F -in my-app.apk -out my-app-enc.apk
```

Listing 3-18: Encrypting an APK file using OpenSSL

Next, we install our encrypted APK by passing the encryption algorithm key (in `javax.crypto.Cipher` transformation string format, which is discussed in Chapter 5) and IV bytes to the `adb install` command as shown in Listing 3-19.

```
$ adb install --algo 'AES/CBC/PKCS5Padding' \
--key 000102030405060708090A0B0C0D0E0F \
--iv 000102030405060708090A0B0C0D0E0F my-app-enc.apk
        pkg: /data/local/tmp/my-app-enc.apk
Success
```

Listing 3-19: Installing an encrypted APK using `adb install`

As the `Success` output indicates, the APK installs without errors. The actual APK file is copied into */data/app/*, and comparing its hash with our encrypted APK reveals that it is in fact a different file. The hash value is exactly the same as that of the original (unencrypted) APK, so we conclude that the APK is decrypted at install time using the provided encryption parameters (algorithm, key, and IV).

Implementation and Encryption Parameters

Let's see how this is implemented. After it has transferred the APK to the device, `adb install` calls the `pm` Android command-line utility with the `install` parameter and the path to the copied APK file. The component responsible for installing apps on Android is `PackageManagerService` and the `pm` command is just a convenient frontend for some of its functionality. When started with the `install` parameter, `pm` calls the method `installPackageWithVerificationAndEncryption()`, converting its options to the relevant parameters as necessary. Listing 3-20 shows the method's full signature.

```
public void installPackageWithVerificationAndEncryption(Uri packageURI,
        IPackageInstallObserver observer, int flags,
        String installerPackageName,
        VerificationParams verificationParams,
        ContainerEncryptionParams encryptionParams) {
--snip--
}
```

Listing 3-20: `PackageManagerService.installPackageWithVerificationAndEncryption()` method signature

We discussed most of the method's parameters in "APK Install Process" earlier, but we have yet to encounter the `VerificationParams` and `ContainerEncryptionParams` classes. As the name implies, the `VerificationParams` class encapsulates a parameter used during package verification, which we will discuss in "Package Verification" on page 83. The `ContainerEncryptionParams` class holds encryption parameters, including the values passed via the `--algo`, `--key`, and `--iv` options of `adb install`. Listing 3-21 shows its data members.

```
public class ContainerEncryptionParams implements Parcelable {
    private final String mEncryptionAlgorithm;
    private final IvParameterSpec mEncryptionSpec;
    private final SecretKey mEncryptionKey;
    private final String mMacAlgorithm;
    private final AlgorithmParameterSpec mMacSpec;
    private final SecretKey mMacKey;
    private final byte[] mMacTag;
    private final long mAuthenticatedDataStart;
    private final long mEncryptedDataStart;
    private final long mDataEnd;
    --snip--
}
```

Listing 3-21: `ContainerEncryptionParams` data members

The `adb install` parameters above correspond to the first three fields of the class. While not available through the `adb install` wrapper, the `pm install` command also takes the `--macalgo`, `--mackey`, and `--tag` parameters, which correspond to the `mMacAlgorithm`, `mMacKey`, and `mMacTag` fields of the `ContainerEncryptionParams` class. In order to use those parameters, we need to calculate the MAC value of the encrypted APK first, which we accomplish with the OpenSSL `dgst` command as shown in Listing 3-22.

```
$ openssl dgst -hmac 'hmac_key_1' -sha1 -hex my-app-enc.apk
HMAC-SHA1(my-app-enc.apk)= 962ecdb4e99551f6c2cf72f641362d657164f55a
```

Listing 3-22: Calculating the MAC of an encrypted APK

NOTE *The* `dgst` *command doesn't allow you to specify the HMAC key using hexadecimal or Base64, so we're limited to ASCII characters. This may not be a good idea for production use, so consider using a real key and calculating the MAC in some other way (for example, using a JCE program).*

Installing an Encrypted APK with Integrity Check

We can now install an encrypted APK and verify its integrity by opening the Android shell using `adb shell` and executing the command shown in Listing 3-23.

```
$ pm install -r --algo 'AES/CBC/PKCS5Padding' \
--key 000102030405060708090A0B0C0D0E0F \
--iv 000102030405060708090A0B0C0D0E0F \
--macalgo HmacSHA1 --mackey 686d61635f6b65795f31 \
--tag 962ecdb4e99551f6c2cf72f641362d657164f55a /sdcard/my-app-enc.apk
        pkg: /sdcard/kr-enc.apk
Success
```

Listing 3-23: Installing an encrypted APK with integrity verification using `pm install`

The app's integrity is checked by comparing the specified MAC tag with the value calculated based on the actual file contents, the contents are decrypted, and the decrypted APK is copied to */data/app/*. (To test that MAC verification is indeed performed, change the tag value slightly. Doing so should result in an install error with error code `INSTALL_FAILED_INVALID_APK`.)

As we saw in Listings 3-19 and 3-23, the APK files that are ultimately copied to */data/app/* are not encrypted and thus the installation process is the same as for unencrypted APKs, except for file decryption and the optional integrity verification. Decryption and integrity verification are performed transparently by the `MediaContainerService` while copying the APK to the application directory. If a `ContainerEncryptionParams` instance is passed to its `copyResource()` method, it uses the provided encryption parameters to instantiate the JCA classes `Cipher` and `Mac` (see Chapter 5) that can perform decryption and integrity checking.

NOTE *The MAC tag and encrypted APK can be bundled in a single file, in which case the* `MediaContainerService` *uses the* `mAuthenticatedDataStart`, `mEncryptedDataStart`, *and* `mDataEnd` *members to extract the MAC and APK data from the file.*

Forward Locking

Forward locking appeared around the time ringtones, wallpapers, and other digital "goods" started selling on feature phones. Because installed APK files are world readable on Android, it's relatively easy to extract apps from even a production device. In an attempt to lock down paid apps (and prevent a user from forwarding them to another user) without losing any of the OS's flexibility, early Android versions introduced forward locking (also called *copy protection*).

The idea behind forward locking was to split app packages into two parts: a world-readable part that contains resources and the manifest (in */data/app/*), and a package that is readable only by the *system* user and which contains executable code (in */data/app-private/*). The code package was protected by filesystem permissions, which made it inaccessible to users on most consumer devices, but it could be extracted from devices with root access, and this early forward locking mechanism was quickly deprecated and replaced with an online application licensing service called Google Play Licensing.

The problem with Google Play Licensing was that it shifted app protection implementation from the OS to app developers, and it had mixed results. The forward locking implementation was redesigned in Android 4.1, and now offers the ability to store APKs in an encrypted container that requires a device-specific key to be mounted at runtime. Let's look at it in a bit more detail.

Android 4.1 Forward Locking Implementation

While the use of encrypted app containers as a forward locking mechanism was introduced in Android version 4.1, encrypted containers were originally introduced in Android 2.2. At that time (mid-2010), most Android devices came with limited internal storage and relatively large (a few gigabytes) external storage, usually in the form of a microSD card. To make file sharing easier, external storage was formatted using the FAT filesystem, which lacks file permissions. As a result, files on the SD card could be read and written by any application.

To prevent users from simply copying paid apps from the SD card, Android 2.2 created an encrypted filesystem image file and stored the APK in it when a user opted to move an app to external storage. The system would then create a mount point for the encrypted image, and mount it using Linux's device-mapper. Android loaded each app's files from its mount point at runtime.

Android 4.1 built on this idea by making the container use the ext4 filesystem, which allows for file permissions. A typical forward-locked app's mount point now looks like Listing 3-24 (timestamps omitted).

```
# ls -l /mnt/asec/com.example.app-1
drwxr-xr-x system   system             lib
drwx------ root     root               lost+found
-rw-r----- system   u0_a96     1319057 pkg.apk
-rw-r--r-- system   system      526091 res.zip
```

Listing 3-24: Contents of a forward-locked app's mount point

Here, the *res.zip* holds app resources and the manifest file and is world readable, while the *pkg.apk* file that holds the full APK is only readable by the system and the app's dedicated user (*u0_a96*). The actual app containers are stored in */data/app-asec/* in files with the *.asec* extension.

Encrypted App Containers

Encrypted app containers are referred to as *Android Secure External Caches*, or *ASEC containers*. ASEC container management (creating, deleting, mounting, and unmounting) is implemented in the system volume daemon (*vold*), and the MountService provides an interface to its functionality to framework services. We can also use the vdc command-line utility to interact with *vold* in order to manage forward-locked apps from Android's shell (see Listing 3-25).

```
# vdc asec list❶
vdc asec list
111 0 com.example.app-1
111 0 org.foo.app-1
200 0 asec operation succeeded

# vdc asec path com.example.app-1❷
vdc asec path com.example.app-1
211 0 /mnt/asec/com.example.app-1

# vdc asec unmount org.example.app-1❸
200 0 asec operation succeeded

# vdc asec mount com.example.app-1 000102030405060708090a0b0c0d0e0f 1000❹
com.example.app-1 000102030405060708090a0b0c0d0e0f  1000
200 0 asec operation succeeded
```

Listing 3-25: Issuing ASEC management commands with vdc

Here, the asec list command ❶ lists the namespace IDs of mounted ASEC containers. Namespace IDs are based on the package name and have the same format as APK filenames for non-forward-locked applications. All other commands take a namespace ID as a parameter.

The asec path command ❷ shows the mount point of the specified ASEC container, while the asec unmount command unmounts it ❸. In addition to a namespace ID, asec mount ❹ requires that you specify the encryption key and the mount point's owner UID (1000 is *system*).

The ASEC container encryption algorithm and the key length are unchanged from the original Android 2.2 apps-to-SD implementation: Twofish with a 128-bit key stored in */data/misc/systemkeys/*, as shown in Listing 3-26.

```
# ls -l /data/misc/systemkeys
-rw------- system   system          16 AppsOnSD.sks
# od -t x1 /data/misc/systemkeys/AppsOnSD.sks
0000000 00 01 02 03 04 05 06 07 08 09 0a 0b 0c 0d 0e 0f
0000020
```

Listing 3-26: ASEC container encryption key location and contents

Forward locking an application is triggered by specifying the -l option of pm install or by specifying the INSTALL_FORWARD_LOCK flag when calling one of PackageManager's installPackage() methods.

Installing Forward-Locked APKs

The install process of forward-locked APKs involves two additional steps: creating and mounting the secure container, and extracting the public resource files from the APK file. As with encrypted APKs, those steps are encapsulated by the `MediaContainerService` and are performed while copying the APK to the application directory. As the `MediaContainerService` does not have enough privileges to create and mount secure containers, it delegates container management to the *vold* daemon by calling the appropriate `MountService` methods (`createSecureContainer()`, `mountSecureContainer()`, and so on).

Encrypted Apps and Google Play

Because installing apps without user interaction, encrypted or otherwise, requires system permissions, only system applications can install applications. Google's own Play Store Android client takes advantage of both encrypted apps and forward locking. While describing exactly how the Google Play client works would require detailed knowledge of the underlying protocol (which is not open and is constantly evolving), a casual look into the implementation of a recent Google Play Store client reveals a few useful pieces of information.

Google Play servers send quite a bit of metadata about the app you are about to download and install, such as download URL, APK file size, version code, and refund window. Among these, the `EncryptionParams` shown in Listing 3-27 looks very similar to the `ContainerEncryptionParams` shown in Listing 3-21.

```
class AndroidAppDelivery$EncryptionParams {
  --snip--
  private String encryptionKey;
  private String hmacKey;
  private int version;
}
```

Listing 3-27: `EncryptionParams` used in the Google Play Store protocol

The encryption algorithm and the HMAC algorithm of paid applications downloaded from Google Play are always set to *AES/CBC/PKCS5Padding* and *HMACSHA1*, respectively. The IV and the MAC tag are bundled with the encrypted APK in a single blob. After all parameters are read and verified, they are essentially converted to a `ContainerEncryptionParams` instance, and the app is installed using the `PackageManager.installPackageWithVerification()` method.

The `INSTALL_FORWARD_LOCK` flag is set when installing a paid app in order to enable forward locking. The OS takes it from here, and the process is as described in the previous two sections: free apps are decrypted and the APKs end up in */data/app/*, while an encrypted container in */data/app-asec/* is created and mounted under */mnt/asec/<package-name>* for paid apps.

How secure is this in practice? Google Play can now claim that paid apps are always transferred and stored in encrypted form, and so can your own app distribution channel if you decide to implement it using the app encryption facilities that Android provides. The APK file contents have to be made available to the OS at some point though, so if you have root access to a running Android device, it's still possible to extract a forward-locked APK or the container encryption key.

Package Verification

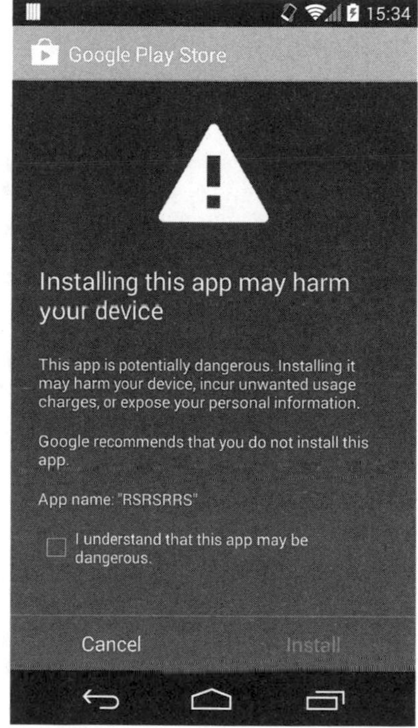

Figure 3-3: Application verification warning dialog

Package verification was introduced as an official Android feature in version 4.2 as *application verification* and was later backported to all versions running Android 2.3 and later and the Google Play Store. The infrastructure that makes package verification possible is built into the OS, but Android doesn't ship with any built-in verifiers. The most widely used package verification implementation is the one built into the Google Play Store client and backed by Google's app analysis infrastructure. It's designed to protect Android devices from what Google calls "potentially harmful applications"[11] (backdoors, phishing applications, spyware, and so on), commonly known simply as *malware.*

When package verification is turned on, APKs are scanned by a verifier prior to installation, and the system shows a warning (see Figure 3-3) or blocks installation if the verifier deems the APK potentially harmful. Verification is on by default on supported devices but requires one-time user approval on first use, as it sends application data to Google. Application verification can be toggled via the Verify Apps option on the system settings Security screen (see Figure 3-2 on page 25).

The following sections discuss the Android package verification infrastructure and then take a brief look at Google Play's implementation.

---

11. Google, *Android Practical Security from the Ground Up*, presented at VirusBulletin 2013. Retrieved from *https://docs.google.com/presentation/d/1YDYUrD22Xq12nKkhBfwoJBfw2Q-OReMr0BrDfHyfyPw*

Android Support for Package Verification

As with most things that deal with application management, package verification is implemented in the PackageManagerService, and has been available since Android 4.0 (API level 14). Package verification is performed by one or more *verification agents*, and has a *required verifier* and zero or more *sufficient verifiers*. Verification is considered complete when the required verifier and at least one of the sufficient verifiers return a positive result. An application can register itself as a required verifier by declaring a broadcast receiver with an intent filter that matches the PACKAGE_NEEDS_VERIFICATION action and the APK file MIME type (*application/vnd.android.package-archive*), as shown in Listing 3-28.

```
<receiver android:name=".MyPackageVerificationReceiver"
          android:permission="android.permission.BIND_PACKAGE_VERIFIER">
    <intent-filter>
        <action
             android:name="android.intent.action.PACKAGE_NEEDS_VERIFICATION" />
        <action android:name="android.intent.action.PACKAGE_VERIFIED" />
        <data android:mimeType="application/vnd.android.package-archive" />
    </intent-filter>
</receiver>
```

Listing 3-28: Required verification declaration in AndroidManifest.xml

In addition, the declaring application needs to be granted the PACKAGE_VERIFICATION_AGENT permission. As this is a signature permission reserved for system applications (signature|system), only system applications can become the required verification agent.

Applications can register sufficient verifiers by adding a <package-verifier> tag to their manifest and listing the sufficient verifier's package name and public key in the tag's attributes, as shown in Listing 3-29.

```
<manifest xmlns:android="http://schemas.android.com/apk/res/android"
        package="com.example.app">
        <package-verifier android:name="com.example.verifier"
                          android:publicKey="MIIB..." />
    <application ...>
     --snip--
    </application>
</manifest>
```

Listing 3-29: Sufficient verifier declaration in AndroidManifest.xml

When installing a package, the PackageManagerService performs verification when a required verifier is installed and the Settings.Global.PACKAGE_VERIFIER_ENABLE system setting is set to true. Verification is enabled by adding the APK to a queue of pending installs and sending the ACTION_PACKAGE_NEEDS_VERIFICATION broadcast to registered verifiers.

The broadcasts contains a unique verification ID, and various metadata about the package being verified. Verification agents respond by calling the `verifyPendingInstall()` method and passing the verification ID and a verification status. Calling the method requires the `PACKAGE_VERIFICATION_AGENT` permission, which guarantees that non-system apps cannot participate in package verification. Each time the `verifyPendingInstall()` is called, the `PackageManagerService` checks to see whether sufficient verification for the pending install has been received. If so, it removes the pending install from the queue, sends the `PACKAGE_VERIFIED` broadcast, and starts the package installation process. If the package is rejected by verification agents, or sufficient verification is not received within the allotted time, installation fails with the `INSTALL_FAILED_VERIFICATION_FAILURE` error.

Google Play Implementation

Google's application verification implementation is built into the Google Play Store client. The Google Play Store app registers itself as a required verification agent and if the Verify apps option is turned on, it receives a broadcast each time an application is about to be installed, whether through the Google Play Store client itself, the `PackgeInstaller` application, or via `adb install`.

The implementation is not open source, and few details are publicly available, but Google's "Protect against harmful apps" Android help page states, "When you verify applications, Google receives log information, URLs related to the app, and general information about the device, such as the Device ID, version of the operating system, and IP address."[12] We can observe that, as of this writing, in addition to this information, the Play Store client sends the APK file's SHA-256 hash value, file size, the app package name, the names of its resources along with their SHA-256 hashes, the SHA-256 hashes of the app's manifest and classes files, its version code and signing certificates, as well as some metadata about the installing application and referrer URLs, if available. Based on that information, Google's APK analysis algorithms determine whether the APK is potentially harmful and return a result to the Play Store client that includes a status code and an error message to display in case the APK is deemed potentially harmful. In turn, the Play Store client calls the `verifyPendingInstall()` method of the `PackageManagerService` with the appropriate status code. Application install is accepted or rejected based on the algorithm described in the previous section.

In practice (at least on "Google experience" devices), the Google Play Store verifier is usually the sole verification agent, so whether the package is installed or rejected depends only on the response of Google's online verification service.

12. Google, *Protect against harmful apps, https://support.google.com/accounts/answer/2812853*

Summary

Android application packages (APK files) are an extension of the JAR file format and contain resources, code, and a manifest file. APK files are signed using the JAR file code signing format, but require that all files are signed with the same set of certificates. Android uses the code signer certificate to establish the same origin of apps and their updates and to establish trust relationships between apps. APK files are installed by copying them to the */data/app/* directory and creating a dedicated data directory for each application under */data/data/*.

Android supports encrypted APK files and secure app containers for forward locked apps. Encrypted apps are automatically decrypted before being copied to the application directory. Forward locked apps are split into a resource and manifest part, which is publicly accessible, and a private code and asset part, which is stored in a dedicated encrypted container, directly accessible only by the OS.

Android can optionally verify apps before installing them by consulting one or more verification agents. Currently, the most widely used verification agent is built into the Google Play Store client applications and uses Google's online app verification service in order to detect potentially harmful applications.

4

USER MANAGEMENT

Android originally targeted personal devices such as smartphones and assumed that each device had only one user. With the increase in popularity of tablets and other shared devices, multi-user support was added in version 4.2 and extended in later versions.

In this chapter, we'll discuss how Android manages users who share devices and data. We begin with a look at the types of users Android supports and how it stores user metadata. We then discuss how Android shares installed applications between users while isolating application data and keeping it private to each user. Finally, we cover how Android implements isolated external storage.

Multi-User Support Overview

Android's multi-user support allows multiple users to share a single device by providing each user with an isolated, personal environment. Each user can have their own home screen, widgets, apps, online accounts, and files that are not accessible to other users.

Users are identified by a unique *user ID* (not to be confused with Linux UIDs) and only the system can switch between users. User switching is normally triggered by selecting a user from the Android lockscreen and (optionally) authenticating using a pattern, PIN, password, and so on (see Chapter 10). Applications can get information about the current user via the `UserManager` API, but typically code modification is not required in order to support a multi-user environment. Applications that need to modify their behavior when used by a restricted profile are an exception: these applications require additional code that checks what restrictions (if any) are imposed on the current user (see "Restricted Profiles" on page 92 for details).

Multi-user support is built into the core Android platform and is thus available on all devices that run Android 4.2 or later. However, the default platform configuration only allows for a single user, which effectively disables multi-user support. In order to enable support for multiple users, the *config_multiuserMaximumUsers* system resource must be set to a value greater than one, typically by adding a device-specific overlay configuration file. For example, on the Nexus 7 (2013), the overlay is placed in the *device/asus/flo/overlay/frameworks/base/core/res/res/values/config.xml* file and the *config_multiuserMaximumUsers* setting is defined as shown in Listing 4-1, to allow a maximum of eight users.

```
<?xml version="1.0" encoding="utf-8"?>
<resources xmlns:xliff="urn:oasis:names:tc:xliff:document:1.2">
    --snip--
    <!-- Maximum number of supported users -->
    <integer name="config_multiuserMaximumUsers">8</integer>
    --snip--
</resources>
```

Listing 4-1: Enabling multi-user support with a resource overlay file

NOTE *The Android Compatibility Definition requires that devices that support telephony (such as mobile phones) must not enable multi-user support because "the behavior of the telephony APIs on devices with multiple users is currently undefined."*[1] *Therefore, in current production builds, all handsets are configured as single-user devices.*

---

1. Google, *Android 4.4 Compatibility Definition,* "9.5. Multi-User Support," *http://static.googleusercontent.com/media/source.android.com/en//compatibility/4.4/android-4.4-cdd.pdf*

When multi-user support is enabled, the system Settings application displays a Users entry that allows the device owner (the first user created, as discussed in the next section) to create and manage users. The user management screen is shown in Figure 4-1.

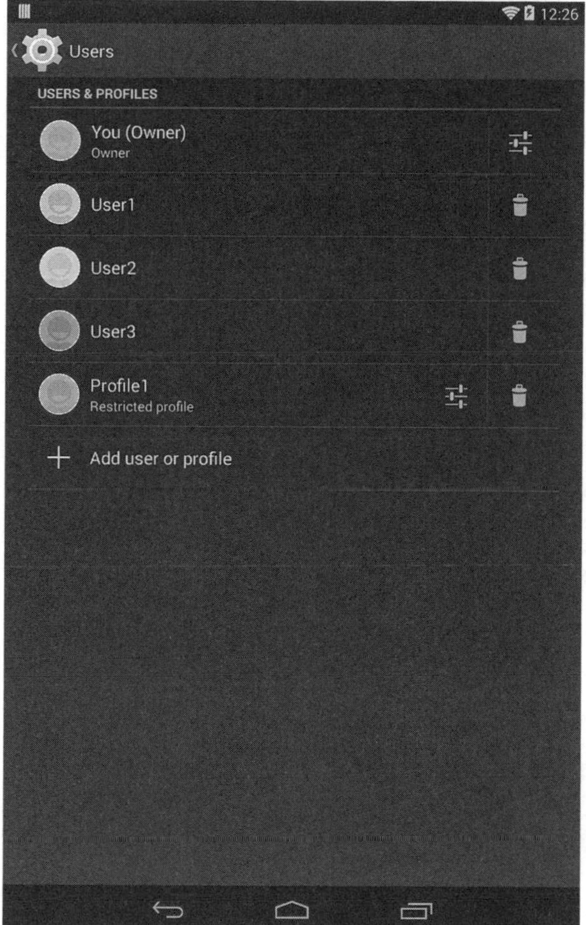

Figure 4-1: User management screen

As soon as more than one user has been created, the lockscreen shows a user widget that displays the current users and allows switching to a different user. Figure 4-2 shows how the lockscreen might look on a device with eight users.

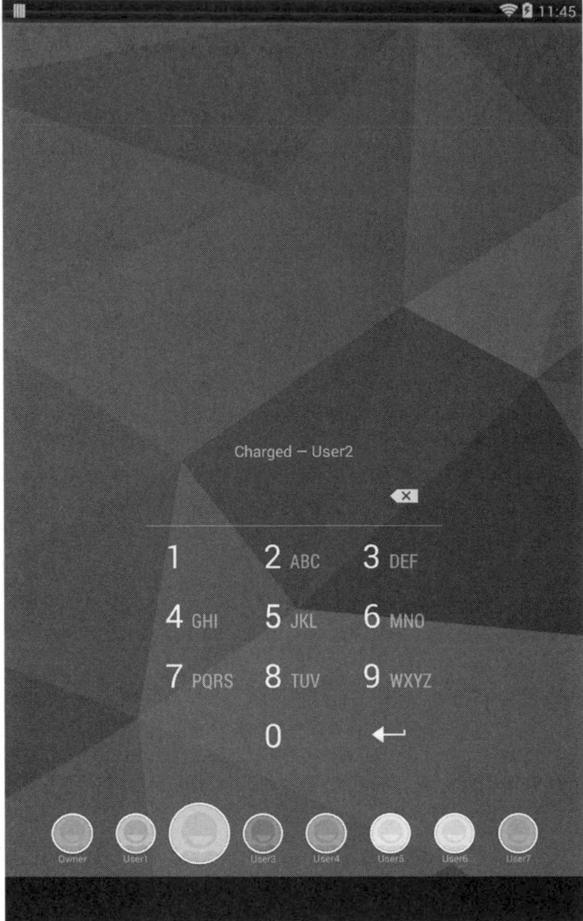

Figure 4-2: Lockscreen with user switcher widget

Types of Users

Even though Android lacks the full user management features of most multi-user operating systems, which typically allow users to add multiple administrators and define user groups, it does support configuring user types with different privileges. Each user type and its privileges will be described in the following sections.

The Primary User (Owner)

The *primary user*, also known as the device *owner*, is the first user created on a multi-user device, or the sole user on single-user devices. The owner is created by default and is always present. The primary user is assigned user ID 0. On single-user devices where the primary user is the only user, Android behaves much like previous versions that lacked multi-user support: directories and UIDs assigned to installed applications maintain the same format and permissions as in previous versions (see "User Management" on page 95 and "Application Sharing" on page 101 for details).

The primary user is assigned all privileges and can create and delete other users, as well as change system settings that affect all users, including settings related to device security, network connectivity, and application management. Device and user management privileges are granted to the primary user by showing the respective settings screens in system settings and hiding them from other users. Additionally, the underlying system services check the identity of the calling user before performing operations that can affect all users, and only allow execution when called by the device owner.

As of Android version 4.4, the following screens in the Wireless and Networks section of system settings are displayed to only the primary user:

- Cell broadcasts
- Manage mobile plan
- Mobile network
- Tethering and portable hotspot
- VPN
- WiMAX (shown if supported by the device)

The following screens in the Security section are also reserved for the primary user:

- Device encryption
- SIM card lock
- Unknown sources (controls app sideloading; see Chapter 3)
- Verify apps (controls package verification; see Chapter 3)

Secondary Users

With the exception of restricted profiles (discussed in the next section), all added users are *secondary users*. Each gets a dedicated user directory (see "User Management" on page 95), their own list of installed apps, and private data directories for each installed app.

Secondary users cannot add or manage users; they can only set their own username via the Users screen (see Figure 4-1). Additionally, they cannot perform any privileged operation reserved for the primary user as listed in the previous sections. Otherwise, secondary users can perform all the operations that a primary user can, including installing and using applications, and changing the system appearance and settings.

Although secondary users are restricted, their actions can still affect device behavior and other users. For example, they can add and connect to a new Wi-Fi network. Because Wi-Fi connectivity state is shared across the system, switching to a different user does not reset the wireless connection, and that user will be connected to the wireless network selected by the previous user. Secondary users can also toggle airplane mode and NFC, and change the global sound and display settings. Most importantly, as application packages are shared across all users (as discussed in "Application Sharing" on page 101), if a secondary user updates an application that adds new permissions, permissions are granted to the application without requiring the consent of other users, and other users are not notified of permission changes.

Restricted Profiles

Unlike secondary users, restricted profiles (added in Android 4.3) are based on the primary user and share its applications, data, and accounts, with certain restrictions. As such, the primary user must set up a lockscreen password in order to protect their data. If no lockscreen password is in place when the primary user creates a restricted profile, Android prompts them to set up one.

User Restrictions

Android defines the following default restrictions in order to control what users are allowed to do. All restrictions are `false` by default. The list below shows their value for restricted users in parentheses.

`DISALLOW_CONFIG_BLUETOOTH` Specifies whether a user is prevented from configuring Bluetooth. (default: `false`)

`DISALLOW_CONFIG_CREDENTIALS` Specifies whether a user is prevented from configuring user credentials. When this restriction is set to `true`, restricted profiles cannot add trusted CA certificates or import private keys into the system credential store; see Chapters 6 and 7 for details. (default: `false`)

`DISALLOW_CONFIG_WIFI` Specifies whether a user is prevented from changing Wi-Fi access points. (default: `false`)

`DISALLOW_INSTALL_APPS` Specifies whether a user is prevented from installing applications. (default: `false`)

`DISALLOW_INSTALL_UNKNOWN_SOURCES` Specifies whether a user is prevented from enabling the Unknown sources setting (see Chapter 3). (default: `false`)

`DISALLOW_MODIFY_ACCOUNTS` Specifies whether a user is prevented from adding and removing accounts. (default: `true`)

`DISALLOW_REMOVE_USER` Specifies whether a user is prevented from removing users. (default: `false`)

`DISALLOW_SHARE_LOCATION` Specifies whether a user is prevented from toggling location sharing. (default: `true`)

`DISALLOW_UNINSTALL_APPS` Specifies whether a user is prevented from uninstalling applications. (default: `false`)

`DISALLOW_USB_FILE_TRANSFER` Specifies whether a user is prevented from transferring files over USB. (default: `false`)

Applying Restrictions

At runtime, applications can use the `UserManager.getUserRestrictions()` method to get a `Bundle` (a universal container class that maps string keys to various value types) containing the restrictions imposed on a user. Restrictions are defined as key-value pairs, where the key is the restriction name and the Boolean value specifies whether it is in effect. Applications can use that value in order to disable certain functionality when running within a restricted profile. For example, the system Settings app checks the value of the `DISALLOW_SHARE_LOCATION` restriction when displaying location preferences. If the value is `true`, it disables the location mode setting. Another example is the `PackageManagerService`: it checks the `DISALLOW_INSTALL_APPS` and `DISALLOW_UNINSTALL_APPS` restrictions before installing or uninstalling apps and returns the `INSTALL_FAILED_USER_RESTRICTED` error code if any of those restrictions are set to `true` for the calling user.

The primary user can select which applications will be available to a restricted profile. When a restricted profile is created, all installed applications are initially disabled, and the owner must explicitly enable the ones that they want to make available to the restricted profile (see Figure 4-3).

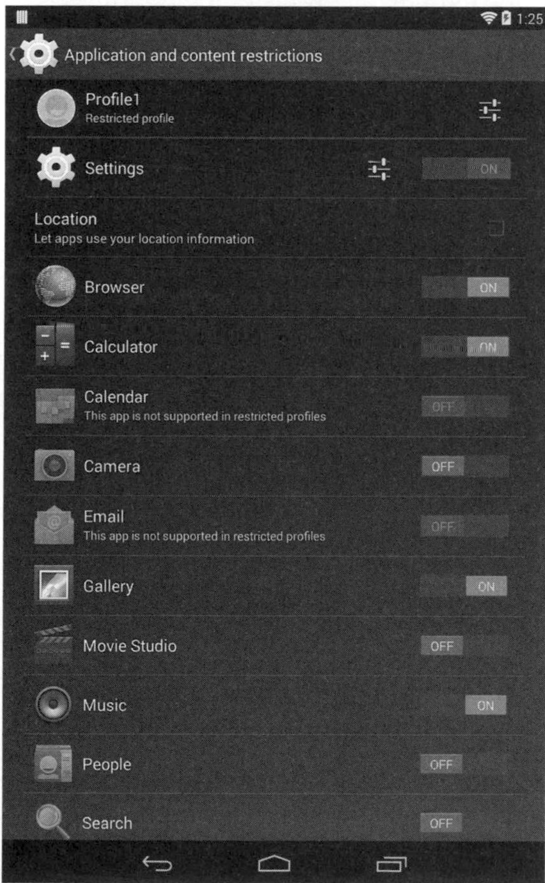

Figure 4-3: Restricted profile management screen

In addition to the built-in restrictions defined by the OS, applications can define custom restrictions by creating a `BroadcastReceiver` that receives the `ACTION_GET_RESTRICTION_ENTRIES` intent. Android invokes this intent to query all apps for available restrictions and automatically builds a UI that allows device owners to toggle the app's custom restrictions.

At runtime, applications can use the `UserManager.getApplicationRestrictions()` method to obtain a `Bundle` that contains saved restrictions as key-value pairs. The application can then disable or modify certain features based on the applied restrictions. The device owner can toggle system and custom restrictions on the same settings screen used to manage applications available to a restricted profile. For example, in Figure 4-3, the single application restriction supported by the Settings app (whether to let apps use location information) is shown below the main application toggle.

Access to Online Accounts

Restricted profiles can also access the online accounts of the primary user via the `AccountManager` API (see Chapter 8), but this access is disabled by default. Applications that need access to accounts when running within a restricted profile must explicitly declare the account types they require using the `restrictedAccountType` attribute of the `<application>` tag, as shown in Listing 4-2.

```
<?xml version="1.0" encoding="utf-8"?>
<manifest xmlns:android="http://schemas.android.com/apk/res/android"
    package="com.example.app" ...>
    <application android:restrictedAccountType="com.google" ... >
        --snip--
    </application>
</manifest>
```

Listing 4-2: Allowing access to the owner's accounts from a restricted profile

On the other hand, applications that do not want to expose account information to restricted profiles can declare this by specifying the account type (an asterisk can be used to match all account types) as the value of the `requiredAccountType` attribute of the `<application>` tag. If the `requiredAccountType` attribute is specified, Android will automatically disable such applications for restricted profiles. For example, because the Android Calendar application declares `android:requiredAccountType="*"` in its manifest, it cannot be made available to restricted profiles and is disabled in the restrictions settings screen (see Figure 4-3).

Guest User

Android supports a single guest user, but this functionality is disabled by default. While the guest user can be enabled by calling the `UserManager.setGuestEnabled()` method, the guest user does not appear to be referenced anywhere other than by the `UserManager` and related classes in current

Android versions. Code comments indicate that the guest user might be transient, but as of this writing its exact purpose is not clear. It appears to be a remnant of a proposed feature that was rejected or never fully implemented.

User Management

Android users are managed by the `UserManagerService`, which is responsible for reading and persisting user information and maintaining the list of active users. Because user management is closely related to package management, the `PackageManagerService` calls the `UserManagerService` to query or modify users when packages are installed or removed. The `android.os.UserManager` class provides a facade to the `UserManagerService` and exposes a subset of its functionality to third-party applications. Applications can get the number of users on a system, a user's serial number, the name and list of restrictions for the current user, as well as the list of restrictions for a package without the need for any special permissions. All other user operations, including querying, adding, removing, or modifying users, require the `MANAGE_USERS` system signature permission.

Command-Line Tools

User management operations can also be performed on the Android shell with the `pm` command. These commands can be run via the shell without root permissions, because the *shell* user (UID 2000) is granted the `MANAGE_USERS` permission. You can use the `pm create-user` command to create a new user, and the `pm remove-user` to remove it. The command `pm get-max-users` returns the maximum number of users supported by the OS, and `pm list users` lists all users. The output of the `pm list users` command might look like Listing 4-3 on a device with five users. The numbers in curly braces are the user ID, name, and flags, in that order.

```
$ pm list users
Users:
        UserInfo{0:Owner:13}
        UserInfo{10:User1:10}
        UserInfo{11:User2:10}
        UserInfo{12:User3:10}
        UserInfo{13:Profile1:18}
```

Listing 4-3: Listing users using the `pm list` command

User States and Related Broadcasts

The `UserManagerService` sends several broadcasts to notify other components of user-related events. When a user is added, it sends the `USER_ADDED` broadcast, and when a user is removed, it sends `USER_REMOVED`. If the username or their profile icon is changed, the `UserManagerService` sends the

USER_INFO_CHANGED broadcast. Switching users triggers the USER_BACKGROUND, USER_FOREGROUND, and USER_SWITCHED broadcasts, all of which contain the relevant user ID as an extra.

While Android supports a maximum of eight users, only three users can be running at a time. A user is started when it is first switched to via the lockscreen user switcher. Android stops inactive users based on a least recently used (LRU) cache algorithm to ensure that no more than three users are active.

When a user is stopped, its processes are killed and it no longer receives any broadcasts. When users are started or stopped, the system sends the USER_STARTING, USER_STARTED, USER_STOPPING, and USER_STOPPED broadcasts. The primary user is started automatically when the system boots and is never stopped.

Starting, stopping, and switching users, as well as targeting a specific user with a broadcast, requires the INTERACT_ACROSS_USERS permission. This is a system permission with signature protection, but it also has the development flag set (see Chapter 2) so it can be dynamically granted to non-system applications that declare it (using the pm grant command). The INTERACT_ACROSS_USERS_FULL signature permission allows sending broadcasts to all users, changing the device administrator, as well as other privileged operations that affect all users.

User Metadata

Android stores user data in the */data/system/users/* directory that hosts metadata about users in XML format, as well as user directories. On a device with five users, its contents may look like Listing 4-4 (timestamps have been omitted).

```
# ls -lF /data/system/users
drwx------ system   system            0❶
-rw------- system   system        230 0.xml❷
drwx------ system   system            10
-rw------- system   system        245 10.xml
drwx------ system   system            11
-rw------- system   system        245 11.xml
drwx------ system   system            12
-rw------- system   system        245 12.xml
drwx------ system   system            13
-rw------- system   system        299 13.xml
-rw------- system   system        212 userlist.xml❸
```

Listing 4-4: Contents of /data/system/users/

The User List File

As shown in Listing 4-4, each user has a dedicated directory called the *user system directory* with a name that matches the assigned user ID (❶ for the primary user) and an XML file that stores metadata about the user, again with a filename based on the user ID (❷ for the primary user). The *userlists.xml* file ❸ holds data about all users created on a system and may look like Listing 4-5 on a system with five users.

```
<users nextSerialNumber="19" version="4">
    <user id="0" />
    <user id="10" />
    <user id="11" />
    <user id="12" />
    <user id="13" />
</users>
```

Listing 4-5: Contents of userlist.xml

The file format is basically a list of <user> tags holding the ID assigned to each user. The root <users> element has a `version` attribute specifying the current file version and a `nextSerialNumber` attribute holding the serial number to be assigned to the next user. The primary user is always assigned user ID 0.

The fact that UIDs assigned to applications are based on the user ID of the owning user ensures that on single-user devices, UIDs assigned to applications are the same as they were before multi-user support was introduced. (For more on application UIDs, see "Application Data Directories" on page 100.) Secondary users and restricted profiles are assigned IDs beginning with the number 10.

User Metadata Files

The attributes of each user are stored in a dedicated XML file. Listing 4-6 shows an example for a restricted profile.

```
<?xml version='1.0' encoding='utf-8' standalone='yes' ?>
<user id="13"
      serialNumber="18"
      flags="24"
      created="1394551856450"
      lastLoggedIn="1394551882324"
      icon="/data/system/users/13/photo.png">❶
    <name>Profile1</name>❷
    <restrictions no_modify_accounts="true" no_share_location="true" />❸
</user>
```

Listing 4-6: User metadata file contents

Here, the <name> tag ❷ holds the user's name and the <restrictions> tag ❸ has attributes for each enabled restriction. (See "Restricted Profiles" on page 92 for a list of built-in restrictions.) Table 4-1 summarizes the attributes of the root <user> element shown at ❶ in Listing 4-6.

Table 4-1: <user> Element Attributes

Name	Format	Description
id	integer	User ID
serialNumber	integer	User serial number
flags	integer	Flags that indicate the type of user
created	milliseconds since the Unix epoch, as per System.currentTimeMillis()	User creation time
lastLoggedIn	milliseconds since the Unix epoch, as per System.currentTimeMillis()	Last login time
icon	string	Full path to the user icon file
partial	Boolean	Indicates that the user is partially initialized. Partial users may not have all of their files and directories created yet.
pinHash	hexadecimal string	The salted SHA1+MD5 PIN hash for PIN-protected restrictions
salt	long integer	The PIN salt for PIN-protected restrictions
failedAttempts	integer	The number of failed PIN entry attempts for PIN-protected restrictions
lastAttemptMs	milliseconds since the Unix epoch, as per System.currentTimeMillis()	The time of the last PIN entry attempt for PIN-protected restrictions (in milliseconds since the Unix epoch, per System.currentTimeMillis())

The flags attribute is one of the most important as it determines the user type. As of this writing, six bits of the flag value are used for the user type and the rest are reserved with the following flags currently defined:

FLAG_PRIMARY (0x00000001) Marks the primary user.

FLAG_ADMIN (0x00000002) Marks administrator users. Administrator can create and delete users.

FLAG_GUEST (0x00000004) Marks the guest user.

FLAG_RESTRICTED (0x00000008) Marks restricted users.

FLAG_INITIALIZED (0x00000010) Marks a user as fully initialized.

While different flag combinations are possible, most combinations don't represent a valid user type or state, and in practice the attributes for the primary owner are set to 19 (0x13 or FLAG_INITIALIZED|FLAG_ADMIN|FLAG_PRIMARY), secondary users have flags 16 (0x10 or FLAG_INITIALIZED), and restricted profiles have flags 24 (0x18 or FLAG_INITIALIZED|FLAG_RESTRICTED).

User System Directory

Each user system directory contains user-specific system settings and data but no application data. As we'll see in the next section, each application that a user installs gets a dedicated data directory under */data*, much like on single-user devices. (See Chapter 3 for more on application data directories.) For example, in the case of a secondary user with user ID 12, the user system directory would be named */data/system/users/12/* and might contain the files and directories listed in Listing 4-7.

```
- accounts.db❶
- accounts.db-journal
- appwidgets.xml❷
- device_policies.xml❸
- gesture.key❹
d inputmethod❺
- package-restrictions.xml❻
- password.key❼
- photo.png❽
- settings.db❾
- settings.db-journal
- wallpaper❿
- wallpaper_info.xml
```

Listing 4-7: Contents of a user directory

The file *accounts.db* ❶ is an SQLite database that holds online account details. (We discuss online account management in Chapter 8.) The file *appwidgets.xml* ❷ holds information about widgets that the user has added to their home screen. The *device_policies.xml* ❸ file describes the current device policy (see Chapter 9 for details), and *gesture.key* ❹ and *password.key* ❼ contain the hash of the currently selected lockscreen pattern or PIN/password, respectively (see Chapter 10 for format details).

The *inputmethod* directory ❺ contains information about input methods. The *photo.png* file ❽ stores the user's profile image or picture. The file *settings.db* ❾ holds system settings specific to that user, and *wallpaper* ❿ is the currently selected wallpaper image. The *package-restrictions.xml* file ❻ defines what applications the user has installed and stores their state. (We discuss application sharing and per-user application data in the next section.)

Per-User Application Management

As mentioned in "Multi-User Support Overview" on page 87, besides dedicated accounts and settings, each user gets their own copy of application data that cannot be accessed by other users. Android achieves this by assigning a new, per-user effective UID for each application and creating a dedicated application data directory owned by that UID. We'll discuss the details of this implementation in the following sections.

Application Data Directories

As we covered in Chapter 3, Android installs APK packages by copying them to the */data/app/* directory, and creates a dedicated data directory for each application under */data/data/*. When multi-user support is enabled, this layout is not changed but extended to support additional users. Application data for the primary user is still stored in */data/data/* for backward compatibility.

If other users exist on the system when a new application is being installed, the `PackageManagerService` creates application data directories for each user. As with the data directory for the primary user, those directories are created with the help of the *installd* daemon (using the `mkuserdata` command) because the *system* user does not have enough privileges to change directory ownership.

User data directories are stored in */data/user/* and named after the user's ID. The device owner directory (*0/*) is a symbolic link to */data/data/*, as shown in Listing 4-8.

```
# ls -l /data/user/
lrwxrwxrwx root      root         0 -> /data/data/
drwxrwx--x system    system       10
drwxrwx--x system    system       11
drwxrwx--x system    system       12
drwxrwx--x system    system       13
```

Listing 4-8: Contents of /data/user/ on a multi-user device

The contents of each application data directory are the same as */data/data/*, but application directories for each user's instance of the same application are owned by a different Linux user, as shown in Listing 4-9.

```
# ls -l /data/data/❶
drwxr-x--x u0_a12    u0_a12                   com.android.apps.tag
drwxr-x--x u0_a0     u0_a0                    com.android.backupconfirm
drwxr-x--x bluetooth bluetooth                com.android.bluetooth
drwxr-x--x u0_a16    u0_a16                   com.android.browser❷
drwxr-x--x u0_a17    u0_a17                   com.android.calculator2
drwxr-x--x u0_a18    u0_a18                   com.android.calendar
--snip--
# ls -l /data/user/13/❸
ls -l /data/user/13
drwxr-x--x u13_system u13_system              android
drwxr-x--x u13_a12   u13_a12                  com.android.apps.tag
drwxr-x--x u13_a0    u13_a0                   com.android.backupconfirm
drwxr-x--x u13_bluetooth u13_bluetooth        com.android.bluetooth
drwxr-x--x u13_a16   u13_a16                  com.android.browser❹
drwxr-x--x u13_a17   u13_a17                  com.android.calculator2
drwxr-x--x u13_a18   u13_a18                  com.android.calendar
--snip--
```

Listing 4-9: Contents of application data directories for the primary user and one secondary user

This listing shows the contents of the app data directories for the primary user ❶ and the secondary user with user ID 13 ❸. As you can see, even though both users have data directories for the same apps, such as the browser app (❷ for the owner and ❹ for the secondary user), those directories are owned by different Linux users: *u0_a16* in the case of the owner and *u13_a16* in the case of the secondary user. If we check the UID for those users using the `su` and `id` commands, we find that *u0_a16* has UID=10016, and *u13_a16* has UID=1310016.

The fact that both UIDs contain the number 10016 is no coincidence. The repeating part is called the *app ID* and is the same as the UID assigned to the app when first installed on a single-user device. On multi-user devices, the app UID is derived from the user ID and the app ID using the following code:

```
uid = userId * 100000 + (appId % 100000)
```

Because the owner's user ID is always 0, the UIDs for the device owner's apps are always the same as their app IDs. When the same application is executed in the context of different users, it executes under the respective UIDs assigned to each user's application instance. For example, if the browser application is executed simultaneously by the device owner and a secondary user with user ID 13, two separate processes running as the *u0_a16* and *u13_a16* Linux users will be created (UID 10016, for the owner ❶ and UID 1310016, for the secondary user ❷) as shown in Listing 4-10.

```
USER      PID   PPID  VSIZE   RSS   WCHAN    PC         NAME
--snip--
u13_a16   1149  180   1020680 72928 ffffffff 4006a58c R com.android.browser❶
--snip--
u0_a16    30500 180   1022796 73384 ffffffff 4006b73c S com.android.browser❷
--snip--
```

Listing 4-10: Process information for the browser application when executed by different device users

Application Sharing

While installed applications have a dedicated data directory for each user, the APK files are shared among all users. The APK files are copied to */data/app/* and are readable by all users; shared libraries used by apps are copied to */data/app-lib/<package name>/* and are symlinked to */data/user/<user ID>/<package name>/lib/*; and the optimized DEX files for each app are stored in */data/dalvik-cache/* and are also shared by all users. Thus once an application is installed, it is accessible to all device users, and an app data directory is automatically created for each user.

Android makes it possible for users to have different applications by creating a *package-restrictions.xml* file (❻ in Listing 4-7) in the system directory of each user, which it uses to track whether an app is enabled for a user or not. Besides the install state of packages, this file contains information about the disabled components of each application, as well as a list of preferred applications to start when processing intents that can be handled by more than one application (such as opening a text file, for example). The contents of *package-restrictions.xml* might look like Listing 4-11 for a secondary user.

```
<?xml version='1.0' encoding='utf-8' standalone='yes' ?>
<package-restrictions>
    <pkg name="com.example.app" inst="false" stopped="true" nl="true" />❶
    <pkg name="com.example.app2" stopped="true" nl="true" />❷
    --snip--
    <pkg name="com.android.settings">
        <disabled-components>
            <item name="com.android.settings.CryptKeeper" />
        </disabled-components>
    </pkg>
    <preferred-activities />
</package-restrictions>
```

Listing 4-11: Contents of the package-restrictions.xml file

Here, the `com.example.app` package is available on the system but is not installed for that secondary user, as expressed by adding a `<pkg>` for the app and setting the `inst` attribute to `false` ❶. Based on this information, the `PackageManagerService` marks the `com.example.app` package as not installed for that user and the package doesn't show up in the launcher or the list of apps in Settings.

Applications can be installed but still marked as stopped, as shown at ❷. Here, the `com.example.app2` package is installed but marked as stopped by setting the `stopped` attribute to `true`. Android has a special state for applications that have never been launched; a state that is persisted with the `nl` attribute of the `<pkg>` tag. The device owner can block a package for a certain user, in which case the `blocked` attribute is set to `true`, though this is not shown in Figure 4-4.

When a device user installs an application, a `<pkg>` tag with `inst="false"` is added to the *package-restrictions.xml* files for all users. When another user installs the same application, the `inst` attribute is removed and the application is considered installed for that user. (Depending on how the second user started the install process, the APK file in */data/app/* may be replaced, as it is in an application update.)

Restricted users cannot install applications, but the same procedure is applied when the device owner enables an app for a restricted user: the application is installed by calling the `PackageManagerService.installExistingPackageAsUser()` method, which sets the installed flag for the package and updates *package-restrictions.xml* accordingly.

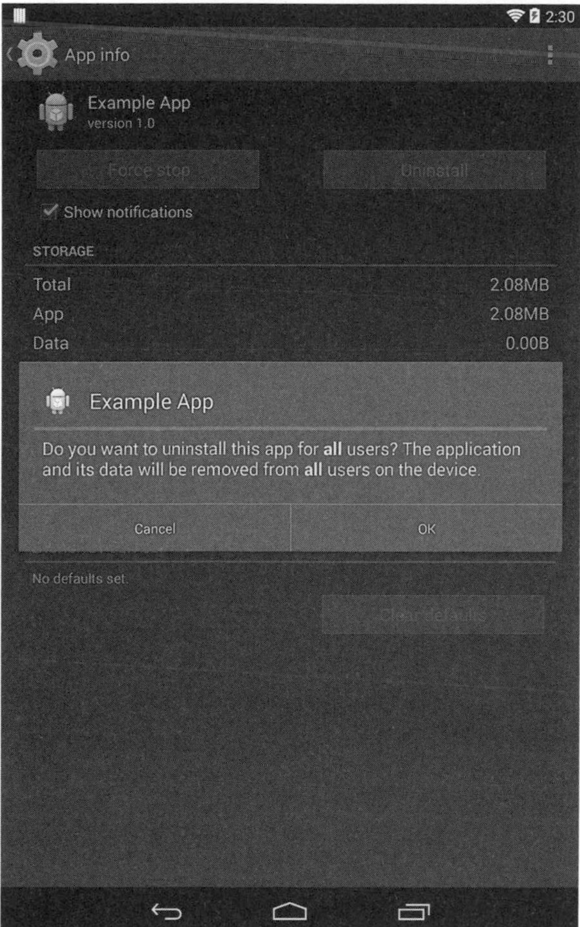

Figure 4-4: Warning shown when the device owner tries to uninstall an app for all users

When a user uninstalls a package, their app data is deleted and the internal per-user package installed flag is set to `false`. This state is then persisted by setting `inst="false"` to the removed package's tag in the user's *package-restrictions.xml* file. The APK file and native library directory are only removed when the last user that has the app installed uninstalls it. However, the owner can see all apps installed on the system in the All tab of the Apps Settings screen, including ones they haven't installed, and they can uninstall those apps for all users. The **`Uninstall for all users`** action is hidden in the overflow menu so that it isn't selected accidentally. It produces the warning shown in Figure 4-4. If the owner selects OK in this warning dialog, app directories for all users are removed and the APK file is deleted from the device.

The app-sharing scheme implemented on multi-user Android devices is backward-compatible with previous versions and saves device space by not copying APK files for all users. However, it has one major disadvantage: any user can update an application, even if it was originally installed by another user.

This scheme is usually not a problem, because every user's app instance has a separate data directory, except when the update adds new permissions. Because Android grants permissions at install time, if a user updates an app and accepts a new permission that affects user privacy (for example, `READ_CONTACTS`), that permission will apply to all users who use the app. Other users are not notified that the app has been granted a new permission and may never notice the change, unless they manually inspect the app's details in system Settings. Android does show a warning that notifies users about this fact when they first enable multi-user support, but does not send subsequent notifications about specific apps.

External Storage

Android has included support for external storage since the first public versions. Because the first few generations of Android devices implemented external storage by simply mounting a FAT-formatted removable SD card, external storage is often referred to as "the SD card." However, the definition of external storage is broader and simply requires that external storage be a "case-insensitive filesystem with immutable POSIX permission classes and modes."[2] The underlying implementation may be anything that satisfies this definition.

External Storage Implementations

Newer devices tend to implement external storage by emulation, and some don't have an SD card slot at all. For example, the last Google Nexus device that had an SD card slot was the Nexus One, released in January 2010, and all Nexus devices released after the Nexus S (which uses a dedicated partition for external storage) implement external storage by emulation. On devices that lack an SD card, external storage is implemented either by directly mounting a FAT-formatted partition, which resides on the same block device as primary storage, or by using a helper daemon to emulate it.

Beginning with Android version 4.4, apps have been able to manage their package-specific directories (*Android/data/com.example.app/* for an app with the `com.example.app` package) on external storage without requiring the `WRITE_EXTERNAL_STORAGE` permission, which grants access to all data on external

2. Google, "External Storage Technical Information," *http://source.android.com/devices/tech/storage/index.html*

storage, including camera pictures, videos, and other media. This feature is called *synthesized permissions* and its AOSP implementation is based on a FUSE daemon that wraps the raw device storage and manages file access and permission based on a specified permission emulation mode.

NOTE *Filesystem in Userspace, or FUSE,[3] is a Linux feature that allows the implementation of a fully functional filesystem in a userspace program. This is achieved by using a generic FUSE kernel module that routes all Virtual Filesystem (VFS) system calls for the target filesystem to its userspace implementation. The kernel module and the userspace implementation communicate via a special file descriptor obtained by opening* /dev/fuse.

As of Android version 4.4, multiple external storage devices can be accessed by applications, but the applications are only allowed to write arbitrary files on *primary external storage* (if they hold the `WRITE_EXTERNAL_STORAGE` permission), and they have only limited access to other external storage devices, referred to as *secondary external storage.* Our discussion will focus on primary external storage as it's most closely related to multi-user support.

Multi-User External Storage

In order to uphold the Android security model in a multi-user environment, the Android Compatibility Definition Document (CDD) places numerous requirements on external storage. The most important of these is that "Each user instance on an Android device MUST have separate and isolated external storage directories."[4]

Unfortunately, implementing this requirement poses a problem because external storage has traditionally been world-readable and implemented using the FAT filesystem, which does not support permissions. Google's implementation of multi-user external storage leverages three Linux kernel features in order to provide backward-compatible, per-user external storage: mount namespaces, bind mounts, and shared subtrees.

Advanced Linux Mount Features

As in other Unix systems, Linux manages all files from all storage devices as part of a single directory tree. Each filesystem is linked to a specific subtree by mounting it at a specified directory, called the *mount point.* Traditionally, the directory tree has been shared by all processes, and each process sees the same directory hierarchy.

---

3. "Filesystem in Userspace," *http://fuse.sourceforge.net/*

4. Google, *Android 4.4 Compatibility Definition,* "9.5. Multi-User Support," *http://static.googleusercontent.com/media/source.android.com/en//compatibility/4.4/android-4.4-cdd.pdf*

Linux 2.4.19 and later versions added support for per-process mount namespaces, which allows each process to have its own set of mount points and thus use a directory hierarchy different from that of other processes.[5] The current list of mounts for each process can be read from the */proc/PID/mounts* virtual file, where *PID* is the process ID. A forked Linux process can request a separate mount namespace by specifying the `CLONE_NEWNS` flag to the Linux-specific `clone()`[6] and `unshare()`[7] system calls. In this case, the namespace of the parent process is referred to as the *parent namespace*.

A *bind mount* allows a directory or file to be mounted at another path in the directory tree, making the same file or directory visible at multiple locations. A bind mount is created by specifying the `MS_BIND` flag to the `mount()` system call, or by passing the `--bind` parameter to the `mount` command.

Finally, *shared subtrees*,[8] which were first introduced in Linux 2.6.15, provide a way to control how filesystem mounts are propagated across mount namespaces. Shared subtrees make it possible for a process to have its own namespace but still access filesystems that are mounted after it starts. Shared subtrees provide four different mount types, of which Android uses the shared and slave mount. A *shared mount* created in a parent namespace propagates to all child namespaces and is thus visible to all processes that have cloned off a namespace. A *slave mount* has a master mount that is a shared mount, and also propagates new mounts. However, the propagation is one-way only: mounts at the master propagate to the slave, but mounts at the slave do not propagate to the master. This scheme allows a process to keep its mounts invisible to any other process, while still being able to see shared system mounts. Shared mounts are created by passing the `MS_SHARED` flag to the `mount()` system call, while creating slave mounts requires passing the `MS_SLAVE` flag.

Android Implementation

Since Android 4.4, mounting external storage directly is no longer supported but is emulated using the FUSE *sdcard* daemon, even when the underlying device is a physical SD card. We'll base our discussion on a configuration that is backed by a directory on internal storage, which is typical for devices without a physical SD card. (The official documentation[9] contains more details on other possible configurations.)

On a device where primary external storage is backed by internal storage, the *sdcard* FUSE daemon uses the */data/media/* directory as a source and

---

5. Michael Kerrisk, *The Linux Programming Interface: A Linux and UNIX System Programming Handbook*, No Starch Press, 2010, pp. 261

6. Ibid., 598

7. Ibid., 603

8. Linux Kernel, *Shared Subtrees*, *https://www.kernel.org/doc/Documentation/filesystems/sharedsubtree.txt*

9. Google, "External Storage: Typical Configuration Examples," *http://source.android.com/devices/tech/storage/config-example.html*

creates an emulated filesystem at */mnt/shell/emulated*. Listing 4-12 shows how the *sdcard* service is declared in the device-specific *init.rc* file in this case ❼.

```
--snip--
on init
    mkdir /mnt/shell/emulated 0700 shell shell❶
    mkdir /storage/emulated 0555 root root❷

    export EXTERNAL_STORAGE /storage/emulated/legacy❸
    export EMULATED_STORAGE_SOURCE /mnt/shell/emulated❹
    export EMULATED_STORAGE_TARGET /storage/emulated❺

    # Support legacy paths
    symlink /storage/emulated/legacy /sdcard❻
    symlink /storage/emulated/legacy /mnt/sdcard
    symlink /storage/emulated/legacy /storage/sdcard0
    symlink /mnt/shell/emulated/0 /storage/emulated/legacy
# virtual sdcard daemon running as media_rw (1023)
service sdcard /system/bin/sdcard -u 1023 -g 1023 -l /data/media /mnt/shell/emulated❼
    class late_start
--snip--
```

Listing 4-12: sdcard service declaration for emulated external storage

Here, the `-u` and `-g` options specify the user and group the daemon should run as, and `-l` specifies the layout used for emulated storage (discussed later in this section). As you can see at ❶, the */mnt/shell/emulated/* directory (available via the `EMULATED_STORAGE_SOURCE` environment variable ❹) is owned and only accessible by the *shell* user. Its contents might look like Listing 4-13 on a device with five users.

```
# ls -l /mnt/shell/emulated/
drwxrwx--x root     sdcard_r         0
drwxrwx--x root     sdcard_r         10
drwxrwx--x root     sdcard_r         11
drwxrwx--x root     sdcard_r         12
drwxrwx--x root     sdcard_r         13
drwxrwx--x root     sdcard_r         legacy
drwxrwx--x root     sdcard_r         obb
```

Listing 4-13: Contents of /mnt/shell/emulated/

As with app data directories, each user gets a dedicated external storage data directory named after their user ID. Android uses a combination of mount namespaces and bind mounts in order to make each user's external storage data directory available only to the applications that the user starts, without showing them other users' data directories. Because all applications are forked off the *zygote* process (discussed in Chapter 2), external storage setup is implemented in two steps: the first one is common to all processes, and the second is specific to each process. First, mount points that are shared by all forked app processes are set up in the unique *zygote* process. Then dedicated mount points, which are visible only to that process, are set up as part of each app's process specialization.

Let's first look at the shared part in the *zygote* process. Listing 4-14 shows an excerpt of the initZygote() function (found in *dalvik/vm/Init.cpp*) that highlights mount point setup.

```
static bool initZygote()
{
   setpgid(0,0);

   if (unshare(CLONE_NEWNS) == -1) {❶
        return -1;
   }

    // Mark rootfs as being a slave so that changes from default
    // namespace only flow into our children.
    if (mount("rootfs", "/", NULL, (MS_SLAVE | MS_REC), NULL) == -1) {❷
        return -1;
    }

    const char* target_base = getenv("EMULATED_STORAGE_TARGET");
    if (target_base != NULL) {
        if (mount("tmpfs", target_base, "tmpfs", MS_NOSUID | MS_NODEV,❸
                "uid=0,gid=1028,mode=0751") == -1) {
            return -1;
        }
    }
    --snip--
    return true;
}
```

Listing 4-14: Mount point setup in zygote

Here, *zygote* passes the CLONE_NEWNS flag to the unshare() system call ❶ in order to create a new, private mount namespace that will be shared by all its children (app processes). It then marks the root filesystem (mounted at */*) as a slave by passing the MS_SLAVE flag to the mount() system call ❷. This ensures that changes from the default mount namespace, such as mounting encrypted containers or removable storage, only propagate to its children, while at the same time making sure that any mounts created by children do not propagate into the default namespace. Finally, *zygote* creates the memory-backed EMULATED_STORAGE_TARGET (usually */storage/emulated/*) mount point by creating a *tmpfs* filesystem ❸, which children use to bind mount external storage into their private namespaces.

Listing 4-15 shows the process-specific mount point setup found in *dalvik/vm/native/dalvik_system_Zygote.cpp* that is executed when forking each app process off *zygote*. (Error handling, logging, and some variable declarations have been omitted.)

```
static int mountEmulatedStorage(uid_t uid, u4 mountMode) {
    userid_t userid = multiuser_get_user_id(uid);❶

    // Create a second private mount namespace for our process
    if (unshare(CLONE_NEWNS) == -1) {❷
        return -1;
    }

    // Create bind mounts to expose external storage
    if (mountMode == MOUNT_EXTERNAL_MULTIUSER
            || mountMode == MOUNT_EXTERNAL_MULTIUSER_ALL) {
        // These paths must already be created by init.rc
        const char* source = getenv("EMULATED_STORAGE_SOURCE");❸
        const char* target = getenv("EMULATED_STORAGE_TARGET");❹
        const char* legacy = getenv("EXTERNAL_STORAGE");❺
        if (source == NULL || target == NULL || legacy == NULL) {
            return -1;
        }
        --snip--
        // /mnt/shell/emulated/0
        snprintf(source_user, PATH_MAX, "%s/%d", source, userid);❻
        // /storage/emulated/0
        snprintf(target_user, PATH_MAX, "%s/%d", target, userid);❼
        --snip--
        if (mountMode == MOUNT_EXTERNAL_MULTIUSER_ALL) {
            // Mount entire external storage tree for all users
            if (mount(source, target, NULL, MS_BIND, NULL) == -1) {
                return -1;
            }
        } else {
            // Only mount user-specific external storage
            if (mount(source_user, target_user, NULL, MS_BIND, NULL) == -1) {❽
                return -1;
            }
        }
        --snip--
        // Finally, mount user-specific path into place for legacy users
        if (mount(target_user, legacy, NULL, MS_BIND | MS_REC, NULL) == -1) {❾
            return -1;
        }

    } else {
        return -1;
    }

    return 0;
}
```

Listing 4-15: External storage setup for app processes

Here, the mountEmulatedStorage() function first obtains the current user ID from the process UID ❶, then uses the unshare() system call to create a new mount namespace for the process by passing the CLONE_NEWNS flag ❷. The function then obtains the values of the EMULATED_STORAGE_SOURCE ❸, EMULATED_STORAGE_TARGET ❹, and EXTERNAL_STORAGE ❺ environment variables, which are all initialized in the device-specific *init.rc* file (see ❸, ❹, and ❺ in Listing 4-12). It then prepares the mount source ❻ and target ❼ directory paths based on the values of EMULATED_STORAGE_SOURCE, EMULATED_STORAGE_TARGET, and the current user ID.

The directories are created if they don't exist, and then the method bind mounts the source directory (such as */mnt/shell/emulated/0* for the owner user) at the target path (for example, */storage/emulated/0* for the owner user) ❽. This ensures that external storage is accessible from the Android shell (started with the *adb shell* command), which is used extensively for application development and debugging.

The final step is to recursively bind mount the target directory at the fixed legacy directory (*/storage/emulated/legacy/*) ❾. The legacy directory is symlinked to */sdcard/* in the device-specific *init.rc* file (❻ in Listing 4-12) for backward compatibility with apps that hardcode this path (normally obtained using the android.os.Environment.getExternalStorageDirectory() API).

After all steps have been executed, the newly created app process is guaranteed to see only the external storage allotted to the user that started it. We can verify this by looking at the list of mounts for two app process executed by different users as shown in Listing 4-16.

```
# cat /proc/7382/mounts
--snip--
/dev/fuse /mnt/shell/emulated fuse rw,nosuid,nodev,relatime,user_id=1023,
group_id=1023,default_permissions,allow_other 0 0❶
/dev/fuse /storage/emulated/0 fuse rw,nosuid,nodev,relatime,user_id=1023,
group_id=1023,default_permissions,allow_other 0 0❷
/dev/fuse /storage/emulated/legacy fuse rw,nosuid,nodev,relatime,user_id=1023,
group_id=1023,default_permissions,allow_other 0 0❸

# cat /proc/7538/mounts
--snip--
/dev/fuse /mnt/shell/emulated fuse rw,nosuid,nodev,relatime,user_id=1023,
group_id=1023,default_permissions,allow_other 0 0❹
/dev/fuse /storage/emulated/10 fuse rw,nosuid,nodev,relatime,user_id=1023,
group_id=1023,default_permissions,allow_other 0 0❺
/dev/fuse /storage/emulated/legacy fuse rw,nosuid,nodev,relatime,user_id=1023,
group_id=1023,default_permissions,allow_other 0 0❻
```

Listing 4-16: List of mount points for process started by different users

Here, the process started by the owner user with PID 7382 has a */storage/emulated/0* mount point ❷, which is a bind mount of */mnt/shell/emulated/0/*, and process 7538 (started by a secondary user) has a */storage/emulated/10* mount point ❺, which is a bind mount of */mnt/shell/emulated/10/*.

Because neither process has a mount point for the other process's external storage directory, each process can only see and modify its own files.

Both processes have a */storage/emulated/legacy* mount point (❸ and ❻), but because it is bound to different directories (*/storage/emulated/0/* and */mnt/shell/emulated/10/*, respectively), each process sees different contents. Both process can see */mnt/shell/emulated/* (❶ and ❹), but because this directory is only accessible to the *shell* user (permissions 0700), app processes cannot see its contents.

External Storage Permissions

In order to emulate the FAT filesystem that was originally used for external storage, the *sdcard* FUSE daemon assigns fixed owner, group, and access permissions to each file or directory on external storage. Additionally, permissions are not changeable, and symlinks and hardlinks are not supported. The assigned owner and permission are determined by the permission derivation mode that the *sdcard* daemon uses.

In legacy mode (specified with the `-l` option), which is backward-compatible with previous Android versions and which is still the default in Android 4.4, most files and directories are owned by the root user and their group is set to *sdcard_r*. Applications that are granted the `READ_EXTERNAL_STORAGE` permission have *sdcard_r* as one of their supplementary groups, and thus can read most files on external storage even if they were originally created by a different application. Listing 4-17 shows the owner and permission of files and directories in the root of external storage.

```
# ls -l /sdcard/
drwxrwx--- root      sdcard_r          Alarms
drwxrwx--x root      sdcard_r          Android
drwxrwx--- root      sdcard_r          DCIM
--snip--
-rw-rw---- root      sdcard_r        5 text.txt
```

Listing 4-17: Owner and permissions of files on external storage

In previous versions of Android, all files and directories on external storage were assigned the same owner and permissions, but Android 4.4 treats the application-specific external files directory (*Android/data/<package-name>/*, the exact path is returned by the `Context.getExternalFilesDir()` method) differently. Applications don't have to hold the `WRITE_EXTERNAL_STORAGE` permission in order to read and write files in this directory because it is owned by the creating application.

That said, even in Android 4.4, the application's external files directory is accessible by any application that holds the `READ_EXTERNAL_STORAGE` or `WRITE_EXTERNAL_STORAGE` permissions because the group of the directory is set to *sdcard_r*, as shown in Listing 4-18.

```
$ ls -l Android/data/
drwxrwx--- u10_a16  sdcard_r          com.android.browser
```

Listing 4-18: Owner and permissions of an app's external files directory

Android 4.4 supports a more flexible permission derivation mode that is based on directory structure, and which is specified by passing the -d option to the *sdcard* daemon. This derivation mode sets dedicated groups to the directories *Pictures/* and *Music/* (*sdcard_pics* ❶ and *sdcard_av* ❷, as shown in Listing 4-19), which allows for fine-grained control over which files applications can access. As of this writing, Android doesn't support such fine-grained access control, but it can easily be implemented by defining additional permissions that map to the *sdcard_pics* and *sdcard_av* groups. In the directory-structure-based permission mode, user directories are hosted under *Android/user/* ❸.

NOTE *While this new permission derivation mode is supported in Android 4.4, as of this writing, Nexus devices still use the legacy permission mode.*

```
rwxrwx--x root:sdcard_rw      /
rwxrwx--- root:sdcard_pics    /Pictures❶
rwxrwx--- root:sdcard_av      /Music❷

rwxrwx--x root:sdcard_rw      /Android
rwxrwx--x root:sdcard_rw      /Android/data
rwxrwx--- u0_a12:sdcard_rw    /Android/data/com.example.app
rwxrwx--x root:sdcard_rw      /Android/obb/
rwxrwx--- u0_a12:sdcard_rw    /Android/obb/com.example.app

rwxrwx--- root:sdcard_all     /Android/user❸
rwxrwx--x root:sdcard_rw      /Android/user/10
rwxrwx--- u10_a12:sdcard_rw   /Android/user/10/Android/data/com.example.app
```

Listing 4-19: Directory owners and permission in the new permission derivation mode

Other Multi-User Features

Besides dedicated app directories, external storage and settings, other Android features also support a multi-user device configuration. For example, as of version 4.4, Android's credential storage (which allows for secure management of cryptographic keys) lets each user have their own key storage. (We discuss credential storage in more detail in Chapter 7.)

In addition, Android's online account database, accessible via the AccountManager API, has been extended to allow secondary users to have their own accounts, as well as to allow restricted profiles to share some of the primary user's accounts (if the app that needs account access supports it). We discuss online account support and the AccountManager API in Chapter 8.

And finally, Android allows setting different device administration policies for each user. As of version 4.4, it also supports setting up per-user VPNs that only route a single user's traffic and which are not accessible by other users. (We discuss device administration, VPNs, and other enterprise features in Chapter 9.)

Summary

Android allows multiple users to share a device by providing dedicated internal and external storage to each user. Multi-user support follows the established security model and each user's applications are assigned a unique UID and run in dedicated processes that cannot access other user's data. User isolation is achieved by combining a UID assignment scheme that takes into account the user ID and storage mounting rules that allow each user to only see their own storage.

As of this writing, multi-user support is only available on devices without telephony support (usually tablets), as the behavior of telephony in a multi-user environment is currently undefined. Most Android features, including account database management, credential storage, device policies, and VPN support are multi-user-aware and allow each user to have their own configuration.

5

CRYPTOGRAPHIC PROVIDERS

This chapter introduces Android's cryptographic provider architecture and discusses the built-in providers and the algorithms they support. Because Android builds on the *Java Cryptography Architecture (JCA)*, we introduce its design in brief, starting with the *cryptographic service provider (CSP)* framework. We then discuss the main JCA classes and interfaces, and the cryptographic primitives they implement. (We will briefly introduce each cryptographic primitive, but a thorough discussion is beyond the scope of this book and some familiarity with basic cryptography is assumed.) Next, we present Android's JCA providers and cryptographic libraries as well as the algorithms each provider supports. Finally, we show how to use additional cryptography algorithms by installing a custom JCA provider.

JCA Provider Architecture

JCA provides an extensible cryptographic provider framework and a set of APIs covering the major cryptographic primitives in use today (block ciphers, message digests, digital signatures, and so on). This architecture aims to be implementation-independent and extensible. Applications that use the standard JCA APIs only need to specify the cryptographic algorithm they want to use and (in most cases) do not depend on a particular provider implementation. Support for new cryptographic algorithms can be added by simply registering an additional provider that implements the required algorithms. Additionally, cryptographic services offered by different providers are generally interoperable (with certain restrictions when keys are hardware-protected or key material is otherwise not directly available) and applications are free to mix and match services from different providers as needed. Let's look at JCA's architecture in more detail.

Cryptographic Service Providers

JCA splits cryptographic functionality into a number of abstract cryptographic services called *engines* and defines APIs for each service in the form of an *engine class*. For example, digital signatures are represented by the `Signature` engine class, and encryption is modeled with the `Cipher` class. (You'll find a comprehensive list of engine classes in the next section.)

In the context of JCA, a *cryptographic service provider* (*CSP*, or simply *provider*) is a package (or set of packages) that provides a concrete implementation of certain cryptographic services. Each provider advertises the services and algorithms it implements, allowing the JCA framework to maintain a registry of supported algorithms and their implementing providers. This registry maintains a preference order for providers, so if a certain algorithm is offered by more than one provider, the one with higher preference order is returned to the requesting application. An exception to this rule is made for engine classes that support *delayed provider selection* (`Cipher`, `KeyAgreement`, `Mac`, and `Signature`). With delayed provider selection, the provider is selected not when an instance of the engine class is created, but when the engine class is initialized for a particular cryptographic operation. Initialization requires a `Key` instance, which the system uses to find a provider that can accept the specified `Key` object. Delayed provider selection is helpful when using keys that are stored in hardware because the system cannot find the hardware-backed provider based on the algorithm name alone. However, concrete `Key` instances passed to initialization methods usually have enough information to determine the underlying provider.

NOTE *Current Android versions don't support delayed provider selection, but some related work is being done in the master branch, and delayed provider selection will likely be supported in a future version.*

Let's look at an example using the provider configuration illustrated in Figure 5-1.

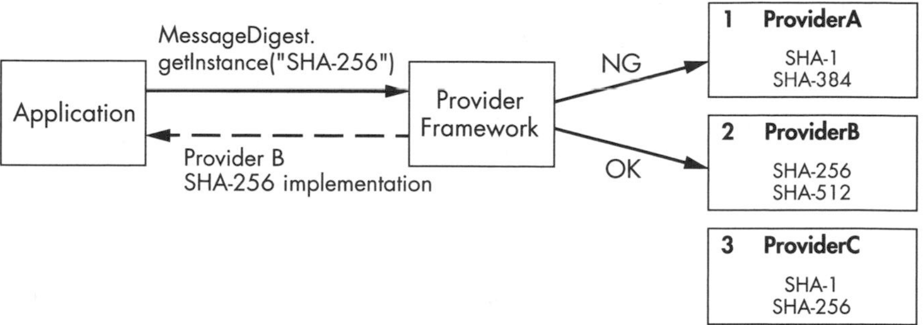

Figure 5-1: JCA algorithm implementation selection when provider is not specified

If an application requests an implementation of the SHA-256 digest algorithm without specifying a provider (as shown in Listing 5-1), the provider framework returns the implementation found in *ProviderB* (number 2 in the list in Figure 5-1), not the one in *ProviderC*, which also supports SHA-256, but which is number 3 in the list in Figure 5-1.

```
MessageDigest md = MessageDigest.getInstance("SHA-256");
```

Listing 5-1: Requesting a SHA-256 implementation without specifying a provider

On the other hand, if the application specifically requests *ProviderC* (as shown in Listing 5-2), its implementation will be returned even though *ProviderB* has a higher preference order.

```
MessageDigest md = MessageDigest.getInstance("SHA-256", "ProviderC");
```

Listing 5-2: Requesting a SHA-256 implementation from a specific provider

Generally, applications should not explicitly request a provider unless they include the requested provider as part of the application or can handle fallback if the preferred provider is not available.

Provider Implementation

The JCA framework guarantees implementation independence by requiring all implementations of a particular cryptographic service or algorithm to conform to a common interface. For each engine class that represents a particular cryptographic service, the framework defines a corresponding abstract *Service Provider Interface (SPI)* class. Providers that offer a particular cryptographic service implement and advertise the corresponding SPI class. For example, a provider that implements a given encryption algorithm would have an implementation of the `CipherSpi` class that corresponds to the `Cipher` engine class. When an application calls the `Cipher.getInstance()` factory method, the JCA framework finds the appropriate provider by using the process outlined in "Cryptographic Service Providers" on page 116 and returns a `Cipher` instance that routes all of its method calls to the `CipherSpi` subclass implemented in the selected provider.

In addition to SPI implementation classes, each provider has a subclass of the abstract `java.security.Provider` class that defines the name and version of the provider and, more importantly, a list of the supported algorithms and matching SPI implementation classes. The JCA provider framework uses this `Provider` class to build the provider registry, and queries it when searching for algorithm implementations to return to its clients.

Static Provider Registration

In order for a provider to be visible to the JCA framework, it must be registered first. There are two ways to register a provider: statically and dynamically. Static registration requires editing the system security properties file and adding an entry for the provider. (On Android, this properties file is called *security.properties* and is only present inside the *core.jar* system library. Therefore, it cannot be edited and static provider registration is not supported. We describe it here only for completeness.)

A provider entry in the security properties file is formatted as shown in Listing 5-3.

```
security.provider.n=ProviderClassName
```

Listing 5-3: Static registration of a JCA provider

Here, *n* is the provider's preference order that is used when searching for requested algorithms (when no provider name is specified). The order is 1-based; that is, 1 is the most preferred, followed by 2, and so on. `ProviderClassName` is the name of the `java.security.Provider` class implementation described in "Provider Implementation" on page 117.

Dynamic Provider Registration

Providers are registered dynamically (at runtime) with the `addProvider()` and `insertProviderAt()` methods of the `java.security.Security` class. These methods return the actual position in which the provider was added, or –1 if the provider was not added because it was already installed. Providers can also be removed dynamically by calling the `removeProvider()` method.

The `Security` class manages the list of security `Providers` and effectively acts as the provider registry described in the previous sections. In Java SE, programs require special permissions in order to register providers and modify the provider registry because by inserting a new provider at the top of the provider list, they can effectively replace the system security implementation. In Android, modifications to the provider registry are limited to the current app process and cannot affect the system or other applications. Therefore, no special permissions are required in order to register a JCA provider.

Dynamic modifications to the provider registry are typically placed in a static block to ensure that they are executed before any application code. Listing 5-4 shows an example of replacing the default (top priority) provider with a custom one.

```
static {
    Security.insertProviderAt(new MyProvider(), 1);
}
```

Listing 5-4: Dynamically inserting a custom JCA provider

If the class is loaded more than once (for example, by different class loaders), the static block may be executed multiple times. You can work around this by checking whether the provider is already available or by using a holder class that is loaded only once.

JCA Engine Classes

An engine class provides the interface to a specific type of cryptographic service. JCA engines provide one of the following services:

- Cryptographic operations (encrypt/decrypt, sign/verify, hash, and so on)
- Generation or conversion of cryptographic material (keys and algorithm parameters)
- Management and storage of cryptographic objects, such as keys and digital certificates

Obtaining an Engine Class Instance

In addition to providing a unified interface to cryptographic operations, engine classes decouple client code from the underlying implementation, which is why they cannot be instantiated directly; instead, they provide a static factory method called `getInstance()` that lets you request an implementation indirectly. The `getInstance()` method typically has one of the signatures shown in Listing 5-5.

```
static EngineClassName getInstance(String algorithm)❶
    throws NoSuchAlgorithmException
static EngineClassName getInstance(String algorithm, String provider)❷
    throws NoSuchAlgorithmException, NoSuchProviderException
static EngineClassName getInstance(String algorithm, Provider provider)❸
    throws NoSuchAlgorithmException
```

Listing 5-5: JCA engine class factory method signatures

Usually, you would use the signature at ❶ and specify only the algorithm name. The signatures at ❷ and ❸ allow you to request an implementation from a specific provider. All variants throw a `NoSuchAlgorithmException` if an implementation for the requested algorithm is not available and ❷ throws `NoSuchProviderException` if a provider with the specified name is not registered.

Algorithm Names

The string `algorithm` parameter that all factory methods take maps to a particular cryptographic algorithm or transformation, or specifies an implementation strategy for higher-level objects that manage collections of certificates or keys. Usually, the mapping is straightforward. For example, *SHA-256* maps to an implementation of the SHA-256 hashing algorithm and *AES* requests an implementation of the AES encryption algorithm. However, some algorithm names have structure and specify more than one parameter of the requested implementation. For example, *SHA256withRSA* specifies a signature implementation that uses SHA-256 for hashing the signed message and RSA to perform the signature operation. Algorithms can also have aliases, and more than one algorithm name can map to the same implementation.

Algorithm names are case-insensitive. The standard algorithm names supported by each JCA engine class are defined in the *JCA Standard Algorithm Name Documentation* (sometimes referred to as just *Standard Names*).[1] In addition to those, providers can define their own algorithm names and aliases. (See each provider's documentation for details.) You can use the code in Listing 5-6 to list all providers, the algorithm names of cryptographic services offered by each provider, and the implementation classes they map to.

```
Provider[] providers = Security.getProviders();
for (Provider p : providers) {
     System.out.printf("%s/%s/%f\n", p.getName(), p.getInfo(), p.getVersion());
     Set<Service> services = p.getServices();
     for (Service s : services) {
         System.out.printf("\t%s/%s/%s\n", s.getType(),
              s.getAlgorithm(), s.getClassName());
    }
}
```

Listing 5-6: Listing all JCA providers and the algorithms they support

We will show the format for the algorithm name of major engine classes as we introduce them in the following sections.

SecureRandom

The `SecureRandom` class represents a cryptographic *Random Number Generator (RNG)*. While you may not directly use it too often, it is used internally by most cryptographic operations to generate keys and other cryptographic material. The typical software implementation is usually a *Cryptographically Secure Pseudo Random Number Generator (CSPRNG)*, which produces a sequence of numbers that approximate the properties of true random numbers based on an initial value called a *seed*. As the quality of random numbers produced

1. Oracle, *Java™ Cryptography Architecture Standard Algorithm Name Documentation, http://docs.oracle.com/javase/7/docs/technotes/guides/security/StandardNames.html*

by a CSPRNG largely depends on its seed, it is chosen carefully, usually based on the output of a true RNG.

On Android, CSPRNG implementations are seeded by reading seed bytes from the standard Linux */dev/urandom* device file, which is an interface to the kernel CSPRNG. As the kernel CSPRNG itself may be in a fairly predictable state right after starting, Android periodically saves the state (which is 4096 bytes as of Android 4.4) of the kernel CSPRNG to the */data/system/entropy.dat* file. The contents of that file are written back to */dev/urandom* on boot in order to carry over the previous CSPRNG state. This is performed by the `EntropyMixer` system service.

Unlike most engine classes, `SecureRandom` has public constructors that you can use to create an instance. The recommended way to get a properly seeded instance on Android is to use the default (no argument) constructor (❶ in Listing 5-7). If you use the `getInstance()` factory method, you need to pass *SHA1PRNG* as the algorithm name, which is the only universally supported algorithm name for `SecureRandom`. Because *SHA1PRNG* is not exactly a cryptographic standard, implementations from different providers might behave differently. To have `SecureRandom` generate random bytes, you pass a byte array to its `nextBytes()` method (❷ in Listing 5-7). It will generate as many bytes as the array length (16 in Listing 5-7) and store them in it.

```
SecureRandom sr = new SecureRandom();❶
byte[] output = new byte[16];
sr.nextBytes(output);❷
```

Listing 5-7: Using `SecureRandom` to generate random bytes

Seeding `SecureRandom` manually is not recommended because seeding the system CSPRNG improperly may result in it producing a predictable sequence of bytes, which could compromise any higher-level operations that require random input. However, if you need to manually seed `SecureRandom` for some reason (for example, if the default system seeding implementation is known to be flawed), you can do so by using the `SecureRandom(byte[] seed)` constructor or by calling the `setSeed()` method. When seeding manually, make sure that the seed you are using is sufficiently random; for example, by reading it from */dev/urandom.*

Additionally, depending on the underlying implementation, calling `setSeed()` may not replace, but instead only add to the internal CSPRNG state; so two `SecureRandom` instances seeded with the same seed value may not produce the same number sequence. Therefore, `SecureRandom` should not be used when deterministic values are required. Instead, use a cryptographic primitive that is designed to produce deterministic output from a given input, such as a hash algorithm or a key derivation function.

MessageDigest

The `MessageDigest` class represents the functionality of a cryptographic message digest, also referred to as a hash function. A cryptographic message digest takes an arbitrarily long sequence of bytes and generates a fixed-size byte sequence called a *digest* or *hash*. A good hash function guarantees that even a small change in its input results in completely different output and that it is very difficult to find two inputs that are different but produce the same hash value (*collision resistance*), or generate an input that has a given hash (*pre-image resistance*). Another important property of hash functions is second pre-image resistance. In order to withstand second pre-image attacks, a hash function should make it difficult to find a second input m_2 that hashes to the same value as a given input m_1.

Listing 5-8 shows how to use the `MessageDigest` class.

```
MessageDigest md = MessageDigest.getInstance("SHA-256");❶
byte[] data = getMessage();
byte[] digest = md.digest(data);❷
```

Listing 5-8: Using `MessageDigest` to hash data

A `MessageDigest` instance is created by passing the hash algorithm name to the `getInstance()` factory method ❶. Input may be provided in chunks by using one of the `update()` methods, and then calling one of the `digest()` methods to get the calculated hash value. Alternatively, if the input data size is fixed and relatively short, it can be hashed in one step by using the `digest(byte[] input)` method ❷, as shown in Listing 5-8.

Signature

The `Signature` class provides a common interface for digital signature algorithms based on asymmetric encryption. A digital signature algorithm takes an arbitrary message and a private key and produces a fixed-sized byte string called a *signature*. Digital signatures typically apply a digest algorithm to the input message, encode the calculated hash value, and then use a private key operation to produce the signature. The signature can then be verified using the corresponding public key by applying the reverse operation, calculating the hash value of the signed message, and comparing it to the one encoded in the signature. Successful verification guarantees the integrity of the signed message and, on the condition that the signing private key has remained indeed private, its authenticity.

`Signature` instances are created with the standard `getInstance()` factory method. The algorithm name used is generally in the form *<digest>with<encryption>*, where *<digest>* is a hash algorithm name as used by `MessageDigest` (such as *SHA256*), and *<encryption>* is an asymmetric encryption algorithm (such as *RSA* or *DSA*). For example, a *SHA512withRSA* `Signature` would first use the SHA-512 hash algorithm to produce a digest value and then encrypt the encoded digest with an RSA private key to produce the signature. For signature algorithms that use a mask generation function such as RSA-PSS, the algorithm name takes the form *<digest>with<encryption>and<mgf>* (for example, *SHA256withRSAandMGF1*).

Listing 5-9 shows how to use the `Signature` class to generate and verify a cryptographic signature.

```
PrivateKey privKey = getPrivateKey();
PublicKey pubKey = getPublicKey();
byte[] data = "sign me".getBytes("ASCII");

Signature sig = Signature.getInstance("SHA256withRSA");
sig.initSign(privKey);❶
sig.update(data);❷
byte[] signature = sig.sign();❸

sig.initVerify(pubKey);❹
sig.update(data);
boolean valid = sig.verify(signature);❺
```

Listing 5-9: Generating and verifying a signature with the `Signature` *class*

After obtaining an instance, the `Signature` object is initialized for either signing, by passing a private key to the `initSign()` method (❶ in Listing 5-9), or verification, by passing a public key or certificate to the `initVerify()` method ❹ for verification.

Signing is similar to calculating a hash with `MessageDigest`: the data to be signed is fed in chunks to one of the `update()` methods ❷ or in bulk to the `sign()` method ❸, which returns the signature value. To verify a signature, the signed data is passed to one of the `update()` methods. Finally, the signature is passed to the `verify()` method ❺, which returns `true` if the signature is valid.

Cipher

The `Cipher` class provides a common interface to encryption and decryption operations. Encryption is the process of using some algorithm (called a *cipher*) and a key to transform data (called *plaintext*, or *plaintext message*) into a randomly looking form (called *ciphertext*). The inverse operation, called *decryption*, transforms the ciphertext back into the original plaintext.

The two major types of encryption widely used today are *symmetric encryption* and *asymmetric encryption*. Symmetric, or *secret key*, encryption uses the same key to encrypt and decrypt data. Asymmetric encryption uses a pair of keys: a *public key* and a *private key*. Data encrypted with one of the keys can only be decrypted with the other key of the pair. The `Cipher` class supports both symmetric and asymmetric encryption.

Depending on how they process input, ciphers can be *block* or *stream*. Block ciphers work on fixed-sized chunks of data called *blocks*. If the input cannot be divided into an integral number of blocks, the last block is *padded* by adding the necessary number of bytes to match the block size. Both the operation and the added bytes are called *padding*. Padding is removed in the decryption process and is not included in the decrypted plaintext. If a padding algorithm is specified, the `Cipher` class can add and remove padding automatically. On the other hand, stream ciphers process input data one byte (or even bit) at a time and do not require padding.

Block Cipher Modes of Operation

Block ciphers employ different strategies when processing input blocks in order to produce the final ciphertext (or plaintext when decrypting). Those strategies are called *modes of operation*, *cipher modes*, or simply *modes*. The simplest processing strategy is to split the plaintext into blocks (padding as necessary), apply the cipher to each block, and then concatenate the encrypted blocks to produce the ciphertext. This mode is called *Electronic Code Book (ECB)* mode, and while it's straightforward and easy to use, it has the major disadvantage that identical plaintext blocks produce identical ciphertext blocks. Thus, plaintext structure is reflected in the ciphertext, which compromises message confidentiality and facilitates cryptanalysis. This has often been illustrated with the infamous "ECB Penguin" from the Wikipedia entry on block cipher modes.[2] We present our Android version in Figure 5-2.[3] Here, ❶ is the original image, ❷ is the image encrypted in ECB mode, and ❸ is the same image encrypted in CBC mode. As you can see, the pattern of the original image is distinguishable in ❷, while ❸ looks like random noise.

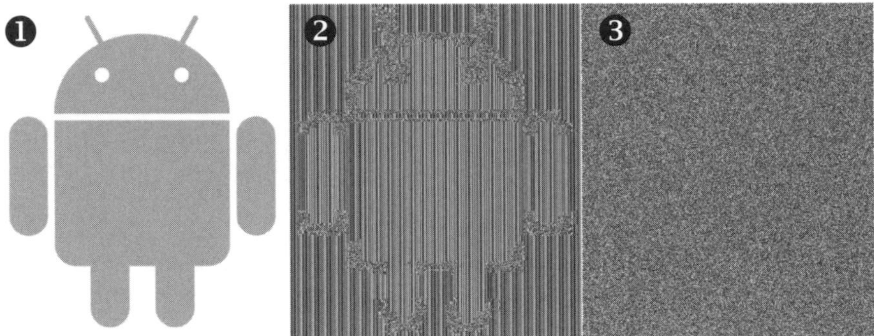

Figure 5-2: Ciphertext patterns produced by different cipher modes

Feedback modes add randomness to the ciphertext by combining the previous encrypted block with the current plaintext block before encrypting. In order to produce the first cipher block, they combine the first plaintext block with a block-sized string of bytes not found in the original plain text, called an *initialization vector (IV)*. When configured to use a feedback mode, the `Cipher` class can use a client-specified IV or generate one automatically. Commonly used feedback modes are *Cipher-block chaining (CBC)*, *Cipher feedback (CFB)*, and *Output feedback (OFB)*.

Another way to add randomness to the ciphertext, employed by the *Counter (CTR)* mode, is to encrypt the successive values of a counter sequence in order to produce a new key for each plaintext block that needs to be encrypted. This effectively turns the underlying block cipher into a stream cipher and no padding is required.

---

2. Wikipedia, "Block cipher mode of operation," *https://en.wikipedia.org/wiki/Block_cipher_mode_of_operation*

3. The Android robot is reproduced or modified from work created and shared by Google and used according to terms described in the Creative Commons 3.0 Attribution License.

Newer cipher modes, such as *Galois/Counter Mode (GCM)*, not only diffuse patterns in the original plaintext but also authenticate the ciphertext, making sure it has not been tampered with. They provide *authenticated encryption (AE)* or *Authenticated Encryption with Associated Data (AEAD)*.[4] The `Cipher` APIs have been extended to support authenticated encryption in Java SE 7, and those extensions have been available since Android 4.4, which has a Java 7–compatible runtime library API. AE ciphers concatenate the authentication tag output by the encryption operation to the ciphertext that operation produces in order to form their final output. In the Java `Cipher` API, the tag is included (or verified, when decrypting) implicitly after calling `doFinal()`, so you should not use the output of `update()` until you're sure the implicit tag at the end validates.

Obtaining a Cipher Instance

Having reviewed the major parameters of a cipher, we can finally discuss how to create `Cipher` instances. Like the other engine classes, `Cipher` objects are created with the `getInstance()` factory method, which requires not just a simple algorithm name, but that you fully specify the cryptographic *transformation* that the requested cipher will perform.

Listing 5-10 shows how to create a `Cipher` instance by passing a transformation string to `getInstance()`.

```
Cipher c = Cipher.getInstance("AES/CBC/PKCS5Padding");
```

Listing 5-10: Creating a `Cipher` *instance*

A transformation needs to specify the encryption algorithm, cipher mode, and padding. The transformation string passed to `getInstance()` is in the *algorithm/mode/padding* format. For example, the transformation string used in Listing 5-10 would create a `Cipher` instance that uses AES as the encryption algorithm, CBC as the cipher mode, and PKCS#5 padding.

NOTE *The term* PKCS *will appear quite a few times in our discussion of JCA providers and engine classes. The acronym stands for* Public Key Cryptography Standard *and refers to a group of cryptography standards that were originally developed and published by RSA Security, Inc. in the early 1990s. Most have evolved into public Internet standard and are now published and maintained as RFCs (Requests for Comments, formal documents describing Internet standards), but they are still referred to by their original name. Notable standards include PKCS#1, which defines the basic algorithms for RSA encryption and signatures; PKCS#5, which defines password-based encryption; PKCS#7, which defines message encryption and signing under a PKI and became the basis of S/MIME; and PKCS#12, which defines a container for keys and certificates. A full list can be found on EMC's website.*[5]

4. D. McGrew, *RFC 5116 – An Interface and Algorithms for Authenticated Encryption, http://www.ietf.org/rfc/rfc5116.txt*

5. RSA Laboratories, *Public-Key Cryptography Standards (PKCS), http://www.emc.com/emc-plus/rsa-labs/standards-initiatives/public-key-cryptography-standards.htm*

A Cipher instance can be created by passing only the algorithm name, but in that case the returned implementation would use provider-specific defaults for the cipher mode and padding. This is not only not portable across providers, but could severely impact the security of the system if, for example, a less-secure-than-intended cipher mode (such as ECB) is used at runtime. This "shortcut" is a major design flaw of the JCA provider framework and should never be used.

Using a Cipher

Once a Cipher instance has been obtained, it needs to be initialized before encrypting or decrypting data. A Cipher is initialized by passing an integer constant that denotes the operation mode (ENCRYPT_MODE, DECRYPT_MODE, WRAP_MODE, or UNWRAP_MODE), a key or certificate, and, optionally, algorithm parameters, to one of the corresponding init() methods. ENCRYPT_MODE and DECRYPT_MODE are used to encrypt and decrypt arbitrary data, while WRAP_MODE and UNWRAP_MODE are specialized modes used when encrypting (*wrapping*) and decrypting (*unwrapping*) the key material of a Key object with another key.

Listing 5-11 shows how to use the Cipher class to encrypt and decrypt data.

```
SecureRandom sr = new SecureRandom();
SecretKey key = getSecretKey();
Cipher cipher = Cipher.getInstance("AES/CBC/PKCS5Padding");❶

byte[] iv = new byte[cipher.getBlockSize()];
sr.nextBytes(iv);
IvParameterSpec ivParams = new IvParameterSpec(iv);❷
cipher.init(Cipher.ENCRYPT_MODE, key, ivParams);❸
byte[] plaintext = "encrypt me".getBytes("UTF-8");
ByteArrayOutputStream baos = new ByteArrayOutputStream();
byte[] output = cipher.update(plaintext);❹
if (output != null) {
    baos.write(output);
}
output = cipher.doFinal();❺
baos.write(output);
byte[] ciphertext = baos.toByteArray();

cipher.init(Cipher.DECRYPT_MODE, key, ivParams);❻
baos = new ByteArrayOutputStream();
output = cipher.update(ciphertext);❼
if (output != null) {
    baos.write(output);
}
output = cipher.doFinal();❽
baos.write(output);
byte[] decryptedPlaintext = baos.toByteArray();❾
```

Listing 5-11: Using the Cipher class to encrypt and decrypt data

In this example, we create a Cipher instance that uses AES in CBC mode and PKCS#5 padding ❶; generate a random IV and wrap it into an IvParameterSpec object ❷; and then initialize the Cipher for encryption by passing ENCRYPT_MODE, the encryption key, and the IV to the init() method ❸. We can then encrypt data by passing data chunks to the update() method ❹, which returns intermediate results (or null if the input data is too short to result in a new block), and obtain the last block by calling the doFinal() method ❺. The final ciphertext is obtained by concatenating the intermediate result(s) with the final block.

To decrypt, we initialize the cipher in DECRYPT_MODE ❻, passing the same key and the IV used for encryption. We then call update() ❼, this time using the ciphertext as input, and finally call doFinal() ❽ to obtain the last chunk of plaintext. The final plaintext is obtained by concatenating the intermediate result(s) with the final chunk ❾.

Mac

The Mac class provides a common interface to *Message Authentication Code (MAC)* algorithms. A MAC is used to check the integrity of messages transmitted over an unreliable channel. MAC algorithms use a secret key to calculate a value, *the MAC* (also called a *tag*), which can be used to authenticate the message and check its integrity. The same key is used to perform verification, so it needs to be shared between the communicating parties. (A MAC is often combined with a cipher to provide both confidentiality and integrity.)

```
KeyGenerator keygen = KeyGenerator.getInstance("HmacSha256");
SecretKey key = keygen.generateKey();
Mac mac = Mac.getInstance("HmacSha256");❶
mac.init(key);❷
byte[] message = "MAC me".getBytes("UTF-8");
byte[] tag = mac.doFinal(message);❸
```

Listing 5-12: Using the Mac class to generate a message authentication code

A Mac instance is obtained with the getInstance() factory method ❶ (as shown in Listing 5-12) by requesting an implementation of the HMAC[6] MAC algorithm that uses SHA-256 as the hash function. It is then initialized ❷ with a SecretKey instance, which may be generated with a KeyGenerator (see "KeyGenerator" on page 131), derived from a password or directly instantiated from raw key bytes. For MAC implementations based on hash functions (such as HMAC SHA-256 in this example), the type of key does not matter, but implementations that use a symmetric cipher may require a matching key type to be passed. We can then pass the message in chunks using one of the update() methods and call doFinal() to obtain the final MAC value, or perform the operation in one step by passing the message bytes directly to doFinal() ❸.

6. H. Krawczyk, M. Bellare, and R. Canetti, *HMAC: Keyed-Hashing for Message Authentication*, *http://tools.ietf.org/html/rfc2104*

Key

The `Key` interface represents *opaque* keys in the JCA framework. Opaque keys can be used in cryptographic operations, but usually do not provide access to the underlying *key material* (raw key bytes). This allows us to use the same JCA classes and interfaces both with software implementations of cryptographic algorithms that store key material on memory, and with hardware-backed ones, where the key material may reside in a hardware token (smart card, HSM,[7] and so on) and is not directly accessible.

The `Key` interface defines only three methods:

`String getAlgorithm()` Returns the name of the encryption algorithm (symmetric or asymmetric) that this key can be used with. Examples are *AES* or *RSA*.

`byte[] getEncoded()` Returns a standard encoded form of the key that can be used when transmitting the key to other systems. This can be encrypted for private keys. For hardware-backed implementations that do not allow exporting key material, this method typically returns `null`.

`String getFormat()` Returns the format of the encoded key. This is usually *RAW* for keys that are not encoded in any particular format. Other formats defined in JCA are *X.509* and *PKCS#8*.

You can obtain a `Key` instance in the following ways:

- Generate keys using a `KeyGenerator` or a `KeyPairGenerator`.
- Convert from some encoded representation using a `KeyFactory`.
- Retrieve a stored key from a `KeyStore`.

We discuss different `Key` types and how they are created and accessed in the next sections.

SecretKey and PBEKey

The `SecretKey` interface represents keys used in symmetric algorithms. It is a marker interface and does not add any methods to those of the parent `Key` interface. It has only one implementation that can be directly instantiated, namely `SecretKeySpec`. It is both a key implementation and a key specification (as discussed in the "KeySpec" section that follows) and allows you to instantiate `SecretKey` instances based on the raw key material.

The `PBEKey` subinterface represents keys derived using *Password Based Encryption (PBE)*.[8] PBE defines algorithms that derive strong cryptographic keys from passwords and passphrases, which typically have low entropy and thus cannot be used directly as keys. PBE is based on two main ideas: using a *salt* to protect from table-assisted (pre-computed) dictionary attacks (*salting*), and using a large iteration count to make the key derivation computationally

---

7. Hardware Security Module

8. B. Kaliski, *PKCS #5: Password-Based Cryptography Specification, Version 2.0, http://www.ietf.org/rfc/rfc2898.txt*

expensive (*key stretching*). The salt and iteration count are used as parameters to PBE algorithms and thus need to be retained in order to generate the same key from a particular password. Thus `PBEKey` implementations are required to implement `getSalt()` and `getIterationCount()` along with `getPassword()`.

PublicKey, PrivateKey, and KeyPair

Public and private keys for asymmetric encryption algorithms are modeled with the `PublicKey` and `PrivateKey` interfaces. They are marker interfaces and do not add any new methods. JCA defines specialized classes for concrete asymmetric algorithms that hold the parameters of the corresponding keys, such as `RSAPublicKey` and `RSAPrivateCrtKey`. The `KeyPair` interface is simply a container for a public key and a private key.

KeySpec

As discussed in "Key" on page 128, the JCA `Key` interface represents opaque keys. On the other hand, `KeySpec` models a *key specification*, which is a *transparent* key representation that allows you to access individual key parameters.

In practice, most `Key` and `KeySpec` interfaces for concrete algorithms overlap considerably because the key parameters need to be accessible in order to implement the encryption algorithms. For example, both `RSAPrivateKey` and `RSAPrivateKeySpec` define `getModulus()` and `getPrivateExponent()` methods. The difference is only important when an algorithm is implemented in hardware, in which case the `KeySpec` will only contain a reference to the hardware-managed key and not the actual key parameters. The corresponding `Key` will hold a handle to the hardware-managed key and can be used to perform cryptographic operations, but it will not hold any key material. For example, an `RSAPrivateKey` that is stored in hardware will return `null` when its `getPrivateExponent()` method is called.

`KeySpec` implementations can hold an encoded key representation, in which case they are algorithm independent. For example, the `PKCS8EncodedKeySpec` can hold either an RSA key or a DSA key in DER-encoded PKCS#8 format.[9] On the other hand, an algorithm-specific `KeySpec` holds all key parameters as fields. For example, `RSAPrivateKeySpec` contains the modulus and private exponent for an RSA key, which can be obtained using the `getModulus()` and `getPrivateExponent()` methods, respectively. Regardless of their type, `KeySpec`s are converted to `Key` objects using a `KeyFactory`.

KeyFactory

A `KeyFactory` encapsulates a conversion routine needed to turn a transparent public or private key representation (some `KeySpec` subclass) into an opaque[10]

---

9. RSA Laboratories, *PKCS #8: Private-Key Information Syntax Standard, http://www.emc.com/emc-plus/rsa-labs/standards-initiatives/pkcs-8-private-key-information-syntax-stand.htm*

10. Some `Key` subclasses, such as `RSAPrivateKey`, expose all key material and thus are not technically opaque.

key object (some Key subclass) that can be used to perform a cryptographic operation, or vice versa. A KeyFactory that converts an encoded key typically parses the encoded key data and stores each key parameter in the corresponding field of the concrete Key class. For example, to parse an X.509-encoded RSA public key, you can use the following code (see Listing 5-13).

```
KeyFactory kf = KeyFactory.getInstance("RSA");❶
byte[] encodedKey = readRsaPublicKey();
X509EncodedKeySpec keySpec = new X509EncodedKeySpec(encodedKey);❷
RSAPublicKey pubKey = (RSAPublicKey) kf.generatePublic(keySpec);❸
```

Listing 5-13: Using a KeyFactory to convert an X.509 encoded key to an RSAPublicKey object

Here we create an RSA KeyFactory by passing *RSA* to KeyFactory.getInstance() ❶. We then read the encoded RSA key, use the encoded key bytes to instantiate an X509EncodedKeySpec ❷, and finally pass the KeySpec to the factory's generatePublic() method ❸ in order to obtain an RSAPublicKey instance.

A KeyFactory can also convert an algorithm-specific KeySpec, such as RSAPrivateKeySpec, to a matching Key (RSAPrivateKey, in this example) instance, but in that case it merely copies the key parameters (or key handle) from one class to the other. Calling the KeyFactory.getKeySpec() method converts a Key object to a KeySpec, but this usage is not very common because an encoded key representation can be obtained simply by calling getEncoded() directly on the key object, and algorithm-specific KeySpecs generally do not provide any more information than a concrete Key class does.

Another feature of KeyFactory is converting a Key instance from a different provider into a corresponding key object compatible with the current provider. The operation is called *key translation* and is performed using the translateKey(Key key) method.

SecretKeyFactory

SecretKeyFactory is very similar to KeyFactory except that it only operates on secret (symmetric) keys. You can use it to convert a symmetric key specification into a Key object and vice versa. In practice though, if you have access to the key material of a symmetric key, it is much easier to use it to instantiate directly a SecretKeySpec that is also a Key, so it is not used very often in this fashion.

A much more common use case is generating a symmetric key from a user-supplied password using PBE (see Listing 5-14).

```
byte[] salt = generateSalt();
int iterationCount = 1000;
int keyLength = 256;
KeySpec keySpec = new PBEKeySpec(password.toCharArray(), salt,
                                 iterationCount, keyLength);❶
```

```
SecretKeyFactory skf = SecretKeyFactory.getInstance("PBKDF2WithHmacSHA1");❷
SecretKey key = skf.generateSecret(keySpec);❸
```

Listing 5-14: Generating a secret key from a password using SecretKeyFactory

In this case, a PBEKeySpec is initialized with the password, a randomly generated salt, iteration count, and the desired key length ❶. A SecretKey factory that implements a PBE key derivation algorithm (in this case, PBKDF2) is then obtained with a call to getInstance() ❷. Passing the PBEKeySpec to generateSecret() executes the key derivation algorithm and returns a SecretKey instance ❸ that can be used for encryption or decryption.

KeyPairGenerator

The KeyPairGenerator class generates pairs of public and private keys. A KeyPairGenerator is instantiated by passing an asymmetric algorithm name to the getInstance() factory method (❶ in Listing 5-15).

```
KeyPairGenerator kpg = KeyPairGenerator.getInstance("ECDH");❶
ECGenParameterSpec ecParamSpec = new ECGenParameterSpec("secp256r1");❷
kpg.initialize(ecParamSpec);❸
KeyPair keyPair = kpg.generateKeyPair();❹
```

Listing 5-15: Initializing KeyPairGenerator with algorithm-specific parameters

There are two ways to initialize a KeyPairGenerator: by specifying the desired key size and by specifying algorithm-specific parameters. In both cases, you can optionally pass a SecureRandom instance to be used for key generation. If only a key size is specified, key generation will use default parameters (if any). To specify additional parameters, you must instantiate and configure an AlgorithmParameterSpec instance appropriate for the asymmetric algorithm you are using and pass it to the initialize() method, as shown in Listing 5-15. In this example, the ECGenParameterSpec initialized in ❷ is an AlgorithmParameterSpec that allows you to specify the curve name used when generating *Elliptic Curve (EC)* cryptography keys. After it is passed to the initialize() method in ❸, the subsequent generateKeyPair() call in ❹ will use the specified curve (*secp256r1*) to generate the key pair.

NOTE *While named curves have been defined by various standards, the Oracle JCA specification does not explicitly define any elliptic curve names. As there is no official JCA standard, curve names supported by Android may vary based on platform version.*

KeyGenerator

The KeyGenerator is very similar to the KeyPairGenerator class, except that it generates symmetric keys. While you can generate most symmetric keys by requesting a sequence of random bytes from SecureRandom, KeyGenerator implementations perform additional checks for weak keys and set key parity bytes where appropriate (for DES and derived algorithms) and can take advantage of available cryptography hardware, so it's best to use KeyGenerator instead of generating keys manually.

Listing 5-16 shows how to generate an AES key using KeyGenerator.

```
KeyGenerator keygen = KeyGenerator.getInstance("AES");❶
kg.init(256);❷
SecretKey key = keygen.generateKey();❸
```

Listing 5-16: Generating an AES key with KeyGenerator

To generate a key using KeyGenerator, create an instance ❶, specify the desired key size with init() ❷, and then call generateKey() ❸ to generate the key.

KeyAgreement

The KeyAgreement class represents a *key agreement protocol* that allows two or more parties to generate a shared key without needing to exchange secret information. While there are different key agreement protocols, the ones most widely used today are based on the *Diffie-Hellman (DH) key exchange*—either the original one based on discrete logarithm cryptography[11] (simply known as *DH*), or the newer variant based on elliptic key cryptography (*ECDH*[12]).

Both variants of the protocol are modeled in JCA using the KeyAgreement class and can be performed in the same way, with the only difference being the keys. For both variants, each communicating party needs to have a key pair, with both key pairs generated with the same key parameters (prime modulus and base generator for DH, and typically the same well-defined named curve for ECDH). Then the parties only need to exchange public keys and execute the key agreement algorithm to arrive at a common secret.

Listing 5-17 illustrates using the KeyAgreement class to generate a shared secret using ECDH.

```
PrivateKey myPrivKey = getPrivateKey();
PublicKey remotePubKey = getRemotePubKey();
KeyAgreement keyAgreement = KeyAgreement.getInstance("ECDH");❶
keyAgreement.init(myPrivKey);❷
keyAgreement.doPhase(remotePubKey, true);❸
byte[] secret = keyAgreement.generateSecret();❹
```

Listing 5-17: Using KeyAgreement to generate a shared secret

A KeyAgreement instance is first created by passing the algorithm name, *ECDH*, to the getInstance() factory method ❶. Then the agreement

11. RSA Laboratories, *PKCS #3: Diffie-Hellman Key-Agreement Standard*, *ftp://ftp.rsasecurity.com/pub/pkcs/ascii/pkcs-3.asc*

12. NIST, *Recommendation for Pair-Wise Key Establishment Schemes Using Discrete Logarithm Cryptography*, *http://csrc.nist.gov/publications/nistpubs/800-56A/SP800-56A_Revision1_Mar08-2007.pdf*

is initialized by passing the local private key to the `init()` method ❷. Next, the `doPhase()` method is called $N - 1$ times, where N is the number of communicating parties, passing each party's public key as the first parameter, and setting the second parameter to `true` when executing the last phase of the agreement ❸. (For two communicating parties, as in this example, the `doPhase()` method needs to be called only once.) Finally, calling the `generateSecret()` method ❹ produces the shared secret.

Listing 5-17 shows the call flow for only one of the parties (*A*), but the other party (*B*) needs to execute the same sequence using its own private key to initialize the agreement, and passing *A*'s public key to `doPhase()`.

Note that while the value (or part of it) returned by `generateSecret()` can be used directly as a symmetric key, the preferred method is to use it as the input for a *key-derivation function (KDF)* and use the output of the KDF as key(s). Directly using the generated shared secret may lead to some loss of entropy, and doing so limits the number of keys that can be produced using a single DH key agreement operation. On the other hand, using a KDF diffuses any structure that the secret may have (such as padding) and allows for generating multiple derived keys by mixing in a salt.

`KeyAgreement` has another `generateSecret()` method which takes an algorithm name as a parameter and returns a `SecretKey` instance that can be used to initialize a `Cipher` directly. If the `KeyAgreement` instance has been created with an algorithm string that includes a KDF specification (for example, *ECDHwithSHA1KDF*), this method will apply the KDF to the shared secret before returning a `SecretKey`. If a KDF has not been specified, most implementations simply truncate the shared secret in order to obtain key material for the returned `SecretKey`.

KeyStore

JCA uses the term *keystore* to refer to a database of keys and certificates. A keystore manages multiple cryptographic objects, referred to as *entries* that are each associated with a string *alias*. The `KeyStore` class offers a well-defined interface to a keystore that defines three types of entries:

`PrivateKeyEntry` A private key with an associated certificate chain. For a software implementation, the private key material is usually encrypted and protected by a user-supplied passphrase.

`SecretKeyEntry` A secret (symmetric) key. Not all `KeyStore` implementations support storing secret keys.

`TrustedCertificateEntry` A public key certificate of another party. `TrustedCertificateEntry`s often contain CA certificates that can be used to establish trust relationships. A keystore that contains only `TrustedCertificateEntry`s is called a *truststore.*

KeyStore Types

A `KeyStore` implementation does not need to be persistent, but most implementations are. Different implementations are identified by a *keystore type* that defines the storage and data format of the keystore, as well as the methods used to protect stored keys. The default `KeyStore` type is set with the `keystore.type` system property.

The default `KeyStore` implementation of most JCA providers is usually a keystore type that stores its data in a file. The file format may be proprietary or based on a public standard. Proprietary formats include the original Java SE *JKS* format and its security enhanced version *JCEKS*, as well as the *Bouncy Castle KeyStore (BKS)* format, which is the default in Android.

PKCS#12 File-Backed KeyStores

The most widely used public standard that allows for bundling private keys and associated certificates in a file is the *Personal Information Exchange Syntax Standard*, commonly referred to as *PKCS#12*. It is a successor of the *Personal Information Exchange Syntax (PFX)* standard, so the terms PKCS#12 and PFX are used somewhat interchangeably, and PKCS#12 files are often called PFX files.

PKCS#12 is a container format that can contain multiple embedded objects, such as private keys, certificates, and even CRLs. Like the previous PKCS standards, which PKCS#12 builds upon, the container contents are defined in *ASN.1*[13] and are essentially a sequence of nested structures. The internal container structures are called `SafeBags`, with different bags defined for certificates (`CertBag`), private keys (`KeyBag`), and encrypted private keys (`PKCS8ShroudedKeyBag`). The integrity of the whole file is protected by a MAC that uses a key derived from an *integrity password*, and each individual private key entry is encrypted with a key derived from a *privacy password*. In practice, the two passwords are usually the same. PKCS#12 can also use public keys to protect the privacy and integrity of the archive contents, but this usage is not very common.

A typical PKCS#12 file that contains a user's encrypted password key and an associated certificate might have structure like that illustrated in Figure 5-3 (note that some of the wrapper structures have been removed for clarity).

Figure 5-3: Structure of a PKCS#12 file holding a private key and an associated certificate

13. *Abstract Syntax Notation One (ASN.1)*: A standard notation that describes rules and structures for encoding data in telecommunications and computer networking. Extensively used in cryptography standards to define the structure of cryptographic objects.

Listing 5-18 shows how to obtain a private key and certificate from a PKCS#12 file.

```
KeyStore keyStore = KeyStore.getInstance("PKCS12");❶
InputStream in = new FileInputStream("mykey.pfx");
keyStore.load(in, "password".toCharArray());❷
KeyStore.PrivateKeyEntry keyEntry =
      (KeyStore.PrivateKeyEntry)keyStore.getEntry("mykey", null);❸
X509Certificate cert = (X509Certificate) keyEntry.getCertificate();❹
RSAPrivateKey privKey = (RSAPrivateKey) keyEntry.getPrivateKey();❺
```

Listing 5-18: Using the `KeyStore` *class to extract a private key and certificate from a PKCS#12 file*

The `KeyStore` class can be used to access the contents of a PKCS#12 file by specifying *PKCS12* as the keystore type when creating an instance (❶ in Listing 5-18). To load and parse the PKCS#12 file, we call the `load()` method ❷, passing an `InputStream` from which to read the file, and the file integrity password. Once the file is loaded, we can obtain a private key entry by calling the `getEntry()` method and passing the key alias ❸ and, optionally, a `KeyStore.PasswordProtection` instance initialized with the password for the requested entry, if it's different from the file integrity password. If the alias is unknown, all aliases can be listed with the `aliases()` method. Once we have a `PrivateKeyEntry`, we can access the public key certificate ❹ or the private key ❺. New entries can be added with the `setEntry()` method and deleted with the `deleteEntry()` method. Changes to the `KeyStore` contents can be persisted to disk by calling the `store()` method, which accepts an `OutputStream` (to which the keystore bytes are written) and an integrity password (which is used to derive MAC and encryption keys) as parameters.

A `KeyStore` implementation does not have to use a single file for storing key and certificate objects. It can use multiple files, a database, or any other storage mechanism. In fact, keys may not be stored on the host system at all, but on a separate hardware device such as a smart card or a *hardware security module (HSM)*. (Android-specific `KeyStore` implementations that provide an interface to the system's trust store and credential storage are introduced in Chapters 6 and 7.)

CertificateFactory and CertPath

`CertificateFactory` acts as a certificate and CRL parser and can build certificate chains from a list of certificates. It can read a stream that contains encoded certificates or CRLs and output a collection (or a single instance) of `java.security.cert.Certificate` and `java.security.cert.CRL` objects. Usually, only an *X.509* implementation that parses X.509 certificates and CRLs is available.

Listing 5-19 shows how to parse a certificate file using `CertificateFactory`.

```
CertificateFactory cf = CertificateFactory.getInstance("X.509");❶
InputStream in = new FileInputStream("certificate.cer");
X509Certificate cert = (X509Certificate) cf.generateCertificate(in);❷
```

Listing 5-19: Parsing an X.509 certificate file with `CertificateFactory`

To create a `CertificateFactory`, we pass *X.509* as the factory type to `getInstance()` ❶, and then call `generateCertificate()`, passing an `InputStream` from which to read ❷. Because this is an *X.509* factory, the obtained object can be safely cast to `java.security.cert.X509Certificate`. If the read file includes multiple certificates that form a certificate chain, a `CertPath` object can be obtained by calling the `generateCertPath()` method.

CertPathValidator and CertPathBuilder

The `CertPathValidator` class encapsulates a certificate chain validation algorithm as defined by the *Public-Key Infrastructure (X.509)* or *PKIX* standard.[14] We discuss PKIX and certificate chain validation in more detail in Chapter 6, but Listing 5-20 shows how to use `CertificateFactory` and `CertPathValidator` to build and validate a certificate chain.

```
CertPathValidator certPathValidator = CertPathValidator.getInstance("PKIX");❶
CertificateFactory cf = CertificateFactory.getInstance("X.509");

X509Certificate[] chain = getCertChain();
CertPath certPath = cf.generateCertPath(Arrays.asList(chain));❷
Set<TrustAnchor> trustAnchors = getTrustAnchors();
PKIXParameters result = new PKIXParameters(trustAnchors);❸
PKIXCertPathValidatorResult result = (PKIXCertPathValidatorResult)
            certPathValidator.validate(certPath, pkixParams);❹
```

Listing 5-20: Building and validating a certificate chain with `CertPathValidator`

As you can see, we first obtain a `CertPathValidator` instance by passing *PKIX* to the `getInstance()` method ❶. We then build a certificate chain using `CertificateFactory`'s `generateCertPath()` method ❷. Note that if the passed list of certificates does not form a valid chain, this method throws a `CertificateException`. If we do not already have all the certificates needed to form a chain, we can use a `CertPathBuilder` initialized with a `CertStore` to find the needed certificates and build a `CertPath` (not shown).

Once we have a `CertPath`, we initialize the `PKIXParameters` class with a set of *trust anchors* (typically, these are trusted CA certificates; see Chapter 6 for details) ❸, and then call `CertPathValidator.validate()` ❹, passing the `CertPath` that we built in ❷ and the `PKIXParameters` instance. If validation succeeds, `validate()` returns a `PKIXCertPathValidatorResult` instance; if not, it throws a `CertPathValidatorException` that contains detailed information about why it failed.

14. D. Cooper et al., *Internet X.509 Public Key Infrastructure Certificate and Certificate Revocation List (CRL) Profile*, May 2008, *http://tools.ietf.org/html/rfc5280*

Android JCA Providers

Android's cryptography providers are based on JCA and follow its architecture with some relatively minor exceptions. While low-level Android components directly use native cryptography libraries (such as OpenSSL), JCA is the main cryptographic API and is used by system components and third-party applications alike.

Android has three core JCA providers that include implementations of the engine classes outlined in the previous section and two *Java Secure Socket Extension (JSSE)* providers that implement SSL functionality. (JSSE is discussed in detail in Chapter 6.)

Let's examine Android's core JCA providers.

Harmony's Crypto Provider

Android's Java runtime library implementation is derived from the retired Apache Harmony project,[15] which also includes a limited JCA provider simply named *Crypto* that provides implementations for basic cryptographic services like random number generation, hashing, and digital signatures. Crypto is still included in Android for backward compatibility but has the lowest priority of all JCA providers, so engine class implementations from Crypto are not returned unless explicitly requested. Table 5-1 shows the engine classes and algorithms that Crypto supports.

Table 5-1: Algorithms Supported by the Crypto Provider as of Android 4.4.4

Engine Class Name	Supported Algorithms
`KeyFactory`	*DSA*
`MessageDigest`	*SHA-1*
`SecureRandom`	*SHA1PRNG*
`Signature`	*SHA1withDSA*

NOTE *While the algorithms listed in Table 5-1 are still available in Android 4.4, all except* SHA1PRNG *have been removed in the Android master branch and may not be available in future versions.*

Android's Bouncy Castle Provider

Before Android version 4.0, the only full-featured JCA provider in Android was the Bouncy Castle provider. The Bouncy Castle provider is part of the Bouncy Castle Crypto APIs,[16] a set of open source Java implementations of cryptographic algorithms and protocols.

15. The Apache Software Foundation, "Apache Harmony," *http://harmony.apache.org/*

16. Legion of the Bouncy Castle Inc., "Bouncy Castle Crypto APIs," *https://www.bouncycastle.org/java.html*

Android includes a modified version of the Bouncy Castle provider, which is derived from the mainstream version by applying a set of Android-specific patches. Those patches are maintained in the Android source tree and updated for each new release of the mainstream Bouncy Castle provider. The main differences from the mainstream version are summarized below.

- Algorithms, modes, and algorithm parameters not supported by Java's reference implementation (RI) have been removed (RIPEMD, SHA-224, GOST3411, Twofish, CMAC, El Gamal, RSA-PSS, ECMQV, and so on).
- Insecure algorithms such as MD2 and RC2 have been removed.
- Java-based implementations of MD5 and the SHA family of digest algorithms have been replaced with a native implementation.
- Some PBE algorithms have been removed (for example, *PBEwithHmacSHA256*).
- Support for accessing certificates stored in LDAP has been removed.
- Support for certificate blacklists has been added (blacklists are discussed in Chapter 6).
- Various performance optimizations have been made.
- The package name has been changed to `com.android.org.bouncycastle` to avoid conflict with apps that bundle in Bouncy Castle (since Android 3.0).

The engine classes and algorithms supported by Android's Bouncy Castle provider as of version 4.4.4 (based on Bouncy Castle 1.49) are listed in Table 5-2.

Table 5-2: Algorithms Supported by Android's Bouncy Castle Provider as of Android 4.4.4

Engine Class Name	Supported Algorithms
`CertPathBuilder`	*PKIX*
`CertPathValidator`	*PKIX*
`CertStore`	*Collection*
`CertificateFactory`	*X.509*
`Cipher`	*AES* *AESWRAP* *ARC4* *BLOWFISH* *DES* *DESEDE* *DESEDEWRAP* *PBEWITHMD5AND128BITAES-CBC-OPENSSL* *PBEWITHMD5AND192BITAES-CBC-OPENSSL* *PBEWITHMD5AND256BITAES-CBC-OPENSSL* *PBEWITHMD5ANDDES* *PBEWITHMD5ANDRC2* *PBEWITHSHA1ANDDES* *PBEWITHSHA1ANDRC2*

Engine Class Name	Supported Algorithms
`Cipher` *(continued)*	*PBEWITHSHA256AND128BITAES-CBC-BC* *PBEWITHSHA256AND192BITAES-CBC-BC* *PBEWITHSHA256AND256BITAES-CBC-BC* *PBEWITHSHAAND128BITAES-CBC-BC* *PBEWITHSHAAND128BITRC2-CBC* *PBEWITHSHAAND128BITRC4* *PBEWITHSHAAND192BITAES-CBC-BC* *PBEWITHSHAAND2-KEYTRIPLEDES-CBC* *PBEWITHSHAAND256BITAES-CBC-BC* *PBEWITHSHAAND3-KEYTRIPLEDES-CBC* *PBEWITHSHAAND40BITRC2-CBC* *PBEWITHSHAAND40BITRC4* *PBEWITHSHAANDTWOFISH-CBC* *RSA*
`KeyAgreement`	*DH* *ECDH*
`KeyFactory`	*DH* *DSA* *EC* *RSA*
`KeyGenerator`	*AES* *ARC4* *BLOWFISH* *DES* *DESEDE* *HMACMD5* *HMACSHA1* *HMACSHA256* *HMACSHA384* *HMACSHA512*
`KeyPairGenerator`	*DH* *DSA* *EC* *RSA*
`KeyStore`	*BKS* (default) *BouncyCastle* *PKCS12*
`Mac`	*HMACMD5* *HMACSHA1* *HMACSHA256* *HMACSHA384* *HMACSHA512* *PBEWITHHMACSHA* *PBEWITHHMACSHA1*
`MessageDigest`	*MD5* *SHA-1* *SHA-256* *SHA-384* *SHA-512*

(continued)

Table 5-2 *(continued)*

Engine Class Name	Supported Algorithms
`SecretKeyFactory`	*DES* *DESEDE* *PBEWITHHMACSHA1* *PBEWITHMD5AND128BITAES-CBC-OPENSSL* *PBEWITHMD5AND192BITAES-CBC-OPENSSL* *PBEWITHMD5AND256BITAES-CBC-OPENSSL* *PBEWITHMD5ANDDES* *PBEWITHMD5ANDRC2* *PBEWITHSHA1ANDDES* *PBEWITHSHA1ANDRC2* *PBEWITHSHA256AND128BITAES-CBC-BC* *PBEWITHSHA256AND192BITAES-CBC-BC* *PBEWITHSHA256AND256BITAES-CBC-BC* *PBEWITHSHAAND128BITAES-CBC-BC* *PBEWITHSHAAND128BITRC2-CBC* *PBEWITHSHAAND128BITRC4* *PBEWITHSHAAND192BITAES-CBC-BC* *PBEWITHSHAAND2-KEYTRIPLEDES-CBC* *PBEWITHSHAAND256BITAES-CBC-BC* *PBEWITHSHAAND3-KEYTRIPLEDES-CBC* *PBEWITHSHAAND40BITRC2-CBC* *PBEWITHSHAAND40BITRC4* *PBEWITHSHAANDTWOFISH-CBC* *PBKDF2WithHmacSHA1* *PBKDF2WithHmacSHA1And8BIT*
`Signature`	*ECDSA* *MD5WITHRSA* *NONEWITHDSA* *NONEwithECDSA* *SHA1WITHRSA* *SHA1withDSA* *SHA256WITHECDSA* *SHA256WITHRSA* *SHA384WITHECDSA* *SHA384WITHRSA* *SHA512WITHECDSA* *SHA512WITHRSA*

AndroidOpenSSL Provider

As mentioned in "Android's Bouncy Castle Provider" on page 137, hash algorithms in Android's Bouncy Castle provider have been replaced with native code for performance reasons. In order to further improve cryptographic performance, the number of supported engine classes and algorithms in the native AndroidOpenSSL provider has been steadily growing with each release since 4.0.

Originally, AndroidOpenSSL was only used to implement SSL sockets, but as of Android 4.4, it covers most of the functionality offered by Bouncy Castle. Because it is the preferred provider (with the highest priority, 1), engine classes that don't explicitly request Bouncy Castle get an implementation from the AndroidOpenSSL provider. As the name implies, its cryptographic functionality is provided by the OpenSSL library. The provider implementation uses JNI to link OpenSSL's native code to the Java SPI classes required to implement a JCA provider. The bulk of the implementation is in the `NativeCrypto` Java class, which is called by most SPI classes.

AndroidOpenSSL is part of Android's *libcore* library, which implements the core part of Android's Java runtime library. Starting with Android 4.4, AndroidOpenSSL has been decoupled from *libcore* so that it can be compiled as a standalone library and included in applications that want a stable cryptographic implementation that does not depend on the platform version. The standalone provider is called *Conscrypt* and lives in the `org.conscrypt` package, renamed to `com.android.org.conscrypt` when built as part of the Android platform.

The engine classes and algorithms supported by the AndroidOpenSSL provider as of version 4.4.4 are listed in Table 5-3.

Table 5-3: Algorithms Supported by the AndroidOpenSSL Provider as of Android 4.4.4

Engine Class Name	Supported Algorithms
`CertificateFactory`	*X509*
`Cipher`	*AES/CBC/NoPadding* *AES/CBC/PKCS5Padding* *AES/CFB/NoPadding* *AES/CTR/NoPadding* *AES/ECB/NoPadding* *AES/ECB/PKCS5Padding* *AES/OFB/NoPadding* *ARC4* *DESEDE/CBC/NoPadding* *DESEDE/CBC/PKCS5Padding* *DESEDE/CFB/NoPadding* *DESEDE/ECB/NoPadding* *DESEDE/ECB/PKCS5Padding* *DESEDE/OFB/NoPadding* *RSA/ECB/NoPadding* *RSA/ECB/PKCS1Padding*
`KeyAgreement`	*ECDH*
`KeyFactory`	*DSA* *EC* *RSA*
`KeyPairGenerator`	*DSA* *EC* *RSA*
`Mac`	*HmacMD5* *HmacSHA1* *HmacSHA256* *HmacSHA384* *HmacSHA512*
`MessageDigest`	*MD5* *SHA-1* *SHA-256* *SHA-384* *SHA-512*

(continued)

Table 5-3 *(continued)*

Engine Class Name	Supported Algorithms
SecureRandom	*SHA1PRNG*
Signature	*ECDSA* *MD5WithRSA* *NONEwithRSA* *SHA1WithRSA* *SHA1withDSA* *SHA256WithRSA* *SHA256withECDSA* *SHA384WithRSA* *SHA384withECDSA* *SHA512WithRSA* *SHA512withECDSA*

OpenSSL

OpenSSL is an open source cryptographic toolkit that implements the SSL and TLS protocols and is widely used as a general purpose cryptography library.[17] It is included in Android as a system library and used to implement the AndroidOpenSSL JCA provider that was introduced in "AndroidOpenSSL Provider" on page 140, as well as by some other system components.

Different Android releases use different OpenSSL versions (generally the latest stable version, which is 1.0.1e in Android 4.4), with an evolving set of patches applied. Therefore, Android does not offer a stable public OpenSSL API, so applications that need to use OpenSSL should include the library and not link to the system version. The only public cryptographic API is the JCA one, which offers a stable interface decoupled from the underlying implementation.

Using a Custom Provider

While Android's built-in providers cover most widely used cryptographic primitives, they do not support some more exotic algorithms and even some newer standards. As mentioned in our discussion of the JCA architecture, Android applications can register custom providers for their own use, but cannot affect system-wide providers.

17. The OpenSSL Project, "OpenSSL: The Open Source toolkit for SSL/TLS," *http://www.openssl.org/*

One of the most widely used and full-featured JCA providers is Bouncy Castle, also the base of one of Android's built-in providers. However, as discussed in "Android's Bouncy Castle Provider" on page 137, the version shipped with Android has had a number of algorithms removed. If you need to use any of those algorithms, you can try simply bundling the full Bouncy Castle library with your application—but that may cause class loading conflicts, especially on versions of Android earlier than 3.0, which do not change the system's Bouncy Castle's package name. To avoid this, you can change the library's root package with a tool such as jarjar,[18] or use Spongy Castle.[19]

Spongy Castle

Spongy Castle is a repackaged version of Bouncy Castle. It moves all package names from `org.bouncycastle.*` to `org.spongycastle.*` in order to avoid class loader conflicts, and changes the provider name from *BC* to *SC*. No class names are changed, so the API is the same as Bouncy Castle. To use Spongy Castle, you simply need to register it with the JCA framework using `Security.addProvider()` or `Security.insertProviderAt()`. You can then request algorithms not implemented by Android's built-in providers simply by passing the algorithm name to the respective `getInstance()` method.

To explicitly request an implementation from Spongy Castle, pass the *SC* string as the provider name. If you bundle the Spongy Castle library with your app, you can also directly use Bouncy Castle's lightweight cryptographic API (which is often more flexible) without going through the JCA engine classes. Additionally, some cryptographic operations, such as signing an X.509 certificate or creating an S/MIME message, have no matching JCA APIs and can only be performed using the lower-level Bouncy Castle APIs.

Listing 5-21 shows how to register the Spongy Castle provider and request an RSA-PSS (originally defined in PKCS#1[20]) `Signature` implementation, which is not supported by any of Android's built-in JCA providers.

```
static {
    Security.insertProviderAt(
        new org.spongycastle.jce.provider.BouncyCastleProvider(), 1);
}
Signature sig = Signature.getInstance("SHA1withRSA/PSS", "SC");
```

Listing 5-21: Registering and using the Spongy Castle provider

18. Chris Nokleberg, "Jar Jar Links," *https://code.google.com/p/jarjar/*

19. Roberto Tyley, "Spongy Castle," *http://rtyley.github.io/spongycastle/*

20. J. Jonsson and B. Kaliski, *Public-Key Cryptography Standards (PKCS) #1: RSA Cryptography Specifications Version 2.1, http://tools.ietf.org/html/rfc3447*

Summary

Android implements the Java Cryptography Architecture (JCA) and comes bundled with a number of cryptographic providers. JCA defines interfaces to common cryptographic algorithms in the form of engine classes. Cryptographic providers offer implementations of those engine classes and allow clients to request an algorithm implementation by name, without having to know about the actual underlying implementation. The two main JCA providers in Android are the Bouncy Castle provider and the AndroidOpenSSL provider. Bouncy Castle is implemented in pure Java, while AndroidOpenSSL is backed by native code and offers better performance. As of Android 4.4, AndroidOpenSSL is the preferred JCA provider.

6

NETWORK SECURITY AND PKI

As discussed in the previous chapter, Android includes various cryptographic providers that implement most modern cryptographic primitives: hashing, symmetric and asymmetric encryption, and message authentication codes. Those primitives can be combined to implement secure communication, but even a subtle mistake can result in serious vulnerabilities, so the preferred way to implement secure communication is to use standard protocols that are designed to protect the privacy and integrity of data transferred across a network.

The most widely used secure protocols are Secure Sockets Layer (SSL) and Transport Layer Security (TLS). Android supports these protocols by providing an implementation of the standard Java Secure Socket Extension (JSSE). In this chapter, we'll briefly discuss the JSSE architecture and then provide some details about Android's JSSE implementation. Our description of Android's SSL stack is focused on certificate validation and trust anchor management, which are tightly integrated into the platform and are one of the biggest differences that set it apart from other JSSE implementations.

NOTE *While TLS and SSL are technically different protocols, we will usually use the more common term* SSL *to refer to both, and will only distinguish between SSL and TLS when discussing protocol differences.*

PKI and SSL Overview

TLS[1] and SSL[2] (its predecessor) are secure point-to-point communication protocols designed to provide (optional) authentication, message confidentiality, and message integrity between two parties communicating over TCP/IP. They use a combination of symmetric and asymmetric encryption to implement message confidentiality and integrity, and rely heavily on public key certificates to implement authentication.

To start a secure SSL channel, a client contacts a server and sends the SSL protocol version it supports, as well as a list of suggested cipher suites. A *cipher suite* is a set of algorithms and key sizes used for authentication, key agreement, encryption, and integrity. In order to establish a secure channel, the server and client negotiate a commonly supported cipher suite, and then verify each other's identity based on their certificates. Finally, the communicating parties agree on a symmetric encryption algorithm and compute a shared symmetric key that is used to encrypt all subsequent communication. Typically, only the server's identity is verified (*server authentication*) and not the client's. The SSL protocol supports verifying client identity as well (*client authentication*), but it is used much more rarely.

NOTE *While anonymous (unauthenticated) cipher suites such as* TLS_DH_anon_WITH_AES_128_CBC_SHA *are defined in SSL specifications, they are vulnerable to man-in-the-middle (MITM) attacks and are typically only employed when SSL is used as part of a more complex protocol that has other means to ensure authentication.*

Public Key Certificates

As mentioned in the previous section, SSL relies on public key certificates to implement authentication. A public key certificate is a construct that binds an identity to a public key. For *X.509 certificates*, which are used in SSL communication, the "identity" is a set of attributes typically including a common name (CN), organization, and location that form the entity's distinguished name (DN). Other major attributes of X.509 certificates are the issuer DN, validity period, and a set of extensions, which may be additional entity attributes or pertain to the certificate itself (for example, intended key usage).

The binding is formed by applying a digital signature over the entity's public key and all additional attributes to produce a digital certificate. The

1. T. Dierks and E. Rescorla, *The Transport Layer Security (TLS) Protocol Version 1.2*, August 2008, *http://tools.ietf.org/html/rfc5246*

2. A. Freier, P. Karlton, and P. Kocher, *The Secure Sockets Layer (SSL) Protocol Version 3.0*, August 2011, *http://tools.ietf.org/html/rfc6101*

signing key used may be the certified entity's own private key, in which case the certificate is referred to as *self-signed*, or it may belong to a trusted third party called a *certificate authority (CA)*.

The contents of a typical X.509 server certificate as parsed by the OpenSSL `x509` command are shown in Listing 6-1. This particular certificate binds the *C=US, ST=California, L=Mountain View, O=Google Inc, CN=*.googlecode.com* DN ❷ and a set of alternative DNS names ❹ to the server's 2048-bit RSA key ❸ and is signed with the private key of the Google Internet Authority G2 CA ❶.

```
Certificate:
    Data:
        Version: 3 (0x2)
        Serial Number:
            09:49:24:fd:15:cf:1f:2e
    Signature Algorithm: sha1WithRSAEncryption
        Issuer: C=US, O=Google Inc, CN=Google Internet Authority G2❶
        Validity
            Not Before: Oct  9 10:33:36 2013 GMT
            Not After : Oct  9 10:33:36 2014 GMT
        Subject: C=US, ST=California, L=Mountain View, O=Google Inc, CN=*.googlecode.com❷
        Subject Public Key Info:
            Public Key Algorithm: rsaEncryption
                Public-Key: (2048 bit)❸
                Modulus:
                    00:9b:58:02:90:d6:50:03:0a:7c:79:06:99:5b:7a:
                    --snip--
                Exponent: 65537 (0x10001)
        X509v3 extensions:
            X509v3 Extended Key Usage:
                TLS Web Server Authentication, TLS Web Client Authentication
            X509v3 Subject Alternative Name:
                DNS:*.googlecode.com, DNS:*.cloud.google.com, DNS:*.code.google.com,❹
                --snip--
            Authority Information Access:
                CA Issuers - URI:http://pki.google.com/GIAG2.crt
                OCSP - URI:http://clients1.google.com/ocsp

            X509v3 Subject Key Identifier:
                65:10:15:1B:C4:26:13:DA:50:3F:84:4E:44:1A:C5:13:B0:98:4F:7B
            X509v3 Basic Constraints: critical
                CA:FALSE
            X509v3 Authority Key Identifier:
                keyid:4A:DD:06:16:1B:BC:F6:68:B5:76:F5:81:B6:BB:62:1A:BA:5A:81:2F
            X509v3 Certificate Policies:
                Policy: 1.3.6.1.4.1.11129.2.5.1
            X509v3 CRL Distribution Points:
                Full Name:
                  URI:http://pki.google.com/GIAG2.crl
    Signature Algorithm: sha1WithRSAEncryption
        3f:38:94:1b:f5:0a:49:e7:6f:9b:7b:90:de:b8:05:f8:41:32:
        --snip--
```

Listing 6-1: X.509 certificate contents, as parsed by OpenSSL

Direct Trust and Private CAs

If an SSL client communicates with a limited number of servers, it can be preconfigured with a set of server certificates that it trusts (called *trust anchors*), and deciding whether to trust a remote party becomes simply a matter of checking whether its certificate is in that set. This model allows for fine-grained control over whom clients trust, but makes it harder to rotate or upgrade server keys, which requires issuing a new self-signed certificate.

This problem can be solved by using a *private CA* and configuring both clients and servers to use it as the single trust anchor. In this model, SSL parties do not check for a particular entity certificate, but trust any certificate issued by the private CA. This allows for transparent key and certificate upgrades, without the need to upgrade SSL clients and servers as long as the CA certificate is still valid. The downside is that at the same time, this single-CA model creates a single point of failure; if the CA key is compromised, whoever has obtained access to it can issue fraudulent certificates that all clients will trust (as we will see later, this is not limited to private CAs). Recovering from this situation requires updating all clients and replacing the CA certificate.

Another problem with this model is that it cannot be used for clients that do not know in advance what servers they will need to connect to—usually generic Internet clients such as web browsers, email applications, and messaging or VoIP clients. Such generic clients are typically configured with a set of trust anchors that includes well-known issuers, which we call *public CAs*. While certain guidelines and requirements exist, the process of selecting public CAs to include as default trust anchors varies widely between browsers and OSes. For example, in order to include a CA certificate as a trust anchor in its products, Mozilla requires that the CA has a public *Certificate Policy and Certification Practice Statement (CP/CPS)* document, enforces multi-factor authentication for operator accounts, and that the CA certificate does not issue end-entity certificates directly.[3] Other vendors can have less stringent requirements. Current versions of most OSes and browsers ship with more than 100 CA certificates included as trust anchors.

Public Key Infrastructure

When certificates are issued by public CAs, some sort of identity verification is performed before issuing the certificate. The verification process varies vastly between CAs and types of certificates issued, ranging from accepting automatic email address confirmation (for cheap server certificates) to requiring multiple forms of government-issued ID and company registration documents (for Extended Validation, or EV, certificates).

Public CAs depend on multiple people, systems, procedures, and policies in order to perform entity verification and to create, manage, and distribute

3. Mozilla, *Mozilla CA Certificate Inclusion Policy (Version 2.2)*, *https://www.mozilla.org/en-US/about/governance/policies/security-group/certs/policy/inclusion/*

certificates. The set of those parties and systems is referred to as a *Public Key Infrastructure (PKI)*. PKIs can be infinitely complex, but in the context of secure communication, and SSL in particular, the most important pieces are the CA certificates, which act as trust anchors and are used when validating the identity of communication parties. Therefore, managing trust anchors will be one of the key points in our discussion of Android's SSL and PKI implementation. Figure 6-1 shows a simplified representation of a typical PKI.

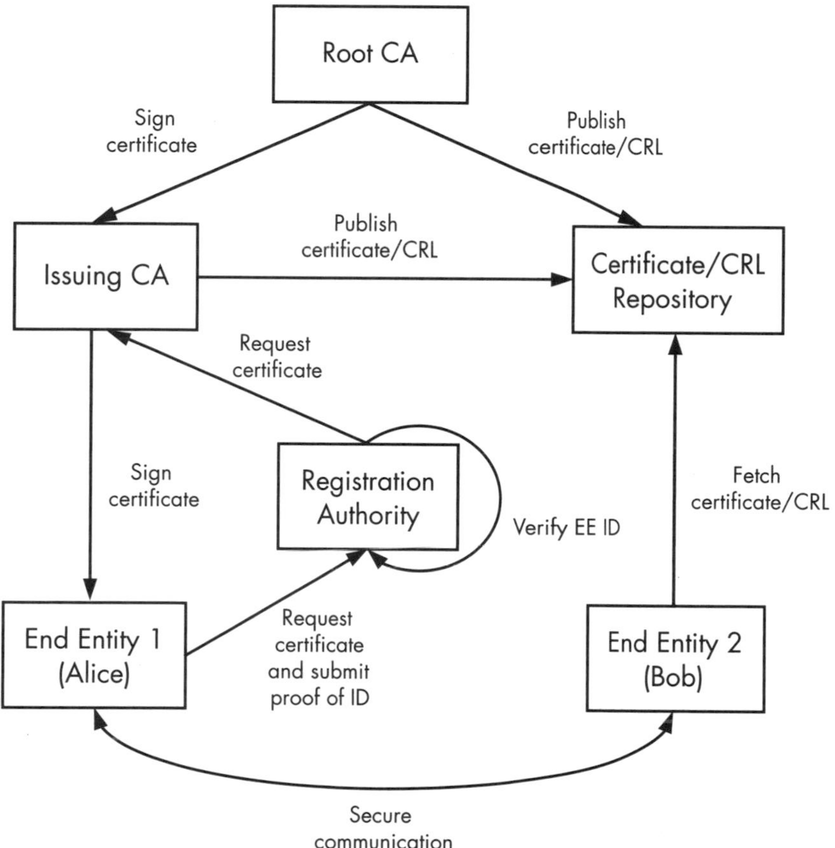

Figure 6-1: PKI entities

Here, a person or server that holds a certificate is referred to as an *end entity (EE)*. To obtain a certificate, an end entity sends a certificate request to a registration authority (RA). The RA obtains some proof of identity from the EE and verifies its identity according to the CA's policy requirements. After the RA has established the identity of the EE, it checks that it matches the contents of the certificate request, and if so, forwards the request to the issuing CA. An issuing CA signs the EE certificate request in order to generate EE certificates and maintains revocation information (discussed in the next section) about the issued certificates. On the other hand, a root CA does not sign EE certificates directly but only signs certificates for issuing CAs and revocation information concerning issuing CAs. A root CA is used very rarely and is usually kept offline in order to increase the security of its keys.

For the PKI sketched in Figure 6-1, an EE certificate is associated with two CA certificates: the issuing CA's certificate, which signed it, and the root CA's certificate, which signed the issuing CA's certificate. The three certificates form a certificate chain (also called a certification path). The chain begins with the EE certificate and terminates with the root CA certificate. In order for an EE certificate to be trusted, its certification path needs to lead to a certificate the system trusts implicitly (trust anchor). While intermediate certificates can be used as trust anchors, this role is usually performed by root CA certificates.

Certificate Revocation

In addition to issuing certificates, CAs can mark a certificate as invalid by revoking it. *Revoking* involves adding the certificate serial number and a revocation reason to a certificate revocation list (CRL) that the CA signs and periodically publishes. Entities validating a certificate can then check to see if it has been revoked by searching for its serial number (which is unique within a given CA) in the issuing CA's current CRL. Listing 6-2 shows the contents of a sample CRL file, issued by the Google Internet Authority G2. In this example, certificates with the serial numbers `40BF8571DD53E3BB` ❶ and `0A9F21196A442E45` ❷ have been revoked.

```
Certificate Revocation List (CRL):
        Version 2 (0x1)
    Signature Algorithm: sha1WithRSAEncryption
        Issuer: /C=US/O=Google Inc/CN=Google Internet Authority G2
        Last Update: Jan 13 01:00:02 2014 GMT
        Next Update: Jan 23 01:00:02 2014 GMT
        CRL extensions:
            X509v3 Authority Key Identifier:
                keyid:4A:DD:06:16:1B:BC:F6:68:B5:76:F5:81:B6:BB:62:1A:BA:5A:81:2F
            X509v3 CRL Number:
                219
Revoked Certificates:
    Serial Number: 40BF8571DD53E3BB❶
        Revocation Date: Sep 10 15:19:22 2013 GMT
        CRL entry extensions:
            X509v3 CRL Reason Code:
                Affiliation Changed
--snip--
    Serial Number: 0A9F21196A442E45❷
        Revocation Date: Jun 12 17:42:06 2013 GMT
        CRL entry extensions:
            X509v3 CRL Reason Code:
                Superseded
    Signature Algorithm: sha1WithRSAEncryption
         40:f6:05:7d:...
```

Listing 6-2: CRL file contents

Revocation status can also be checked without fetching the full list of all revoked certificates by using the Online Certificate Status Protocol (OCSP).[4] CRL and OCSP URIs are often included as extensions in certificates so that verifying parties do not need to know their location in advance. All public CAs maintain revocation information, but in practice a lot of SSL clients either do not check revocation at all or allow connections (possibly with a warning) even if the remote party's certificate is revoked. The main reasons for this lenient behavior of SSL clients are the overhead associated with fetching current revocation information, and ensuring connectivity. While delta CRLs (CRLs that only contain the difference, or *delta*, from the previous CRL version) and local caching alleviate the problem to some extent, CRLs for major CAs are typically huge and need to be downloaded before an SSL connection is established, which adds user-visible latency. OCSP improves this situation but still requires a connection to a different server, which again adds latency.

In either case, revocation information may simply be unavailable, due to a network or configuration problem in a CA's infrastructure. For a major CA, a revocation database outage could disable a large number of secure sites, which translates directly to financial loss for their operators. Lastly, nobody likes connection errors and when faced with a revocation error, most users will simply find another, less strict SSL client that simply "works."

JSSE Introduction

We'll briefly introduce the architecture and main components of JSSE here. (For complete coverage, see the official *JSSE Reference Guide.*[5])

The JSSE API lives in the `javax.net` and `javax.net.ssl` packages and provides classes that represent the following features:

- SSL client and server sockets
- An engine for producing and consuming SSL streams (`SSLEngine`)
- Factories for creating sockets
- A secure socket context class (`SSLContext`) that creates secure socket factories and engines
- PKI-based key and trust managers and factories to create them
- A class for HTTPS (HTTP over TLS, specified in *RFC 2818*[6]) URL connections (`HttpsURLConnection`)

Just as with JCA cryptographic service providers, a JSSE provider supplies implementations for the engine classes defined in the API. Those implementation classes are responsible for creating the underlying sockets,

4. S. Santesson et al., *X.509 Internet Public Key Infrastructure Online Certificate Status Protocol - OCSP*, June 2013, *http://tools.ietf.org/html/rfc6960*

5. Oracle, *Java™ Secure Socket Extension (JSSE) Reference Guide*, *http://docs.oracle.com/javase/7/docs/technotes/guides/security/jsse/JSSERefGuide.html*

6. E. Rescorla, *HTTP Over TLS*, May 2000, *http://tools.ietf.org/html/rfc2818*

and key and trust managers required to establish a connection, but JSSE API users never directly interact with them, only with the respective engine classes. Let's briefly review the key classes and interfaces in the JSSE API, as well as how they relate to each other.

Secure Sockets

JSSE supports both stream-based, blocking I/O using sockets and NIO (New I/O) channel-based, nonblocking I/O. The central class for stream-based communication is `javax.net.ssl.SSLSocket`, which is created either by an `SSLSocketFactory` or by calling the `accept()` method of the `SSLServerSocket` class. In turn, `SSLSocketFactory` and `SSLServerSocketFactory` instances are created by calling the appropriate factory methods of the `SSLContext` class. SSL socket factories encapsulate the details of creating and configuring SSL sockets, including authentication keys, peer certificate validation strategies, and enabled cipher suites. Those details are typically common for all SSL sockets that an application uses and are configured when initializing the application's `SSLContext`. They are then passed to all SSL socket factories created by the shared `SSLContext` instance. If an `SSLContext` is not explicitly configured, it uses the system defaults for all SSL parameters.

Nonblocking SSL I/O is implemented in the `javax.net.ssl.SSLEngine` class. This class encapsulates an SSL state machine and operates on byte buffers supplied by its clients. While `SSLSocket` hides much of the complexity of SSL, in order to offer greater flexibility, `SSLEngine` leaves I/O and threading to the calling application. Therefore, `SSLEngine` clients are expected to have some understanding of the SSL protocol. `SSLEngine` instances are created directly from an `SSLContext` and inherit its SSL configuration, just like SSL socket factories.

Peer Authentication

Peer authentication is an integral part of the SSL protocol and relies on the availability of a set of trust anchors and authentication keys. In JSSE, peer authentication configuration is provided with the help of the `KeyStore`, `KeyManagerFactory`, and `TrustManagerFactory` engine classes. A `KeyStore` represents a storage facility for cryptographic keys and certificates and can be used to store both trust anchors certificates, and end entity keys along with their associated certificates. `KeyManagerFactory` and `TrustManagerFactory` create `KeyManagers` or `TrustManagers`, respectively, based on a specified authentication algorithm. While implementations based on different authentication strategies are possible, in practice SSL uses only a X.509-based PKI (PKIX)[7] for authentication, and the only algorithm supported by those factory classes is *PKIX* (aliased to *X.509*). An `SSLContext` can be initialized with a set of

7. D. Cooper et al., *Internet X.509 Public Key Infrastructure Certificate and Certificate Revocation List (CRL) Profile*, May 2008, *http://tools.ietf.org/html/rfc5280*

KeyManager and TrustManager instances by calling the following method. All parameters are optional, and if null is specified, the system default is used (see Listing 6-3).

```
void init(KeyManager[] km, TrustManager[] tm, SecureRandom random);
```

Listing 6-3: SSLContext initialization method

A TrustManager determines whether the presented peer authentication credentials should be trusted. If they are, the connection is established; if not, the connection is terminated. In the context of PKIX, this translates to validating the certificate chain of the presented peer certificate based on the configured trust anchors. This is also reflected in the X509TrustManager interface JSSE uses (see Listing 6-4):

```
void checkClientTrusted(X509Certificate[] chain, String authType);
void checkServerTrusted(X509Certificate[] chain, String authType);
X509Certificate[] getAcceptedIssuers();
```

Listing 6-4: X509TrustManager interface methods

Certificate chain validation is performed using the system Java Certification Path API (or CertPath API) implementation,[8] which is responsible for building and validating certificate chains. While the API has a somewhat algorithm-independent interface, in practice it's closely related to PKIX and implements the chain building and validation algorithms defined in PKIX standards. The default PKIX TrustManagerFactory implementation can create an X509TrustManager instance that preconfigures the underlying CertPath API classes with the trust anchors stored in a KeyStore object.

The KeyStore object is typically initialized from a system keystore file referred to as a *trust store*. When more fine-grained configuration is required, a CertPathTrustManagerParameters instance that contains detailed CertPath API parameters can be used to initialize the TrustManagerFactory as well. When the system X509TrustManager implementation cannot be configured as required using the provided APIs, a custom instance can be created by implementing the interface directly, possibly delegating base cases to the default implementation.

A KeyManager determines which authentication credentials to send to the remote host. In the context of PKIX, this means selecting the client authentication certificate to send to an SSL server. The default KeyManagerFactory can create a KeyManager instance that uses a KeyStore to search for client authentication keys and related certificates. Just as with TrustManagers, the concrete interfaces, X509KeyManager (shown in Listing 6-5) and X509ExtendedKeyManager

8. Oracle, *Java™ PKI Programmer's Guide, http://docs.oracle.com/javase/7/docs/technotes/guides/security/certpath/CertPathProgGuide.html*

(which allows for connection-specific key selection), are PKIX-specific and select a client certificate based on the list of trusted issuers that the server has provided. If the default KeyStore-backed implementation is not sufficiently flexible, a custom implementation can be provided by extending the abstract X509ExtendedKeyManager class.

```
String chooseClientAlias(String[] keyType, Principal[] issuers, Socket socket);
String chooseServerAlias(String keyType, Principal[] issuers, Socket socket);
X509Certificate[] getCertificateChain(String alias);
String[] getClientAliases(String keyType, Principal[] issuers);
PrivateKey getPrivateKey(String alias);
String[] getServerAliases(String keyType, Principal[] issuers);
```

Listing 6-5: X509KeyManager interface

In addition to support for "raw" SSL sockets, JSSE also provides support for HTTPS with the HttpsURLConnection class. HttpsURLConnection uses the default SSLSocketFactory to create secure sockets when opening a connection to a web server. If additional SSL configuration such as specifying app-private trust anchors or authentication keys is required, the default SSLSocketFactory can be replaced for all HttpsURLConnection instances by calling the static setDefaultSSLSocketFactory() method. Alternatively, you can configure the socket factory for a particular instance by calling its setSSLSocketFactory() method.

Hostname Verification

While SSL verifies server identity by checking its certificate, the protocol does not mandate any hostname verification, and when using raw SSL sockets, the certificate subject is not matched against the server hostname. The HTTPS standard does mandate such a check however, and HttpsURLConnection performs one internally. The default hostname verification algorithm can be overridden by assigning a HostnameVerifier instance to the class or on a per-instance basis. The verify() callback it needs to implement is shown in Listing 6-6. The SSLSession class used in the callback encapsulates details about the current SSL connection, including selected protocol and cipher suite, local and peer certificate chains, and peer hostname and connection port number.

```
boolean verify(String hostname, SSLSession session);
```

Listing 6-6: HostnameVerifier hostname verification callback

We have discussed the major classes and interfaces that form the JSSE API and introduced how they related to each other. Their relationships can be visualized as shown in Figure 6-2.

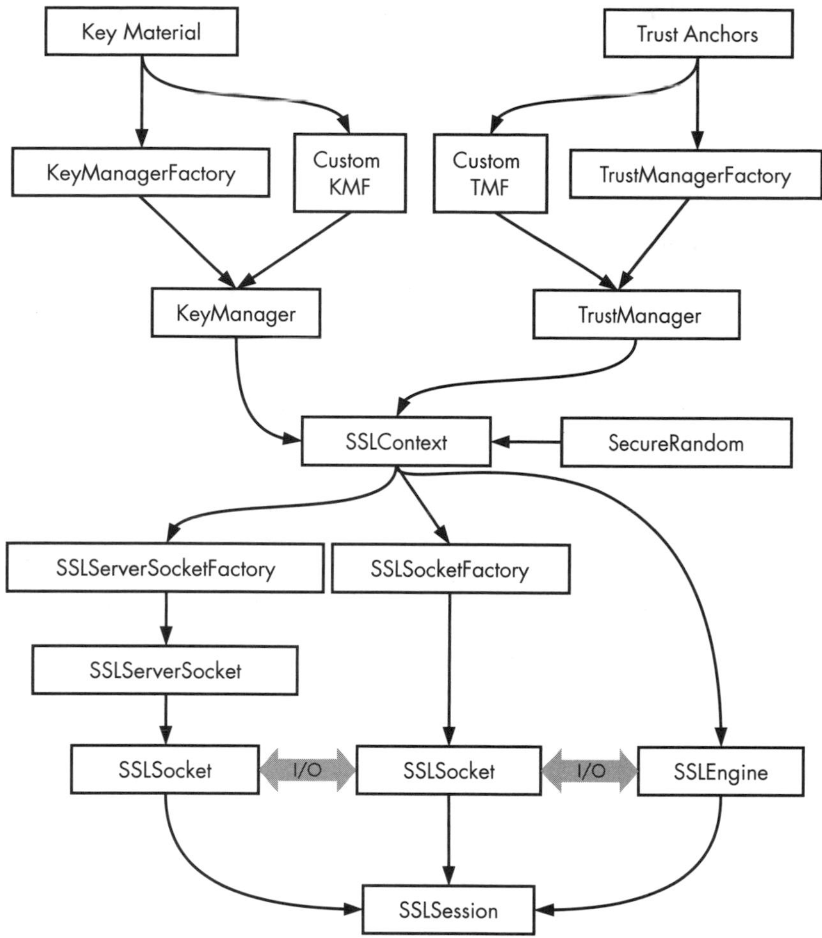

Figure 6-2: JSSE classes and their relationships

Android JSSE Implementation

Android comes with two JSSE providers: the Java-based HarmonyJSSE and the AndroidOpenSSL provider, which is implemented largely in native code bridged to the public Java API using JNI. HarmonyJSSE builds on Java sockets and JCA classes in order to implement SSL, while AndroidOpenSSL implements most of its functionality by using OpenSSL library calls. As discussed in Chapter 5, AndroidOpenSSL is the preferred JCA provider in Android, and it also provides the default `SSLSocketFactory` and `SSLServerSocketFactory` implementations that are returned by `SSLSocketFactory.getDefault()` and `SSLServerSocketFactory.getDefault()`, respectively.

Both JSSE providers are part of the core Java library (found in `core.jar` and `libjavacore.so`), and the native part of the AndroidOpenSSL provider is compiled into `libjavacrypto.so`. HarmonyJSSE provides only SSLv3.0 and TLSv1.0 support, while AndroidOpenSSL supports TLSv1.1 and TLSv1.2 as well. While the SSL socket implementation is different, both providers share the same `TrustManager` and `KeyManager` code.

NOTE *The HarmonyJSSE provider is still available in Android 4.4, but it is considered deprecated and is not actively maintained. It may be removed in future Android versions.*

In addition to current TLS protocol versions, the OpenSSL-based provider supports the *Server Name Indication (SNI)* TLS extension (defined in *RFC 3546*[9]), which allows SSL clients to specify the intended hostname when connecting to servers hosting multiple virtual hosts. SNI is used by default when establishing a connection using the `HttpsURLConnection` class in Android 3.0 and later versions (version 2.3 has partial SNI support). However, SNI is not supported when using the Apache HTTP client library bundled with Android (in the `org.apache.http` package).

Before Android 4.2, the HTTP stack in Android's core Java library, including `HttpsURLConnection`, was based on Apache Harmony code. In Android 4.2 and later, the original implementation is replaced with Square's HTTP & SPDY client library, *OkHttp*.[10]

Certificate Management and Validation

Android's JSSE implementations mostly conform to the JSSE API specification, but there are some notable differences as well. The biggest one is how Android handles the system trust store. In Java SE JSSE implementations, the system trust store is a single keystore file (typically called *cacerts*) whose location can be set with the `javax.net.ssl.trustStore` system property, but Android follows a different strategy. Recent versions of Android also provide modern certificate validation features such as blacklisting and pinning that are not specified in the original JSSE architecture document. We will discuss Android's trust store implementation and advanced certificate validation features in the next sections.

System Trust Stores

As discussed in "Peer Authentication" on page 152, JSSE implementations use a trust store to authenticate connection peers. While SSL does support encryption-only, non-authenticated connections, in practice raw SSL clients usually perform server authentication and it is mandatory for HTTPS. When a per-application trust store is not explicitly provided, JSSE

---

9. S. Blake-Wilson et al., *Transport Layer Security (TLS) Extensions*, June 2003, *http://tools.ietf.org/html/rfc3546*

10. Square, Inc., *OkHttp: An HTTP & SPDY client for Android and Java applications*, *http://square.github.io/okhttp/*

uses the system trust store to perform SSL peer authentication. The system trust store is especially important for generic Internet clients such as browsers, because they typically do not manage their own trust store on mobile devices (desktop versions of Mozilla clients do maintain private credential and certificate stores, but not on Android). Because system trust stores are central to the security of all applications that use JSSE, we will look into their implementation in detail.

Until Android 4.0, the OS trust store was hardwired into the system and users had no control over it whatsoever. Certificates bundled in the store were chosen solely by the device manufacturer or carrier. The only way to make changes was to root your device, repackage the trusted certificates file, and replace the original one—a procedure that's obviously not too practical, and a major obstacle to using Android in enterprise PKIs. In the wake of the compromise of multiple major CAs, third-party tools that could change the system-trusted certificates were developed, but using them still required a rooted phone. Fortunately, Android 4.0 made managing the trust store much more flexible, and gave the much-needed control over who to trust to the user.

Android 4.x System Trust Store

Prior to Android 4.0, the system trust store was a single file: */system/etc/security/cacerts.bks*, a Bouncy Castle (one of the cryptographic providers used in Android; see Chapter 5 for details) native keystore file. It contained all the CA certificates that Android trusts and was used both by system apps such as the email client and browser, and third-party apps. Because it resided on the read-only *system* partition, it could not be changed even by system applications.

Android 4.0 introduced a new, more flexible `TrustedCertificateStore` class that allows for maintaining built-in trust anchors and adding new ones. It still reads system-trusted certificates from */system/etc/security/*, but adds two new, mutable locations to store CA certificates in */data/misc/keychain/*: the *cacerts-added/* and *cacerts-removed/* directories. Listing 6-7 shows what their contents looks like:

```
# ls -l /data/misc/keychain
drwxr-xr-x system   system            cacerts-added
drwxr-xr-x system   system            cacerts-removed
-rw-r--r-- system   system         81 pubkey_blacklist.txt
-rw-r--r-- system   system          7 serial_blacklist.txt
# ls -l /data/misc/keychain/cacerts-added
-rw-r--r-- system   system        653 30ef493b.0❶
# ls -l /data/misc/keychain/cacerts-removed
-rw-r--r-- system   system       1060 00673b5b.0❷
```

Listing 6-7: Contents of the cacerts-added/ *and* cacerts-removed/ *directories*

Each file in these directories contains one CA certificate. The file names may look familiar: they are based on the MD5 hashes of the CA subject names (computed using OpenSSL's `X509_NAME_hash_old()` function), as used in *mod_ssl* and other cryptographic software implemented using OpenSSL. This makes it easy to quickly find certificates without scanning the entire store by directly converting the DN to a filename.

Also note the permissions of the directories: *0775 system system* guarantees that only the *system* user is able to add or remove certificates, but anyone can read them. As expected, adding trusted CA certificates is implemented by storing the certificate in the *cacerts-added/* directory under the appropriate file name. The certificate stored in the *30ef493b.0* file (❶ in Listing 6-7) will also be displayed in the User tab of the Trusted credentials system application (**Settings ▸ Security ▸ Trusted credentials**).

But how are OS-trusted certificates disabled? Because preinstalled CA certificates are still stored in */system/etc/security/* (which is mounted read-only), a CA is marked as not trusted by placing a copy of its certificate in the *cacerts-removed/* directory. Re-enabling is performed by simply removing the file. In this particular case, *00673b5b.0* (❷ in Listing 6-7) is the *thawte Primary Root CA*, shown as disabled in the System tab (see Figure 6-3).

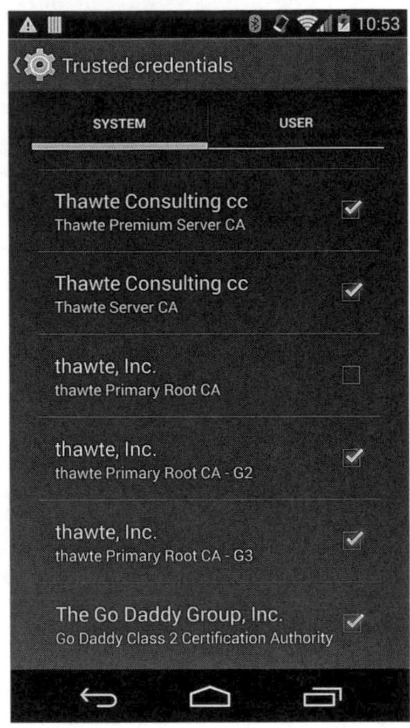

Figure 6-3: Preinstalled CA certificate marked as untrusted

Using the System Trust Store

`TrustedCertificateStore` is not part of the Android SDK, but it has a wrapper (`TrustedCertificateKeyStoreSpi`) accessible via the standard JCA `KeyStore` API that applications can use (see Listing 6-8).

```
KeyStore ks = KeyStore.getInstance("AndroidCAStore");❶
ks.load(null, null);❷
Enumeration<String> aliases = ks.aliases();❸
while (aliases.hasMoreElements()) {
    String alias = aliases.nextElement();
    Log.d(TAG, "Certificate alias: " +  alias);
    X09Certificate cert = (X509Certificate) ks.getCertificate(alias);❹
    Log.d(TAG, "Subject DN: " + cert.getSubjectDN().getName());
    Log.d(TAG, "Issuer DN: " + cert.getIssuerDN().getName());
}
```

Listing 6-8: Listing trusted certificates using AndroidCAStore

To get a list of the current trusted certificates, we:

1. Create a `KeyStore` instance by specifying *AndroidCAStore* as the `type` parameter ❶.
2. Call its `load()` method and pass `null` for both parameters ❷.
3. Get a list of certificate aliases with the `aliases()` method ❸.
4. Pass each alias to the `getCertificate()` method to get the actual certificate object ❹.

When you examine the output of this code, you'll notice that certificate aliases start with either the *user:* (for user-installed certificates) or *system:* (for preinstalled ones) prefix, followed by the subject's hash value.

The *AndroidCAStore* `KeyStore` implementation lets us easily access the OS's trusted certificates, but a real-world application would be more interested in whether it should trust a particular server certificate, not what the current trust anchors are. Android makes this very easy by integrating the `TrustedCertificateKeyStoreSpi` with its JSSE implementation. The default `TrustManagerFactory` uses it to get a list of trust anchors, and thus automatically validates server certificates against the system's currently trusted certificates. Higher-level code that uses `HttpsURLConnection` or `HttpClient` (both built on top of JSSE) should thus work without needing to worry about creating and initializing a custom `SSLSocketFactory`.

In order to install our own CA certificate (such as one from a private enterprise CA) into the system trust store, we need to convert it to DER (binary) format and copy it to the device. On versions prior to Android 4.4.1, the certificate file needs to be copied to the root of external storage with a *.crt* or *.cer* extension. Android 4.4.1 and later uses the storage access framework introduced in Android 4.4 and allow you to select a certificate file from any storage backend that the device can access, including integrated cloud providers like Google Drive. We can then import the certificate using the system Settings app by selecting **Settings ▸ Personal ▸ Security ▸ Credential storage ▸ Install from storage**. A list of available certificate files is displayed and tapping on a filename brings up the import dialog, as shown in Figure 6-4.

The imported certificate will be displayed in the User tab of the Trusted credentials screen (see Figure 6-5). You can view certificate details by tapping the list entry, and remove it by scrolling down to the bottom of the details screen and tapping the Remove button.

NOTE *If the certificate is successfully imported, the certificate file in external storage file will be deleted on versions prior to Android 4.4.1.*

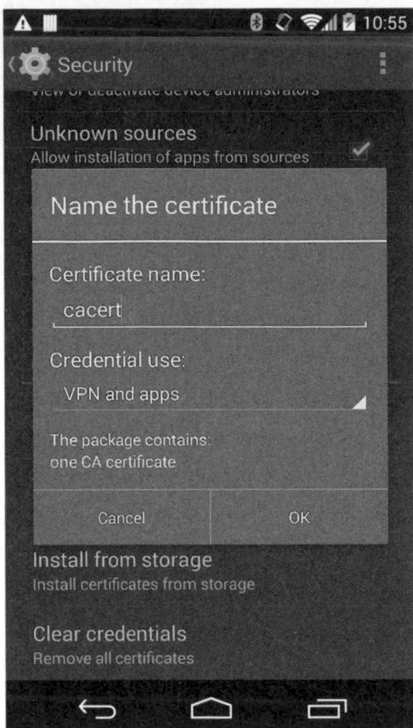

Figure 6-4: CA certificate import dialog

Figure 6-5: User-imported CA certificates

Beginning with Android 4.4, the system displays a notification that warns the user that network activity could be monitored if there are any user-installed trusted certificates. SSL connection monitoring can be accomplished by using an intercepting proxy server that returns automatically generated certificates for the sites that the user is trying to access. As long as those certificates are issued by a CA that Android trusts (such as the one manually installed in the trust store), most applications would not know the difference between a connection to the original host and the intercepting proxy (unless they are have pinned the target host; see "Certificate Pinning" on page 168 for details). A warning icon is shown in Quick Settings and next to the *Security* preference entry in the system Settings. When tapped, the notification displays the warning message shown in Figure 6-6.

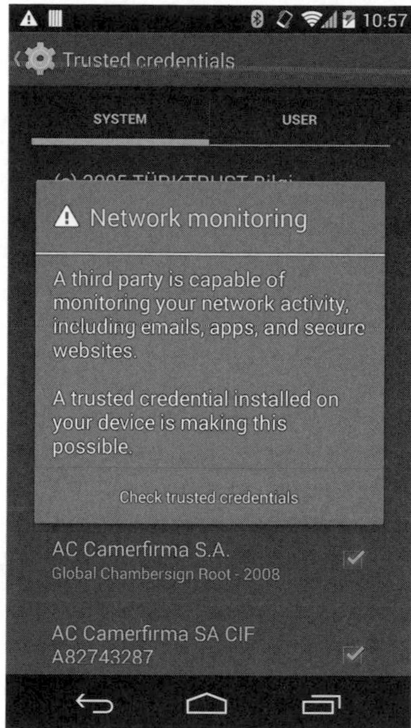

Figure 6-6: Network monitoring warning in Android 4.4

System Trust Store APIs

Third-party applications can prompt the user to import a needed certificate into the system trust store by using the `KeyChain` API, introduced in Android 4.0 as well. (We'll discuss the `KeyChain` API in Chapter 7.) Beginning with Android 4.4, device administrator applications can silently install CA certificates in the system trust store if they hold the *MANAGE_CA_CERTIFICATES* system permission. (We'll introduce device administration and related APIs in Chapter 9.)

Once a CA certificate is imported into the system trust store, we can use it to validate certificates using the JSSE `TrustManager` API as shown in Listing 6-9.

```
// Certificate chain including the end entity (server) certificate
// and any intermediate issuers.
X509Certificate[] chain = { endEntityCert };
TrustManagerFactory tmf = TrustManagerFactory.getInstance("X509");❶
tmf.init((KeyStore) null);❷
```

```
TrustManager[] tms = tmf.getTrustManagers();
X509TrustManager xtm = (X509TrustManager) tms[0];❸
Log.d(TAG, "checking chain with " + xtm.getClass().getName());
xtm.checkServerTrusted(chain, "RSA");❹
Log.d(TAG, "chain is valid");
```

Listing 6-9: Initializing a `TrustManager` with system trust anchors and validating a certificate

To do so, we first get the system PKIX (aliased to *X509*) `TrustManagerFactory` (❶ in Listing 6-9); initialize it using the system trust store by passing `null` to its `init(KeyStore ks)` method ❷; then get the first `TrustManager` implementation for the specified algorithm (there is usually only one, but do check in production code) and cast it to the validation algorithm-specific `X509TrustManager` interface ❸. Finally, we pass the certificate chain and the key exchange algorithm used (*RSA*, *DHE_DSS*, and so on) to the `checkServerTrusted()` method ❹. If a chain leading to a trusted CA certificate can be built, validation passes and the method returns. If any of the certificates in the chain is expired or invalid, or if the chain does not lead to a system trust anchor, the method will throw a `java.security.cert.CertificateException` (or one of its subclasses). Connections established with `SSLSocket` and `HttpsURLConnection` perform similar validation automatically.

This works pretty well, but there is one major problem with this code: it does not check revocation. Android's default `TrustManager` explicitly turns off revocation when validating the certificate chain. So even if the certificate had a CRL Distribution Point (CDP) extension, pointing to a valid CRL, or the OCSP responder URI was included in the Authority Information Access (AIA) extension, and the certificate was actually revoked, it would still validate in Android. What's missing here is *online revocation checking*: the ability to dynamically fetch, cache, and update revocation information as needed, based on information available in certificate extensions.

Certificate Blacklisting

Instead of using online revocation checks, Android relies on CA and end entity certificate blacklisting, which we will discuss in this section. *Certificate blacklisting* refers to the explicit blocking of certain certificates by verifiers, regardless of their state in the PKI's repository. Blacklisting is not part of the original PKI philosophy and is not defined in any of the related standards. So why is it necessary in practice?

In a perfect world, a working PKI takes care of issuing, distributing, and revoking certificates as necessary. All that a system needs to verify the identities of previously unknown machines and users are a few trust anchor certificates: any end entity certificates encountered will be issued by one of the trusted CAs, or one of their subordinate issuing CAs (sub-CA). In practice, though, there are a number of issues, mostly related to handling compromised keys. End entity certificates have a relatively short validity period (usually one year), which limits the time a compromised key can be exploited. However, CA certificates have very long validity (20 or more years is typical) and because CAs are implicitly trusted, a key compromise may go undetected for quite some time. Recent breaches in top-level CAs have shown that CA key compromise is not a theoretical problem, and the consequences of a CA breach can be quite far-reaching.

Handling CA Key Compromises

Probably the biggest PKI issue is that revocation of root certificates is not really supported. Most OSes and browsers come with a preconfigured set of trusted CA certificates (dozens of them!) and when a CA certificate is compromised, there are two main ways to handle it: tell users to remove it from the trust store, or issue an emergency update that removes the affected certificate. Expecting users to handle this is obviously unrealistic, so that leaves the second option.

Windows modifies OS trust anchors by distributing patches via Windows Update, and browser vendors simply release a new patch version. However, even if an update removes a CA certificate from the system trust store, a user can still install it again, especially when presented with a "do this, or you can't access this site" ultimatum.

To make sure removed trust anchors are not brought back, the hashes of their public keys are added to a blacklist and the OS or browser rejects them even if they are in the user trust store. This approach effectively revokes CA certificates (within the scope of the OS or browser, of course) and addresses PKI's inability to handle compromised trust anchors. However, it is not exactly ideal because even an emergency update takes some time to prepare, and after it's released, some users won't update right away no matter how often they're nagged about it. (Fortunately, CA compromises are relatively rare and widely publicized, so it seems to work well in practice—for now, at least.) Other approaches have been proposed as well, but most are not widely used. We discuss some of the proposed solutions in "Radical Solutions" on page 167.

Handling End Entity Key Compromises

While CA breaches are fairly uncommon, end entity (EE) key compromise occurs much more often. Whether due to a server breach, stolen laptop, or a lost smart card, these compromises occur daily. Fortunately, modern PKI systems are designed with this in mind and CAs can revoke certificates and publish revocation information in the form of CRLs, or provide online revocation status using OCSP.

Unfortunately, this doesn't work too well in the real world. Revocation checking generally requires network access to a machine different from the one we are trying to connect to, and as such has a fairly high failure rate. To mitigate this, most browsers try to fetch fresh revocation information, but if that effort fails for some reason, they simply ignore the error (soft-fail), or at best show some visual indication that revocation information is not available.

NOTE *To address this problem, Google Chrome disables online revocation checks*[11] *altogether, and now uses its update mechanism to proactively push revocation information to browsers, without requiring an application update or restart.*[12] *Thus Chrome can have an up-to-date local cache of revocation information, which makes certificate validation both faster and more reliable. This is can be considered yet another blacklist (Chrome calls it a* CRL set*), this time based on information published by each CA. The browser vendor effectively managing revocation data on the user's behalf is quite novel; not everyone thinks it's a good idea, but it has worked well so far.*

An alternative to directly pushing revocation information as part of browser updates is *OCSP stapling*, formerly known as the TLS *Certificate Status Request* extension.[13] Instead of requiring clients to issue an OCSP request for the server certificate, the relevant response is included ("stapled") with the SSL handshake via the Certificate Status Request extension response. Because the response is signed by the CA, the client can trust it just as if it had fetched it directly from the CA's OCSP server. If the server did not include an OCSP response in the SSL handshake, the client is expected to fetch one itself. OCSP stapling is supported by all major HTTP servers, but browser support is still patchy, especially on mobile versions where latency is an issue.

Android Certificate Blacklisting

As we learned in "Android 4.x System Trust Store" on page 157, Android 4.0 added a management UI, as well as an SDK API, that allows for adding and removing trust anchors to the system trust store. This didn't quite solve PKI's number one problem, though: aside from the user manually disabling a compromised trust anchor, an OS update was still required to remove a compromised CA certificate. Additionally, because Android does not perform online revocation checks when validating certificate chains, there was no way to detect compromised end entity certificates, even if they have been revoked.

To solve this problem, Android 4.1 introduced certificate blacklists that can be modified without requiring an OS update. There are now two system blacklists:

- A public key hash blacklist (to handle compromised CAs)
- A serial number blacklist (to handle compromised EE certificates)

The certificate chain validator component takes those two lists into consideration when verifying websites or user certificates. Let's look at how this is implemented in a bit more detail.

---

11. Adam Langley, *Revocation checking and Chrome's CRL*, Feb 2012, *https://www.imperialviolet.org/2012/02/05/crlsets.html*

12. Online revocation checks can still be enabled by setting the *EnableOnlineRevocationChecks* option to *true* (default is *false*).

13. D. Eastlake 3rd, *Transport Layer Security (TLS) Extensions: Extension Definitions*, Section 8, January 2011, *http://tools.ietf.org/html/rfc6066#section-8*

Android uses a content provider to store OS settings in a system database. Some of those settings can be modified by third-party apps holding the necessary permissions, while some are reserved for the system and can only be changed in the system Settings, or by another system application. The settings reserved for the system are known as *secure settings*. Android 4.1 adds two new secure settings under the following URIs:

- *content://settings/secure/pubkey_blacklist*
- *content://settings/secure/serial_blacklist*

As the names imply, the first one stores public key hashes of compromised CAs and the second one a list of EE certificate serial numbers. Additionally, the system server now starts a `CertBlacklister` component that registers itself as a `ContentObserver` for the two blacklist URIs. Whenever a new value is written to any of the blacklist secure settings, the `CertBlacklister` is notified and writes the value to a file on disk. The files are comprised of a comma-delimited list of hex-encoded public key hashes or certificate serial numbers. The files are:

- Certificate blacklist: */data/misc/keychain/pubkey_blacklist.txt*
- Serial number blacklist: */data/misc/keychain/serial_blacklist.txt*

Why write the files to disk when they are already available in the settings database? Because the component that actually uses the blacklists is a standard Java CertPath API class that doesn't know anything about Android and its system databases. The certificate path validator class, `PKIXCertPathValidatorSpi`, is part of the Bouncy Castle JCA provider modified to handle certificate blacklists, which are an Android-specific feature and not defined in the standard CertPath API. The PKIX certificate validation algorithm that the class implements is rather complex, but what Android 4.1 adds is fairly straightforward:

- When verifying an EE (leaf) certificate, check to see if its serial number is in the serial number blacklist. If so, return the same error (exception) as if the certificate has been revoked.
- When verifying a CA certificate, check to see if the hash of its public key is in the public key blacklist. If so, return the same error as if the certificate has been revoked.

NOTE *Using the unqualified serial number to index blacklisted EE certificates could be a problem if two or more certificates from different CAs happen to have the same serial number. In this case, blacklisting just one of the certificates will effectively blacklist all others with the same serial number. In practice, though, most public CAs use long and randomly generated serial numbers so the probability of collision is quite low.*

The certificate path validator component is used throughout the whole system, so blacklists affect applications that use HTTP client classes, as well as the native Android browser and `WebView`. As mentioned above, modifying the blacklists requires system permissions, so only core system apps can change it. There are no apps in the AOSP source that actually call those APIs, but a good candidate to manage blacklists are the Google services components, available on "Google Experience" devices (that is, devices with the Play Store client preinstalled). These manage Google accounts and access to Google services, and provide push-style notifications via Google Client Messaging (GCM). Because GCM allows for real-time server-initiated push notifications, it's a safe bet that those will be used to trigger certificate blacklist updates.

Reexamining the PKI Trust Model

Android has taken steps to make its trust store more flexible by allowing on-demand modification of both trust anchors and certificate blacklists without requiring a system update. While certificate blacklisting does make Android more resilient to some PKI-related attacks and vulnerabilities, it doesn't quite solve all problems related to using certificates issued by public CAs. We present some of those problems and the proposed solutions next. We then conclude our discussion of PKI and SSL with a description of Android's implementation of one of those solutions: certificate pinning.

Trust Problems in Today's PKI

In the highly unlikely case that you haven't heard about it, the trustworthiness of the existing public CA model has been severely compromised in recent years. It has been suspect for a while, but recent high profile CA security breaches have brought this problem into the spotlight. Attackers have managed to issue certificates for a wide range of sites, including Windows Update servers and Gmail. Although not all were used (or at least they were not detected) in real attacks, the incidents have shown just how much of current Internet technology depends on certificates.

Fraudulent certificates can be used for anything from installing malware to spying on Internet communication, all while fooling users into thinking that they are using a secure channel or installing a trusted executable. Unfortunately, better security for CAs is not a solution because major CAs have willingly issued hundreds of certificates for unqualified names such as *localhost*, *webmail*, and *exchange*.[14] Certificates issued for unqualified host names can be used to launch a MITM attack against clients that accesses internal servers using their unqualified name, thus making it easy to eavesdrop on internal corporate traffic. And, of course, there is also the matter of compelled certificate creation, where a government agency could compel a CA to issue a false certificate to be used for intercepting secure traffic.

Clearly the current PKI system, which is largely based on a preselected set of trusted CAs (whose certificates are preinstalled as trust anchors), is problematic, but what are some of the actual problems? There are different takes on this, but for starters, there are too many public CAs. The

14. Electronic Frontier Foundation, *Unqualified Names in the SSL Observatory*, April 2011, *https://www.eff.org/deeplinks/2011/04/unqualified-names-ssl-observatory*

Electronic Frontier Foundation's SSL Observatory project[15] has shown that more than 650 public CAs are trusted by major browsers. Recent Android versions ship with more than 100 trusted CA certificates and until version 4.0, the only way to remove a trusted certificate was through a vendor-initiated OS update.

Additionally, there is generally no technical restriction on which certificates CAs can issue. As the Comodo and DigiNotar attacks, as well as the recent ANNSI[16] intermediate CA incident, have shown, anyone can issue a certificate for **.google.com* (name constraints don't apply to root CAs and don't really work for a public CA). Furthermore, because CAs don't publicize the certificates they have issued, there is no way for site operators (in this case, Google) to know when someone issues a new, possibly fraudulent certificate for one of their sites and take appropriate action (certificate transparency standards[17] aim to address this). In short, with the current system, if any of the built-in trust anchors are compromised, an attacker could issue a certificate for any site, and neither users accessing it nor the site's owner would notice.

Radical Solutions

Proposed solutions range from radical—scrap the whole PKI idea altogether and replace it with something new and better (DNSSEC is a usual favorite); to moderate—use the current infrastructure but do not implicitly trust CAs; to evolutionary—maintain compatibility with the current system but extend it in ways that limit the damage of CA compromise.

Unfortunately, DNSSEC is still not universally deployed, although the key TLD domains have already been signed. Additionally, it is inherently hierarchical—with country top-level domains controlled by the respective countries—and actually more rigid than PKI, so it doesn't really fit the bill too well. Improving the current PKI situation is an area of active research, and other viable radical solutions have yet to emerge.

Moving toward the moderate side, the SSH model has also been suggested (sometimes called *Trust on First Use*, or *TOFU*). In this model, no sites or CAs are initially trusted, and users decide which site to trust on first access. Unlike SSH however, the number of sites that you access directly or indirectly (via CDNs, embedded content, and so on) is virtually unlimited, and user-managed trust is quite unrealistic.

Convergence and Trust Agility

In a similar vein but much more practical is Convergence.[18] *Convergence* is a system based on the idea of *trust agility*, defined as "the ability to easily

---

15. Electronic Frontier Foundation, *The EFF SSL Observatory*, *https://www.eff.org/observatory*

16. *Agence nationale de la sécurité des systèmes d'information*, French Network and Information Security Agency

17. B. Laurie, A. Langley, and E. Kasper, *Certificate Transparency*, June 2013, *http://tools.ietf.org/html/rfc6962*

18. Thoughtcrime Labs, *Convergence*, *http://convergence.io/*

choose who you trust and to revise that decision at any time." It both abolishes the browser (or OS) preselected trust anchor set, and recognizes that users cannot be relied on to independently make trust decisions about all the sites they visit. Trust decisions are delegated to a set of notaries that can vouch for a site by confirming that the certificate you receive from a site is one they have seen before. If multiple notaries point out that the same certificate as correct, users can be reasonably sure that it is genuine and therefore trustworthy.

Convergence is not a formal standard, but a working implementation has been released, including a Firefox plugin (client) and server-side notary software. While this system is promising, the number of available notaries is currently limited, and Google has publicly stated that it won't add it to Chrome. Additionally, it cannot currently be implemented as a browser extension, because Chrome does not allow third-party extensions to override the default certificate validation module.

Certificate Pinning

That leads us to the current evolutionary solutions, which have been deployed to a fairly large user base, mostly courtesy of the Chrome browser. One is certificate blacklisting, which we already discussed, and the other is certificate pinning.

Certificate pinning (or more accurately, *public key pinning*) takes a converse to the blacklisting approach: it whitelists the keys that are trusted to sign certificates for a particular site. Pinning was introduced in Google Chrome version 13 in order to limit the CAs that can issue certificates for Google properties. It is implemented by maintaining a list of public keys that are trusted to issue certificates for a particular DNS name. The list is consulted when validating the certificate chain for a host, and if the chain doesn't include at least one of the whitelisted keys, validation fails. In practice, the browser keeps a list of SHA-1 hashes of the `SubjectPublicKeyInfo` (SPKI) field of trusted certificates. Pinning the public keys instead of the actual certificates allows for updating host certificates without breaking validation and requiring pinning information updates.

However, a hardcoded pin list doesn't really scale and a couple of new Internet standards have been proposed to help solve this scalability problem: Public Key Pinning Extension for HTTP (PKPE)[19] by Google and Trust Assertions for Certificate Keys (TACK)[20] by Moxie Marlinspike. The first one is simpler and proposes a new HTTP header (`Public-Key-Pin`, or *PKP*) that holds pinning information about a host's certificate. The header value can include public key hashes, pin lifetime, and a flag that specifies whether pinning should be applied to subdomains of the current host. Pinning information (or simply *pins*) is cached by the browser and used when making trust decisions until it expires. Pins are required to be

---

19. C. Evans, C. Palmer, and R. Sleevi, *Public Key Pinning Extension for HTTP*, August 7, 2014, *http://tools.ietf.org/html/draft-ietf-websec-key-pinning-20*

20. M. Marlinspike, *Trust Assertions for Certificate Keys*, January 7, 2013, *http://tack.io/draft.html*

delivered over a secure (SSL) connection, and the first connection that includes a PKP header is implicitly trusted (or optionally validated against pins built into the client). The protocol also supports an endpoint to report failed validations via the `report-uri` directive and allows for a non-enforcing mode (specified with the `Public-Key-Pins-Report-Only` header), where validation failures are reported but connections are still allowed. This makes it possible to notify host administrators about possible MITM attacks against their sites, so that they can take appropriate action.

The TACK proposal, on the other hand, is somewhat more complex and defines a new TLS extension (also called TACK) that carries pinning information signed with a dedicated *TACK key*. TLS connections to a pinned hostname require the server to present a "tack" containing the pinned key and a corresponding signature over the TLS server's public key. Thus, both pinning information exchange and validation are carried out at the TLS layer. In contrast, PKPE uses the HTTP layer (over TLS) to send pinning information to clients, but also requires validation to be performed at the TLS layer, dropping the connection if validation against the pins fails.

Now that we have an idea how pinning works, let's see how it's implemented on Android.

Certificate Pinning in Android

Pinning is one of the many security enhancements introduced in Android 4.2. The OS doesn't come with any built-in pins, but instead reads them from a file in the */data/misc/keychain/* directory (where user-added certificates and blacklists are stored). The file is simply called *pins* and is in the following format (see Listing 6-10):

```
hostname=enforcing|SPKI SHA512 hash, SPKI SHA512 hash,...
```

Listing 6-10: System pins *file format*

Here, `enforcing` is either `true` or `false` and is followed by a list of SPKI SHA-512 hashes separated by commas. Note that there is no validity period, so pins are valid until deleted. The file is used not only by the browser, but system-wide by virtue of pinning being integrated in *libcore*. In practice, this means that the default (and only) system `X509TrustManager` implementation (`TrustManagerImpl`) consults the pin list when validating certificate chains.

But there's a twist: the standard `checkServerTrusted()` method doesn't consult the pin list. Thus, any legacy libraries that do not know about certificate pinning would continue to function exactly as before, regardless of the contents of the pin list. This has probably been done for compatibility reasons and is something to be aware of: running on Android 4.2 or above doesn't necessarily mean that you get the benefit of system-level certificate pins. The pinning functionality is exposed to third-party libraries and apps via the new `X509TrustManagerExtensions` SDK class. It has a single method, `checkServerTrusted()` (full signature shown in Listing 6-11) that returns a validated chain on success or throws a `CertificateException` if validation fails.

```
List<X509Certificate> checkServerTrusted(X509Certificate[] chain, String authType, String host)
```

Listing 6-11: `X509TrustManagerExtensions` *certificate validation method*

The last parameter, `host`, is what the underlying implementation (`TrustManagerImpl`) uses to search the pin list for matching pins. If one is found, the public keys in the chain being validated will be checked against the hashes in the pin entry for that host. If none matches, validation will fail and you will get a `CertificateException`.

What part of the system uses the new pinning functionality then? The default SSL engine (JSSE provider), namely the client handshake (`ClientHandshakeImpl`), and SSL socket (`OpenSSLSocketImpl`) implementations check their underlying `X509TrustManager` and if it supports pinning, they perform additional validation against the pin list. If validation fails, the connection won't be established, thus implementing pin validation on the TLS layer as required by the standards discussed in the previous section.

The *pins* file is not written directly by the OS. Its updates are triggered by a broadcast (`android.intent.action.UPDATE_PINS`) that contains the new pins in its extras. The extras contain the path to the new pins file, its new version (stored in */data/misc/keychain/metadata/version/*), a hash of the current pins, and a *SHA512withRSA* signature over all the above. The receiver of the broadcast (`CertPinInstallReceiver`) then verifies the version, hash, and signature, and if valid, atomically replaces the current pins file with new content (the same procedure is used for updating the premium SMS numbers list). Signing the new pins ensures that they can only by updated by whoever controls the private signing key. The corresponding public key used for validation is stored as a system secure setting under the *config_update_certificate* key (usually in the secure table of the */data/data/com.android.providers.settings/databases/settings.db*). (As of this writing, the *pins* file on Nexus devices contains more than 40 pin entries, which cover most Google properties, including Gmail, YouTube, and Play Store servers.)

Summary

Android builds on standard Java APIs such as JSSE and CertPath to implement SSL connections and the required authentication mechanisms. Most of the secure sockets functionality is provided by the largely native, OpenSSL-based JSSE implementation, while certificate validation and trust store management are implemented in Java. Android provides a shared system trust store that can be managed via the Settings UI or the `KeyStore` API. All applications that use SSL or certificate validation APIs inherit the system trust anchors, unless an app-specific trust store is explicitly specified. Certificate validation in Android does not use online revocation checking but relies on the system certificate blacklist to detect compromised CA or end entity certificates. Finally, recent versions of Android support system-level certificate pinning in order to be able to constrain the set of certificates that are allowed to issue a server certificate for a particular host.

7

CREDENTIAL STORAGE

The previous chapter introduced PKI and the challenges involved in managing trust. While the most prevalent use of PKI is for authenticating the entity you connect to (*server authentication*), it's also used to authenticate you to those entities (*client authentication*). Client authentication is mostly found in enterprise environments, where it is used for everything from desktop logon to remotely accessing company servers. PKI-based client authentication requires the client to prove that it possesses an authentication key (typically an RSA private key) by performing certain cryptographic operations that the server can verify independently. Therefore, the security of client authentication relies heavily on protecting authentication keys from unauthorized use.

Most operating systems provide a system service that applications can use to securely store and access authentication keys without having to implement key protection themselves. Android has had such a service since version 1.6, and it has improved significantly since Android 4.0.

Android's credential store can be used to store credentials for built-in features such as Wi-Fi and VPN connectivity, as well as for third-party apps. Apps can access the credential store via standard SDK APIs and use it to manage their keys securely. Recent Android versions feature hardware-backed key storage, which provides enhanced key protection. This chapter discusses the architecture and implementation of Android's credential store and introduces the public APIs that it provides.

VPN and Wi-Fi EAP Credentials

Virtual Private Networks (VPNs) are the preferred way to offer remote access to private enterprise services. We'll discuss VPNs and related technologies in more detail in Chapter 9, but simply put, a VPN allows a remote client to join a private network by creating an encrypted tunnel between it and a public tunnel endpoint. VPN implementations differ in their use of tunneling technology, but all need to authenticate the client before they establish a secure connection. While some VPNs use a shared key or password for authentication, enterprise solutions often rely on PKI-based client authentication.

Extensible Authentication Protocol (EAP) is an authentication framework frequently used in wireless networks and point-to-point (P2P) connections. (EAP is discussed in more detail in Chapter 9.) Like VPN, EAP can use many different authentication methods, but EAP-Transport Layer Security (EAP-TLS) is preferred in enterprise environments, especially when a company PKI has already been deployed.

Authentication Keys and Certificates

In the case of both EAP-TLS and PKI-based VPNs, clients have an authentication key and are issued a matching certificate, often by the company certificate authority (CA). Keys are sometimes stored in a portable, tamper-resistant device such as a smart card or USB token. This greatly increases security because keys cannot be exported or extracted from the device and thus authentication requires both physical possession of the token and the knowledge of the associated PIN or passphrase.

When the security policy allows using authentication keys that are not protected by a hardware device, keys and associated certificates are typically stored in the standard PKCS#12 file format. Private keys stored in PKCS#12 files are encrypted with a symmetric key derived from a user-supplied password, and thus extracting the keys requires knowledge of the password. Some applications use PKCS#12 files as secure containers and only extract keys and certificates into memory when required, but typically they're imported into a system- or application-specific credential storage before use. This is how Android works as well.

The user-facing implementation of importing credentials on Android is rather simple: to import an authentication key and related certificates, users copy their PKCS#12 files (and, if necessary, any related CA certificates) to the device's external storage (often an SD card) and select **Install from storage** from the **Security** system settings screen. Android searches the root of the external storage for matching files (with the *.pfx* or *.p12* extensions) and presents an import dialog (see Figure 7-1). If the correct password is supplied, keys are extracted from the PKCS#12 file and imported into the system credential store.

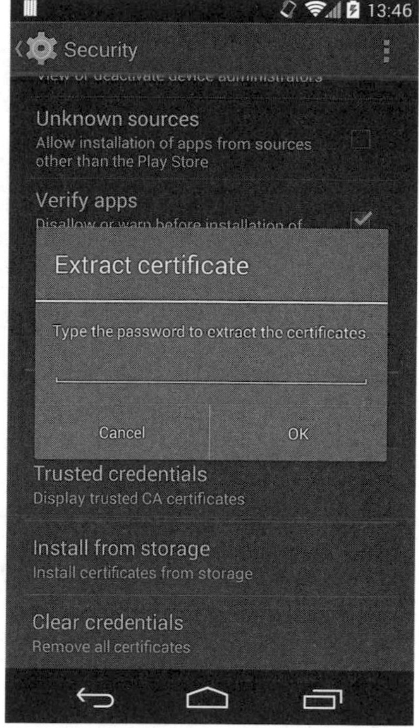

Figure 7-1: PKCS#12 file password dialog

The System Credential Store

The system credential store is a system service that encrypts imported credentials before storing them on disk. The encryption key is derived from a user-supplied password: a dedicated credential store protection password in pre-4.0 versions, or the device unlock swipe pattern, PIN, or password in post-4.0 versions of Android. Additionally, the credential store system service regulates access to stored credentials and guarantees that only apps explicitly granted access can access keys.

The original credential store was introduced in Android 1.6 and was limited to storing VPN and Wi-Fi EAP credentials. Only the system—not third-party apps—could access stored keys and certificates. Additionally, the only supported way to import credentials was to go through the system settings UI outlined in the previous section, and no public APIs for credential store management were available.

APIs for accessing the system credential store were first introduced in Android 4.0. The system credential store was later extended to support hardware-backed credential storage and to offer not only shared system keys, but app-private keys as well. Table 7-1 shows a summary of the major credential store enhancements added in each Android version. We'll introduce these enhancements and the related APIs in the following sections.

Table 7-1: Credential Store Feature Progression

Android version	API level	Credential store changes
1.6	4	Added credential store for VPN and Wi-Fi.
4.0	14	Added public API for credential store (`KeyChain` API).
4.1	16	Added the ability to generate and use keys without exporting them. Introduced keymaster HAL module and initial support for hardware-backed RSA key storage.
4.3	18	Added support for generating and accessing app-private keys using the *AndroidKeyStore* JCA provider, and APIs to check whether the device supports hardware-backed key storage for RSA keys.
4.4	19	Added ECDSA and DSA support to the *AndroidKeyStore* JCA provider.

Credential Storage Implementation

We now know that Android can encrypt imported credentials and manage access to them. Let's see how this is implemented under the hood.

The keystore Service

Credential storage management in Android was originally implemented by a single native daemon called *keystore*. Its functionality was initially limited to storing arbitrary blobs in encrypted form and verifying the credential store password, but it was extended with new features as Android evolved. It offered a local socket-based interface to its clients, and each client was responsible for managing their own state and socket connections. The *keystore* daemon was replaced with a centralized Binder service in Android 4.3 in order to better integrate it with other framework services and facilitate extension. Let's see how this *keystore* service works.

The *keystore* service is defined in *init.rc*, as shown in Listing 7-1.

```
service keystore /system/bin/keystore /data/misc/keystore
    class main
    user keystore
    group keystore drmrpc
```

Listing 7-1: keystore *service definition in* init.rc

As you can see, the *keystore* service runs as a dedicated *keystore* user and stores its files in */data/misc/keystore/*. Let's peek into */data/misc/keystore/* first. If you're using a single-user device, such as a phone, you will only find a single *user_0/* directory inside the *keystore/* directory (see Listing 7-2, timestamps removed), but on multi-user enabled devices you should find one directory for each Android user.

```
# ls -la /data/misc/keystore/user_0
-rw------- keystore keystore      84 .masterkey
-rw------- keystore keystore     980 1000_CACERT_cacert
-rw------- keystore keystore     756 1000_USRCERT_test
-rw------- keystore keystore     884 1000_USRPKEY_test
-rw------- keystore keystore     724 10019_USRCERT_myKey
-rw------- keystore keystore     724 10019_USRCERT_myKey1
```

Listing 7-2: Sample contents of the keystore *directory on a single-user device*

In this example, each file name consists of the UID of the app that created it (1000 is *system*), the entry type (CA certificate, user certificate, or private key), and the key name (alias), all connected with underscores. Since Android 4.3, system and app-private keys are supported as well, and the UID reflects the Android user ID as well as the app ID. On multi-user devices the user ID is `UID / 100000`, as discussed in Chapter 4.

In addition to system or app-owned key blobs, there is also a single *.masterkey* file, which we'll discuss shortly. When an app that owns store-managed keys is uninstalled for a user, only keys created by that user are deleted. If an app is completely removed from the system, its keys are deleted for all users. Because key access is tied to the app ID, this feature prevents a different app that happens to get the same UID from accessing an uninstalled app's keys. (Keystore reset, which deletes both key files and the master key, also affects only the current user.)

In the default software-based implementation, these files have the following contents (contents may be different for hardware-backed implementations; instead of encrypted key material, they often store only a reference to hardware-managed key objects):

- The master key (stored in *.masterkey*) is encrypted with a 128-bit AES key derived from the screen unlock password by applying the *PBKDF2* key derivation function with 8192 iterations and a randomly generated 128-bit salt. The salt is stored in the *.masterkey* file's info header.
- All other files store key blobs. A *key blob* (binary large object) contains a serialized, optionally encrypted key along with some data that describes the key (metadata). Each keystore key blob contains a metadata header, the initial vector (IV) used for encryption, and a concatenation of an MD5 hash value of the data with the data itself, encrypted with the 128-bit AES master key in CBC mode. Or more concisely: `metadata || Enc(MD5(data) || data)`.

In practice, this architecture means that the Android keystore is pretty secure for a software solution. Even if you had access to a rooted device and managed to extract the key blobs, you would still need the keystore password to derive the master key. Trying different passwords in an attempt to decrypt the master key would require at least 8192 iterations to derive a key, which is prohibitively expensive. In addition, because the derivation function is seeded with a 128-bit random number, pre-calculated password tables cannot be used. However, the MD5-based integrity mechanism used does not employ a standard Message Authentication Code (MAC) algorithm such as HMAC and is a remnant of the original implementation. It's kept for backward compatibility, but may be replaced in a future version.

Key Blob Versions and Types

Beginning with Android 4.1, two fields were added to key blobs: *version* and *type*. The current version (as of Android 4.4) is *2* and keys blobs are automatically upgraded to the latest version when an application first accesses them. As of this writing, the following key types are defined:

- `TYPE_ANY`
- `TYPE_GENERIC`
- `TYPE_MASTER_KEY`
- `TYPE_KEY_PAIR`

`TYPE_ANY` is a meta key type that matches any key type. `TYPE_GENERIC` is used for key blobs that are saved using the original get/put interface, which stores arbitrary binary data, and `TYPE_MASTER_KEY` is, of course, only used for the keystore master key. The `TYPE_KEY_PAIR` type is used for key blobs created using the `generate_keypair` and `import_keypair` operations, newly introduced in Android 4.1. We'll discuss these in the "keymaster Module and keystore Service Implementation" section.

Android 4.3 is the first version to use the `flags` field of key blobs. It uses this field to distinguish encrypted (the default) from non-encrypted key blobs. Key blobs that are protected by a hardware-based implementation (available on some devices) are stored without additional encryption.

Access Restrictions

Key blobs are owned by the *keystore* user, so on a regular (not rooted) device, you need to go through the *keystore* service in order to access them. The *keystore* service applies the following access restrictions:

- The *root* user cannot lock or unlock the keystore, but can access system keys.
- The *system* user can perform most keystore management operations (like initialization, reset, and so on) in addition to storing keys. However, the *system* user cannot use or retrieve other users' keys.
- Non-system users can insert, delete, and access keys, but can only see their own keys.

Now that we know what the *keystore* service does, let's look at the actual implementation.

keymaster Module and keystore Service Implementation

While the original daemon-based implementation included both key blob management and encryption in a single binary, Android 4.1 introduced a new *keymaster Hardware Abstraction Layer (HAL)* system module responsible for generating asymmetric keys and signing/verifying data without the need to export the keys first.

The *keymaster* module is meant to decouple the *keystore* service from the underlying asymmetric key operations implementation and to allow for easier integration of device-specific, hardware-backed implementations. A typical implementation would use a vendor-provided library to communicate with the crypto-enabled hardware and provide a "glue" HAL library, which the *keystore* daemon links with.

Android also comes with a default *softkeymaster* module that performs all key operations in software only (using the system OpenSSL library). This module is used on the emulator and included in devices that lack dedicated cryptographic hardware. The key size of generated keys was initially fixed at 2048 bits and only RSA keys were supported. Android 4.4 added support for specifying key size, as well as the Digital Signature Algorithm (DSA) and Elliptic Curve DSA (ECDSA) algorithms and their respective keys.

As of this writing, the default *softkeymaster* module supports RSA and DSA keys with sizes between 512 and 8192 bits. If the key size is not explicitly specified, DSA keys default to 1024 bits, and RSA ones to 2048 bits. For EC keys, the key size is mapped to a standard curve with the respective field size. For example, when 384 is specified as the key size, the *secp384r1* curve is used to generate keys. Currently the following standard curves are supported: *prime192v1*, *secp224r1*, *prime256v1*, *secp384r1*, and *secp521r1*. Keys for each of the supported algorithms can be imported as well if they are converted to the standard PKCS#8 format.

The HAL module interface is defined in *hardware/keymaster.h* and defines the operations listed below.

- `generate_keypair`
- `import_keypair`
- `sign_data`
- `verify_data`
- `get_keypair_public`
- `delete_keypair`
- `delete_all`

All asymmetric key operations exposed by the *keystore* service are implemented by calling the system *keymaster* module. Thus if the *keymaster* HAL module is backed by a hardware cryptographic device, all upper-level commands and APIs that use the *keystore* service interface automatically get to use hardware crypto. Aside from asymmetric key operations, all other credential store operations are implemented by the *keystore* system service and do not depend on HAL modules. The service registers itself to Android's `ServiceManager` with the *android.security.keystore* name and is started at boot. Unlike most Android services, it is implemented in C++ and the implementation resides in *system/security/keystore/*.

Nexus 4 Hardware-Backed Implementation

To give some perspective to the whole "hardware-backed" idea, let's briefly discuss how it's implemented on the Nexus 4. The Nexus 4 is based on Qualcomm's Snapdragon S4 Pro APQ8064 system on a chip (SoC). Like most recent ARM SoCs, it is TrustZone-enabled, with Qualcomm's Secure Execution Environment (QSEE) implemented on top of that.

ARM's TrustZone technology provides two virtual processors backed by hardware-based access control, which allows a SoC system to be partitioned into two virtual "worlds": the *Secure world* for the security subsystem, and the *Normal world* for everything else. Applications running in the Secure world are referred to as *trusted applications* and can only be accessed by Normal world applications (which the Android OS and apps run in) through a limited interface that they explicitly expose. Figure 7-2 shows a typical software configuration for a TrustZone-enabled system.

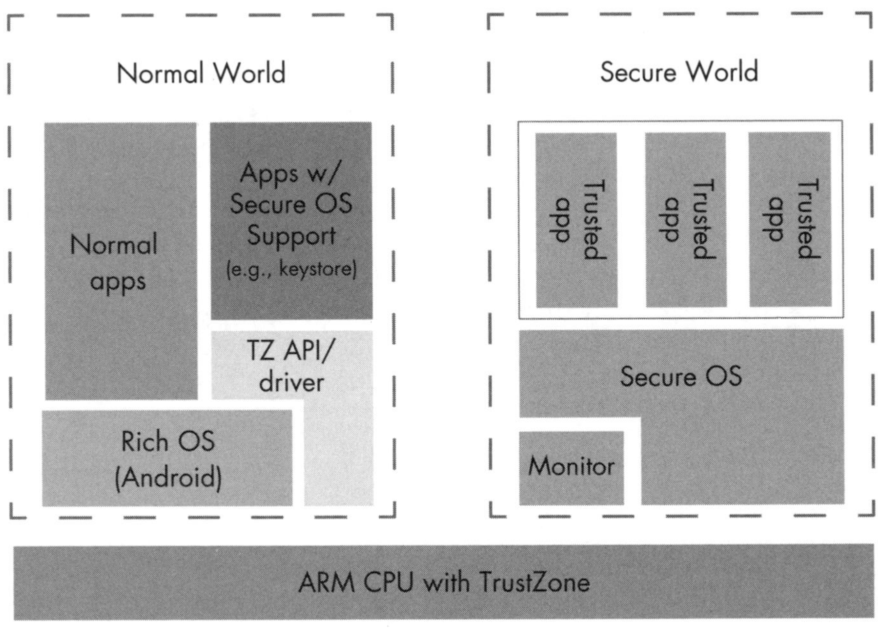

Figure 7-2: TrustZone software architecture

As usual, implementation details are quite scarce, but on the Nexus 4 the only way to interact with trusted applications is through the controlled interface that the */dev/qseecom* device provides. Android applications that wish to interact with the QSEE load the proprietary *libQSEEComAPI.so* library and use its functions to send commands to the QSEE.

As with most other SEEs, the *QSEECom* communication API is quite low level and basically only allows for exchanging opaque blobs (typically commands and replies), the contents of which depend entirely on the secure app you're communicating with. In the case of the Nexus 4 *keymaster*, the commands used are: `GENERATE_KEYPAIR`, `IMPORT_KEYPAIR`, `SIGN_DATA`, and

VERIFY_DATA. The *keymaster* implementation merely creates command structures, sends them via the *QSEECom* API, and parses the replies. It does not contain any cryptographic code.

One interesting detail is that the QSEE *keystore* trusted app (which may not be a dedicated app, but part of a more general-purpose trusted application) doesn't return simple references to protected keys; it uses proprietary encrypted key blobs. In this model, the only thing that is actually protected by hardware is some form of master key-encryption key (KEK); user-generated keys are only indirectly protected by being encrypted with the KEK.

This method allows for a practically unlimited number of protected keys, but it has the disadvantage that if the KEK is compromised, all externally stored key blobs are compromised as well. (Of course, the actual implementation might generate a dedicated KEK for each key blob created, or the key can be fused in hardware; either way no details are available about the internal implementation.) That said, Qualcomm *keymaster* key blobs are defined in AOSP code (shown in Listing 7-3) and the definition suggests that private exponents are encrypted using AES ❶, most probably in CBC mode, with an added HMAC-SHA256 ❷ to check encrypted data integrity.

```
#define KM_MAGIC_NUM     (0x4B4D4B42)    /* "KMKB" Key Master Key Blob in hex */
#define KM_KEY_SIZE_MAX  (512)           /* 4096 bits */
#define KM_IV_LENGTH     (16)          ❶/* AES128 CBC IV */
#define KM_HMAC_LENGTH   (32)          ❷/* SHA2 will be used for HMAC  */

struct  qcom_km_key_blob {
  uint32_t magic_num;
  uint32_t version_num;
  uint8_t  modulus[KM_KEY_SIZE_MAX];❸
  uint32_t modulus_size;
  uint8_t  public_exponent[KM_KEY_SIZE_MAX];❹
  uint32_t public_exponent_size;
  uint8_t  iv[KM_IV_LENGTH];❺
  uint8_t  encrypted_private_exponent[KM_KEY_SIZE_MAX];❻
  uint32_t encrypted_private_exponent_size;
  uint8_t  hmac[KM_HMAC_LENGTH];❼
};
```

Listing 7-3: QSEE keymaster *blob definition (for Nexus 4)*

As you can see in Listing 7-3, the QSEE key blob contains the key modulus ❸, public exponent ❹, the IV ❺ used for private exponent encryption, the private exponent itself ❻, and the HMAC value ❼.

Since the QSEE used in the Nexus 4 is implemented using the TrustZone functions of the processor, in this case the "hardware" of the hardware-backed credential store is simply the ARM SoC. Are other implementations possible? Theoretically, a hardware-backed *keymaster* implementation does not need to be based on TrustZone. Any dedicated device that can generate and store keys securely can be used, with the usual candidates being embedded Secure Elements (SE) and Trusted Platform Modules (TPMs).

We'll discuss SEs and other tamper-resistant devices in Chapter 11, but as of this writing no mainstream Android devices have dedicated TPMs and recent flagship devices have begun shipping without embedded SEs. Therefore, implementations using dedicated hardware are unlikely to show up in mainstream devices.

NOTE *Of course, all mobile devices have some form of* Universal Integrated Circuit Card (UICC), *colloquially known as a SIM card, which typically can generate and store keys, but Android still doesn't have a standard API to access the UICC even though vendor firmware often includes one. So while one could theoretically implement a UICC-based* keymaster *module, it would only work on custom Android builds and would depend on network operators to include support in their UICCs.*

Framework Integration

While managing credentials securely is the key feature of Android's credential storage, its main purpose is to provide this service seamlessly to the rest of the system. Let's briefly discuss how it integrates with the rest of Android before presenting the public APIs that are available for third-party apps.

Because the *keystore* service is a standard Binder service, in order to use it potential clients only need to get a reference to it from the `ServiceManager`. The Android framework provides the singleton `android.security.KeyStore` hidden class, which is responsible for obtaining a reference to the *keystore* service and serves as a proxy to the `IKeystoreService` interface it exposes. Most system applications, such as the PKCS#12 file importer (see Figure 7-1), and the implementations of some of the public APIs use the `KeyStore` proxy class to communicate with the *keystore* service.

In the case of lower-level libraries that are not part of the Android framework, such as native libraries and JCA classes in the core Java library, integration with the system credential store is provided indirectly through an OpenSSL engine called the *Android keystore engine*.

An OpenSSL engine is a pluggable cryptographic module implemented as a dynamic shared library. The *keystore* engine is one such module that implements all of its operations by calling the system *keymaster* HAL module. It supports only loading and signing with RSA, DSA, or EC private keys, but that's enough to implement key-based authentication (such as SSL client authentication). The *keystore* engine makes it possible for native code that uses OpenSSL APIs to use private keys saved in the system credential store without the need for code modifications. It also has a Java wrapper (`OpenSSLEngine`), which is used to implement access to keystore-managed private keys in the JCA framework.

Public APIs

While system applications can access the *keystore* daemon AIDL interface directly or through the `android.security.KeyStore` proxy class, those interfaces are too closely coupled with the implementation to be part of the public API. Android provides higher-level abstractions for third-party apps with the `KeyChain` API and the *AndroidKeyStoreProvider* JCA provider. We'll show how these APIs are used and provide some implementation details in the following sections.

The KeyChain API

Android has offered a system-wide credential store since version 1.6, but it was only usable by built-in VPN and Wi-Fi EAP clients. It was possible to install a private key/certificate pair using the Settings app, but the installed keys were not accessible by third-party applications.

Android 4.0 introduced SDK APIs for both trusted certificate management and secure credential storage via the `KeyChain` class. This feature was extended in Android 4.3 to support the newly introduced hardware-backed features. We'll discuss how it's used and review its implementation in the following sections.

The KeyChain Class

The `KeyChain` class is quite simple: it offers six public static methods, which are sufficient for most certificate- and key-related tasks. We'll look at how to install a private key/certificate pair and then use that pair to access the credential-store-managed private key.

The `KeyChain` API lets you install a private key/certificate pair bundled in a PKCS#12 file. The `KeyChain.createInstallIntent()` factory method is the gateway to this functionality. It takes no parameters and returns a system intent that can parse and install keys and certificates. (This is actually the same intent that is used internally by the Settings system app.)

Installing a PKCS#12 File

To install a PKCS#12 file, you have to read it to a byte array, store it under the `EXTRA_PKCS12` key in the intent's extras, and start the associated activity (see Listing 7-4):

```
Intent intent = KeyChain.createInstallIntent();
byte[] p12 = readFile("keystore-test.pfx");
intent.putExtra(KeyChain.EXTRA_PKCS12, p12);
startActivity(intent);
```

Listing 7-4: Installing a PKCS#12 file using the `KeyChain` API

This should prompt you for the PKCS#12 password in order to extract and parse the key and certificate. If the password is correct, you should be prompted for a certificate name, as shown in Figure 7-3. If the PKCS#12 has a friendly name attribute, it will be shown as the default; if not, you'll just get a long hexadecimal hash string. The string you enter here is the key or certificate alias you can use later to look up and access keys via the KeyChain API. You should be prompted to set a lock screen PIN or password to protect the credential storage if you haven't already set one.

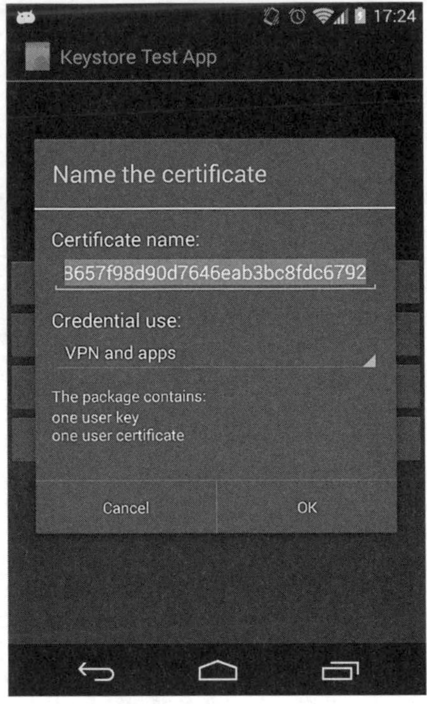

Figure 7-3: Private key and certificate import dialog

Using a Private Key

To use a private key stored in the system credential store, you need to obtain a reference to the key using its alias and request key access permission from the user. If you've never accessed a key before and don't know its alias, you need to first call `KeyChain.choosePrivateKeyAlias()` and provide a callback implementation that receives the selected alias as shown in Listing 7-5.

```
public class KeystoreTest extends Activity implements OnClickListener,
KeyChainAliasCallback {
    @Override
    public void onClick(View v) {
        KeyChain.choosePrivateKeyAlias(❶this, ❷(KeyChainAliasCallback)this,
           ❸new String[] { "RSA" }, ❹null, ❺null, ❻-1, ❼null);
    }
    @Override
    public void alias(final String alias) {❽
        Log.d(TAG, "Thread: " + Thread.currentThread().getName());
        Log.d(TAG, "selected alias: " + alias);
    }
}
```

Listing 7-5: Using a private key stored in the system credential store

The first parameter ❶ is the current context; the second ❷ is the callback to invoke; and the third and fourth specify the acceptable keys ❸ (`RSA`, `DSA`, or `null` for any) and acceptable certificate issuers ❹ for the certificate matching the private key. The next two parameters are the host ❺ and port number ❻ of the server requesting a certificate, and the last one ❼ is the alias to preselect in the key selection dialog. We leave all but the key type as unspecified (`null` or `-1`) here in order to be able to select from all available certificates. Note that the `alias()` ❽ callback will not be called on the main thread, so don't try to directly manipulate the UI from it. (It's called on a binder thread.)

Using the key requires user authorization, so Android should display a key selection dialog (see Figure 7-4) which also serves to grant access to the selected key. Once the user has granted key access to an app, it can look up that key directly without going through the key selection dialog.

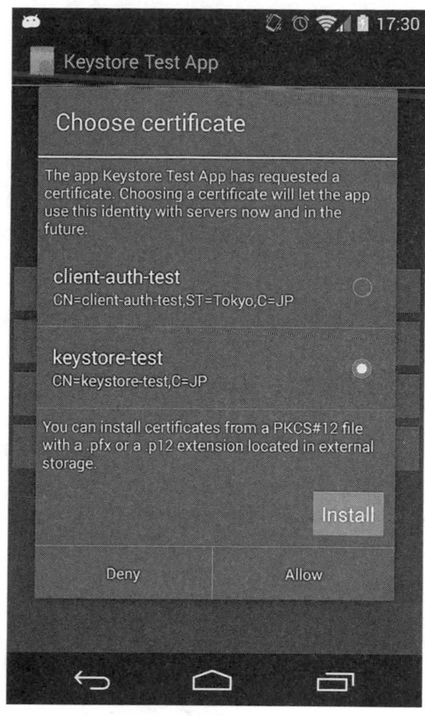

Figure 7-4: Key selection dialog

Listing 7-6 shows how to use the `KeyChain` API to obtain a reference to a private key managed by the system keystore.

```
PrivateKey pk =   KeyChain.getPrivateKey(context, alias);❶
X509Certificate[] chain =   KeyChain.getCertificateChain(context, alias);❷
```

Listing 7-6: Getting a key instance and its certificate chain

To get a reference to a private key, you need to call the `KeyChain .getPrivateKey()` ❶ method, passing it the key alias name received in the previous step. If you try to call this method on the main thread, you'll get an exception, so make sure to call it from a background thread like the one created by the `AsyncTask` utility class. The `getCertificateChain()` ❷ method returns the certificate chain associated with the private key (see Listing 7-6). If a key or certificate with the specified alias doesn't exist, the `getPrivateKey()` and `getCertificateChain()` methods will return `null`.

Installing a CA Certificate

Installing a CA certificate is not very different from installing a PKCS#12 file. To do so, load the certificate in a byte array and pass it as an extra to the install intent under the `EXTRA_CERTIFICATE` key, as shown in Listing 7-7.

```
Intent intent = KeyChain.createInstallIntent();
intent.putExtra(KeyChain.EXTRA_CERTIFICATE, cert);
startActivity(intent);
```

Listing 7-7: Installing a CA certificate using the `KeyChain` *API*

Android parses the certificate, and if its *Basic Constraints* extension is set to `CA:TRUE`, considers it a CA certificate and imports it into the user trust store. You need to authenticate in order to import the certificate.

Unfortunately, the import dialog (see Figure 7-5) shows neither the certificate DN nor its hash value. The user has no way of knowing what they're importing until it's done. Very few people bother to check a certificate's validity, so this could be a potential security threat because malicious applications could trick people into installing rogue certificates.

After the certificate is imported, it should show up in the Trusted credentials screen's User tab (Settings ▸Security ▸Trusted credentials). Tap the certificate entry to display a details dialog where you can check the subject, issuer, validity period, serial number, and SHA-1/SHA-256 fingerprints. To remove a certificate, press the **Remove** button (see Figure 7-6).

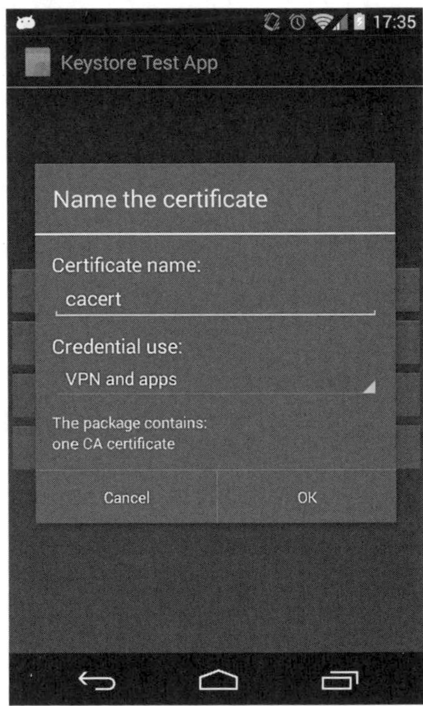

Figure 7-5: CA certificate import dialog

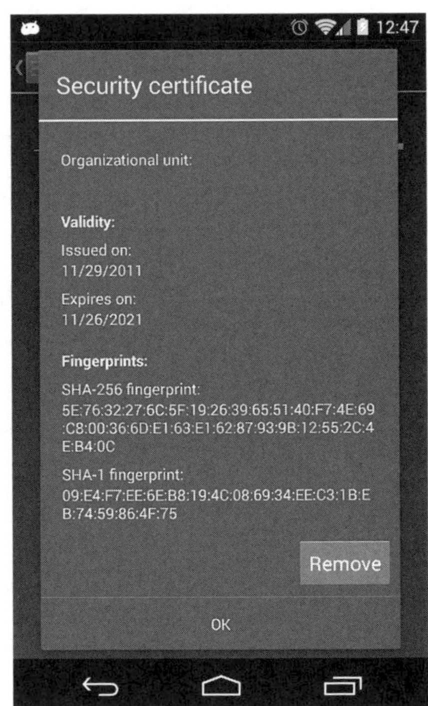

Figure 7-6: Certificate details dialog

Deleting Keys and User Certificates

While you can delete individual CA certificates, there is no way to delete individual keys and user certificates, although the Clear credentials option in the Credential Storage section of the security settings will delete all keys and user certificates.

NOTE *As long as you have keys in the credential store, you can't remove the screen lock because it is used to protect access to the keystore.*

Getting Information about Supported Algorithms

Android 4.3 added two methods to the `KeyChain` class related to the newly introduced hardware support. According to the API documentation, `isBoundKeyAlgorithm(String algorithm)` "returns `true` if the current device's `KeyChain` implementation binds any `PrivateKey` of the given algorithm to the device once imported or generated." In other words, if you pass the string *RSA* to this method, it should return `true` if generated or imported RSA keys have hardware protection and cannot simply be copied off the device. The `isKeyAlgorithmSupported(String algorithm)` method should return `true` if the current `KeyChain` implementation supports keys of the specified type (RSA, DSA, EC, and so on).

We've introduced the main features of the `KeyChain` API. Now let's look at the underlying Android implementation.

KeyChain API Implementation

The public `KeyChain` class and supporting interfaces reside in the `android.security` Java package. The package also contains two hidden AIDL files: `IKeyChainService.aidl` and `IKeyChainAliasCallback`. This is a hint that the actual keystore functionality, like most Android OS services, is implemented as a remote service to which the public APIs bind. The interface `IKeyChainAliasCallback` is called when you select a key via `KeyStore.choosePrivateKeyAlias()`, so it's of little interest. `IKeyChainService.aidl` defines the actual system interface that services use, so we'll describe it in more detail.

The `IKeyChainService` interface has one implementation, the `KeyChainService` class in the `KeyChain` system application. In addition to `KeyChainService`, the application includes an activity, `KeyChain`, and a broadcast receiver, `KeyChainBroadcastReceiver`. The `KeyChain` application has its `sharedUserId` is set to *android.uid.system* and therefore inherits all privileges of the *system* user. This allows its components to send management commands to the native *keystore* service. Let's examine the service first.

The `KeyChainService` is a wrapper for the `android.security.KeyStore` proxy class that directly communicates with the native *keystore* service. It provides four main services:

- Keystore management: methods for getting private keys and certificates.
- Trust store management: methods for installing and deleting CA certificates in the user trust store.

- Key and trust store initialization: a reset() method that deletes all keystore entries, including the master key, thus returning the keystore to an uninitialized state; it also removes all user-installed trusted certificates.
- Methods for querying and adding entries to the key access grant database.

Controlling Access to the Keystore

Since the KeyChain application runs as the *system* user, any process that binds to its remote interface would technically be able to perform all key and trust store operations. To prevent this, the KeyChainService imposes additional access control on its users by controlling access to credential store operations based on the caller's UID and using a key access grant database to regulate access to individual keys. Only the *system* user can delete a CA certificate and reset the key and trust stores (operations typically called via the Settings app's UI, which runs as *system*). By the same token, only the *system* user or the certificate installer application (com.android.certinstaller package) can install a trusted CA certificate.

Controlling access to individual keys in the credential store is a little bit more interesting than operation restrictions. The KeyChainService maintains a grants database (in */data/data/com.android.keychain/databases/grants.db*) that maps UIDs to the key aliases they are allowed to use. Let's have a look inside in Listing 7-8.

```
# sqlite3 grants.db
sqlite> .schema
.schema
CREATE TABLE android_metadata (locale TEXT);
CREATE TABLE grants (alias STRING NOT NULL, uid INTEGER NOT NULL, UNIQUE (alias,uid));
sqlite> select * from grants;
select * from grants;
❶test|10044❷
❸key1|10044
```

Listing 7-8: Schema and contents of the grants database

In this example, the application with UID *10044* ❷ is granted access to the keys with the test ❶ and key1 ❸ aliases.

Each call to getPrivateKey() or getCertificate() is subject to a check against the grants database, and results in an exception if a grant for the required alias is not found. As stated before, KeyChainService has APIs for adding and querying grants, and only the *system* user can call them. But who is responsible for actually granting and revoking access?

Remember the private key selection dialog (Figure 7-4)? When you call KeyChain.choosePrivateKeyAlias(), it starts the KeyChainActivity (introduced above), which checks to see if the keystore is unlocked; if so, KeyChainActivity shows the key selection dialog. Clicking the **Allow** button returns to the KeyChainActivity, which then calls KeyChainService.setGrant() with the selected alias, adding it to the grants database. Thus, even if the activity requesting access to a private key has the needed permissions, the user must unlock the keystore and explicitly authorize access to each individual key.

Besides controlling private key storage, the `KeyChainService` also offers trust store management by using the newly added `TrustedCertificateStore` class (part of *libcore*). This class provides both the ability to add user-installed trusted CA certificates and remove (mark as not trusted) system (preinstalled) CAs. Chapter 6 discusses the details of its implementation.

KeyChainBroadcastReceiver

The last component of the KeyChain app is the `KeyChainBroadcastReceiver`. It listens for the `android.intent.action.PACKAGE_REMOVED` system broadcast and simply forwards control to the `KeyChainService`. On receiving the `PACKAGE_REMOVED` action, the service does some grant database maintenance: it goes through all entries and deletes any referencing packages that are no longer available (that is, ones that have been uninstalled).

Credential and Trust Store Summary

Android 4.0 introduces a new service that grants access to both the system keystore (managed by the *keystore* system service) and the trust store (managed by the `TrustedCertificateStore` class) that backs the `KeyChain` API exposed in the public SDK. This feature makes it possible to control access to keys based on both the calling process's UID and the key access grant database, thus allowing for fine-grained, user-driven control over which keys each application can access. The components of Android's credential and trust store and their relationship are presented in Figure 7-7.

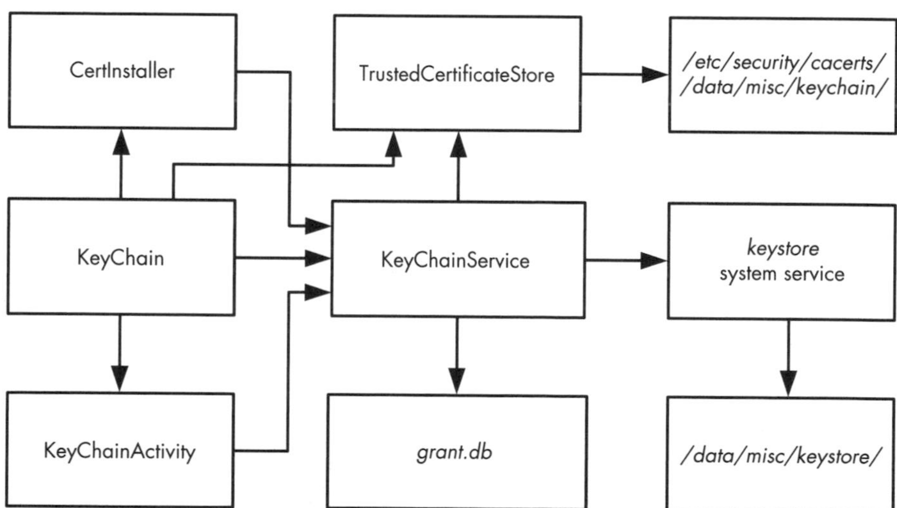

Figure 7-7: System credential store components

Android Keystore Provider

While the KeyChain API introduced in Android 4.0 allows applications to import keys into the system credential store, those keys are owned by the *system* user and any application can request access to them. Android 4.3 adds support for *app-private* keys, which allows any app to generate and save private keys that can only be accessed and used by itself and are not visible to other apps.

Instead of introducing yet another Android-specific API, keystore access is exposed via standard JCA APIs, namely java.security.KeyPairGenerator and java.security.KeyStore. Both are backed by a new Android JCA provider, *AndroidKeyStoreProvider*, and are accessed by passing *AndroidKeyStore* as the type parameter of the respective factory methods. Listing 7-9 shows how to generate and access RSA keys using the *AndroidKeyStoreProvider*.

```
// generate a key pair
Calendar notBefore = Calendar.getInstance()
Calendar notAfter = Calendar.getInstance();
notAfter.add(1, Calendar.YEAR);
KeyPairGeneratorSpec spec = new KeyPairGeneratorSpec.Builder(ctx)
                .setAlias("key1")
                .setKeyType("RSA")
                .setKeySize(2048)
                .setSubject(new X500Principal("CN=test"))
                .setSerialNumber(BigInteger.ONE).setStartDate(notBefore.getTime())
                .setEndDate(notAfter.getTime()).build();❶
KeyPairGenerator kpGenerator = KeyPairGenerator.getInstance("RSA",
                                "AndroidKeyStore");
kpGenerator.initialize(spec);❷
KeyPair kp = kpGenerator.generateKeyPair();❸
// in another part of the app, access the keys
KeyStore ks = KeyStore.getInstance("AndroidKeyStore");
ks.load(null);
KeyStore.PrivateKeyEntry keyEntry = (KeyStore.PrivateKeyEntry)keyStore.getEntry("key1", null);❹
RSAPublic pubKey = (RSAPublicKey)keyEntry.getCertificate().getPublicKey();
RSAPrivateKey privKey = (RSAPrivateKey) keyEntry.getPrivateKey();
```

Listing 7-9: Generating and accessing RSA keys using the AndroidKeyStoreProvider

First ❶ you create a KeyPairGeneratorSpec describing the keys you want to generate and the automatically created self-signed certificate each key is associated with. You can specify the key type (*RSA*, *DSA*, or *EC*) using the setKeyType() method, and key size with the setKeySize() method.

NOTE *Each* PrivateKeyEntry *managed by a* KeyStore *object needs to be associated with a certificate chain. Android automatically creates a self-signed certificate when you generate a key, but you can replace the default certificate with one signed by a CA later.*

Next, you initialize a `KeyPairGenerator` ❷ with the `KeyPairGeneratorSpec` instance and then generate the keys by calling `generateKeyPair()` ❸.

The most important parameter is the alias. You pass the alias to `KeyStore.getEntry()` ❹ in order to get a reference to the generated keys later. The returned key object does not contain the actual key material; it is only a pointer to a hardware-managed key object. Therefore, it is not usable with cryptographic providers that rely on key material being directly accessible.

If the device has a hardware-backed keystore implementation, keys will be generated outside the Android OS and won't be directly accessible even to the system (or *root*) user. If the implementation is software only, keys will be encrypted with a per-user key-encryption master key derived from the unlock PIN or password.

Summary

As you've learned in this chapter, Android has a system credential store that can be used to store credentials for built-in features such as Wi-Fi and VPN connectivity, as well as for use by third-party apps. Android 4.3 and later versions provide standard JCA APIs for generating and accessing app-private keys, which makes it easier for non-system apps to store their keys securely without needing to implement key protection themselves. Hardware-backed key storage, which is available on supported devices, guarantees that even apps with *system* or *root* privileges cannot extract the keys. Most current hardware-backed credential storage implementations are based on ARM's TrustZone technology and do not use dedicated tamper-resistant hardware.

8

ONLINE ACCOUNT MANAGEMENT

While enterprise services usually employ PKI for user authentication, most publicly available online services rely on passwords to authenticate their users. However, typing complex passwords on a touch screen mobile device multiple times a day for different sites is not a very pleasant exercise.

In an effort to improve the user experience when accessing online services, Android provides a centralized registry of user accounts that can cache and reuse credentials. This account registry can be accessed by third-party applications, allowing them to access web services on behalf of the device user without the need for apps to handle passwords directly. In this chapter, we discuss how Android manages a user's online account credentials and the APIs that applications can use to take advantage of cached credentials and to register custom accounts. We then show how Google experience devices (devices on which the Google Play Store is preinstalled) store Google account information and allow access to Google APIs and other online services by using the stored credentials.

Android Account Management Overview

While early Android devices had built-in support for Google accounts and automatic background data synchronization with Google services such as Gmail, no APIs for this functionality were originally provided. Android 2.0 (API Level 5) introduced the concept of centralized account management with a public API. The central piece in the API is the `AccountManager` class, which "provides access to a centralized registry of the user's online accounts. The user enters credentials (username and password) once per account, granting applications access to online resources with 'one-click' approval."[1] Another major feature of the class is that it lets you get an authentication token for supported accounts, allowing third-party applications to authenticate to online services without needing to actually handle the user password. On some older Android versions, the `AccountManager` would also monitor your SIM card and wipe cached credentials if you swapped cards, but this feature was removed in Android 2.3.4 and later versions.

Account Management Implementation

As with most Android system APIs, the `AccountManager` is just a facade for the `AccountManagerService`, which does the actual work. The service doesn't provide an implementation for any particular form of authentication, though. It merely coordinates a number of pluggable authenticator modules for different account types (Google, Twitter, Microsoft Exchange, and so on). Any application can register an authenticator module by implementing an account authenticator and related classes, if needed. We show how to write and register a custom authenticator module in "Adding an Authenticator Module" on page 203.

Registering a new account type with the system lets you take advantage of a number of Android infrastructure services, including the ability to:

- Use a centralized credential storage in a system database
- Issue tokens to third-party apps
- Take advantage of Android's automatic background synchronization (via a sync adapter)

Figure 8-1 shows the main components of Android's account management subsystems and their relationships. Each component and its role will be described in the following sections.

1. Google, *Android API Reference*, "AccountManager," *http://developer.android.com/reference/android/accounts/AccountManager.html*

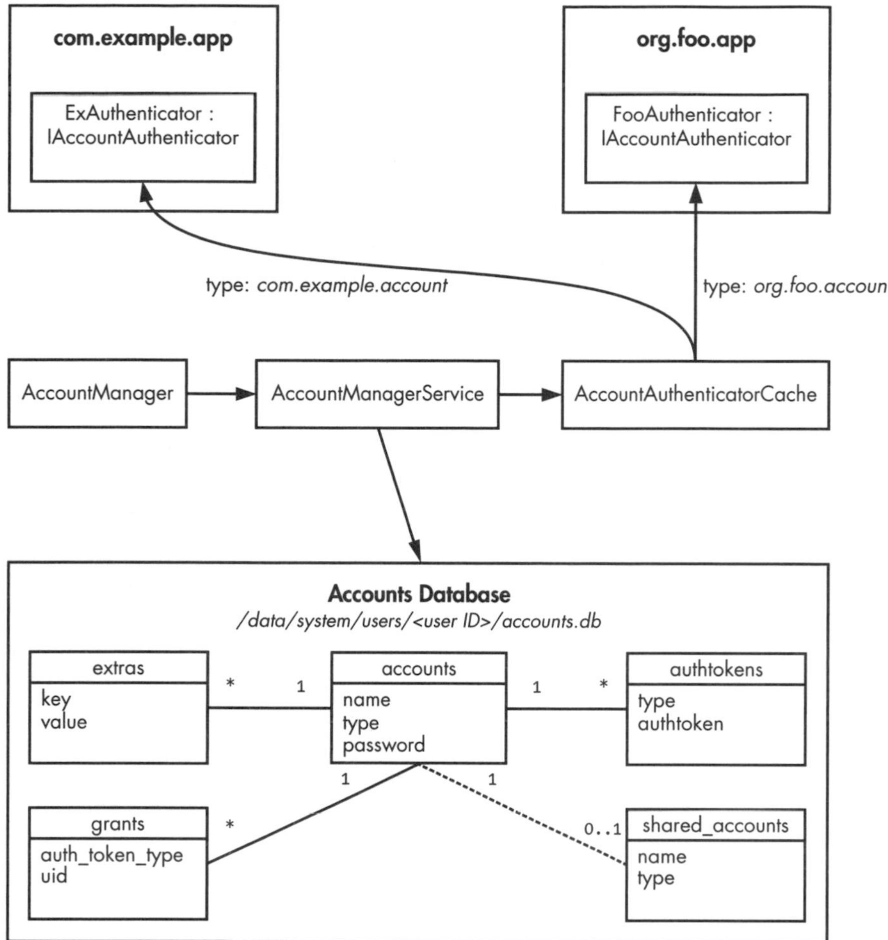

Figure 8-1: Account management components

AccountManagerService and AccountManager

The central piece here is the `AccountManagerService`, which coordinates all other components and persists account data in the accounts database. The `AccountManager` class is the facade that exposes a subset of its functionality to third-party applications. It starts worker threads for asynchronous methods and posts the results (or error details) back to the caller. Additionally, `AccountManager` shows an account chooser when the requested token or feature can be provided by more than one account. However, it doesn't enforce any permissions; all caller permissions are checked by the `AccountManagerService` and we'll discuss the concrete permissions shortly.

Authenticator Modules

As mentioned above, the functionality of each registered account is provided by a pluggable authenticator module, but what exactly is an authenticator module? *Authenticator modules* are defined and hosted by applications, and each is simply a bound service that implements the `android.accounts.IAccountAuthenticator` AIDL interface. This interface has methods for adding an account, prompting the user for their credentials, getting an authentication token, and for updating account metadata. In practice, applications don't implement this interface directly, but instead extend the `android.accounts.AbstractAccountAuthenticator` class which links implementation methods to an internal AIDL stub.

The `AbstractAccountAuthenticator` also ensures that all callers of the AIDL stub hold the `ACCOUNT_MANAGER` permission; a system signature permission that only allows system components to call authenticator modules directly. All other clients need to go through the `AccountManagerService`.

Each authenticator module implements an account identified uniquely by a string called the *account type*. Account types are typically in reverse domain notation (like Java packages) and are usually named using the base package name of the defining application concatenated with the account type, or the *account* or *auth* strings (Android does not enforce this rule, however, and there are no explicit guidelines). For example, in Figure 8-1, the `com.example.app` application defines an account with type `com.example.account`, and the `org.foo.app` application defines an account with type `org.foo.account`.

Authenticator modules are implemented by adding a service that can be bound to by using the *android.accounts.AccountAuthenticator* intent action to the host application. The account type, as well as other metadata, is linked to the service by adding a `<meta-data>` tag to the service declaration. The `resource` attribute of the tag points to an XML file that contains account metadata (see Listing 8-8 for an example).

NOTE *A `<meta-data>` tag allows a name-value pair containing arbitrary data to be associated with its parent component. The data can be a literal value, such as a string or an integer, or a reference to an Android resource file. Multiple `<meta-data>` tags per component are also supported. The values from all `<meta-data>` tags are collected in a single `Bundle` object and made available as the `metaData` field of the `PackageItemInfo` class (the base class of concrete classes that encapsulate component attribute values, such as `ServiceInfo`). The interpretation of the associated metadata is component-specific.*

The Authenticator Module Cache

"Pluggability" is provided by the `AccountAuthenticatorCache` class, which scans for packages that define authenticator modules and makes them available to the `AccountManagerService`. The `AccountAuthenticatorCache` is one implementation of the more general registered service cache facility that Android provides. The cache is built on demand (lazily) by interrogating the `PackageManagerService` about installed packages that register a particular intent action and metadata file. The cache is kept up-to-date by a broadcast receiver that triggers an update when packages are added, updated, or removed. The cache is persistent and written to disk each time a change is detected, with cache files written to the */data/system/registered_services/* directory and named after the intent action they scan for. The authenticator module cache is saved to the *android.accounts.AccountAuthenticator.xml* file and might look like Listing 8-1.

```
<?xml version='1.0' encoding='utf-8' standalone='yes' ?>
<services>
    <service uid="10023" type="com.android.exchange" />❶
    <service uid="10023" type="com.android.email" />❷
    <service uid="10069" type="com.example.account" />❸
    <service uid="10074" type="org.foo.account" />❹
    --snip--
    <service uid="1010023" type="com.android.email" />❺
    <service uid="1010023" type="com.android.exchange" />❻
    <service uid="1010069" type="com.example.account" />❼
    --snip--
</services>
```

Listing 8-1: Contents of the AccountAuthenticator.xml *registered services cache file*

Here, the *com.android.exchange* and *com.android.email* account types (❶ and ❷) are registered by the stock Email application, and *com.example.account* and *org.foo.account* (❸ and ❹) are registered by third-party applications. On a multi-user device, the cache file will have entries for the accounts available to each user.

In this example, the first secondary user (user ID 10) can use *com.android.exchange*, *com.android.email*, and *com.example.account* (❺, ❻, and ❼), but not the *org.foo.account* account (because there is no entry for it in the file). When the `AccountManagerService` needs to perform an action with a particular account, it queries the `AccountAuthenticatorCache` for the implementing service by passing the account type. If an account implementation for that type is registered for the current user, `AccountAuthenticatorCache` returns details about the implementing service that contain the name of the implementing component and the UID of the host package. The `AccountManagerService` uses this information to bind to the service in order to be able to call methods of the `IAccountAuthenticator` interface that the service implements.

AccountManagerService Operations and Permissions

As shown in Figure 8-1, `AccountManagerService` implements its functionality by either calling into authenticator modules or by using cached data from the accounts database. Third-party components can only use the API that `AccountManagerService` exposes; they can't access authenticator modules or the accounts database. This centralized interface guarantees operation workflow and enforces access rules for each operation.

`AccountManagerService` implements access control using a combination of permissions and caller UID and signature checks. Let's look at the operations it provides and the respective permission checks.

Listing and Authenticating Accounts

Clients can get a list of accounts that match certain criteria (including type, declaring package, and other features) by calling one of the `getAccounts()` methods, and they can check to see if a particular account has the required features by calling the `hasFeatures()` method. These operations require the `GET_ACCOUNTS` permission, which has the *normal* protection level. A new account of a particular type can be added by calling the `addAccount()` method (which starts an implementation-specific *authenticator activity* that collects credentials from the user) or silently by calling the `addAccountExplicitly()` method, which takes the account, password, and any associated user data as parameters. The first method requires callers to hold the `MANAGE_ACCOUNTS` permission, and the second requires that they both hold the `AUTHENTICATE_ACCOUNTS` permission and have the same UID as the account's authenticator. Both permissions have protection level *dangerous* and therefore require user confirmation when the app is installed. Requiring callers of `addAccountExplicitly()` to have the same UID as the authenticator ensures that only the same app, or apps that belong to the same shared user ID (see Chapter 2 for details), can add accounts without user interaction.

Other operations that require the caller to both hold the `AUTHENTICATE_ACCOUNTS` permission and have the same UID as the account's authenticator are listed below. (We've omitted `AccountManager` method parameters here and in the following sections for clarity. See the reference documentation of the `AccountManager` class[2] for full method signatures and additional information.)

`getPassword()` Returns the raw cached password.

`getUserData()` Returns authenticator-specific account metadata that matches a specified key.

`peekAuthToken()` Returns a cached token of the specified type (if available).

`setAuthToken()` Adds or replaces an authentication token for an account.

`setPassword()` Sets or clears the cached password for an account.

`setUserData()` Sets or clears the metadata entry with the specified key.

Managing Accounts

Just as when adding a new account, removing an existing account requires the `MANAGE_ACCOUNTS` permission. However, if the calling device user has the `DISALLOW_MODIFY_ACCOUNTS` restriction set (see Chapter 4 for more details on user restrictions), they cannot add or remove accounts, even if the calling application holds the `MANAGE_ACCOUNTS` permission. Other methods that require this permission are those that modify account properties or credentials as listed next.

2.Google, *Android API Reference*, "AccountManager," *http://developer.android.com/reference/android/accounts/AccountManager.html.*

clearPassword() Clears a cached password.

confirmCredentials() Explicitly confirms that the user knows the password (even if it is already cached) by showing a password entry UI.

editProperties() Shows a UI that allows the user to change global authenticator settings.

invalidateAuthToken() Removes an authentication token from the cache. (This can also be called if the caller holds the `USE_CREDENTIALS` permission.)

removeAccount() Removes an existing account.

updateCredentials() Asks the user the enter the current password and updates the saved credentials accordingly.

Using Account Credentials

The final permission the `AccountManagerService` might require its clients to hold is `USE_CREDENTIALS`. This permission protects methods that return or modify *authentication tokens*, a service-dependent credential string that clients can use to authenticate requests to the server without sending their password with each request.

Typically, servers return an authentication token after the client successfully authenticates with their username and password (or other permanent credentials). The token is identified by a string called the *token type*, which describes what type of access the token grants (for example, read-only or read-write). The token is reusable and can be used for sending multiple requests, but might have a limited validity period. Additionally, if a user account is believed to have been compromised, or if a user changes their password, all existing authentication tokens for that user are usually invalidated on the server. In this case, requests that use cached authentication tokens will fail with an authentication error. Because the `AccountManagerService` is protocol- and application-agnostic, it doesn't automatically invalidate cached tokens, even if they have expired or been invalidated on the server. Applications are responsible for cleaning up such invalid cached tokens by calling the `invalidateAuthToken()` method.

These are the methods that require `USE_CREDENTIALS`:

getAuthToken() Gets an authentication token of the specified type for a particular account.

invalidateAuthToken() Removes an authentication token from the cache. (This can also be called if the caller holds the `MANAGE_ACCOUNTS` permission.)

Requesting Authentication Token Access

Besides holding the `USE_CREDENTIALS` permission, in order to obtain an authentication token of a particular type, callers of the `getAuthToken()` (or any of its wrapper methods as provided by the `AccountManager` facade class) must explicitly be granted access to the requested token type. This is accomplished by showing a confirmation dialog like the one shown in Figure 8-2. The dialog shows both the name of the requesting application (in the first bullet, "Account Requestor," in this example), the account type and name (in the second bullet, "Example" and "example_user", respectively), and a short description (below the bullets, "Full access to example data") of the type of data access that will be permitted if the access request is granted. If the user grants access, this decision is cached and the dialog won't be shown if a token of the same type is requested again. Applications running under the same UID as the authenticator module are allowed access to its tokens without showing a confirmation dialog. Additionally, privileged system applications are implicitly allowed access to all token types without user confirmation, so the dialog is not shown if the token request comes from a privileged application.

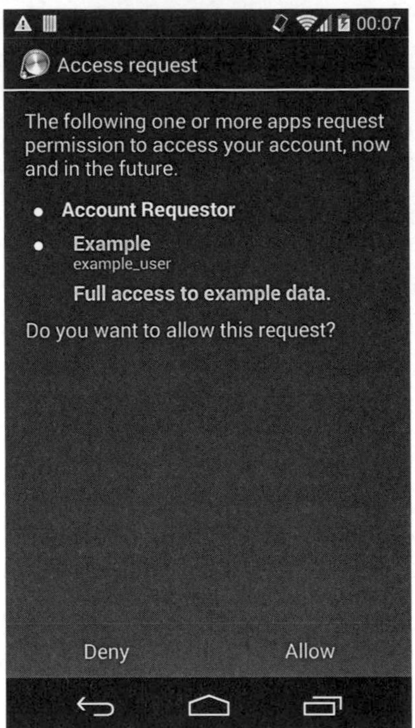

Figure 8-2: Account access request dialog

The Accounts Database

We've introduced authenticator modules, the authenticator cache, and the main features of the `AccountManagerService`. Now let's see how this service uses the *accounts database*, an SQLite database stored in each user's system directory with the *accounts.db* filename, to register accounts and cache credentials.

The accounts database is found at */data/system/users/0/accounts.db* on single-user devices. On multi-user devices, this file stores account information for the primary user, and secondary users each have their own instance at */data/system/users/<user ID>/accounts.db*. The database consists of six tables: `accounts`, `extras`, `authtokens`, `grants`, `shared_users`, and `meta`. As of this writing, the `meta` table appears to be unused; all other tables and their relationships are shown in Figure 8-1.

Table Schema

The accounts table stores the name, type, and password of registered accounts, and all other tables directly or indirectly link to it. It might contain data similar to Listing 8-2.

```
sqlite> select * from accounts;
_id|name              |type                      |password
1  |user1@gmail.com   |com.google                |1/......❶
2  |user1@example.com|com.google.android.pop3|password❷
3  |example_user      |com.example.account       |pass1234❸
```

Listing 8-2: Contents of the accounts table

Here, ❶ is a Google account (type *com.google*) which allows access to Gmail, the Google Play Store, and other Google services. Google accounts depend on proprietary system components and are only available on Google experience devices. (You'll find more details on Google accounts in "The Google Login Service" on page 206.) The account at ❷ is a POP3 mail account (type *com.google.android.pop3*) registered by the stock email application, and ❸ is a custom account (type *com.example.account*) registered by a third-party application. Each account can be associated with zero or more metadata key-value pairs that are stored in the extras table and link to the account by using its primary key (in the _id column). For example, if our custom application (❸ in Listing 8-2, _id=3) does background data synchronization, it might have entries similar to those in Listing 8-3.

```
sqlite> select * from extras where accounts_id=3;
_id|accounts_id|key      |value
11 |3          |device_id|0123456789
12 |3          |last_sync|1395297374
13 |3          |user_id  |abcdefghij
14 |3          |option1  |1
```

Listing 8-3: Contents of the extras table

The authtokens table stores tokens that have been issued for an account. For our custom application, it might look like Listing 8-4.

```
sqlite> select * from authtokens where accounts_id=3;
_id|accounts_id|type            |authtoken
16 |3          |com.example.auth|abcdefghij0123456789
```

Listing 8-4: Contents of the authtokens table

The grants table associates application UIDs with the types of tokens they're allowed to use. Grants are added when the user OK's the access confirmation dialog for a particular account type and token (see Figure 8-2). For example, if an application with UID 10291 has requested and been granted access to tokens of type *com.example.auth* as in our sample application (see

Listing 8-4), the grant will be represented by the following row in the grants table (see Listing 8-5). A new row is added for each combination of account ID, token type, and granted application UID.

```
sqlite> select * from grants;
accounts_id|auth_token_type |uid
3          |com.example.auth|10291
```

Listing 8-5: Contents of the grants table

The shared_accounts table is used when sharing the device owner's accounts with one of the restricted users on the device. (You'll find more details on its contents and usage in "Multi-User Support" on page 201.)

Table Access

Now we'll examine the relationship between tables and data in the accounts database and the key methods of the AccountManagerService. At a high level the relationship is fairly straightforward (if we ignore caching and synchronization): methods that retrieve or manipulate account details access the accounts table, and methods that handle user data associated with an account access the extras table. APIs that handle authentication tokens access the authtokens table, and save per-application token access grants in the grants table. We describe each method and the data it accesses next.

When you add an account of a particular type by calling one of the addAccount() methods, the AccountManagerService inserts a row in the accounts table containing its type, username, and password. Calling one of the getPassword(), setPassword(), or clearPassword() methods results in the AccountManagerService accessing or updating the password column of the accounts table. If you get or set user data for the account using the getUserdata() or setUserdata() methods, the AccountManagerService fetches the matching entry from or saves it to the extras table.

When you request a token for a particular account, things become a bit more complex. If a token with the specified type has never been issued before, AccountManagerService shows a confirmation dialog (see Figure 8-2) asking the user to approve access for the requesting application. If they accept, the UID of the requesting app and the token type are saved to the grants table. (Authenticators can declare that they use custom tokens by setting the customTokens account metadata attribute to true. In this case, they're responsible for managing tokens, and Android neither shows the token access dialog nor automatically saves tokens to the authtokens table). If a grant already exits, AccountManagerService checks the authtokens table for tokens matching the request. If a valid one exists, it's returned. If a matching token is not found, the AccountManagerService finds the authenticator for the specified account type in the cache and calls its getAuthToken() method to request a token. This usually involves the authenticator fetching the username and password from the accounts table (via the getPassword() method) and calling its respective online service to get a fresh token. When a token is returned, it gets cached in the authtokens table and then is returned to the requesting app (usually asynchronously via a callback). Invalidating a token results in deleting the row that stores it from the `authtokens` table. Finally, when an account is removed by calling the `removeAccount()` method, its row is deleted from the `accounts` table and a database trigger cleans up all linked rows from the `authtokens`, `extras`, and `grants` tables.

Password Security

One thing to note is that while credentials (usually usernames and passwords) are stored in a central database under */data/system/* that is only accessible to system applications, credentials are not encrypted; encrypting or otherwise protecting credentials is left to the authenticator module to implement as necessary. In fact, if you have a rooted device, you'll likely find that a listing of the contents of the accounts table will show certain passwords in cleartext, especially for the stock email application (the `com.android.email` or `com.google.android.email` package). For example, in Listing 8-2, the strings *password* ❷ and *pass1234* ❸ are the cleartext passwords for a POP account used by the stock application and a custom *com.example.account* account, respectively.

NOTE *Email applications may need to store the password instead of a password hash or an authentication token in order to support several challenge-response authentication methods that take the password as input, such as DIGEST-MD5 and CRAM-MD5.*

Because the `AccountManger.getPassword()` method can be called only by apps with the same UID as the account's authenticator, cleartext passwords are not accessible to other applications at runtime, but they may be included in backups or device dumps. In order to avoid this potential security risk, applications can encrypt passwords with a device-specific key or choose to replace a password with a revokable master token after initial authentication succeeds. For example, the official Twitter client does not store the user password in the `accounts` table, but only saves obtained authentication tokens (in the `authtokens` table). Google accounts are another example (account type *com.google*): as shown in "The Google Login Service" on page 206, instead of the user password, Google accounts store a master token that is exchanged for service-specific authentication tokens.

Multi-User Support

Recall from Chapter 4 that on multi-user devices, Android allows each user to have their own set of applications, application data, and system settings. This user isolation extends to online accounts as well and users can have their own accounts registered with the system's account manager service. Android 4.3 added support for restricted profiles, which are not fully independent users but share installed applications with the primary user. Additionally, restricted profiles can have a number of restrictions applied. Apps that use the `AccountManager` APIs can add explicit support for restricted profiles, thus allowing restricted profiles to see and use a subset of the primary user's accounts within supported apps. We explain this feature in detail in "Shared Accounts" below.

The following sections discuss how Android implements account isolation and sharing on multi-user devices.

Per-User Account Databases

As mentioned in "The Accounts Database" on page 198, the accounts databases that `AccountManagerServices` uses to store account information and cache authentication tokens are stored in each user's system directory in */data/system/users/<user ID>/accounts.db*. This allows each user to have dedicated account storage, and different users might even have separate instances of the same type of online account. Aside from the database location, everything else works in exactly the same way as it does for the owner user, including permissions, access grants, and so on. When a user is removed, the system deletes all of its data, including the accounts database.

Shared Accounts

Primary user accounts are shared with a restricted profile by simply cloning the account data into the restricted profile's accounts database. Thus, restricted profiles do not access the primary user's account data directly, but have their own copy. When a new restricted profile is added, the name and type of all current accounts of the primary user are copied into the `shared_accounts` table of the restricted profile's accounts database. However, because the new user is not started yet, the `accounts` table is empty at this point and the shared accounts are not yet usable.

The `shared_accounts` table has the same structure as the `accounts` table, without the `password` column. It might look like Listing 8-6 for a restricted profile.

```
sqlite> select * from shared_accounts;
_id|name              |type
1  |user1@gmail.com   |com.google
2  |user1@example.com|com.google.android.pop3
3  |example_user      |com.example.account
```

Listing 8-6: Contents of the shared_accounts table

Shared accounts are not cloned directly by copying data from the owner's `accounts` table; instead, cloning is performed via the authenticator that declared the account. By default, the `AbstractAccountAuthenticator`, which all authenticator classes derive from, does not support account cloning.

Implementations that want to support shared accounts for restricted profiles need to do so explicitly, by overriding a couple of methods that were introduced in Android 4.3, along with restricted profile support: `getAccountCredentialsForCloning()`, which returns a `Bundle` containing all data needed to clone the account, and `addAccountFromCredentials()`, which receives this `Bundle` as a parameter and is responsible for creating the account based on credentials in the Bundle. The AccountManagerService delays the cloning of a shared account until a restricted user is actually started. If the owner user adds any new accounts, they are added to the shared_accounts table and similarly cloned.

Even when accounts are successfully cloned, they may not be available to an application started by a restricted profile. Recall from Chapter 4 that if an application wants to support shared accounts, it must explicitly declare the account type it requires with the restrictedAccountType attribute of the <application> manifest tag. The AccountManagerServices uses the value of the restrictedAccountType attribute to filter accounts before passing them to applications running within a restricted profile. As of this writing, an application can declare only one type of account with this attribute.

NOTE *Secondary users do not share accounts with the owner, and therefore their* shared_accounts *tables are always empty and owner accounts are never cloned.*

Adding an Authenticator Module

In "Authenticator Modules" on page 194, we showed that an authentcator module is a bound service that implements the android.accounts.IAccountAuthenticator AIDL interface and which can be bound to by using the *android.accounts.AccountAuthenticator* intent action. In this section, we'll show how an application can implement and declare an authenticator module.

Most of the authenticator logic, including adding accounts, checking user-supplied credentials, and fetching authentication tokens, is implemented in an authenticator class derived from the base class that Android provides—namely, AbstractAccountAuthenticator.[3] The authenticator class needs to provide implementation of all abstract methods, but if not all functionality is needed, implemented methods can return null or throw UnsupportedOperationException. In order to store the account password, an implementation should implement at least the addAccount() method and display a UI that collects the password from the user. The password can then be added to the accounts database by calling the addAccountExplicitly() method of AccountManager. Activities that implement credential collection and login can extend from the AccountAuthenticatorActivity,[4] which provides a convenience method to pass back collected credentials to the AccountManager.

NOTE *Remember that the* addAccountExplicitly() *method does not encrypt or otherwise protect the password that is stored in cleartext by default. If required, encryption should be implemented separately, and the encrypted password or token should be passed to* addAccountExplicitly() *instead of the cleartext version.*

---

3. Google, *Android API Reference*, "AbstractAccountAuthenticator," *http://developer.android.com/reference/android/accounts/AbstractAccountAuthenticator.html*

4. Google, *Android API Reference*, "AccountAuthenticatorActivity," *http://developer.android.com/reference/android/accounts/AccountAuthenticatorActivity.html*

Once you have an account authenticator implementation, you simply create a service that returns its Binder interface when invoked with the *android.accounts.AccountAuthenticator* intent action, as shown in Listing 8-7 (`AbstractAccountAuthenticator` method implementations have been omitted).

```
public class ExampleAuthenticatorService extends Service {

    public static class ExampleAuthenticator extends
            AbstractAccountAuthenticator{
        // ...
    }

    private ExampleAuthenticator authenticator;

    @Override
    public void onCreate() {
        super.onCreate();
        authenticator = new ExampleAuthenticator(this);
    }

    @Override
    public IBinder onBind(Intent intent) {
        if (AccountManager.ACTION_AUTHENTICATOR_INTENT.equals(intent.
                getAction())) {
            return authenticator.getIBinder();
        }
        return null;
    }
}
```

Listing 8-7: Account authenticator service implementation

In order to be picked up by the `AccountAuthenticatorCache` and made available via the `AccountManagerService`, the service needs to declare the *android.accounts.AccountAuthenticator* intent action and matching metadata as shown in Listing 8-8. Permissions needed to access accounts and tokens need to be added to the manifest as well. In this example, we only add the `AUTHENTICATE_ACCOUNTS` permission, which is the minimum required in order to be able to add an account with `addAccountExplicitly()`.

```
<?xml version="1.0" encoding="utf-8"?>
<manifest xmlns:android="http://schemas.android.com/apk/res/android"
    package="com.example.app"
    android:versionCode="1" android:versionName="1.0" >

    <uses-permission android:name="android.permission.AUTHENTICATE_ACCOUNTS" />

    <application ...>
        --snip--
        <service android:name=".ExampleAuthenticatorService" >
            <intent-filter>
                <action android:name="android.accounts.AccountAuthenticator" />
            </intent-filter>
```

```
        <meta-data
            android:name="android.accounts.AccountAuthenticator"
            android:resource="@xml/authenticator" />
    </service>
  </application>
</manifest>
```

Listing 8-8: Declaring an account authenticator service in AndroidManifest.xml

Finally, the account type, label, and icons must be declared in the referenced XML resource file as shown in Listing 8-9. Here, the account type is *com.example.account* and we're simply using the app icon as the account icon.

```
<?xml version="1.0" encoding="utf-8"?>
<account-authenticator
    xmlns:android="http://schemas.android.com/apk/res/android"
    android:accountType="com.example.account"
    android:label="@string/account_label"
    android:icon="@drawable/ic_launcher"
    android:smallIcon="@drawable/ic_launcher"/>
```

Listing 8-9: Declaring account metadata in an XML resource file

After the application that declares our new account is installed, *com.example.account* accounts can be added via the `AccountManager` API or the system Settings UI by selecting **Add an account**. The new account should show up in the list of supported accounts, as shown in Figure 8-3.

Custom accounts can be used for convenience only by the declaring application, or when creating a sync adapter, which requires a dedicated account. In order to allow third-party applications to authenticate using your custom account, you must implement authentication tokens, because as we saw in "Listing and Authenticating Accounts" on page 196, third-party applications cannot access an account password via the `AccountManager.getPassword()` API, unless they are signed with the same key and certificate as the application hosting the target account's authenticator module.

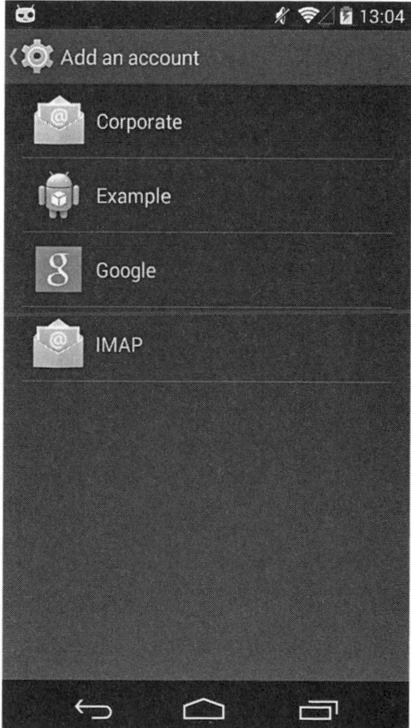

Figure 8-3: Adding a custom account via the system Settings UI

Google Accounts Support

The main goal of Android's account management facility is to make it easier to integrate online services into the OS, and to allow for seamless access to user data via background synchronization. The first versions of the system account management service were built to support Android integration with Google online services, and the service was later decoupled and made part of the OS. In Android versions 2.0 and later, Google account and online service support is bundled as a set of components that provide account authenticators (for the *com.google* account type) and sync adapters (for Gmail, Calendar, contacts, and so on), using standard OS APIs. However, there are a few notable differences from other third-party authenticator modules and sync adapters:

- The Google accounts components are bundled with the system and thus are granted extra permissions.
- A lot of the actual functionality is implemented on the server side.
- The account authenticator does not store passwords in plain text on the device.

The Google Login Service

The two main components that implement Google account and service support are the Google Services Framework (GSF) and the Google Login Service (GLS, displayed as *Google Account Manager* in recent versions). The former provides common services to all Google apps, such as centralized settings and feature toggle management, while the latter implements the authentication provider for Google accounts and will be the main topic of this section.

Google provides numerous online services, and supports a handful of different methods to authenticate to those services, both via a user-facing web UI and several dedicated authentication APIs. Android's Google Login Service, however, doesn't call those public authentication APIs directly, but rather via a dedicated online service, which lives at *https://android.clients.google.com*. It has endpoints both for authentication, authorization token issuing, and different data feeds (mail, calendar, and so on) that are used for data synchronization.

While a lot of the authentication and authorization logic is implemented on the server side, some sort of locally stored credentials are also required, especially for background syncing. On-device credential management is one of the services GLS provides, and while as of this writing there is no source code or reference documentation publicly available, we can observe what data GLS stores on the device and infer how authentication is implemented.

As mentioned earlier, GLS plugs into the system account framework, so cached credentials, tokens, and associated extra data are stored in the system's accounts database of the current user, just as it is for other account types. Unlike most other applications, however, GLS doesn't store Google account passwords directly. Instead, in place of a password, GLS stores an opaque master token (probably some form of an OAuth refresh token) in the `password` column of the `accounts` table and exchanges it for authentication tokens for different Google services by calling an associated web service endpoint. The token is obtained when a Google account is first added to the device by sending the username and password entered in the sign-in activity shown in Figure 8-4.

If the target Google account is using the default password-only authentication method and the correct password is entered, the GLS online service returns the master token and the account is added to the user's accounts database. All subsequent authentication requests use the master token to obtain service- or scope-specific tokens that are used for synchronization or automatic web login. If the Google account is set to use two-factor authentication (2FA), the user is prompted to enter their one-time password (OTP, called *verification code* in the web UI) in an embedded web view like the one shown in Figure 8-5.

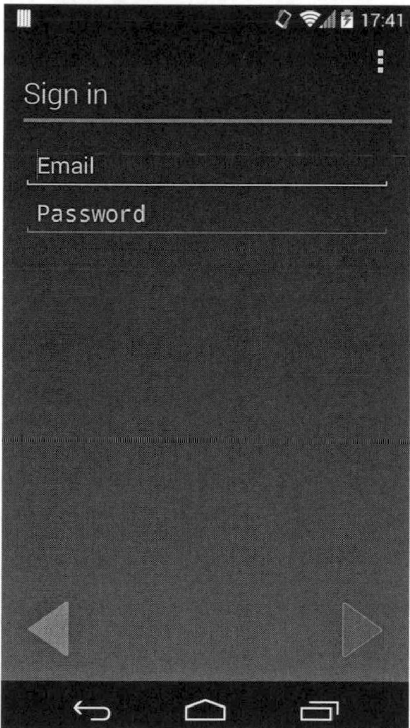

Figure 8-4: Google account sign-in activity

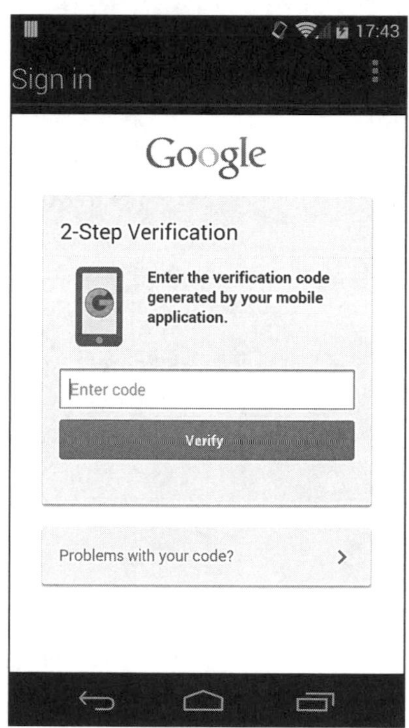

Figure 8-5: One-time password entry as part of adding a Google account

If the OTP is successfully verified, the master token is added to the accounts database and a list of services that support background synchronization is shown (see Figure 8-6).

Note that only the initial login process differs for Google accounts that have 2FA enabled: all subsequent authentication requests use the cached master token and do not require entering an OTP. Thus, once cached, the master token grants full access to a Google account and can be used not only for data synchronization, but for other types of account access as well, including web login.

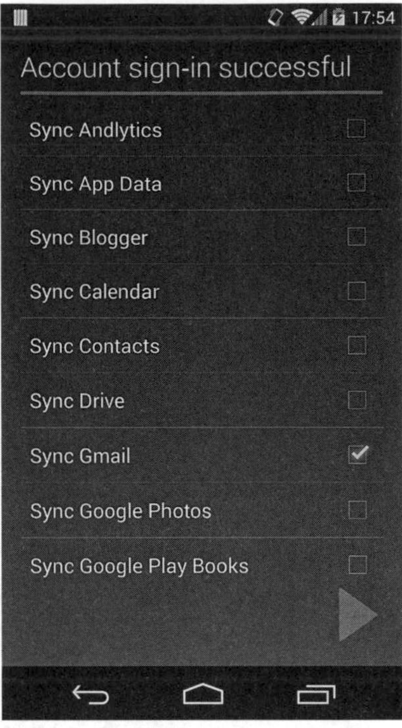

Figure 8-6: List of Google services that support background synchronization

While it's very handy to have an all-powerful authentication token cached, this trade-off in favor of convenience has enabled several attacks on Google accounts, and as a result many Google services now require additional authentication when sensitive data is displayed or account settings are changed. The master token can be invalidated by changing the Google account password, by enabling two-factor authentication, or by removing the Android device from the *Account Permissions* page of the associated Google account (see Figure 8-7). Any of these actions will require the user to reauthenticate with their new credentials on the device the next time it tries to get a Google authentication token via the `AccountManager` API.

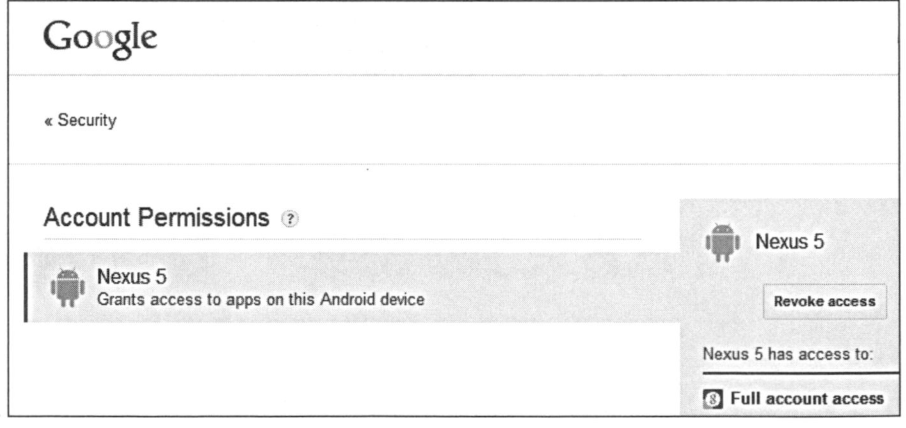

Figure 8-7: Android device entry in the Account Permissions page of a Google account

Google Services Authentication and Authorization

Besides user-facing online services with a web UI such as Gmail, Google Calendar and, of course, search, Google provides programmatic access to many of its services via different web APIs. Most of these require authentication, either in order to be able to access a subset of a particular user's data, or for quota and billing purposes. Several standard or Google-proprietary authentication and authorization methods have been used over the years, with the current trend being to migrate everything to OAuth 2.0[5] and OpenID Connect.[6] However, many services still use older, proprietary protocols, so we'll briefly look into those as well.

Most authentication protocols have two variations: one for web applications and one for the so-called installed applications. Web applications run in a browser and are expected to be able to take advantage of all standard browser features including rich UI, free-form user interaction, cookie store, and the ability to follow redirects. Installed applications, on the other hand, don't have a native way to preserve session information, and may not have the full web capabilities of a browser. Android native applications (mostly) fall into the "installed applications" category, so let's see what protocols are available for them.

ClientLogin

The oldest and, as of this writing, still widely used authorization protocol for installed applications is *ClientLogin*.[7] This protocol assumes that the application has access to the user's account name and password and lets you get an authorization token for a particular service that can be saved and used for accessing that service on behalf of the user. Services are identified by proprietary service names, such as *cl* for Google Calendar and *ah* for Google App engine. You'll find a list of many supported service names in the Google Data API reference,[8] but here are a few Android-specific ones not listed in the reference: *ac2dm*, *android*, *androidsecure*, *androiddeveloper*, and *androidmarket*.

The authorization tokens for these services can be fairly long-lived (up to two weeks), but cannot be refreshed and the application must obtain a new token when the current token expires. Unfortunately, there is no way to validate a token short of accessing the associated service: if you get an *OK* HTTP status (200) the token is valid, but if 403 is returned you need to consult the additional error code and retry or get a new token.

Another limitation of ClientLogin authorization tokens is that they don't offer fine-grained access to a service's resources: access is all or nothing, and you cannot specify read-only access or access to a particular resource only.

---

5. D. Hardt, *The OAuth 2.0 Authorization Framework*, *http://tools.ietf.org/html/rfc6749*

6. N. Sakimura et al., *OpenID Connect Core 1.0*, *http://openid.net/specs/openid-connect-core-1_0.html*

7. Google, *Google Accounts Authentication and Authorization*, "ClientLogin for Installed Applications," *https://developers.google.com/accounts/docs/AuthForInstalledApps*

8. Google, *Google Data APIs*, "Frequently Asked Questions," *https://developers.google.com/gdata/faq#clientlogin*

The biggest drawback for mobile apps though is that ClientLogin requires access to the actual user password. Therefore, unless you want to force users to enter their password each time a new token is required, the password must be saved on the device, which poses various problems and potential security issues. Android avoids storing the raw password by storing a master token on the device and uses GLS and the associated online service to exchange the master token for ClientLogin tokens. Getting a token is as simple as calling the appropriate `AccountManger` method, which either returns a cached token or issues an API request to fetch a fresh one.

Despite its many limitations, the ClientLogin protocol is easy to understand and straightforward to implement, so it has been widely used. It was officially deprecated in April 2012 though, and apps using it are encouraged to migrate to OAuth 2.0.

OAuth 2.0

The OAuth 2.0 authorization framework became an official Internet standard in late 2012. It defines different *authorization flows* for different use cases, but we won't try to present all of them here. We'll only discuss how OAuth 2.0 relates to native mobile applications. (For more detail on the actual protocol, see RFC 6749.)

The OAuth 2.0 specification defines four basic flows for getting an authorization token for a resource. It also defines two that don't require the client (in our scenario, an Android app) to directly handle user credentials (such as the Google account username and password), namely the *authorization code grant* flow and the *implicit grant* flow. Both of these require the authorization server (Google's) to authenticate the resource owner (the Android app user) in order to establish whether to grant or deny the access request (say, read-only access to profile information). In a typical browser-based web application, this is straightforward: the user is redirected to an authentication page, then to an access grant page that basically says "Do you allow app X to access data Y and Z?" If the user agrees, another redirect, which includes an authorization token, takes the user back to the original application. The browser simply needs to pass the token in the next request in order to gain access to the target resource.

Things are not so simple with a native app. A native app can either use the system browser to handle the grant permission step, or embed a `WebView` or a similar control in the app's UI. Using the system browser requires launching a third-party application (the browser), detecting success or failure, and finally figuring out a way to return the token back to the calling application. Embedding a `WebView` is a bit more user-friendly, as it doesn't involve switching back and forth between applications, but still results in showing a non-native web UI, and requires complex code to detect success and extract the access token. Neither option is ideal, and both are confusing to the user.

This integration complexity and UI impedance mismatch are the problems that OAuth 2.0 support via native Android APIs aims to solve. Android offers two APIs that can be used to obtain OAuth 2.0 tokens: the platform `AccountManager` via the special *oauth2:scope* token type syntax, and Google Play Services (discussed in the next section). When using either of those APIs to obtain a token, user authentication is implemented transparently by passing the saved master token to the server-side component of GLS, which produces the native `AccountManager` access grant dialog (see Figure 8-8) instead of a `WebView` with a permission grant page. If you grant token access to the requesting application, a second request is sent to convey this to the server, which returns the requested token. The access token is then directly delivered to the app, without passing through an intermediary component such as a `WebView`. This is essentially the same flow as for web applications, except that it doesn't require context switching from native to browser and back, and it's much more user-friendly. Of course, this native authorization flow only works for Google accounts, and writing a client for some other online service that uses OAuth 2.0 still requires integrating its web interface into your app. For example, Twitter clients often use `WebView` to process the permission grant callback URL returned by the Twitter API.

Google Play Services

Google Play Services (GPS)[9] was announced at Google I/O 2012 as an easy-to-use platform that offers third-party Android apps a way to integrate with Google products. Since then, it has grown into a giant all-in-one package (with over 14,000 Java methods!) that provides access to Google APIs and proprietary OS extensions.

As mentioned in the previous section, getting OAuth 2.0 tokens via the standard `AccountManager` interface has been supported since Android 2.2 and higher, but it didn't work reliably across different Android builds because their different bundled GLS versions resulted in slightly different behavior between devices. Additionally, the permission grant dialog shown when requesting a token was not particularly user friendly because it showed the raw OAuth 2.0 scope in some cases, which meant little to most users (see Figure 8-8). While

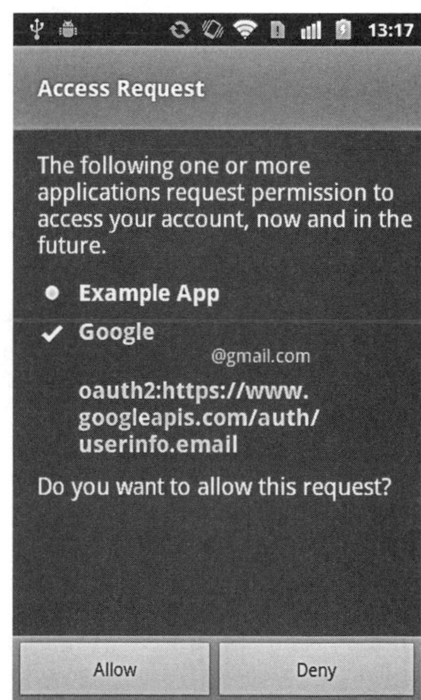

Figure 8-8: OAuth token access request dialog

9. Google, "Google Play Services," *http://developer.android.com/google/play-services/index.html*

human-readable aliases for certain scopes were partially supported (for example, the *Manage your tasks* string was displayed instead of the raw OAuth scope *oauth2:https://www.googleapis.com/auth/tasks* in some versions), that solution was neither ideal nor universally available, as it too depended on the pre-installed GLS version.

Generally, while Android's account management framework is well-integrated into the OS and extensible via third-party authenticator modules, its API is not particularly flexible, and adding support for multi-step authentication or authorization flows such as those used in OAuth 2.0 is far from straightforward. GPS manages to achieve this with the help of an online service, which does its best to hide the complexity of OAuth 2.0 and provides web APIs compatible with Android's account management framework. We discuss the details of this integration next.

GPS adds universal supports for displaying a user-friendly OAuth scope description by making token issuance a two-step process:

1. Much like before, the first request includes the account name, master token, and requested service, in the *oauth2:scope* format. GPS adds two new parameters to the request: the app's package name and the SHA-1 hash of its signing certificate. The response includes some human-readable details about the requested scope and requesting application, which GPS shows in a permission grant dialog like the one shown in Figure 8-9.
2. If the user grants permission, that decision is recorded in the `extras` table in a proprietary format that includes the requesting app's package name, signing certificate hash, and granted OAuth 2.0 scope. (Note that the `grants` table is not used.) GPS then resends the authorization request, setting the *has_permission* parameter to 1. On success, this results in an OAuth 2.0 token and its expiration date in the response. The expiration date is saved in the `extras` table, and the token is cached in the `authtokens` table in a similar format.

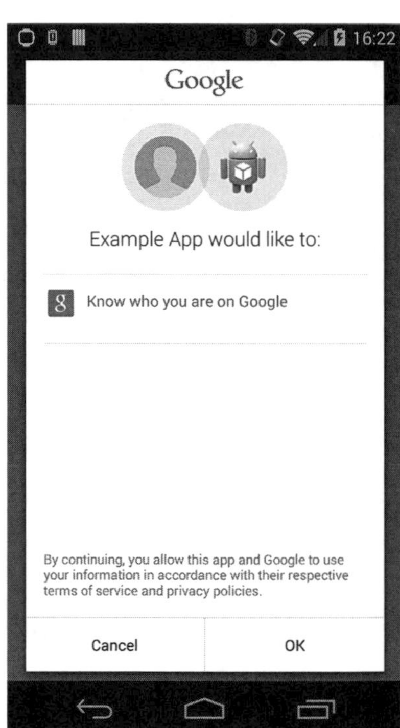

Figure 8-9: Google Play Services account access permission dialog

The GPS app has the same shared user ID as the GSF and GLS packages (*com.google.uid.shared*), so it can directly interact with those services. This allows it, among other things, to directly get and write Google account credentials and tokens to the accounts database. As can be expected, GPS runs in a remote service that's accessed by a client library which is linked into apps that use GPS. The major selling point against the legacy `AccountManager` API is that while its underlying authenticator modules (GLS and GSF) are part of the system (and as such cannot be updated without an OTA), GPS is a user-installable app that can be easily updated via Google Play. In fact, it is auto-updating, so app developers presumably won't have to rely on users to update it if they want to use newer features (unless GPS is disabled altogether). This update mechanism is designed to provide "agility in rolling out new platform capabilities," but as GPS has come to integrate very diverse APIs and functionalities that require extensive testing, updates have been infrequent. That said, if your app uses OAuth 2.0 tokens to authenticate to Google APIs (the preferred method as of this writing), you should definitely consider using GPS over "raw" `AccountManager` access.

NOTE *In order to be able to actually use a Google API, you must register your app's package name and signing key in Google's API console. The registration lets services validating the token query Google about what app the token was issued for, thus identifying the calling app. This validation process has one subtle but important side effect: you don't have to embed an API key in your app and send it with every request. Of course, for a third-party published app, you can easily discover both the package name and the signing certificate so it's not particularly hard to get a token issued in the name of some other app (though not via the official API, of course).*

Summary

Android provides a centralized registry of user online accounts via the `AccountManager` class, which lets you get tokens for existing accounts without having to handle the raw user credentials and register your own custom account types. Registering a custom account type gives you access to powerful system features, such as authentication token caching and automatic background synchronization. Google experience devices include built-in support for Google accounts, which lets third-party apps access Google online services without having to directly request authentication information from the user. The Google Play Services app and companion client library further improve support for Google accounts by making it easy to use OAuth 2.0 tokens from third-party applications.

9

ENTERPRISE SECURITY

Initial Android versions were mostly consumer-oriented, with limited enterprise features. However, as the platform has grown in popularity, Android devices have entered the workplace and are increasingly used to access corporate email, customer information, and other company data. As a result of this trend, the need for increased platform security and tools that allow effective management of employee devices has steadily grown. While Android's primary focus remains general-purpose consumer devices, recent versions have introduced numerous enterprise features and Android will likely become even more enterprise-friendly as it develops.

In this chapter, we discuss Android's major enterprise-oriented features and demonstrate how they can be used to both increase device security and provide centralized device policy management. We'll begin with device administration, and show how it can be integrated into third-party applications. We then look into Android's VPN support and describe the APIs that allow new VPN solutions to be developed as third-party, user-installed applications. Next we show how Android implements different authentication methods supported by the EAP authentication framework and describe how it manages credentials. Finally, we demonstrate how to add an EAP profile programmatically using the extended Wi-Fi management APIs added in Android 4.3.

Device Administration

Android 2.2 introduced support for a Device Administration API, which makes it possible to develop applications that can both enforce a system-wide security policy and dynamically adapt their features based on the device's current security level. Such applications are called *device administrators*. Device administrators must be explicitly enabled in the device's security settings and cannot be uninstalled if they are active. When enabled, they're granted special privileges that allow them to lock the device, change the lockscreen password, and even wipe the device (delete all user data). Device administrators are often coupled with a specific type of enterprise account (such as a Microsoft Exchange or Google Apps account), which allows enterprise administrators to control access to corporate data by allowing access only to devices that conform to the required security policy. Security policies can be static and built into the device administrator application, or they can be configured on the server side and sent to the device as part of a provisioning or synchronization protocol.

As of version 4.4, Android supports the policy types listed in Table 9-1. The policy constants are defined in the `DeviceAdminInfo` class.[1]

Table 9-1: Supported Device Administration Policies

Policy Constant/XML Tag	Value (bit to set)	Description	API Level
`USES_POLICY_LIMIT_PASSWORD` `<limit-password>`	0	Limit the passwords that the user can select by setting a minimum length or complexity.	8
`USES_POLICY_WATCH_LOGIN` `<watch-login>`	1	Watch login attempts by a user.	8
`USES_POLICY_RESET_PASSWORD` `<reset-password>`	2	Reset a user's password.	8
`USES_POLICY_FORCE_LOCK` `<force-lock>`	3	Force the device to lock, or limit the maximum lock timeout.	8
`USES_POLICY_WIPE_DATA` `<wipe-data>`	4	Factory reset the device, erasing all user data.	8
`USES_POLICY_SETS_GLOBAL_PROXY` `<set-global-proxy>`	5	Specify the device global proxy. (This is hidden from SDK applications.)	9

1. Google, *Android APIs Reference*, "DeviceAdminInfo," *https://developer.android.com/reference/android/app/admin/DeviceAdminInfo.html*

Policy Constant/XML Tag	Value (bit to set)	Description	API Level
`USES_POLICY_EXPIRE_PASSWORD` `<expire-password>`	6	Force the user to change their password after an administrator-defined time limit.	11
`USES_ENCRYPTED_STORAGE` `<encrypted-storage>`	7	Require stored data to be encrypted.	11
`USES_POLICY_DISABLE_CAMERA` `<disable-camera>`	8	Disable the use of all device cameras.	14
`USES_POLICY_DISABLE_KEYGUARD_FEATURES` `<disable-keyguard-features>`	9	Disable the use of keyguard features such as lockscreen widgets or camera support.	17

Each device administration application must list the policies it intends to use in a metadata file (see "Privilege Management" on page 218 for details). The list of supported policies is displayed to the user when they activate the administrator app, as shown in Figure 9-1.

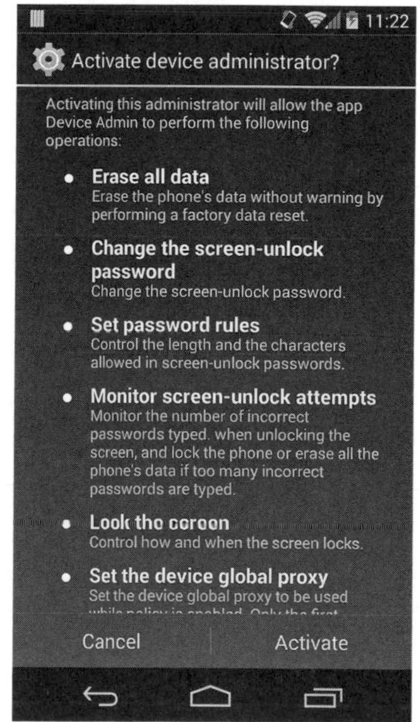

Figure 9-1: Device administrator activation screen

Implementation

Now that we know which policies can be enforced with the Device Administration API, let's look at the internal implementation. Like most public Android APIs, a manager class called `DevicePolicyManager`[2] exposes part of the functionality of the underlying system service, `DevicePolicyManagerService`. However, because the `DevicePolicyManager` facade class defines constants and translates service exceptions to return codes but otherwise adds little functionality, we'll focus on the `DevicePolicyManagerService` class.

Like most system services, `DevicePolicyManagerService` is started by and runs within the *system_server* process as the *system* user, and thus can execute almost all Android privileged actions. Unlike most system services,

2. Google, *Android APIs Reference*, "DevicePolicyManager," *https://developer.android.com/reference/android/app/admin/DevicePolicyManager.html*

it can grant access to certain privileged actions (such as changing the lockscreen password) to third-party applications, which do not need to hold any special system permissions. This makes it possible for users to enable and disable device administrators on demand, and guarantees that device administrators can only enforce policies that they have explicitly declared. However, this level of flexibility cannot be easily implemented with standard Android permissions that are only granted at install time and cannot be revoked (with some exceptions, as discussed in Chapter 2). Therefore, `DevicePolicyManagerService` employs a different method for privilege management.

Another interesting aspect of Android's device administration implementation relates to how policies are managed and enforced. We describe device administrator privilege management and policy enforcement in detail next.

Privilege Management

At runtime, the `DevicePolicyManagerService` keeps an internal, on-memory list of policy structures for each device user. (Policies are also persisted on disk in an XML file, as described in the next section.)

Each policy structure contains the currently effective policy for a certain user and a list of metadata about each active device administrator. Because each user can enable more than one application with device administrator functionality, the currently active policy is calculated by selecting the strictest defined policy among all administrators. The metadata about each active device administrator contains information about the declaring application, and a list of declared policies (represented by a bitmask).

The `DevicePolicyManagerService` decides whether to grant access to privileged operations to a calling application based on its internal list of active policies: if the calling application is currently an active device administrator, and it has requested the policy that corresponds to the current request (API call), only then is the request granted and the operation executed. In order to confirm that an active administrator component really belongs to the calling application, `DevicePolicyManagerService` compares the UID of the calling process (returned by `Binder.getCallingUid()`) with the UID associated with the target administrator component. For example, an application that calls the `resetPassword()` needs to be an active device administrator, have the same UID as the registered administrator component, and have requested the `USES_POLICY_RESET_PASSWORD` policy in order for the call to succeed.

Policies are requested by adding an XML resource file that lists all policies that a device administrator application wants to use as children of the `<uses-policies>` tag. Before a device administrator is activated, the system parses the XML file and displays a dialog similar to the one in Figure 9-1, allowing the user to review the requested policies before enabling the administrator. Much like Android permissions, administrator policies are granted on an all-or-nothing basis, and there is no way to selectively enable only certain policies. A resource file that requests all policies might look like Listing 9-1 (for the policy corresponding to each tag, see the first column of Table 9-1). You can find more details about adding this file to a device administrator application in "Adding a Device Administrator" on page 223.

```
<?xml version="1.0" encoding="utf-8"?>
<device-admin xmlns:android="http://schemas.android.com/apk/res/android">
    <uses-policies>
        <limit-password />
        <watch-login />
        <reset-password />
        <force-lock />
        <wipe-data />
        <expire-password />
        <encrypted-storage />
        <disable-camera />
        <disable-keyguard-features />
        <set-global-proxy />
    </uses-policies>
</device-admin>
```

Listing 9-1: Declaring policies in a device administrator application

In order to be notified about policy-related system events and to be allowed access to the Device Administration API, device administrators must be activated first. This is achieved by calling the `setActiveAdmin()` method of the `DevicePolicyManagerService`. Because this method requires the `MANAGE_DEVICE_ADMINS` permission, which is a system signature permission, only system applications can add a device administrator without user interaction.

User-installed device administrator applications can only request to be activated by starting the `ACTION_ADD_DEVICE_ADMIN` implicit intent with code similar to Listing 9-2. The only handler for this intent is the system Settings application, which holds the `MANAGE_DEVICE_ADMINS` permission. Upon receiving the intent, the Settings applications checks whether the requesting application is a valid device administrator, extracts the requested policies, and builds the confirmation dialog shown in Figure 9-1. The user pressing the Activate button calls the `setActiveAdmin()` method, which adds the application to the list of active administrators for the current device user.

```
Intent intent = new Intent(DevicePolicyManager.ACTION_ADD_DEVICE_ADMIN);
ComponentName admin = new ComponentName(this, MyDeviceAdminReceiver.class);
intent.putExtra(DevicePolicyManager.EXTRA_DEVICE_ADMIN, admin);
intent.putExtra(DevicePolicyManager.EXTRA_ADD_EXPLANATION,
                "Required for corporate email access.");
startActivityForResult(intent, REQUEST_CODE_ENABLE_ADMIN);
```

Listing 9-2: Requesting device administrator activation

Policy Persistence

When a device administrator is activated, deactivated, or its policies are updated, changes are written to the *device_policies.xml* file for the target user. For the owner user, that file is stored under */data/system/*, and for all other users it's written to the user's system directory (*/data/users/<user-ID>/*). The file is owned by and only modifiable by the *system* user (file permissions 0600).

The *device_policies.xml* file contains information about each active administrator and its policies, as well some global information about the current lockscreen password. The file might look like Listing 9-3.

```
<?xml version='1.0' encoding='utf-8' standalone='yes' ?>
<policies>
  <admin name="com.google.android.gms/com.google.android.gms.mdm.receivers.MdmDeviceAdminReceiver">❶
    <policies flags="28" />
  </admin>
  <admin name="com.example.android.apis/com.example.android.apis.app.DeviceAdminSampleReceiver">❷
    <policies flags="1023" />❸
    <password-quality value="327680" />❹
    <min-password-length value="6" />
    <min-password-letters value="2" />
    <min-password-numeric value="2" />
    <max-time-to-unlock value="300000" />
    <max-failed-password-wipe value="100" />
    <encryption-requested value="true" />
    <disable-camera value="true" />
    <disable-keyguard-features value="1" />
</admin>
<admin name="com.android.email/com.android.email.SecurityPolicy$PolicyAdmin">❺
  <policies flags="475" />
</admin>
<password-owner value="10076" />❻
<active-password quality="327680" length="6"
                 uppercase="0" lowercase="3"
                 letters="3" numeric="3" symbols="0" nonletter="3" />❼
</policies>
```

Listing 9-3: Contents of the devices_policies.xml *file*

This example has three active device administrators, each represented by an `<admin>` element (❶, ❷, and ❺). The policies of each administrator app are stored in the `flags` attribute of the `<policies>` tag ❸.

A policy is considered enabled if its corresponding bit is set (see the Value column of Table 9-1). For example, because the *DeviceAdminSample* application has requested all currently available policies, its `flags` attribute has the value 1023 (0x3FF, or 1111111111 in binary).

If the administrator defines password quality restrictions (for example, alphanumeric or complex), they are persisted as the `value` attribute of the `<password-quality>` tag ❹. In this example, the value 327680 (0x50000) corresponds to `PASSWORD_QUALITY_ALPHANUMERIC`. (Password quality constants are defined in the `DevicePolicyManager` class.)

The values of other policy requirements, such as password length and device encryption, are also stored as children of each `<admin>` element. If the password has been set programmatically by using the `resetPassword()` method, *device_policies.xml* contains a `<password-owner>` tag that stores the UID of the application that sets the password in its `value` attribute ❻. Finally, the `<active-password>` tag contains details about the complexity of the current password ❼.

Policy Enforcement

Device administrator policies have different granularity and can be enforced either for the current user or for all users on a device. Some policies are not enforced by the system at all—the system only notifies the declaring administration application, which is then responsible for taking an appropriate action. In this section, we describe how each type of policy is implemented and enforced.

USES_POLICY_LIMIT_PASSWORD

After one or more password restrictions have been set, users cannot enter a password that does not fulfill the current policy. However, the system does not require passwords to be changed immediately, so the current password remains in effect until changed. Administrator applications can prompt the user for a new password by starting an implicit intent with the `DevicePolicyManager.ACTION_SET_NEW_PASSWORD` action.

Because each device user has a separate unlock password, password quality policies are applied per-user. When password quality is set, unlock methods that do not allow for a password of the desired quality are disabled. For example, setting password quality to `PASSWORD_QUALITY_ALPHANUMERIC` disables the Pattern and PIN unlock methods, as shown in Figure 9-2.

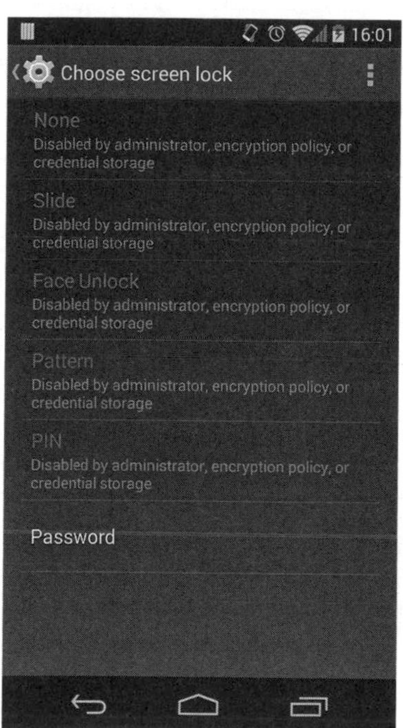

Figure 9-2: Setting a password quality policy disables incompatible unlock methods

USES_POLICY_WATCH_LOGIN

This policy enables device administrators to receive notifications about the outcome of login attempts. Notifications are sent with the `ACTION_PASSWORD_FAILED` and `ACTION_PASSWORD_SUCCEEDED` broadcasts. Broadcast receivers that derive from `DeviceAdminReceiver` are automatically notified via the `onPasswordFailed()` and `onPasswordSucceeded()` methods.

USES_POLICY_RESET_PASSWORD

This policy enables administrator applications to set the current user's password via the `resetPassword()` API. The specified password must satisfy the current password quality requirements and takes effect immediately. Note that if the device is encrypted, setting the lockscreen password for the owner user also changes the device encryption password. (Chapter 10 provides more detail on device encryption.)

USES_POLICY_FORCE_LOCK

This policy allows administrators to lock the device immediately by calling the `lockNow()` method, or to specify the maximum time for user inactivity until the device locks automatically via `setMaximumTimeToLock()`. Setting the maximum time to lock takes effect immediately and limits the inactivity sleep time that users can set via the system Display settings.

USES_POLICY_WIPE_DATA

This policy allows device administrators to wipe user data by calling the `wipeData()` API. Applications that also request the `USES_POLICY_WATCH_LOGIN` policy can set the number of failed login attempts before the device is wiped automatically via the `setMaximumFailedPasswordsForWipe()` API. When the number of failed passwords is set to a value greater than zero, the lockscreen implementation notifies the `DevicePolicyManagerService` and displays a warning dialog after each failed attempt, and triggers a data wipe once the threshold is reached. If the wipe is triggered by an unsuccessful login attempt by the owner user, a full device wipe is performed. If, on the other hand, the wipe is triggered by a secondary user, only that user (and any associated data) is deleted and the device switches to the owner user.

NOTE *Full device wipe is not immediate, but is implemented by writing a* `wipe_data` *command in the* cache *partition and rebooting into recovery mode. The recovery OS is responsible for executing the actual device wipe. Therefore, if the device has a custom recovery image that ignores the wipe command, or if the user manages to boot into a custom recovery and delete or modify the command file, the device wipe might not be executed. (Chapters 10 and 13 discuss recovery images in more detail.)*

USES_POLICY_SETS_GLOBAL_PROXY

As of Android 4.4, this policy is not available to third-party applications. It allows device administrators to set the global proxy server host (`Settings.Global.GLOBAL_HTTP_PROXY_HOST`), port (`GLOBAL_HTTP_PROXY_PORT`), and the list of excluded hosts (`GLOBAL_HTTP_PROXY_EXCLUSION_LIST`) by writing to the global system settings provider. Only the device owner is allowed to set global proxy settings.

USES_POLICY_EXPIRE_PASSWORD

This policy allows administrators to set the password expiration timeout via the `setPasswordExpirationTimeout()` API. If an expiration timeout is set, the system registers a daily alarm that checks for password expiration. If the password has already expired, `DevicePolicyManagerService` posts daily password change notifications until it is changed. Device administrators are notified about password expiration status via the `DeviceAdminReceiver.onPasswordExpiring()` method.

USES_ENCRYPTED_STORAGE

This policy allows administrators to request that device storage be encrypted via the `setStorageEncryption()` API. Only the owner user can request storage encryption. Requesting storage encryption does not automatically start the device encryption process if the device is not encrypted; device administrators must check the current storage status by using the `getStorageEncryptionStatus()` API (which checks the *ro.crypto.state* read-only system property), and start the encryption process. Device encryption can be kicked off by starting the associated system activity with the `ACTION_START_ENCRYPTION` implicit intent.

USES_POLICY_DISABLE_CAMERA

This policy allows device administrators to disable all cameras on the device via the `setCameraDisabled()` API. Camera is disabled by setting the *sys.secpolicy.camera.disabled* system property to 1. The native system `CameraService` checks this property and disallows all connections if it is set to 1, effectively disabling the camera for all users of the device.

USES_POLICY_DISABLE_KEYGUARD_FEATURES

This policy allows administrators to disable keyguard customizations such as lockscreen widgets by calling the `setKeyguardDisabledFeatures()` method. The system keyguard implementation checks if this policy is in effect and disables the corresponding features for the target user.

Adding a Device Administrator

As with other applications, device administrators can either be included in the system image or they can be installed by users. If an administrator is part of the system image, it can be set as the *device owner app* in Android 4.4 and later, which is a special kind of device admin that cannot be disabled by the user and cannot be uninstalled. In this section, we'll show how to implement a device admin app and then demonstrate how a system app can be set as the device owner.

Implementing a Device Administrator

A device administrator application needs to declare a broadcast receiver that requires the BIND_DEVICE_ADMIN permission (❶ in Listing 9-4), declares an XML resource file that lists the policies it uses ❷, and responds to the ACTION_DEVICE_ADMIN_ENABLED intent ❸. Listing 9-1 shows a sample policy declaration.

```
<?xml version="1.0" encoding="utf-8"?>
<manifest xmlns:android="http://schemas.android.com/apk/res/android"
    package="com.example.deviceadmin">
    --snip--
    <receiver android:name=".MyDeviceAdminReceiver"
        android:label="@string/device_admin"
        android:description="@string/device_admin_description"
        android:permission="android.permission.BIND_DEVICE_ADMIN">❶
        <meta-data android:name="android.app.device_admin"
                   android:resource="@xml/device_admin_policy" />❷
        <intent-filter>
            <action android:name="android.app.action.DEVICE_ADMIN_ENABLED" />❸
        </intent-filter>
    </receiver>
    --snip--
</manifest>
```

Listing 9-4: Device administrator broadcast receiver declaration

The Android SDK provides a base class that you can derive your receiver from, namely android.app.admin.DeviceAdminReceiver. This class defines a number of callback methods that you can override in order to handle the device policy-related broadcasts sent by the system. The default implementations are empty, but at a minimum you should override the onEnabled() and onDisabled() methods in order to be notified when the administrator is enabled or disabled. Device administrators cannot use any privileged APIs before onEnabled() is called or after onDisabled() is called.

You can use the isAdminActive() API at any time to see if an application is currently an active device administrator. As mentioned in "Privilege Management" on page 218, an administrator cannot activate itself automatically, but must start a system activity to prompt for user confirmation with code similar to Listing 9-2. However, when already active, an administrator can deactivate itself by calling the removeActiveAdmin() method.

NOTE *See the official Device Administration API guide[3] for more details and a full working example application.*

Setting the Device Owner

A device administrator application that's part of the system image (that is, its APK file is installed on the *system* partition) can be set as the device owner by

3. Google, *API Guides*, "Device Administration," *https://developer.android.com/guide/topics/admin/device-admin.html*

calling the setDeviceOwner(String packageName, String ownerName) method (not visible in the public SDK API). The first parameter in this method specifies the package name of the target application, and the second specifies the name of the owner to be displayed in the UI. While this method requires no special permissions, it can only be called before a device is provisioned (that is, if the global setting Settings.Global.DEVICE_PROVISIONED is set to 0), which means that it can only be called by system applications that execute as part of device initialization.

A successful call to this method writes a *device_owner.xml* file (like the one in Listing 9-5) to */data/system/*. Information about the current device owner can be obtained using the getDeviceOwner(), isDeviceOwner() (which is exposed as isDeviceOwnerApp() in the Android SDK API) and getDeviceOwnerName() methods.

```
<?xml version='1.0' encoding='utf-8' standalone='yes' ?>
<device-owner package="com.example.deviceadmin" name="Device Owner" />
```

Listing 9-5: Contents of the device_owner.xml *file*

When a device owner is activated, either as part of the provisioning process or by the user, it cannot be disabled and uninstalled, as shown in Figure 9-3.

Figure 9-3: A device owner administrator cannot be disabled.

Managed Devices

A device with an owner administrator installed is called a *managed device*, and it reacts differently to configuration changes that affect device security than unmanaged devices. As discussed in Chapters 6 and 7, Android allows users to install certificates in the system trust store either via the system Settings application, or by using third-party applications that call the `KeyChain` API. If there are user-installed certificates in the system trust store, as of version 4.4 Android shows a warning (see Figure 6-6 on page 161) notifying users that their communications can be monitored.

Enterprise networks often require trusted certificates (for example, the root certificate of a corporate PKI) to be installed in order to access enterprise services. Such certificates can be silently installed or removed by device administrators that hold the `MANAGE_CA_CERTIFICATES` system permissions via the `installCaCert()` and `uninstallCaCert()` methods of the `DevicePolicyManager` class (these methods are reserved for system applications and aren't visible in the public SDK API). If an additional trusted certificate is installed on a managed device, the network monitoring warning changes to a less scary information message, as shown in Figure 9-4.

Figure 9-4: Network monitoring information message shown on managed devices

Enterprise Account Integration

As mentioned in "Device Administration" on page 216, device administrator applications are often coupled with enterprise accounts, in order to allow some control over devices that access company data. In this section, we'll discuss two such implementations: one in the stock Email application, which works with Microsoft Exchange ActiveSync accounts, and the other in the dedicated Google Apps Device Policy application, which works with corporate Google accounts.

Microsoft Exchange ActiveSync

Microsoft Exchange ActiveSync (usually abbreviated as *EAS*) is a protocol that supports email, contacts, calendar, and task synchronization from a groupware server to a mobile device. It's supported both by Microsoft's own Exchange Server, and by most competing products, including Google Apps.

The Email application included in Android supports ActiveSync accounts and data synchronization via dedicated account authenticators (see Chapter 8) and sync adapters. In order to allow enterprise administrators to enforce a security policy on devices that access email and other corporate data, the Email application doesn't allow synchronization until the built-in device administrator is enabled by the user. The administrator can set lockscreen password rules, erase all data, require storage encryption, and disable device cameras, as shown in Figure 9-5. However, the policies are not built into the app but fetched from the service using the EAS Provision protocol.

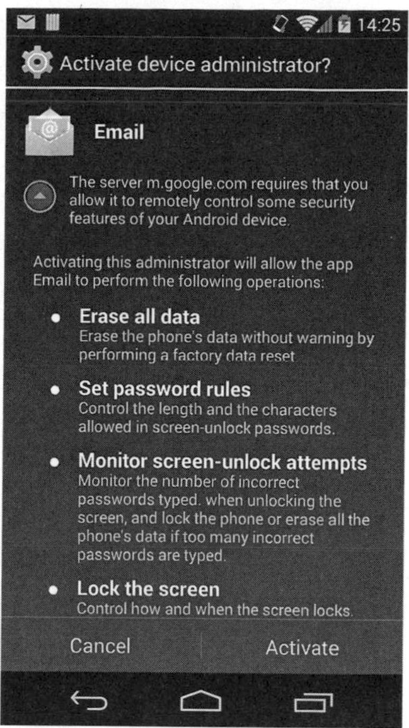

Figure 9-5: Device administrator policies required for using an EAS account

Google Apps

The corporate version of Google's Gmail service, Google Apps, also supports setting mobile device security policies. If the feature is enabled by the domain administrator, Google Apps account holders can also remotely locate, ring, lock, or wipe their Android devices. Domain administrators can also selectively delete a Google Apps account and all of its associated content from a managed device, without performing a full wipe. Both security policy enforcement and remote device management are implemented in the dedicated Google Apps Device Policy application (see ❺ in Listing 9-3 on page 220).

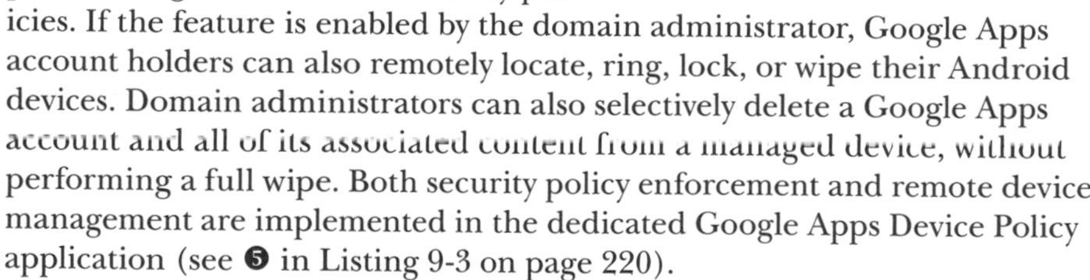

When first started, the application requests that the user enable the built-in device administrator and displays the current domain policy settings as shown in Figure 9-6.

Domain administrators define policies in the Google Apps admin console (see Figure 9-7), and policy settings are pushed to devices using Google's proprietary sync protocol.

While free Google accounts do not support setting a device policy, Google experience devices can use the basic device administrator built into Google Play Services (see ❶ in Listing 9-3 on page 220). This administrator allows Google account holders to remotely locate or wipe their devices using the Android Device Manager website or the associated Android application.

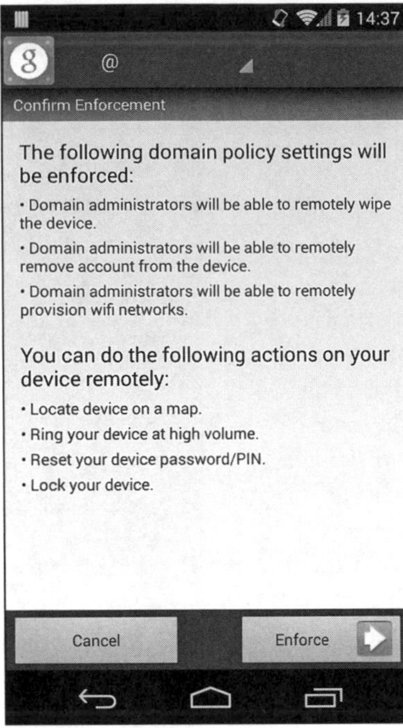

Figure 9-6: Policy enforcement confirmation in the Google Apps Device Policy application

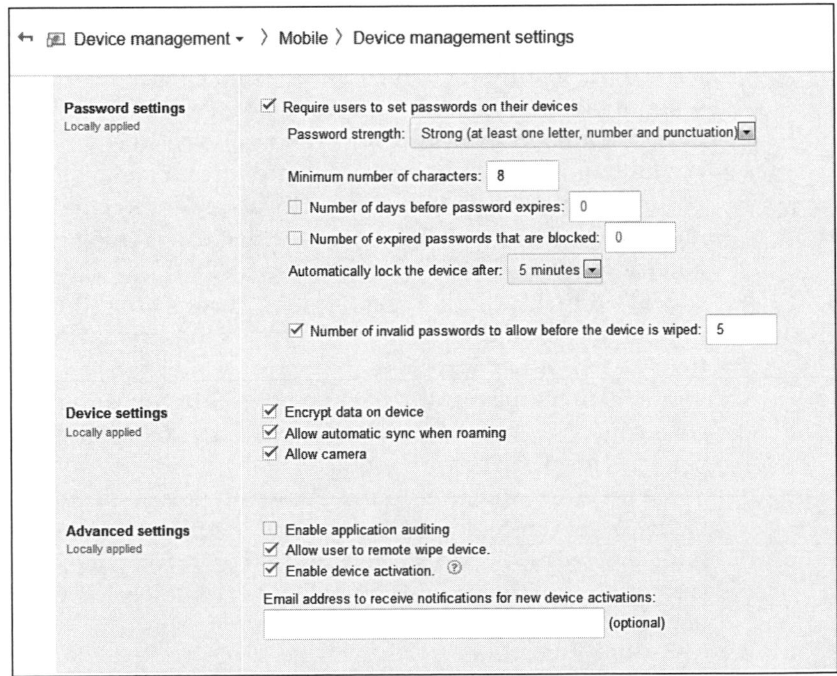

Figure 9-7: Google Apps device policy management UI

VPN Support

A *Virtual Private Network (VPN)* allows a private network to be extended across a public network without requiring a dedicated physical connection, thus enabling all connected devices to send and receive data as if colocated and physically connected to the same private network. When a VPN is used to allow individual devices to connect to a target private network, it's referred to as a *remote access VPN*, and when used to connect two remote networks, as a *site-to-site VPN*.

Remote-access VPNs can connect fixed devices with a static IP address, such as a computer in a remote office, but configurations where mobile clients use variable network connections and dynamic addresses are much more common. Such a configuration is often called a *road warrior* configuration and is the configuration most commonly used with Android VPN clients.

In order to ensure that data transmitted over a VPN remains private, VPNs typically authenticate remote clients and provide data confidentiality and integrity by using a secure tunneling protocol. VPN protocols are complex because they work at multiple network layers simultaneously and often involve multiple levels of encapsulation in order to be compatible with various network configurations. A thorough discussion of them is beyond the scope of his book, but in the following sections you'll find a brief overview of the major types of VPN protocols, with a focus on the ones available on Android.

PPTP

The *Point-to-Point Tunneling Protocol (PPTP)* uses a TCP control channel to establish connections and the Generic Routing Encapsulation (GRE) tunneling protocol to encapsulate Point-to-Point Protocol (PPP) packets. Several authentication methods such as Password Authentication Protocol (PAP), Challenge-Handshake Authentication Protocol (CHAP), and its Microsoft extension MS-CHAP v1/v2, as well as EAP TLS, are supported, but only EAP-TLS is currently considered secure.

The PPP payload can be encrypted using the Microsoft Point-to-Point Encryption (MPPE) protocol, which uses the RC4 stream cipher. Because MPPE does not employ any form of ciphertext authentication, it is vulnerable to bit-flipping attacks. In addition, multiple problems with the RC4 cipher have been uncovered in recent years, which further reduces the security of MMPE and PPTP.

L2TP/IPSec

The *Layer 2 Tunneling Protocol (L2TP)* is similar to PPTP and exists at the data link layer (Layer 2 in the OSI model). Because L2TP provides no encryption or confidentiality of its own (it relies on the tunneled protocol to implement these features), an L2TP VPN is typically implemented using a combination of L2TP and the Internet Protocol Security (IPSec) protocol suite, which adds authentication, confidentiality, and integrity.

In an L2TP/IPSec configuration, a secure channel is first established using IPSec, and an L2TP tunnel is then established over the secure channel. L2TP packets are always wrapped inside IPSec packets and are therefore secure. An IPSec connection requires establishing a *Security Association (SA)*, which is a combination of cryptographic algorithm and mode, encryption key, and other parameters required to establish a secure channel.

SAs are established using the Internet Security Association and Key Management Protocol (ISAKMP). ISAKMP does not define a particular key exchange method and is typically implemented either by manual configuration of pre-shared secrets, or by using the Internet Key Exchange (IKE and IKEv2) protocol. IKE uses X.509 certificates for peer authentication (much like SSL), and a Diffie-Hellman key exchange in order to establish a shared secret, which is used to derive the actual session encryption keys.

IPSec Xauth

IPSec Extended Authentication (Xauth) extends IKE to include additional user authentication exchanges. This allows an existing user database or a RADIUS infrastructure to be used to authenticate remote access clients, and makes it possible to integrate two-factor authentication.

Mode-configuration (Modecfg) is another IPSec extension that is often used in a remote access scenario. Modecfg allows VPN servers to push network configuration information such as the private IP address and DNS server addresses to clients. When used in combination, Xauth and Modecfg make it possible to create a pure-IPSec VPN solution, which doesn't rely on additional protocols for authentication and tunneling.

SSL-Based VPNs

SSL-based VPNs use SSL or TLS (see Chapter 6) to establish a secure connection and tunnel network traffic. No single standard defines SSL-based VPNs, and different implementations use different strategies in order to establish a secure channel and encapsulate packets.

OpenVPN is a popular open source application that uses SSL for authentication and key exchange (preconfigured shared static keys are also supported), and a custom encryption protocol[4] to encrypt and authenticate packets. OpenVPN multiplexes the SSL session used for authentication and key exchange, and the encrypted packets stream over a single UDP (or TCP) port. The multiplexing protocol provides a reliable transport layer for SSL on top of UDP, but it tunnels encrypted IP packets over UDP without adding reliability. Reliability is provided by the tunneled protocol itself, which is usually TCP.

The main advantages of OpenVPN over IPSec are that it is much simpler and can be implemented entirely in userspace. IPSec, on the other hand, requires kernel-level support and implementation of multiple interoperating

4. OpenVPN Technologies, Inc, "OpenVPN Security Overview," *http://openvpn.net/index.php/open-source/documentation/security-overview.html*

protocols. Additionally, it's easier to get OpenVPN traffic through firewalls, NAT, and proxies because it uses the common network protocols TCP and UDP and can multiplex tunneled traffic over a single port.

The following sections examine Android's built-in VPN support and the APIs it provides for applications that want to implement additional VPN solutions. We'll also review the components that make up Android's VPN infrastructure and show how it protects VPN credentials.

Legacy VPN

Prior to Android 4.0, VPN support was entirely built into the platform and wasn't extensible. Support for new VPN types could only be added as part of platform updates. To distinguish it from application-based implementations, built-in VPN support is referred to as *legacy VPN*.

Early Android versions supported different VPN configurations based on PPTP and L2TP/IPsec, with support for "pure-IPSec" VPNs using IPSec Xauth added in version 4.0. In addition to new built-in VPN configurations, Android 4.0 also introduced application-based VPNs by supplying the base platform class `VpnService`, which applications could extend in order to implement a new VPN solution.

Legacy VPN is controlled via the system Settings application and is only available to the owner (also called the primary user) on multi-user devices. Figure 9-8 shows the dialog for adding a new IPSec legacy VPN profile.

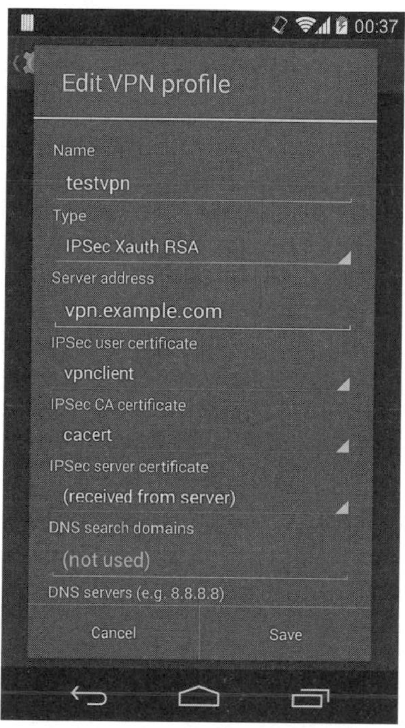

Figure 9-8: Legacy VPN profile definition dialog

Implementation

Legacy VPNs are implemented using a combination of kernel drivers as well as native daemons, commands, and system services. The lower-level implementation of PPTP and L2TP tunneling uses an Android-specific PPP daemon called *mtpd* and the PPPoPNS and PPPoLAC (only available in Android kernels) kernel drivers.

Because legacy VPNs support only a single VPN connection per device, *mtpd* can create only a single session. IPSec VPNs leverage the built-in kernel support for IPSec and a modified *racoon* IKE key management daemon (part of the IPSec-Tools[5] utilities package that complements the Linux kernel IPSec implementation; *racoon* supports only IKEv1). Listing 9-6 shows how these two daemons are defined in *init.rc*.

```
service racoon /system/bin/racoon❶
    class main
    socket racoon stream 600 system system❷
    # IKE uses UDP port 500. Racoon will setuid to vpn after binding the port.
    group vpn net_admin inet❸
    disabled
    oneshot

service mtpd /system/bin/mtpd❹
    class main
    socket mtpd stream 600 system system❺
    user vpn
    group vpn net_admin inet net_raw❻
    disabled
    oneshot
```

Listing 9-6: racoon *and* mtpd *definition in* init.rc

Both *racoon* ❶ and *mtpd* ❹ create control sockets (❷ and ❺), which are only accessible by the *system* user and are not started by default. Both daemons have *vpn*, *net_admin* (mapped by the kernel to the `CAP_NET_ADMIN` Linux capability), and *inet* added to their supplementary groups (❸ and ❻), which allow them to create sockets and control network interface devices. The *mtpd* daemon also receives the *net_raw* group (mapped to the `CAP_NET_RAW` Linux capability), which allows it to create GRE sockets (used by PPTP).

When a VPN is started via the system Settings app, Android starts the *racoon* and *mtpd* daemons and sends them control commands via their local sockets in order to establish the configured connection. The daemons create the requested VPN tunnel, and then create and configure a tunnel network interface with the received IP address and network mask. While *mtpd* performs interface configuration internally, *racoon* uses the helper command `ip-up-vpn` to bring up the tunnel interface, which is usually *tun0*.

In order to communicate connection parameters back to the framework, VPN daemons write a *state* file in */data/misc/vpn/* as shown in Listing 9-7.

```
# cat /data/misc/vpn/state
tun0❶
10.8.0.1/24❷
192.168.1.0/24❸
192.168.1.1❹
example.com❺
```

Listing 9-7: Contents of the VPN state file

5. IPSec-Tools, *http://ipsec-tools.sourceforge.net/*

The file contains the tunnel interface name ❶, its IP address and mask ❷, configured routes ❸, DNS servers ❹, and search domains ❺, with each on a new line.

After the VPN daemons start running, the framework parses the *state* file and calls the system `ConnectivityService` in order to configure routing, DNS servers, and search domains for the newly established VPN connection. In turn, `ConnectivityService` sends control commands via the local control socket of the *netd* daemon, which can modify the kernel's packet filtering and routing tables because it runs as root. Traffic from all applications started by the owner user and restricted profiles is routed through the VPN interface by adding a firewall rule that matches the application UID and corresponding routing rules. (We discuss per-application traffic routing and multi-user support in detail in "Multi-User Support" on page 239).

Profile and Credential Storage

Each VPN configuration created via the Settings app is called a *VPN profile* and is saved on disk in encrypted form. Encryption is performed by the Android credential storage daemon *keystore*, with a device-specific key. (See Chapter 7 for more on credential storage implementation.)

VPN profiles are serialized by concatenating all configured properties, which are delimited by a *NUL* character (*\0*) in a single profile string that is saved to the system keystore as a binary blob. VPN profile filenames are generated by appending the current time in milliseconds (in hexadecimal format) to the *VPN_* prefix. For example, Listing 9-8 shows the *keystore* directory of a user with three configured VPN profiles (file timestamps omitted):

```
# ls -l /data/misc/keystore/user_0
-rw------- keystore keystore      980 1000_CACERT_cacert❶
-rw------- keystore keystore       52 1000_LOCKDOWN_VPN❷
-rw------- keystore keystore      932 1000_USRCERT_vpnclient❸
-rw------- keystore keystore     1652 1000_USRPKEY_vpnclient❹
-rw------- keystore keystore      116 1000_VPN_144965b85a6❺
-rw------- keystore keystore       84 1000_VPN_145635c88c8❻
-rw------- keystore keystore      116 1000_VPN_14569512c80❼
```

Listing 9-8: Contents of the keystore directory when VPN profiles are configured

The three VPN profiles are stored in the *1000_VPN_144965b85a6* ❺, *1000_VPN_145635c88c8* ❻, and *1000_VPN_14569512c80* ❼ files. The *1000_* prefix represents the owner user, which is *system* (UID 1000). Because VPN profiles are owned by the *system* user, only system applications can retrieve and decrypt profile contents.

Listing 9-9 shows the decrypted contents of the three VPN profile files. (The *NUL* character has been replaced with vertical bar [|] for readability.)

```
psk-vpn|1|vpn1.example.com|test1|pass1234||||true|l2tpsecret|l2tpid|PSK|||❶
pptpvpn|0|vpn2.example.com|user1|password||||true||||||❷
certvpn|4|vpn3.example.com|user3|password||||true||||vpnclient|cacert|❸
```

Listing 9-9: Contents of VPN profile files

The profile files contain all fields shown in the VPN profile edit dialog (see Figure 9-8), with missing properties represented by an empty string. The first five fields represent the name of the VPN, the type of VPN, the VPN gateway host, the username, and the password, respectively. In Listing 9-9, the first VPN profile ❶ is for an L2TP/IPsec VPN with pre-shared key (type 1); the second profile ❷ is for a PPTP VPN (type 0), and the last one ❸ is for a IPSec VPN that uses certificates and Xauth authentication (type 4).

In addition to the username and password, VPN profile files also contain all other credentials required to connect to the VPN. In the case of the first VPN profile ❶ in Listing 9-9, the additional credential is the pre-shared key required to establish an IPSec secure connection (represented by the *PSK* string in this example). In the case of the third profile ❸, the additional credentials are the user's private key and certificate. However, as you can see in the listing, the full key and certificate are not included; instead, the profile contains only the alias (*vpnclient*) of the key and certificate (both share a common alias). The private key and certificate are stored in the system credential store, and the alias included in the VPN profile serves only as an identifier, which is used to access or retrieve the key and certificate.

Accessing Credentials

The *racoon* daemon, which originally used keys and certificates stored in PEM files, was modified to use Android's *keystore* OpenSSL engine. As discussed in Chapter 7, the *keystore* engine is a gateway to the system credential store, which can take advantage of hardware-backed credential store implementations when available. When passed a key alias, it uses the corresponding private key to sign authentication packets, without extracting the key from the keystore.

The VPN profile ❸ in Listing 9-9 also contains the alias of the CA certificate (*cacert*), which is used as a trust anchor when validating the server's certificate. At runtime, the framework retrieves the client certificate (❸ in Listing 9-8) and the CA certificate (❶ in Listing 9-8) from the system keystore and passes them to *racoon* via the control socket, along with other connection parameters. The private key blob (❹ in Listing 9-8) is never directly passed to the *racoon* daemon, only its alias (*vpnclient*).

NOTE *While private keys are protected by hardware on devices with a hardware-backed keystore, pre-shared keys or passwords stored in a VPN profile content are not. The reason for this is that as of this writing, Android doesn't support importing symmetric keys in the hardware-backed keystore; it only supports asymmetric keys (RSA, DSA, and EC). As a result, credentials for VPNs that use pre-shared keys are stored in the VPN profile in plaintext form and can be extracted from devices that allow root access after the profile is decrypted on memory.*

Always-On VPN

Android 4.2 and later supports an *always-on* VPN configuration, which blocks all network connections from applications until a connection to the specified VPN profile is established. This prevents applications from sending data across insecure channels, such as public Wi-Fi networks.

Setting up an always-on VPN requires setting up a VPN profile that specifies the VPN gateway as an IP address, and specifies an explicit DNS server IP address. This explicit configuration is required in order to make sure that DNS traffic isn't sent to the locally configured DNS server, which is blocked when an always-on VPN is in effect. The VPN profile selection dialog is shown in Figure 9-9.

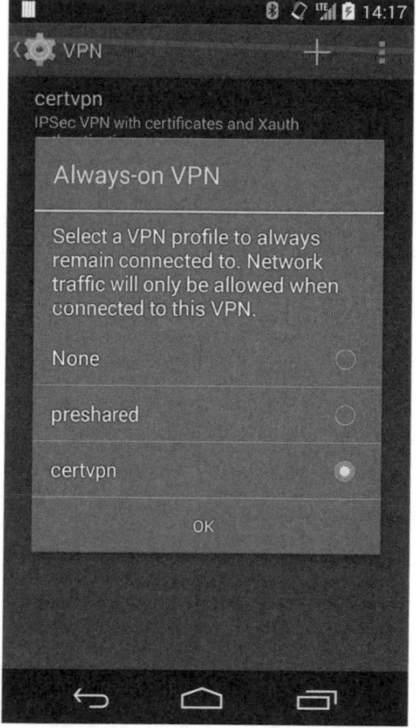

Figure 9-9: Always-on VPN profile selection dialog

The profile selection is saved with other VPN profiles in the encrypted file *LOCKDOWN_VPN* (❷ in Listing 9-8) which contains only the name of the selected profile; in our example, *144965b85a6*. If the *LOCKDOWN_VPN* file is present, the system automatically connects to the specified VPN when the device boots. If the underlying network connection reconnects or changes (for example, when switching Wi-Fi hotspots), the VPN is automatically restarted.

An always-on VPN guarantees that all traffic goes through the VPN by installing firewall rules that block all packets except those which go through the VPN interface. The rules are installed by the `LockdownVpnTracker` class (always-on VPN is referred to as *lockdown VPN* in Android source code), which monitors VPN state and adjusts the current firewall state by sending commands to the *netd* daemon, which in turn executes the `iptables` utility in order to modify the kernels packet filtering tables. For example, when an always-on L2TP/IPSec VPN has connected to a VPN server with IP address 11.22.33.44 and has created a tunnel interface *tun0* with IP address 10.1.1.1, the installed firewall rules (as reported by `iptables`; some columns have been omitted for brevity) might look like Listing 9-10.

```
# iptables -v -L n
--snip--
Chain fw_INPUT (1 references)
 target     prot opt in     out     source        destination
 RETURN     all  --  *      *       0.0.0.0/0     10.1.1.0/24❶
 RETURN     all  --  tun0   *       0.0.0.0/0     0.0.0.0/0❷
```

```
RETURN     udp  --  *     *      11.22.33.44  0.0.0.0/0    udp spt:1701❸
RETURN     tcp  --  *     *      11.22.33.44  0.0.0.0/0    tcp spt:1701
RETURN     udp  --  *     *      11.22.33.44  0.0.0.0/0    udp spt:4500
RETURN     tcp  --  *     *      11.22.33.44  0.0.0.0/0    tcp spt:4500
RETURN     udp  --  *     *      11.22.33.44  0.0.0.0/0    udp spt:500
RETURN     tcp  --  *     *      11.22.33.44  0.0.0.0/0    tcp spt:500
RETURN     all  --  lo    *      0.0.0.0/0    0.0.0.0/0
DROP       all  --  *     *      0.0.0.0/0    0.0.0.0/0❹

Chain fw_OUTPUT (1 references)
 target    prot opt in    out    source       destination
 RETURN    all  --  *     *      10.1.1.0/24  0.0.0.0/0❺
 RETURN    all  --  *     tun0   0.0.0.0/0    0.0.0.0/0❻
 RETURN    udp  --  *     *      0.0.0.0/0    11.22.33.44  udp dpt:1701❼
 RETURN    tcp  --  *     *      0.0.0.0/0    11.22.33.44  tcp dpt:1701
 RETURN    udp  --  *     *      0.0.0.0/0    11.22.33.44  udp dpt:4500
 RETURN    tcp  --  *     *      0.0.0.0/0    11.22.33.44  tcp dpt:4500
 RETURN    udp  --  *     *      0.0.0.0/0    11.22.33.44  udp dpt:500
 RETURN    tcp  --  *     *      0.0.0.0/0    11.22.33.44  tcp dpt:500
 RETURN    all  --  *     lo     0.0.0.0/0    0.0.0.0/0
 REJECT    all  --  *     *      0.0.0.0/0    0.0.0.0/0   reject-with icmp-port-unreachable❽
--snip--
```

Listing 9-10: Always-on VPN firewall rules

As you can see in the listing, all traffic to and from the VPN network is allowed (❶ and ❺), as is all traffic on the tunnel interface (❷ and ❻). Traffic to and from the VPN server (❸ and ❼) is allowed only on the ports used by IPSec (500 and 4500) and L2TP (1701). All other incoming traffic is dropped ❹, and all other outgoing traffic is rejected ❽.

Application-Based VPNs

Android 4.0 added a `VpnService` public API[6] that third-party applications can use to build VPN solutions that are neither built into the OS nor require system-level permissions. The `VpnService` and associated `Builder` class let applications specify network parameters such as interface IP address and routes, which the system uses to create and configure a virtual network interface. Applications receive a file descriptor associated with that network interface and can tunnel network traffic by reading from or writing to the file descriptor of the interface.

Each read retrieves an outgoing IP packet, and each write injects an incoming IP packet. Because raw access to network packets effectively lets applications intercept and modify network traffic, application-based VPNs cannot be started automatically and always require user interaction. Additionally, an ongoing notification is shown while a VPN is connected. The connection warning dialog for an application-based VPN might look like Figure 9-10.

6. Google, *Android APIs Reference*, "VpnService," *https://developer.android.com/reference/android/net/VpnService.html*

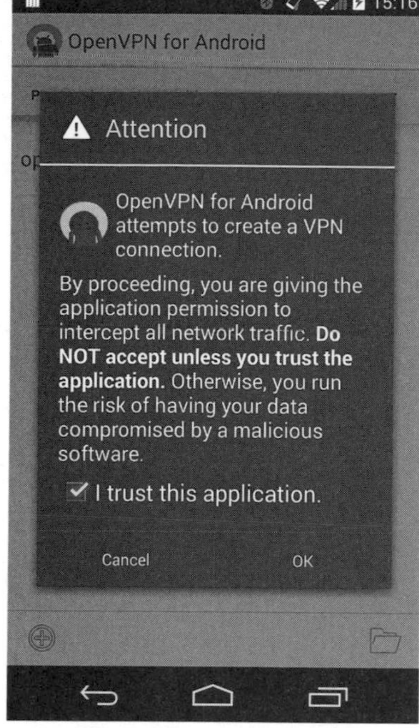

Figure 9-10: Application-based VPN connection warning dialog

Declaring a VPN

An application-based VPN is implemented by creating a service component that extends the VpnService base class and registering it in the application manifest, as shown in Listing 9-11.

```
<?xml version="1.0" encoding="utf-8"?>
<manifest xmlns:android="http://schemas.android.com/apk/res/android"
    package="com.example.vpn">
    --snip--
    <application android:label="@string/app">
        --snip--
        <service android:name=".MyVpnService"
                android:permission="android.permission.BIND_VPN_SERVICE">❶
            <intent-filter>
                <action android:name="android.net.VpnService"/>❷
            </intent-filter>
        </service>
    </application>
</manifest>:
```

Listing 9-11: Registering a VPN service in the application manifest

The service must have an intent filter that matches the *android.net.VpnService* intent action ❷ so that the system can bind to the service and control it. In addition, the service must require the `BIND_VPN_SERVICE` system signature permission ❶, which guarantees that only system applications can bind to it.

Preparing the VPN

To register a new VPN connection with the system, the application first calls `VpnService.prepare()` in order to be granted permission to run, and then calls the `establish()` method in order to create a network tunnel (discussed in the next section). The `prepare()` method returns an intent that's used to start the warning dialog shown in Figure 9-10. The dialog serves to obtain the user's permission and ensure that only one VPN connection per user is running at any time. If `prepare()` is called while a VPN connection created by another application is running, that connection is terminated. The `prepare()` method saves the package name of the calling application, and only that application is allowed to start a VPN connection until the method is called again, or the system tears down the VPN connection (for example, if the VPN app's process crashes). When a VPN connection is deactivated for any reason, the system calls the `onRevoke()` method of the current VPN application's `VpnService` implementation.

Establishing a VPN Connection

After a VPN application has been prepared and granted permission to run, it can start its `VpnService` component, which would then typically create a tunnel to the VPN gateway and negotiate the network parameters for the VPN connection. Next, it sets up the `VpnService.Builder` class using those parameters and calls `VpnService.establish()` in order to receive a file descriptor to read and write packets. The `establish()` method first ensures that it's being called by the application currently granted permission to establish a VPN connection by comparing the UID of the caller to the granted application's UID. `establish()` then checks whether the current Android user is allowed to create VPN connections, and verifies that the service requires the `BIND_VPN_SERVICE` permission; if the service doesn't require that permission, it's considered insecure and a `SecurityException` is thrown. Next, the `establish()` method creates and configures a tunnel interface using native code, and sets up routing and DNS servers.

Notifying the User About the VPN Connection

The last step in establishing a VPN connection is to show an ongoing notification that tells the user that network traffic is been tunneled through a VPN, which allows them to monitor and control the connection via the associated control dialog. The dialog for the OpenVPN for Android application is shown in Figure 9-11.

This dialog is part of the dedicated package `com.android.vpndialogs`, which is the only package explicitly allowed to manage application-based VPN connections, other than the *system* user. This ensures that a VPN connection can only be started and managed via the system-mandated UI.

Using the application-based VPN framework, applications are free to implement network tunneling, with any required authentication and encryption methods. Because all packets the device sends or receives pass through the VPN application, it can be used not only for tunneling but also for traffic logging, filtering, or modification (such as removing advertisements).

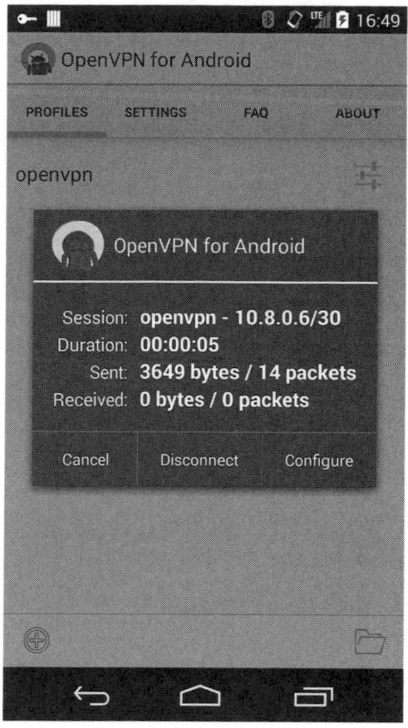

Figure 9-11: Application-based VPN management dialog

NOTE *For a full-featured implementation of an application-based VPN that takes advantage of Android's credential store to manage authentication keys and certificates, see the source code for OpenVPN for Android.*[7] *This application implements an SSL VPN client that is fully compatible with the OpenVPN server.*

Multi-User Support

As mentioned earlier, on multi-user devices, legacy VPNs can be controlled only by the owner user. However, with its introduction of multi-user support, Android 4.2 and higher allows all secondary users (with the exception of restricted profiles, which must share the primary user's VPN connection) to start application-based VPNs. While this change technically allowed each user to start their own VPN, because only one application-based VPN could be activated at a time, traffic for all device users was routed through the currently active VPN regardless of who started it. Android 4.4 finally brought full multi-user VPN support by introducing *per-user VPN*, which allows traffic from any user to be routed through their VPN, thus isolating it from other users' traffic.

Linux Advanced Routing

Android uses several advanced packet filtering and routing features of the Linux kernel in order to implement per-user VPNs. These features (implemented by the *netfilter* kernel framework) include the *owner* module

7. Arne Schwabe, "Openvpn for Android 4.0+," *https://code.google.com/p/ics-openvpn/*

of the Linux *iptables* tool, which allows matching of locally generated packets based on the UID, GID, or PID of the process that created them. For example, the command shown at ❶ in Listing 9-12 creates a packet-filtering rule that drops all outgoing packets generated by the user with UID 1234.

```
# iptables -A OUTPUT -m owner --uid-owner 1234 -j DROP❶
# iptables -A PREROUTING -t mangle -p tcp --dport 80 -j MARK --set-mark 0x1❷
# ip rule add fwmark 0x1 table web❸
# ip route add default via 1.2.3.4 dev em3 table web❹
```

Listing 9-12: Using owner matching and packet marking with iptables

Another important netfilter feature is the ability to mark packets that match a certain selector with a specified number (called a *mark*). For example, the rule at ❷ marks all packets destined for port 80 (which is typically used by a web server) with the mark 0x1. This mark can then be matched in later filtering or routing rules in order to, for example, send marked packets through a particular interface by adding a routing rule that sends marked packets to a predefined routing table, which is *web* in our example ❸. Finally, a route that sends packets matching the *web* table to the *em3* interface can be added with the command shown at ❹.

Multi-User VPN Implementation

Android uses these packet filtering and routing features to mark packets originating from all apps of a particular Android user and send them through the tunneling interface created by the VPN app started by that user. When the owner user starts a VPN, that VPN is shared with any restricted profiles on the device that cannot start their own VPNs by matching all packets originating from restricted profiles and routing them through the owner's VPN tunnel.

This split-routing is implemented at the framework level by the `NetworkManagementService`, which provides APIs to manage package matching and routing by UID or UID range. `NetworkManagementService` implements those APIs by sending commands to the native *netd* daemon which runs as root, and thus can modify the kernel's packet filtering and routing tables. *netd* manipulates the kernel's filtering and routing configuration by calling the *iptables* and *ip* userland utilities.

Let's illustrate Android's per-user VPN routing with an example as shown in Listing 9-13. The primary user (user ID 0) and the first secondary user (user ID 10) have each started an application-based VPN. The owner user's VPN is assigned the *tun0* tunneling interface, and the secondary user's VPN is assigned the *tun1* interface. The device also has a restricted profile with user ID 13. Listing 9-13 shows the state of the kernel's packet filtering tables when both VPNs are connected (with some details omitted).

```
# iptables -t mangle -L -n
--snip--
Chain st_mangle_OUTPUT (1 references)
target     prot opt source               destination
```

```
RETURN     all  --  0.0.0.0/0            0.0.0.0/0           mark match 0x1❶
RETURN     all  --  0.0.0.0/0            0.0.0.0/0           owner UID match 1016❷
--snip--
st_mangle_tun0_OUTPUT  all  --  0.0.0.0/0            0.0.0.0/0           [goto]  owner UID match
0-99999❸
st_mangle_tun0_OUTPUT  all  --  0.0.0.0/0            0.0.0.0/0           [goto]  owner UID match
1300000-1399999❹
st_mangle_tun1_OUTPUT  all  --  0.0.0.0/0            0.0.0.0/0           [goto]  owner UID match
1000000-1099999❺

Chain st_mangle_tun0_OUTPUT (3 references)
target     prot opt source               destination
MARK       all  --  0.0.0.0/0            0.0.0.0/0           MARK and 0x0
MARK       all  --  0.0.0.0/0            0.0.0.0/0           MARK set 0x3c❻

Chain st_mangle_tun1_OUTPUT (2 references)
target     prot opt source               destination
MARK       all  --  0.0.0.0/0            0.0.0.0/0           MARK and 0x0
MARK       all  --  0.0.0.0/0            0.0.0.0/0           MARK set 0x3d❼
```

Listing 9-13: Packet matching rules for VPNs started by two different device users

Outgoing packets are first sent to the *st_mangle_OUTPUT* chain, which is responsible for matching and marking packets. Packets exempt from per-user routing (those already marked with 0x1 ❶), and packets originating from legacy VPNs (UID 1016 ❷, assigned to the built-in *vpn* user, which both *mtd* and *racoon* run as) pass without modification.

Next, packets created by processes running with UIDs between 0 and 99999 (the range of UIDs assigned to apps started by the primary user, as discussed in Chapter 4) are matched and sent to the *st_mangle_tun0_OUTPUT* chain ❸. Packets originating from UIDs 1300000–1399999, the range assigned to our restricted profile (user ID 13), are sent to the same chain ❹. Thus, traffic originating from the owner user and the restricted profile is treated the same way. Packets originating from the first secondary user (user ID 10, UID range 1000000-1099999) are, however, sent to a different chain, *st_mangle_tun1_OUTPUT* ❺. The target chains themselves are simple: *st_mangle_tun0_OUTPUT* first clears the packet mark and then marks them with *0x3c* ❻; *st_mangle_tun1_OUTPUT* does the same but uses the mark *0x3d* ❼. After packets have been marked, the marks are used to implement and match different routing rules, as shown in Listing 9-14.

```
# ip rule ls
0:      from all lookup local
100:    from all fwmark 0x3c lookup 60❶
100:    from all fwmark 0x3d lookup 61❷
--snip--
# ip route list table 60
default dev tun0  scope link❸
# ip route list table 61
default dev tun1  scope link❹
```

Listing 9-14: Routing rules for VPNs started by two different device users

Notice that two rules that match each mark have been created, and that they're associated with different routing tables. Packets marked with *0x3c* go to routing table 60 (0x3c in hexadecimal ❶), while those marked with *0x3d* go to table 61 (0x3d in hexadecimal ❷). Table 60 routes everything through the *tun0* tunneling interface ❸, which was created by the owner user, and table 61 routes everything through the *tun1* interface ❹, created by the secondary user.

NOTE *While the VPN traffic routing method introduced in Android 4.4 offers greater flexibility and allows user VPN traffic to be isolated, as of this writing the implementation appears to have some problems, especially related to switching between different physical networks (for example, mobile to Wi-Fi or vice versa). Those problems should be addressed in future versions, possibly by modifying how packet filtering chains are associated with interfaces, but the basic implementation strategy is likely to remain the same.*

Wi-Fi EAP

Android supports different wireless network protocols, including Wi-Fi Protected Access (WPA) and Wi-Fi Protected Access II (WPA2), which are currently deployed on most wireless devices. Both protocols support a simple *pre-shared key (PSK)* mode, also referred to as *Personal mode,* in which all devices that access the network must be configured with the same 256-bit authentication key.

Devices can be configured either with the raw key bytes or with an ASCII passphrase that's used to derive the authentication key using the PBKDF2 key derivation algorithm. While the PSK mode is simple, it doesn't scale as the number of network users increases. If access for a certain user needs to be revoked, for example, the only way to cancel their network credentials is to change the shared passphrase, which would force all other users to reconfigure their devices. Additionally, as there is no practical way to distinguish users and devices, it is difficult to implement flexible access rules or accounting.

To address this problem, both WPA and WPA2 support the IEEE 802.1X network access control standard, which offers an encapsulation of the Extensible Authentication Protocol (EAP). Authentication in a wireless network that uses 802.1X and involves a supplicant, an authenticator, and an authentication server is shown in Figure 9-12.

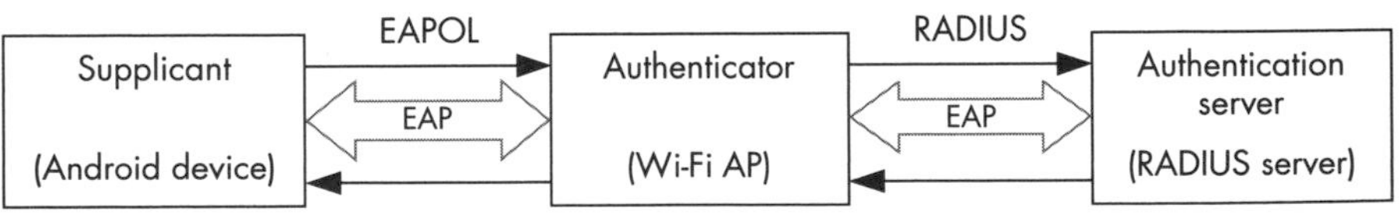

Figure 9-12: 802.1X authentication participants

The *supplicant* is a wireless device such as an Android phone that wants to connect to the network, and the *authenticator* is the gateway to the network that validates the supplicant's identity and provides authorization. In a typical Wi-Fi configuration, the authenticator is the wireless access point (AP). The *authentication server*, typically a RADIUS server, verifies client credentials and decides whether they should be granted access based on a preconfigured access policy.

Authentication is implemented by exchanging EAP messages between the three nodes. These are encapsulated in a format suitable for the medium connecting each two nodes: EAP over LAN (EAPOL) between the supplicant and the authenticator, and RADIUS between the authenticator and the authentication server.

Because EAP is an authentication framework that supports different concrete authentication types and not a concrete authentication mechanism, the supplicant and authentication server (with the help of the authenticator) need to negotiate a commonly supported authentication method before authentication can be performed. There are various standard and proprietary EAP authentication methods, and current Android versions support most of the methods used in wireless networks.

The sections below offer a brief overview of the EAP authentication methods that Android supports, and show how it protects credentials for each method. We'll also demonstrate how to configure access to a Wi-Fi network that uses EAP for authentication using Android's wireless network management APIs.

EAP Authentication Methods

As of version 4.4, Android supports the PEAP, EAP-TLS, EAP-TTLS, and EAP-PWD authentication methods. Before exploring how Android stores credentials for each authentication method, let's briefly discuss how each one works.

PEAP

The Protected Extensible Authentication Protocol (PEAP) transmits EAP messages through an SSL connection in order to provide confidentiality and integrity. It uses PKI and a server certificate to authenticate the server and establish an SSL connection (Phase 1), but does not mandate how clients are authenticated. Clients are authenticated using a second, inner (Phase 2) authentication method, which is transmitted inside the SSL tunnel. Android supports the MSCHAPv2 (specified in PEAPv0[8]) and Generic Token Card (GTC, specified in PEAPv2[9]) methods for Phase 2 authentication.

8. Vivek Kamath, Ashwin Palekar, and Mark Woodrich, *Microsoft's PEAP version 0 (Implementation in Windows XP SP1)*, *https://tools.ietf.org/html/draft-kamath-pppext-peapv0-00/*

9. Ashwin Palekar et al., *Protected EAP Protocol (PEAP) Version 2*, *https://tools.ietf.org/html/draft-josefsson-pppext-eap-tls-eap-10/*

EAP-TLS

The EAP-Transport Layer Security (EAP-TLS) method[10] uses TLS for mutual authentication and was formerly the only EAP method certified for use with WPA Enterprise. EAP-TLS uses both a server certificate to authenticate the server to supplicants, and a client certificate that the authentication server verifies in order to establish supplicant identity. Granting network access requires issuing and distributing X.509 client certificates, and thus maintaining a public key infrastructure. Existing clients can be blocked from accessing the network by revoking their supplicant certificates. Android supports EAP-TLS and manages client keys and certificates using the system credential store.

EAP-TTLS

Like EAP-TLS, the EAP-Tunneled Transport Layer Security (EAP-TTLS) protocol[11] is based on TLS. However, EAP-TTLS does not require client authentication using X.509 certificates. Clients can be authenticated either using a certificate during the handshake phase (Phase 1), or with another protocol during the tunnel phase (Phase 2). Android does not support authentication during Phase 1, but supports the PAP, MSCHAP, MSCHAPv2, and GTC protocols for Phase 2.

EAP-PWD

The EAP-PWD authentication method[12] uses a shared password for authentication. Unlike legacy schemes that rely on a simple challenge-response mechanism, EAP-PWD is designed to be resistant to passive attacks, active attacks, and dictionary attacks. The protocol also provides forward secrecy and guarantees that even if a password is compromised, earlier sessions cannot be decrypted. EAP-PWD is based on discrete logarithm cryptography and can be implemented using either finite fields or elliptic curves.

Android Wi-Fi Architecture

Like most hardware support in Android, Android's Wi-Fi architecture consists of a kernel layer (WLAN adapter driver modules), native daemon (*wpa_supplicant*), a Hardware Abstraction Layer (HAL), system services, and a system UI. Wi-Fi adapter kernel drivers are usually specific to the system on a chip (SoC) that an Android device is built upon, and are typically closed source and loaded as kernel modules. The *wpa_supplicant*[13] is a WPA supplicant daemon that implements key negotiation with a WPA authenticator and

---

10. D. Simon, B. Aboba, and R. Hurst, *The EAP-TLS Authentication Protocol, http://tools.ietf.org/html/rfc5216/*

11. P. Funk and S. Blake-Wilson, *Extensible Authentication Protocol Tunneled Transport Layer Security Authenticated Protocol Version 0 (EAP-TTLSv0), https://tools.ietf.org/html/rfc5281/*

12. D. Harkins and G. Zorn, *Extensible Authentication Protocol (EAP) Authentication Using Only a Password, https://tools.ietf.org/html/rfc5931/*

13. Jouni Malinen, *Linux WPA/WPA2/IEEE 802.1X Supplicant, http://hostap.epitest.fi/wpa_supplicant/*

controls 802.1X association of the WLAN driver. However, Android devices rarely include the original *wpa_supplicant* code; the included implementation is often modified for better compatibility with the underlying SoC.

The HAL is implemented in the *libhardware_legacy* native library and is responsible for relaying commands from the framework to *wpa_supplicant* via its control socket. The system service that controls Wi-Fi connectivity is `WifiService`, which offers a public interface via the `WifiManager` facade class. The `WifiService` delegates Wi-Fi state management to a rather complex `WifiStateMachine` class, which can go through more than a dozen states while connecting to a wireless network.

WLAN connectivity is controlled via the Wi-Fi screen of the system Settings app, and connectivity status is displayed in the status bar and Quick Settings, both of which are part of the SystemUI package.

Android stores Wi-Fi-related configuration files in the */data/misc/wifi/* directory because wireless connectivity daemons persist configuration changes directly to disk and thus need a writable directory. The directory is owned by the *wifi* user (UID 1010), which is also the user that the *wpa_supplicant* runs as. Configurations files, including *wpa_supplicant.conf*, have permissions set to 0660 and are owned by the *system* user, and their group is set to *wifi*. This ensures that both system applications and the supplicant daemon can read and modify configurations files, but they are not accessible to other applications. The *wpa_supplicant.conf* file contains configuration parameters formatted as key-value pairs, both global and specific to a particular network. Network-specific parameters are enclosed in network blocks, which may look like Listing 9-15 for a PSK configuration.

```
network={
    ssid="psk-ap"❶
    key_mgmt=WPA-PSK❷
    psk="password"❸
    priority=805❹
}
```

Listing 9-15: PSK network configuration block in wpa_supplicant.conf

As you can see, the `network` block specifies the network SSID ❶, authentication key management protocol ❷, the pre-shared key itself ❸, and a priority value ❹. The PSK is saved in plaintext, and while the *wpa_supplicant .conf* access bits disallow non-system applications from accessing it, it can be easily extracted from devices that allow root access.

EAP Credentials Management

In this section, we'll examine how Android manages Wi-Fi credentials for each of the supported EAP authentication methods and discuss the Android-specific *wpa_supplicant* changes that allow the supplicant daemon to take advantage of Android's system credential store.

Listing 9-16 shows the network block in *wpa_supplicant.conf* for a network configured to use PEAP.

```
network={
    ssid="eap-ap"
    key_mgmt=WPA-EAP IEEE8021X❶
    eap=PEAP❷
    identity="android1"❸
    anonymous_identity="anon"
    password="password"❹
    ca_cert="keystore://CACERT_eapclient"❺
    phase2="auth=MSCHAPV2"❻
    proactive_key_caching=1
}
```

Listing 9-16: PEAP network configuration block in wpa_supplicant.conf

Here, the key management mode is set to *WPA-EAP IEEE8021X* ❶, the EAP method to *PEAP* ❷, and Phase 2 authentication to MSCHAPv2 ❻. Credentials, namely the identity ❸ and password ❹, are stored in plaintext in the configuration file, as they are in PSK mode.

One notable difference from a general-purpose *wpa_supplicant.conf* is the format of the CA certificate path ❺. The CA certificate path (*ca_cert*) is used when validating the server certificate, and in Android *ca_cert* is in a URI-like format with the *keystore* scheme. This Android-specific extension allows the *wpa_supplicant* daemon to retrieve certificates from the system credential store. When the daemon encounters a certificate path that starts with *keystore://*, it connects to the `IKeystoreService` remote interface of the native *keystore* service and retrieves the certificate bytes using the URI path as the key.

EAP-TLS configuration is similar to the PEAP one, as shown in Listing 9-17.

```
network={
    ssid="eap-ap"
    key_mgmt=WPA-EAP IEEE8021X
    eap=TLS
    identity="android1"
    ca_cert="keystore://CACERT_eapclient"
    client_cert="keystore://USRCERT_eapclient"❶
    engine_id="keystore"❷
    key_id="USRPKEY_eapclient"❸
    engine=1
    priority=803
    proactive_key_caching=1
}
```

Listing 9-17: EAP-TLS network configuration block in wpa_supplicant.conf

New here is the addition of a client certificate URI ❶, an engine ID ❷, and a key ID ❸. The client certificate is retrieved from the system credential store, just like the CA certificate. The engine ID refers to the OpenSSL engine that should be used for cryptographic operations when connecting to the SSID configured in the `network` block. The *wpa_supplicant* has native support for configurable OpenSSL engines, and is often used with an PKCS#11 engine in order to use keys stored in a smart card or other hardware device.

As discussed in Chapter 7, Android's *keystore* engine uses keys stored in the system credential store. If a device supports hardware-backed credential storage, the *keystore* engine can transparently take advantage of it by virtue of the intermediate *keymaster* HAL module. The key ID in Listing 9-17 references the alias of the private key to use for authentication.

As of version 4.3, Android allows you to select the owner of private keys and certificates when importing them. Previously, all imported keys were owned by the *system* user, but if you set the Credential use parameter to Wi-Fi in the import dialog (see Figure 9-13), the key owner is set to the *wifi* user (UID 1010), and the key can only be accessed by system components that run as the *wifi* user, like *wpa_supplicant*.

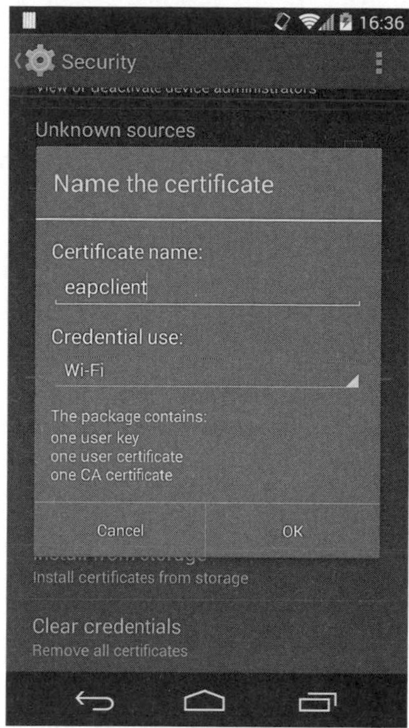

Figure 9-13: Setting the credential owner to Wi-Fi in the PKCS#12 import dialog

Because Android does not support client authentication when using the EAP-TTLS authentication method, the configuration only contains a CA certificate reference ❷, as shown in Listing 9-18. The password ❶ is stored in plaintext.

```
network={
    ssid="eap-ap"
    key_mgmt=WPA-EAP IEEE8021X
    eap=TTLS
    identity="android1"
    anonymous_identity="anon"
    password="pasword"❶
    ca_cert="keystore://CACERT_eapclient"❷
    phase2="auth=GTC"
    proactive_key_caching=1
}
```

Listing 9-18: EAP-TTLS network configuration block in wpa_supplicant.conf

The EAP-PWD method does not depend on TLS to establish a secure channel and thus requires no certificate configuration, as shown in Listing 9-19. Credentials are stored in plaintext (❶ and ❷), as with other configurations that use passwords.

```
network={
    ssid="eap-ap"
    key_mgmt=WPA-EAP IEEE8021X
    eap=PWD
    identity="android1"❶
    password="password"❷
    proactive_key_caching=1
}
```

Listing 9-19: EAP-PWD network configuration block in wpa_supplicant.conf

To sum up, configurations for all EAP methods that use a password for authentication store credential information in plaintext in the *wpa_supplicant.conf* file. When using EAP-TLS, which relies on client authentication, the client key is stored in the system keystore, and thus offers the highest level of credential protection.

Adding an EAP Network with WifiManager

While Android supports a number of WPA Enterprise authentication methods, setting them up properly might challenge some users because of the number of parameters that need to be configured and the need to install and select authentication certificates. Because Android's official API for managing Wi-Fi networks, called `WifiManager`, did not support EAP configurations prior to Android 4.3, the only way to set up an EAP network was to add it via the system Settings app and configure it manually. Android 4.3 (API level 18) extended the `WifiManager` API to allow for programmatic EAP configuration, thus enabling automatic network provisioning in enterprise environments. In this section, we'll show how to use `WifiManager` to add an EAP-TLS network and discuss the underlying implementation.

`WifiManager` allows an app that holds the `CHANGE_WIFI_STATE` permission (protection level *dangerous*) to add a Wi-Fi network by initializing a `WifiConfiguration` instance with the network's SSID, authentication algorithms, and credentials, and pass it to the `addNetwork()` method of `WifiManager`. Android 4.3 extends this API by adding an `enterpriseConfig` field of type `WifiEnterpriseConfig` to the `WifiConfiguration` class, which allows you to configure the EAP authentication method to use, client and CA certificates, the Phase 2 authentication method (if any), and additional credentials such as username and password. Listing 9-20 shows how to use this API to add a network that uses EAP-TLS for authentication.

```
X509Certificate caCert = getCaCert();
PrivateKey clientKey = getClientKey();
X509Certificate clientCert = getClientCert();

WifiEnterpriseConfig enterpriseConfig = new WifiEnterpriseConfig();
enterpriseConfig.setCaCertificate(caCert);❶
enterpriseConfig.setClientKeyEntry(clientKey, clientCert);❷
enterpriseConfig.setEapMethod(WifiEnterpriseConfig.Eap.TLS);❸
enterpriseConfig.setPhase2Method(WifiEnterpriseConfig.Phase2.NONE);❹
enterpriseConfig.setIdentity("android1");❺
```

```
WifiConfiguration config = new WifiConfiguration();
config.enterpriseConfig = enterpriseConfig;❻
config.SSID = "\"eap-ap\"";
config.allowedKeyManagement.set(WifiConfiguration.KeyMgmt.IEEE8021X);❼
config.allowedKeyManagement.set(WifiConfiguration.KeyMgmt.WPA_EAP);❽

int netId = wm.addNetwork(config);❾
if (netId != -1) {
    boolean success = wm.saveConfiguration();❿
}
```

Listing 9-20: Adding an EAP-TLS network using `WifiManager`

In order to set up EAP-TLS authentication, we first need to obtain the CA certificate used to verify the server's identity, and the client's private key and certificate. Because these are typically distributed as a PKCS#12 file, we can use a `KeyStore` of type *PKCS12* to extract them (not shown). (Android will automatically import the specified keys and certificates into the system keystore when you add an EAP profile that uses them, so you don't need to import the PKCS#12 file.) After we have the CA certificate and client credentials, we set them to our `WifiEnterpriseConfig` instance using the `setCaCertificate()` ❶ and `setClientKeyEntry()` ❷ methods. We then set the EAP method to `Eap.TLS` ❸ and the Phase 2 method to `NONE` ❹, as EAP-TLS authenticates users as part of establishing an SSL connection (Phase 1). Android also requires us to set the identity ❺ even though it might not be used by the authentication server. After we've configured the `WifiEnterpriseConfig` object, we can add it to the main `WifiConfiguration` instance ❻. The set of key management protocols also needs to be configured (❼ and ❽) because it defaults to WPA PSK. Finally, we can add the network ❾ and save the configuration ❿, which updates the *wpa_supplicant.conf* file to include the newly configured network.

Android automatically generates aliases for the configured private key and certificates, and then imports the PKI credentials into the system keystore. The aliases are based on the AP name, key management scheme, and EAP authentication method. A programmatically configured network is automatically shown in the Wi-Fi screen of the system Settings application, and might look like Figure 9-14 for the example shown in Listing 9-20.

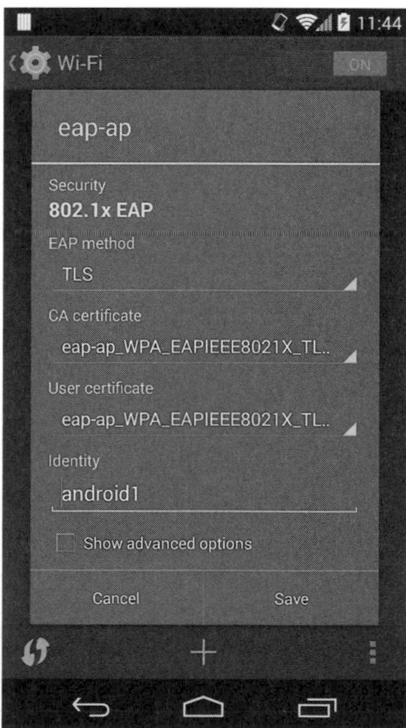

Figure 9-14: An EAP-TLS network added using `WifiManager`

Summary

Android supports a Device Administration API that allows device administration apps to configure a security policy, which can include requirements for lockscreen password complexity, device encryption, and camera usage. Device administrators are often used with corporate accounts, such as those for Microsoft Exchange and Google Apps, in order to limit access to corporate data based on the policy and device settings. The Device Administration API also provides features that enable remote device locking and data wipe.

Android devices can connect to various types of VPNs, including PPTP, L2TP/IPSec, and SSL-based VPNs. Support for PPTP and L2TP/IPSec is built into the platform and can only be extended through OS updates. Android 4.0 adds support for application-based VPNs, which allows third-party applications to implement custom VPN solutions.

In addition to the widely used pre-shared key Wi-Fi authentication mode, Android supports various WPA Enterprise configurations, namely PEAP, EAP-TLS, EAP-TTLS, and EAP-PWD. Certificates and private keys for EAP authentication methods that use SSL to establish a secure channel or authenticate users are stored in the system keystore and can use hardware protection when available. Wi-Fi networks that use EAP for authentication can be automatically provisioned using the `WifiManager` API in recent Android versions, beginning with Android 4.3.

10

DEVICE SECURITY

Until now, we've focused on how Android implements sandboxing and privilege separation in order to isolate applications from one another and the core OS. In this chapter, we look at how Android ensures OS integrity and protects device data from attackers that have physical access to a device. We start with a brief description of Android's bootloader and recovery OS, then discuss Android's verified boot feature, which guarantees that the *system* partition is not modified by malicious programs. Next we look at how Android encrypts the *userdata* partition, which hosts OS configuration files and application data. This guarantees that the device can't be booted without the decryption password and that user data can't be extracted even by direct access to the device's flash memory. We then show how Android's screen locking functionality is implemented, and how unlock patterns, PINs, and passphrases are hashed and stored on the device.

We'll also discuss secure USB debugging, which authenticates hosts that connect to the *Android Debug Bridge (ADB)* daemon over USB and requires users to explicitly allow access for each host. Because ADB access over USB allows execution of privileged operations such as application installation, full backup, and filesystem access (including full access to external storage), this feature helps prevent unauthorized access to device data and applications on devices that have ADB debugging enabled. Finally, we describe the implementation and archive encryption format of Android's full backup feature.

Controlling OS Boot-Up and Installation

Given physical access to a device, an attacker can access or modify user and system data not only via higher-level OS constructs such as files and directories, but also by accessing memory or raw disk storage directly. Such direct access can be achieved by physically interfacing with the device's electronic components by, for example, disassembling the device and connecting to hidden hardware debug interfaces or desoldering flash memory and reading the contents with a specialized device.

NOTE *Such hardware attacks are beyond the scope of this book; see Chapter 10 of the* Android Hacker's Handbook *(Wiley, 2014) for an introduction to this topic.*

A less intrusive, but still powerful way to gain access to this data is to use the device update mechanism to modify system files and remove access restrictions, or boot an alternative operating system that allows direct access to storage devices. Most consumer Android devices are locked down by default so that those techniques are either not possible or require possession of a code signing key, typically available only to the device manufacturer.

In the next sections, we briefly discuss how Android's bootloader and recovery OS regulate access to boot images and device update mechanisms. (We'll explore bootloader and recovery functionality in more detail in Chapter 13.)

Bootloader

A *bootloader* is a specialized, hardware-specific program that executes when a device is first powered on (coming out of reset for ARM devices). Its purpose is to initialize device hardware, optionally provide a minimal device configuration interface, and then find and start the operating system.

Booting a device typically requires going through different stages, which may involve a separate bootloader for each stage—but we'll refer to a single, aggregate bootloader that includes all boot stages, for the sake of simplicity. Android bootloaders are typically proprietary and specific to the system on a chip (SoC) that the device is built upon. Device and SoC manufacturers provide different functionality and levels of protection in their bootloaders, but most bootloaders support a *fastboot*, or more generally, *download mode*, which allows for the writing (usually called *flashing*) of raw partition images to the device's persistent storage, as well as booting transient system images (without flashing them to the device). Fastboot mode is enabled by a special hardware key combination applied while the device is booting, or by sending the *reboot bootloader* command via ADB.

In order to ensure device integrity, consumer devices are shipped with locked bootloaders, which either disallow flashing and booting system images completely or allow it only for images that have been signed by the device manufacturer. Most consumer devices allow for unlocking the bootloader, which removes fastboot restrictions and image signature checks. Unlocking the bootloader typically requires formatting the *userdata* partition, thus ensuring that a malicious OS image cannot get access to existing user data.

On some devices, unlocking the bootloader is an irreversible procedure, but most devices provide a way to relock the bootloader and return it to its original state. This is typically implemented by storing a bootloader state flag on a dedicated system partition (typically called `param` or `misc`) that hosts various device metatdata. Relocking the bootloader simply resets the value of this flag.

Recovery

A more flexible way to update a device is via its recovery OS. The *recovery OS*, or simply *recovery*, is a minimal Linux-based OS that includes a kernel, RAM disk with various low-level tools, and a minimal UI that is typically operated using the device's hardware buttons. The recovery is used to apply post-ship updates, generally delivered in the form of over-the-air (OTA) update packages. OTA packages include the new versions (or a binary patch) of updated system files and a script that applies the update. As we learned in Chapter 3, OTA files are also code signed with the private key of the device manufacturer. The recovery includes the public part of that key and verifies OTA files before applying them. This ensures that only OTA files that originate from a trusted party can modify the device OS.

The recovery OS is stored on a dedicated partition, just like the main Android OS. Therefore, it can be replaced by putting the bootloader into download mode and flashing a custom recovery image, which replaces the embedded public key, or does not verify OTA signatures at all. Such a recovery OS allows the main OS to be completely replaced with a build produced by a third party. A custom recovery OS can also allow unrestricted root access via ADB, as well as raw partition data acquisition. While the *userdata* partition could be encrypted (see "Disk Encryption" on page 258), making direct data access impossible, it is trivial to install a malicious program (rootkit) on the *system* partition while in recovery mode. The rootkit can then enable remote access to the device when the main OS is booted and thus allow access to user data that is transparently decrypted when the main OS boots. Verified boot (discussed in the next section) can prevent this, but only if the device verifies the *boot* partition using an unmodifiable verification key, stored in hardware.

An unlocked bootloader allows booting or flashing custom system images and direct access to system partitions. While Android security features such as verified boot and disk encryption can limit the damage that a malicious system image flashed via an unlocked bootloader can do, controlling access to the bootloader is integral to protecting an Android device. Therefore the bootloader should only be unlocked on test or development devices, or relocked and returned to its original state immediately after modifying the system.

Verified Boot

Android's verified boot implementation is based on the dm-verity device-mapper block integrity checking target.[1] *Device-mapper*[2] is a Linux kernel framework that provides a generic way to implement virtual block devices. It's the basis of Linux's Logical Volume Manager (LVM), and it's used to implement full-disk encryption (using the dm-crypt target), RAID arrays, and even distributed replicated storage.

Device-mapper works by essentially mapping a virtual block device to one or more physical block devices and optionally modifying transferred data in transit. For example, dm-crypt (which is also the basis of Android's *userdata* partition encryption, as discussed in "Disk Encryption" on page 258) decrypts read physical blocks and encrypts written blocks before committing them to disk. Thus, disk encryption is transparent to users of the virtual dm-crypt block device. Device-mapper targets can be stacked on top of each other, making it possible to implement complex data transformations.

dm-verity Overview

Because dm-verity is a block integrity checking target, it transparently verifies the integrity of each device block as it's being read from disk. If the block checks out, the read succeeds; if not, the read generates an I/O error as if the block were physically corrupted.

Under the hood, dm-verity is implemented using a precalculated hash tree (also called a *Merkle tree*) that includes the hashes of all device blocks. The leaf nodes of the tree include hashes of physical device blocks, while intermediate nodes are hashes of their child nodes (hashes of hashes). The root node is called the *root hash* and is based on all hashes in lower levels, as shown in Figure 10-1. Thus, a change even in a single device block will result in a change of the root hash, and in order to verify that a hash tree is genuine we only need to verify its root hash.

At runtime, dm-verity calculates the hash of each block when it's read and verifies it by traversing the precalculated hash tree. Because reading data from a physical device is already a time-consuming operation, the

---

1. Milan Broz, "dm-verity: device-mapper block integrity checking target," *https://code.google.com/p/cryptsetup/wiki/DMVerity*

2. Red Hat, Inc., "Device-Mapper Resource Page," *https://www.sourceware.org/dm/*

latency added by hashing and verification is relatively low. Furthermore, once verified, disk blocks are cached, and subsequent reads of the same block do not trigger integrity verification.

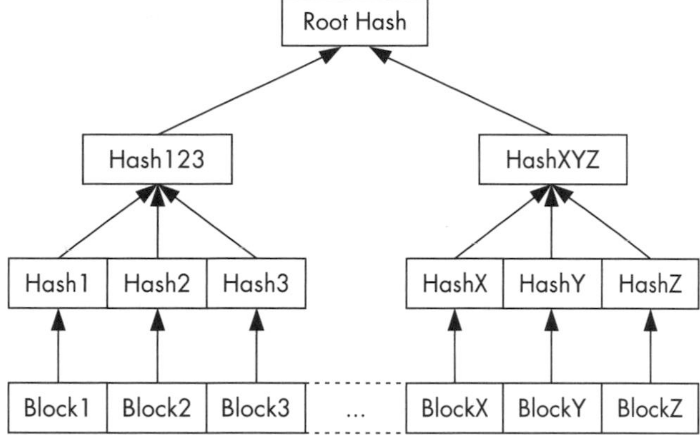

Figure 10-1: dm-verity hash tree

Because dm-verity depends on a precalculated hash tree over all blocks of a device, the underlying device must be mounted read-only in order for verification to be possible. Most filesystems record mount times and other metadata in their superblock, so even if no files are changed at runtime, block integrity checks will fail if the underlying block device is mounted read-write. Even though this can be seen as a limitation, it works well for devices or partitions that hold system files, which are only changed by OS updates. Any other change indicates either OS or disk corruption, or that a malicious program is trying to modify the OS or masquerade as a system file.

Ultimately, dm-verity's read-only requirement fits well with Android's security model, which hosts only application data on a read-write partition and keeps OS files on the read-only *system* partition.

Android Implementation

The dm-verity device-mapper target was originally developed in order to implement verified boot in Chrome OS and was integrated into the mainline Linux kernel in version 3.4. It's enabled with the `CONFIG_DM_VERITY` kernel configuration item.

Like Chrome OS, Android 4.4 also uses the dm-verity target, but the cryptographic verification of the root hash and mounting of verified partitions are implemented differently. The RSA public key used for verification is embedded in the boot partition under the *verity_key* filename and is used to verify the dm-verity mapping table, which holds the locations of the target device and the offset of the hash table, as well as the root hash and salt.

The mapping table and its signature are part of the verity metadata block, which is written to disk directly after the last filesystem block of the target device. A partition is marked as verifiable by adding the `verify` flag to the Android-specific *fs_mgr_flags* field of the device's *fstab* file. When Android's filesystem manager encounters the `verify` flag in *fstab*, it loads the verity metadata from the block device specified in *fstab* and verifies its signature using the included verity key. If the signature check succeeds, the filesystem manager parses the dm-verity mapping table and passes it to the Linux device-mapper, which uses the information contained in the mapping table in order to create a virtual dm-verity block device. This virtual block device is then mounted at the mount point specified in *fstab* in place of the corresponding physical device. As a result, all reads from the underlying physical device are transparently verified against the pre-generated hash tree. Modifying or adding files, or even remounting the partition as read-write results in an integrity verification and an I/O error.

NOTE *Because dm-verity is a kernel feature, in order for its integrity protection to be effective, the kernel that the device boots needs to be trusted. On Android, this requires verifying the boot partition, which also contains the root filesystem RAM disk* (initrd) *and the verity public key. Kernel or boot image verification is a device-specific process, which is typically implemented in the device bootloader and relies on an unmodifiable signature verification key stored in hardware.*

Enabling Verified Boot

The official Android documentation describes the procedure required to enable verified boot on Android as a multi-step process, which involves generating a hash tree, creating a dm-verity mapping table for the hash tree, signing the table, and generating and writing a verity metadata block to the target device.[3] In this section, we briefly describe the key steps of this process.

A dm-verity hash tree is generated with the `veritysetup` program, which is part of the *cryptsetup* cryptographic volume management tools package. The `veritysetup` program can operate directly on block devices or generate a hash tree using a filesystem image, and write the hash table to a file. Android's dm-verity implementation expects that the hash tree data to be stored on the same device as the target filesystem, so an explicit hash offset that points to a location after the verity metadata block must be specified when invoking `veritysetup`. Figure 10-2 shows the layout of a disk partition prepared for use with dm-verity.

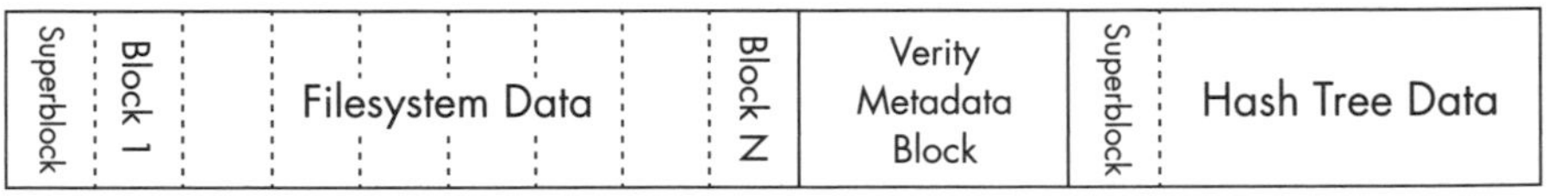

Figure 10-2: Layout of a disk partition prepared for dm-verity verification

Generating the hash tree produces the root hash, which is used to build the dm-verity mapping table for the target device. A sample mapping table is shown in Listing 10-1.

3. Google, "dm-verity on boot," *https://source.android.com/devices/tech/security/dm-verity.html*

```
1❶ /dev/block/mmcblk0p21❷ /dev/block/mmcblk0p21❸ 4096❹ 4096❺
204800❻ 204809❼ sha256❽
1F951588516c7e3eec3ba10796aa17935c0c917475f8992353ef2ba5c3f47bcb❾
5f061f591b51bf541ab9d89652ec543ba253f2ed9c8521ac61f1208267c3bfb1❿
```

Listing 10-1: Android dm-verity device mapping table

As shown in the listing, the table is a single line (split across multiple lines for readability) that, besides the root hash ❾, contains the dm-verity version ❶, name of the underlying data and hash device (❷ and ❸), data and hash block sizes (❹ and ❺), data and hash disk offsets (❻ and ❼), hash algorithm ❽, and salt ❿.

The mapping table is signed using a 2048-bit RSA key, and along with the resulting PKCS#1 v1.5 signature, is used to form the 32 KB verity metadata block. Table 10-1 shows the contents and size of each field of the metadata block.

Table 10-1: Verity Metadata Block Contents

Field	Description	Size	Value
Magic number	Used by fs_mgr as a sanity check	4 bytes	0xb001b001
Version	Metadata block version	4 bytes	Currently 0
Signature	Mapping table signature (PKCS#1 v1.5)	256 bytes	
Mapping table length	Mapping table length in bytes	4 bytes	
Mapping table	dm-verity mapping table	variable	
Padding	Zero-byte padding to 32k byte length	variable	

The RSA public key used for verification needs to be in mincrypt format (a minimalistic cryptographic library, also used by the stock recovery when verifying OTA file signatures), which is a serialization of mincrypt's `RSAPublicKey` structure. The interesting thing about this structure is that it doesn't simply include the key's modulus and public exponent values, but contains pre-computed values used by mincrypt's RSA implementation (based on Montgomery reduction). The public key is included in the root of the boot image under the *verity_key* filename.

The last step needed to enable verified boot is to modify the device's *fstab* file in order to enable block integrity verification for the *system* partition. This is simply a matter of adding the `verify` flag, as shown in Listing 10-2 (example *fstab* file for Nexus 4).

```
/dev/block/platform/msm_sdcc.1/by-name/system /system ext4 ro,barrier=1 wait,verify
```

Listing 10-2: fstab *entry for a dm-verity-formatted partition verified*

When the device boots, Android automatically creates a virtual dm-verity device based on the *fstab* entry and the information in the mapping table (contained in the metadata block), and mounts it at */system* as shown in Listing 10-3.

```
# mount|grep system
/dev/block/dm-0 /system ext4 ro,seclabel,relatime,data=ordered 0 0
```

Listing 10-3: dm-verity virutal block device mounted at /system

Now, any modifications to the system partition will result in read errors when reading the corresponding file(s). Unfortunately, system modifications by file-based OTA updates, which modify file blocks without updating verity metadata, also invalidate the hash tree. As mentioned in the official documentation, in order to be compatible with dm-verity-based verified boot, OTA updates should operate at the block level, ensuring that both file blocks and the hash tree and metadata are updated. This requires changing the current OTA update infrastructure, which is probably one of the reasons verified boot has yet to be deployed to production devices.

Disk Encryption

Android 3.0 introduced disk encryption along with device administrator policies (see Chapter 9 for details) that can enforce mandatory device encryption as one of the several "enhancements for the enterprise" included in that release. Disk encryption has been available in all subsequent versions with relatively few changes until version 4.4, which introduced a new key derivation function (scrypt). This section describes how Android implements disk encryption and how encryption keys and metadata are stored and managed.

NOTE *The Android Compatibility Definition requires that "IF the device has lockscreen, the device MUST support full-disk encryption."*[4]

Disk encryption uses an encryption algorithm to convert every bit of data that goes to disk to ciphertext, ensuring that data cannot be read from the disk without the decryption key. *Full-disk encryption (FDE)* promises that everything on disk is encrypted, including operating system files, cache, and temporary files. In practice, a small part of the OS, or a separate OS loader, must be kept unencrypted so that it can obtain the decryption key and then decrypt and mount the disk volume(s) used by the main OS. The disk decryption key is usually stored encrypted and requires an additional key encryption key (KEK) in order to be decrypted. The KEK can either be stored in a hardware module, such as a smart card or a TPM, or derived

4. Google, *Android 4.4 Compatibility Definition*, "9.9. Full-Disk Encryption," *https://static.googleusercontent.com/media/source.android.com/en//compatibility/4.4/android-4.4-cdd.pdf*

from a passphrase obtained from the user on each boot. When stored in a hardware module, the KEK can also be protected by a user-supplied PIN or password.

Android's FDE implementation encrypts only the *userdata* partition, which stores system configuration files and application data. The *boot* and *system* partitions, which store the kernel and OS files, are not encrypted, but *system* can optionally be verified using the dm-verity device-mapper target as described earlier in "Verified Boot" on page 254. Android's disk encryption is not enabled by default, and the disk encryption process must be triggered either by the user or by a device policy on managed devices. We examine Android's disk encryption implementation in the following sections.

Cipher Mode

Android's disk encryption uses dm-crypt,[5] currently the standard disk encryption subsystem in the Linux kernel. Like dm-verity, dm-crypt is a device-mapper target that maps an encrypted physical block device to a virtual device-mapper device. All data access to the virtual device is decrypted (for reads) or encrypted (for writes) transparently.

The encryption mechanism employed in Android uses a randomly generated 128-bit key together with AES in CBC mode. As we learned in Chapter 5, CBC mode requires an initialization vector (IV) that needs to be both random and unpredictable in order for encryption to be secure. This presents a problem when encrypting block devices, because blocks are accessed non-sequentially, and therefore each sector (or device block) requires a separate IV.

Android uses the encrypted salt-sector initialization vector (ESSIV) method with the SHA-256 hash algorithm (ESSIV:SHA256) in order to generate per-sector IVs. ESSIV employs a hash algorithm to derive a secondary key *s* from the disk encryption key *K*, called a *salt*. It then uses the salt as an encryption key and encrypts the sector number *SN* of each sector to produce a per-sector IV. In other words, $IV(SN) = AES_s(SN)$, where $s = SHA256(K)$.

Because the IV of each sector depends on a secret piece of information (the disk encryption key), per-sector IVs cannot be deduced by an attacker. However, ESSIV does not change CBC's malleability property and does not ensure the integrity of encrypted blocks. In fact, it's been demonstrated that an attacker who knows the original plaintext stored on disk can manipulate stored data and even inject a backdoor on volumes that use CBC for disk encryption.[6]

---

5. Milan Broz, "dm-crypt: Linux kernel device-mapper crypto target," *https://code.google.com/p/cryptsetup/wiki/DMCrypt*

6. Jakob Lell, "Practical malleability attack against CBC-Encrypted LUKS partitions," *http://www.jakoblell.com/blog/2013/12/22/practical-malleability-attack-against-cbc-encrypted-luks-partitions/*

ALTERNATIVE CIPER MODES: XTS

This particular attack against the ESSIV mode can be avoided by switching to a tweakable encryption cipher mode such as XTS (XEX-based tweaked-codebook mode with ciphertext stealing), which uses a combination of the sector address and index of the cipher block inside the sector to derive a unique "tweak" (variable parameter) for each sector.

Using a distinct tweak for each sector has the same effect as encrypting each sector with a unique key: the same plaintext will result in different ciphertext when stored in different sectors, but has much better performance than deriving a separate key (or IV) for each sector. However, while better than the CBC ESSIV mode, XTS is still susceptible to data manipulation in some cases and does not provide ciphertext authentication.

As of this writing, Android does not support the XTS mode for disk encryption. However, the underlying dm-crypt device-mapper target supports XTS, and it can easily be enabled with some modifications to Android's volume daemon (*vold*) implementation.

Key Derivation

The disk encryption key (called the "master key" in Android source code) is encrypted with another 128-bit AES key (KEK), derived from a user-supplied password. In Android versions 3.0 to 4.3, the key derivation function used was PBKDF2 with 2,000 iterations and a 128-bit random salt value. The resulting encrypted master key and the salt are stored, along with other metadata like the number of failed decryption attempts, in a footer structure occupying the last 16 KB of the encrypted partition, called a *crypto footer*. Storing an encrypted key on disk instead of using a key derived from the user-supplied password directly allows for changing the decryption password quickly, because the only thing that needs to be re-encrypted with the key derived from the new password is the master key (16 bytes).

While using a random salt makes it impossible to use precomputed tables to speed up key cracking, the number of iterations (2,000) used for PBKDF2 is not sufficiently large by today's standards. (The keystore key derivation process uses 8,192 iterations as discussed in Chapter 7. Backup encryption uses 10,000 iterations, as discussed later in "Android Backup" on page 283.) Additionally, PBKDF2 is an iterative algorithm, based on standard and relatively easy to implement hash functions, which makes it possible for PBKDF2 key derivation to be parallelized, taking full advantage of the processing power of multi-core devices such as GPUs. This allows even fairly complex alphanumeric passphrases to be brute-forced in a matter of days, or even hours.

In order to make it harder to brute-force disk encryption passwords, Android 4.4 introduced support for a new key derivation function called *scrypt*.[7] Scrypt employs a key derivation algorithm specifically designed to require large amounts of memory, as well as multiple iterations (such an algorithm is called *memory hard*). This makes it harder to mount brute-force attacks on specialized hardware such as ASICs or GPUs, which typically operate with a limited amount of memory.

Scrypt can be tuned by specifying the variable parameters *N*, *r*, and *p*, which influence the required CPU resources, memory amount, and parallelization cost, respectively. The values used in Android by default are $N = 32768$ (2^{15}), $r = 8$, and $p = 2$. They can be changed by setting the value of the *ro.crypto.scrypt_params* system property using the *N_factor:r_factor:p_factor* format; for example, *15:3:1* (the default). The value of each parameter is computed by raising 2 to the power of the respective factor. Android 4.4 devices automatically update the key derivation algorithm in the crypto footer from PBKDF2 to scrypt and re-encrypt the master key using a scrypt-derived encryption key. When the encrypted master key is updated, the *N*, *r*, and *p* parameters that were used for KEK derivation are written to the crypto footer.

NOTE *On the same desktop machine, brute-forcing a 4-digit PIN (using a naive, single-threaded algorithm that generates all possible PINs starting from 0000) takes about 5 milliseconds per PIN when using PBKDF2, and about 230 milliseconds per PIN when using scrypt as the KEK derivation function. In other words, brute-forcing PBKDF2 is almost 50 times cheaper (that is, faster) compared to scrypt.*

Disk Encryption Password

As discussed in the previous section, the KEK used to encrypt the disk encryption key is derived from a user-supplied password. When you first start the device encryption process, you're asked to either confirm your device unlock PIN or password, or set one if you haven't already or you're using the pattern screen lock (see Figure 10-3). The entered password or PIN is then used to derive the master key encryption key, and you're required to enter the password or PIN each time you boot the device, and then once more to unlock the screen after it starts.

Android doesn't have a dedicated setting to manage the encryption password after the device is encrypted, and changing the screen lock password or PIN will also silently change the device encryption password. This is most probably a usability-driven decision: most users would be confused by having to remember and enter two different passwords at different times and would probably quickly forget the less frequently used, and possibly more complex, disk encryption password. While this design is good for usability, it effectively forces users to use a simple disk encryption password, because they have to enter it each time they unlock the device, usually dozens of times a day. No one wants to enter a complex password that many times, and thus most users opt for a simple numeric PIN (unless a device policy requires otherwise).

7. C. Percival and S. Josefsson, *The scrypt Password-Based Key Derivation Function*, *http://tools.ietf.org/html/draft-josefsson-scrypt-kdf-01/*

Additionally, passwords are limited to 16 characters (a limit that is hardwired in the framework and not configurable), so using a passphrase is not an option.

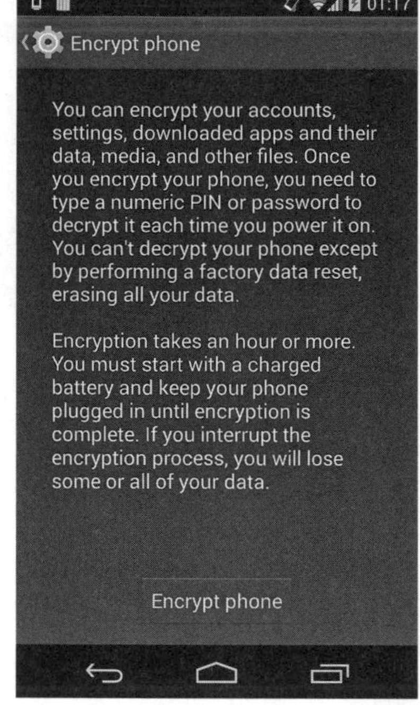

Figure 10-3: Device encryption screen

What's the problem with using the same password for both disk encryption and the lockscreen? After all, to get to the data on the phone you need to guess the lockscreen password anyway, so why bother with a separate one for disk encryption? The reason is that the two passwords protect your phone against two different types of attack. Most screen lock attacks would be online, brute-force ones: essentially someone trying out different passwords on a running device when they get brief access to it. After a few unsuccessful attempts, Android will lock the screen for 30 seconds (rate limiting), and even wipe the device if there are more failed unlock attempts (if required by device policy). Thus, even a relatively short screen-lock PIN offers adequate protection against online attacks in most cases (see "Brute-Force Attack Protection" on page 276 for details).

Of course, if someone has physical access to the device or a disk image of it, they can extract password hashes and crack them offline without worrying about rate-limiting or device wiping. This, in fact, is the scenario that full disk encryption is designed to protect against: when a device is stolen or confiscated, the attacker can either brute-force the actual device, or copy its data and analyze it even after the device is returned or disposed of. As mentioned earlier in "Key Derivation" on page 260, the encrypted master key is stored on disk, and if the password used to derive its encryption key is based on a short numeric PIN, it can be brute-forced in minutes[8] (or even seconds on pre-4.4 devices that use PBKDF2 for key derivation). A remote wipe solution could prevent this attack by deleting the master key, which only takes a moment and renders the device useless, but this is often not an option because the device might be offline or turned off.

Changing the Disk Encryption Password

The user-level part of disk encryption is implemented in the *cryptfs* module of Android's volume management daemon (*vold*). *crypfs* has commands for

8. Demonstrated by viaForensics in the "Into The Droid" talk, presented at DEF CON 20. Slides are available at *https://www.defcon.org/images/defcon-20/dc-20-presentations/Cannon/DEFCON-20-Cannon-Into-The-Droid.pdf*

both creating and mounting an encrypted volume, and for verifying and changing the master key encryption password. Android system services communicate with *cryptfs* by sending commands to *vold* through a local socket (also named *vold*), and *vold* sets system properties that describe the current state of the encryption or mount process based on the received command. (This results in a fairly complex boot procedure, described in detail in "Enabling Encryption" below and "Booting an Encrypted Device" on page 265.)

Android does not provide a UI to change only the disk encryption password, but one can do so by communicating directly with the *vold* daemon using the `vdc` command-line utility. However, access to the *vold* control socket is limited to the root user and members of the *mount* group, and furthermore, *cryptfs* commands are only available to the *root* and *system* users. If you're using an engineering build, or your device provides root access via a "superuser" app (see Chapter 13), you can send the *cryptfs* command shown in Listing 10-4 to *vold* in order to change the disk encryption password.

```
# vdc cryptfs changepw <newpass>
200 0 0
```

Listing 10-4: Changing the disk encryption password using vdc

NOTE *If you change your lockscreen password, the disk encryption password will be changed automatically. (This does not apply to secondary users on multi-user devices.)*

Enabling Encryption

As mentioned in the previous section, the user-level part of Android's disk encryption is implemented by a dedicated *cryptfs* module of the *vold* daemon. *cryptfs* provides the `checkpw`, `restart`, `cryptocomplete`, `enablecrypto`, `changepw`, `verifypw`, `getfield`, and `setfield` commands, which the framework sends at various points of the encryption or encrypted volume mount process. In addition to the permissions set on the *vold* local socket, *crypfs* explicitly checks the identity of the command sender, and only allows access to the *root* and *system* users.

Controlling Device Encryption Using System Properties

The *vold* daemon sets a number of system properties in order to trigger the various stages of device encryption or mounting and to communicate the current encryption state to framework services. The *ro.crypto.state* property holds the current encryption state, which is set to *encrypted* when the data partition has been successfully encrypted, and to *unencrypted* when it has not yet been encrypted. The property can also be set to *unsupported* if the device does not support disk encryption. The *vold* daemon also sets various predefined values to the *vold.decrypt* property in order to signal the current state of device encryption or mounting. The *vold.encrypt_progress* property holds the current encryption progress (from 0 to 100), or an error string if an error occurred during device encryption or mounting.

The *ro.crypto.fs_crypto_blkdev* system property contains the name of the virtual device allocated by the device mapper. After successfully decrypting the disk encryption key, this virtual device is mounted at */data* in place of the underlying physical volume, as shown in Listing 10-5 (with output split for readability).

```
# mount|grep '/data'
/dev/block/dm-0 /data ext4 rw,seclabel,nosuid,nodev,noatime,
errors=panic,user_xattr,barrier=1,nomblk_io_submit,data=ordered 0 0
```

Listing 10-5: Encrypted virtual block device mounted at /data

Unmounting /data

The Android framework expects */data* to be available, but it needs to be unmounted in order to be encrypted. This creates a catch-22 situation, which Android solves by unmounting the physical *userdata* partition and mounting an on-memory filesystem (tempfs) in its place while performing encryption. Switching partitions at runtime in turn requires stopping and restarting certain system services, which *vold* triggers by setting the value of the *vold.decrypt* system property to *trigger_restart_framework*, *trigger_restart_min_framework*, or *trigger_shutdown_framework*. These values trigger different parts of *init.rc*, as shown in Listing 10-6.

```
--snip--
on post-fs-data❶
    chown system system /data
    chmod 0771 /data
    restorecon /data
    copy /data/system/entropy.dat /dev/urandom
--snip--
on property:vold.decrypt=trigger_reset_main❷
    class_reset main

on property:vold.decrypt=trigger_load_persist_props
    load_persist_props

on property:vold.decrypt=trigger_post_fs_data❸
    trigger post-fs-data

on property:vold.decrypt=trigger_restart_min_framework❹
    class_start main

on property:vold.decrypt=trigger_restart_framework❺
    class_start main
    class_start late_start

on property:vold.decrypt=trigger_shutdown_framework❻
    class_reset late_start
    class_reset main
--snip-
```

Listing 10-6: vold.decrypt *triggers in* init.rc

Triggering the Encryption Process

When the user starts the encryption process via the system Settings UI with Security ▸ Encrypt phone, the Settings app calls `MountService`, which in turn sends the `cryptfs enablecrypto inplace` *password* command to *vold*, where *password* is the lockscreen password. In turn, *vold* unmounts the *userdata* partition and sets *vold.decrypt* to *trigger_shutdown_framework* (❻ in Listing 10-6), which shuts down most system services except for those that are part of the *core* service class. The *vold* daemon then unmounts */data,* mounts a tempfs filesystem in its place, and then sets *vold.encrypt_progress* to 0 and *vold.decrypt* to *trigger_restart_min_framework* (❹ in Listing 10-6). This starts a few more system services (in the *main* class) that are required for showing the encryption progress UI.

Updating the Crypto Footer and Encrypting Data

Next, *vold* sets up the virtual dm-crypt device and writes the crypto footer. The footer can be written to the end of the *userdata* partition or to a dedicated partition or file, and its location is specified in the *fstab* file as the value of the `encryptable` flag. For example, on the Nexus 5 the crypto footer is written to the dedicated partition *metadata,* as shown in Listing 10-7 as ❶ (with the single line broken for readability). When the crypto footer is written at the end of the encrypted partition, the `encryptable` flag is set to the string *footer.*

```
--snip--
/dev/block/platform/msm_sdcc.1/by-name/userdata  /data  ext4
noatime,nosuid,nodev,barrier=1,data=ordered,nomblk_io_submit,noauto_da_alloc,errors=panic
wait,check,encryptable=/dev/block/platform/msm_sdcc.1/by-name/metadata❶
--snip--
```

Listing 10-7: The `encryptable` fstab *flag specifies the location of the crypto footer*

The crypto footer contains the encrypted disk encryption key (master key), the salt used for KEK derivation, and other key derivation parameters and metadata. Its *flags* field is set to `CRYPT_ENCRYPTION_IN_PROGRESS` (0x2) to signal that device encryption has started but not been completed.

Finally, each block is read from the physical *userdata* partition and written to the virtual dm-crypt device, which encrypts read blocks and writes them to disk, thus encrypting the *userdata* partition in place. If encryption completes without errors, *vold* clears the `CRYPT_ENCRYPTION_IN_PROGRESS` flag and reboots the device.

Booting an Encrypted Device

Booting an encrypted device requires asking the user for the disk encryption password. Rather then use a specialized bootloader UI, Android sets the *vold.decrypt* system property to 1 and then starts a minimal set of system services in order to show a standard Android UI. As with device encryption, this again requires mounting a tmpfs filesystem at */data* in order to allow core system services to start. When the core framework is up, Android detects that *vold.decrypt* is set to 1 and starts the *userdata* partition mount process.

Obtaining the Disk Encryption Password

The first step in this process is to check whether the partition has been successfully encrypted by sending the `cryptfs cryptocomplete` command to *vold*, which in turn checks whether the crypto footer is properly formatted and that the `CRYPT_ENCRYPTION_IN_PROGRESS` flag is not set. If the partition is found to be successfully encrypted, the framework launches the password entry UI shown in Figure 10-4 provided by `CryptKeeper`, part of the system Settings app. This activity acts as a home screen (launcher), and because it has higher priority than the default launcher, it's started first after the device boots.

If the device is unencrypted, `CryptKeeper` disables itself and finishes, which causes the system activity manager to launch the default home screen application. If the device is encrypted or in the process of being encrypted (that is, the *vold.crypt* property is not empty or set to *trigger_restart_framework*), the `CryptKeeper` activity starts and hides the status and system bars. In addition, `CryptKeeper` ignores hardware back button presses, thus disallowing navigation away from the password input UI.

If the encrypted device is corrupted, or the encryption process interrupted and the *userdata* partition left only partially encrypted, the device cannot be booted. In this case, `CryptKeeper` displays the UI shown in Figure 10-5, allowing the user to trigger a factory reset, which reformats the *userdata* partition.

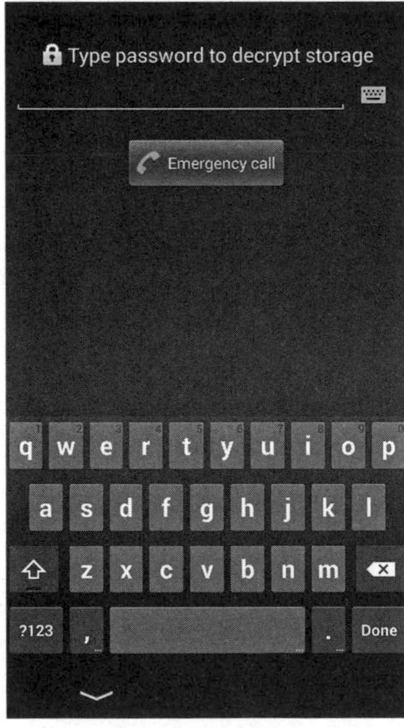

Figure 10-4: Device encryption password input UI

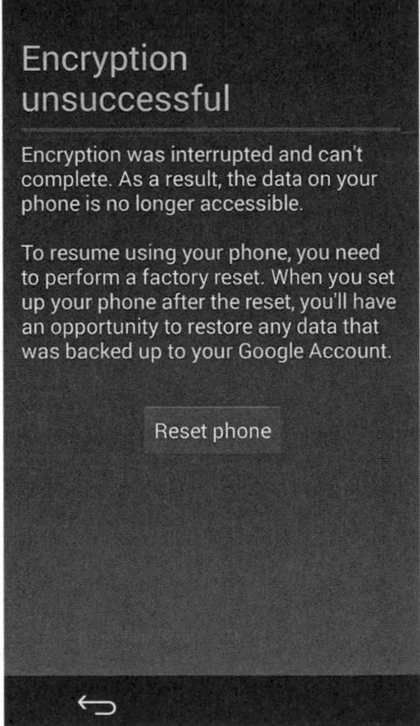

Figure 10-5: UI shown if device encryption fails

Decrypting and Mounting /data

When the user enters their password, `CryptKeeper` sends the `cryptfs checkpw` command to *vold* by calling the `decryptStorage()` method of the system `MountService`. This instructs *vold* to check whether the entered password is correct by trying to mount the encrypted partition at a temporary mount point and then unmounting it. If the procedure succeeds, *vold* sets the name of the virtual block device allocated by the device-mapper as the value of *ro.crypto.fs_crypto_blkdev* property and returns control to `MountService`, which in turn sends the `cryptfs restart` command, instructing *vold* to restart all system services in the *main* class (❷ in Listing 10-6). This allows the tempfs filesystem to be unmounted, and the newly allocated virtual dm-crypt block device to be mounted at */data*.

Starting All System Services

After the encrypted partition is mounted and prepared, *vold* sets *vold.decrypt* to *trigger_post_fs_data* (❸ in Listing 10-6), thus triggering the *post-fs-data* ❶ section of *init.rc*. The commands in this section set up file and directory permissions, restore SELinux contexts, and create required directories under */data* if necessary.

Finally, *post-fs-data* sets the *vold.post_fs_data_done property* to 1, which *vold* polls periodically. When *vold* detects a value of 1, it sets the *vold.decrypt* property to *trigger_restart_framework* (❺ in Listing 10-6), which restarts all services in the *main* class, and starts all delayed services (class *late_start*). At this point, the framework is fully initialized and the device boots using the decrypted view of the *userdata* partition mounted at */data*. From this point on, all data written by applications or the system is automatically encrypted before being committed to disk.

LIMITATIONS OF DISK ENCRYPTION

Disk encryption only protects data at rest; that is, when the device is turned off. Because disk encryption is transparent and implemented at the kernel level, after an encrypted volume is mounted, it is indistinguishable from a plaintext volume to user-level processes. Therefore disk encryption does not protect data from malicious programs running on the device. Applications that deal with sensitive data should not rely solely on full-disk encryption, but should implement their own, file-based encryption instead. The file encryption key should be encrypted with a KEK derived from a user-supplied password, or some unchangeable hardware property if the data needs to be bound to the device. To ensure file integrity, encrypted data must be authenticated using either an authenticated encryption scheme like GCM, or an additional authentication function such as HMAC.

Screen Security

One way to control access to an Android device is by requiring user authentication in order to access the system UI and applications. User authentication is implemented by showing a *lockscreen* each time the device boots or its screen is turned on. The lockscreen on a single-user device, configured to require a numeric PIN to unlock, might look like Figure 10-6.

Figure 10-6: PIN lockscreen

In early Android versions, the lockscreen was only designed to protect access to the device's UI. As the platform evolved, the lockscreen has been extended with features that display widgets that show up-to-date device or application state, allow switching between users on multi-user devices, and the ability to unlock the system keystore. Similarly, the screen unlock PIN or password is now used to derive the credential storage encryption key (for software implementations), as well as the disk encryption key KEK.

Lockscreen Implementation

Android's lockscreen (or *keyguard*) is implemented like regular Android applications: with widgets laid out on a window. It's special because its window lives on a high window layer that other applications cannot draw on top of or control. Additionally, the keyguard intercepts the normal navigation buttons, which makes it impossible to bypass and thus "locks" the device.

The keyguard window layer is not the highest layer, however; dialogs originating from the keyguard itself, and the status bar, are drawn over the keyguard. You can see a list of the currently shown windows using the Hierarchy Viewer tool available with the ADT. When the screen is locked, the active window is the Keyguard window, as shown in Figure 10-7.

NOTE *Prior to Android 4.0, third-party applications could show windows in the keyguard layer, which allowed applications to intercept the Home button and implement "kiosk"-style applications. However, because this functionality was abused by certain malware applications, since Android 4.0 adding windows to the keyguard layer requires the* `INTERNAL_SYSTEM_WINDOW` *signature permission, which is available only to system applications.*

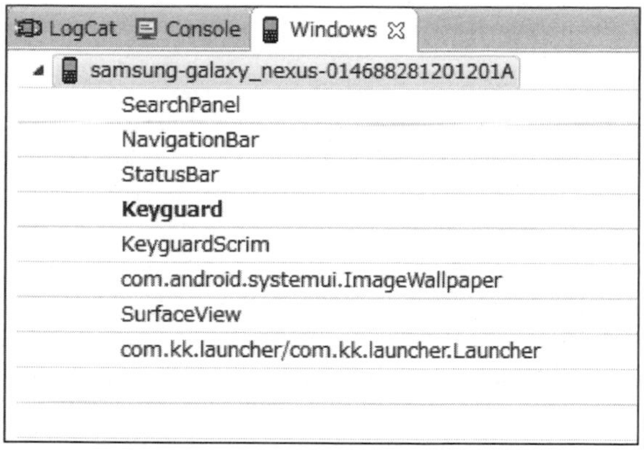

LogCat Console Windows

samsung-galaxy_nexus-014688281201201A
SearchPanel
NavigationBar
StatusBar
Keyguard
KeyguardScrim
com.android.systemui.ImageWallpaper
SurfaceView
com.kk.launcher/com.kk.launcher.Launcher

Figure 10-7: Keyguard window position in Android's window stack

For a long time, the keyguard was an implementation detail of Android's window system and was not separated into a dedicated component. With the introduction of lockscreen widgets, dreams (that is, screensavers), and support for multiple users, the keyguard gained quite a lot of new functionality and was eventually extracted in a dedicated system application, `Keyguard`, in Android 4.4. The `Keyguard` app lives in the *com.android.systemui* process, along with the core Android UI implementation.

The UI for each unlock method (discussed next) is implemented as a specialized view component. This component is hosted by a dedicated view container class called `KeyguardHostView`, along with keyguard widgets and other helper UI components. For example, the PIN unlock view shown in Figure 10-6 is implemented in the `KeyguardPINView` class, and password unlock is implemented by the `KeyguardPasswordView` class. The `KeyguardHostView` class automatically selects and displays the appropriate keyguard view for the currently configured unlock method and device state. Unlock views delegate password checks to the `LockPatternUtils` class, which is responsible for comparing user input to saved unlock credentials, as well as for persisting password changes to disk and updating authentication-related metadata.

Besides the implementations of keyguard unlock views, the `Keyguard` system application includes the exported `KeyguardService` service, which exposes a remote AIDL interface, `IKeyguardService`. This service allows its clients to check the current state of the keyguard, set the current user, launch the camera, and hide or disable the keyguard. Operations that change the state of the keyguard are protected by a system signature permission, `CONTROL_KEYGUARD`.

Keyguard Unlock Methods

Stock Android provides several keyguard unlock methods (also called *security modes* in Android's source code). Of these, five can be directly selected in the Choose screen lockscreen: Slide, Face Unlock, Pattern, PIN, and Password, as shown in Figure 10-8.

The Slide unlock method requires no user authentication and its security level is therefore equivalent to selecting None. Both states are represented internally by setting the current security mode to the `KeyguardSecurityModel.SecurityMode.None` enum value. As of this writing, Face Unlock is the only implementation of the `SecurityMode.Biometric` security mode and is internally referred to as "weak biometric" (a "strong biometric" could be implemented with fingerprint or iris recognition in a future version). Unlock methods that are not compatible with the current device security policy (the top three in Figure 10-8) are disabled and cannot be selected. The security policy can be set either explicitly by a device administrator, or implicitly by enabling a security-related OS feature such as credential storage or full-disk encryption.

The Pattern unlock method (`SecurityMode.Pattern`) is Android-specific and requires drawing a predefined pattern on a 3×3 grid to unlock the device, as shown in Figure 10-9.

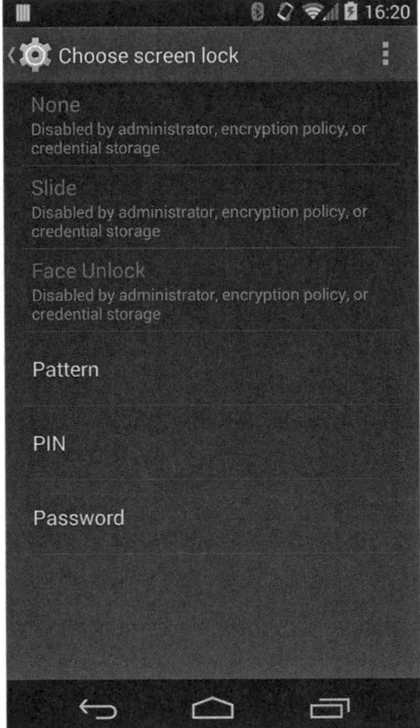

Figure 10-8: Directly selectable keyguard unlock methods

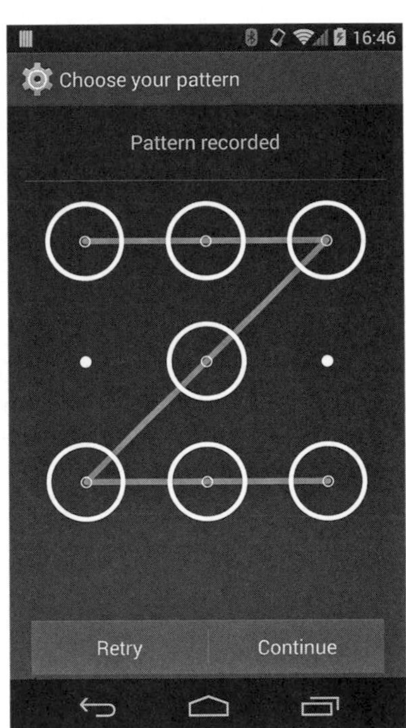

Figure 10-9: Configuring the Pattern unlock method

The PIN (`SecurityMode.PIN`) and Password (`SecurityMode.Password`) unlock methods are implemented similarly, but differ by the scope of allowed characters: only numeric (0-9) for the PIN, or alphanumeric for Password are allowed.

The `SecurityMode` enum defines three more unlock methods that are not directly selectable in the Choose screen lockscreen: `SecurityMode.Account`, `SecurityMode.SimPin`, and `SecurityMode.SimPuk`. The `SecurityMode.Account` method is available only on devices that support Google accounts (Google experience devices) and is not an independent unlock method. It can only be used as a fallback method for another security mode. Similarly, `SecurityMode.SimPin` and `SecurityMode.SimPuk` are not lockscreen unlock methods per se; they're only available if the device's SIM card requires a PIN before use. Because the SIM card remembers the PIN authentication status, the PIN or PUK must be entered only once—when the device boots (or if the SIM card state is otherwise reset). We'll delve deeper into the implementation of each lockscreen security mode in the next sections.

Face Unlock

Face Unlock is a relatively new unlock method introduced in Android 4.0. It uses the device's front-facing camera to register an image of the owner's face (see Figure 10-10) and relies on image recognition technology to recognize the face captured when unlocking the device. Although improvements to Face Unlock's accuracy have been made since its introduction, it's considered the least secure of all unlock methods, and even the setup screen warns users that "someone who looks similar to you could unlock your phone." In addition, Face Unlock requires a backup unlock method—either a pattern or a PIN, to handle situations when face recognition is not possible (such as poor lighting, camera malfunction, and so on). The Face Unlock implementation is based on facial recognition technology developed by the PittPatt (Pittsburgh Pattern Recognition) company, which Google acquired in 2011. The code remains proprietary and no details are available about the format of the stored data or the recognition algorithms employed. As of this writing, the implementation of Face Unlock resides in the `com.android.facelock` package.

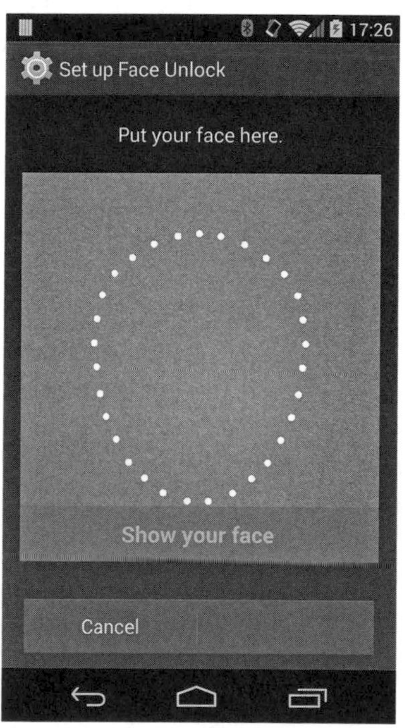

Figure 10-10: Face Unlock setup screen

Pattern Unlock

As shown in Figure 10-9, the code for pattern unlock is entered by joining at least four points on a 3×3 matrix. Each point can be used only once (crossed points are disregarded) and the maximum number of points is nine. Internally, the pattern is stored as a byte sequence, with each point represented by its index, where 0 is top left and 8 is bottom right. Thus the pattern is similar to a PIN with a minimum of four and maximum of nine digits, which uses only nine distinct digits (0 to 8). However, because points cannot be repeated, the number of variations in an unlock pattern is considerably lower compared to those of a nine-digit PIN.

The hash for the pattern lock is stored in */data/system/gesture.key* (*/data/system/users/<user ID>/gesture.key* on multi-user devices) as an unsalted SHA-1 value. By simply dumping this file, we can easily see that the contents of the *gesture.key* file for the pattern in Figure 10-9 (represented as *00010204060708* in hexadecimal) shown in Listing 10-8 matches the SHA-1 hash of the pattern byte sequence, which is *6a062b9b3452e366407181a1bf92ea73e9ed4c48* for this example.

```
# od -t x1 /data/system/gesture.key
0000000 6a 06 2b 9b 34 52 e3 66 40 71 81 a1 bf 92 ea 73
0000020 e9 ed 4c 48
```

Listing 10-8: Contents of the /data/system/gesture.key file

Because a random salt value isn't used when calculating the hash, each pattern is always hashed to the same value, which makes it relatively easy to generate a precomputed table of all possible patterns and their respective hashes. (Such tables are readily available online.) This allows for instant recovery of the pattern once the *gesture.key* file is obtained. However, the file is owned by the *system* user and its permissions are set to 0600, so recovery is not usually possible on production devices. The entered pattern is checked against the saved hash using the `checkPattern()` method of the `LockScreenUtils` class, and the pattern hash is calculated and persisted using the `saveLockPattern()` method of that class. Saving the pattern also sets the current password quality value to `DevicePolicyManager.PASSWORD_QUALITY_SOMETHING`.

Another unfortunate property of the pattern unlock method is that because capacitive touch screens are operated directly using a finger (not with a stylus or a similar tool), drawing the unlock pattern multiple times leaves a distinct trace on a touch screen, making it vulnerable to the so called "smudge attack." Using appropriate lighting and cameras, finger smudges on the screen can be detected, and the unlock pattern can be inferred with a very high probability. For these reasons, the pattern unlock method's security level is considered very low. In addition, because the number of combinations is limited, the unlock pattern is a poor source of entropy and is disallowed when the user's unlock credential is used to derive an encryption key, such as those used for system's keystore and device encryption.

Like Face Unlock, the pattern unlock method supports a backup unlock mechanism that is only made available after the user enters an invalid pattern more than five times. Backup authentication must be manually activated by pressing the Forgot Pattern button shown at the bottom of the lockscreen. After the button is pressed, the device goes into the `SecurityMode.Account` security mode and displays the screen shown in Figure 10-11.

The user can enter the credentials of any Google account registered on the device to unlock it, and then reset or change the unlock method. Therefore, having a Google account with an easy to guess (or shared) password registered on the device could be a potential backdoor to the device's lockscreen.

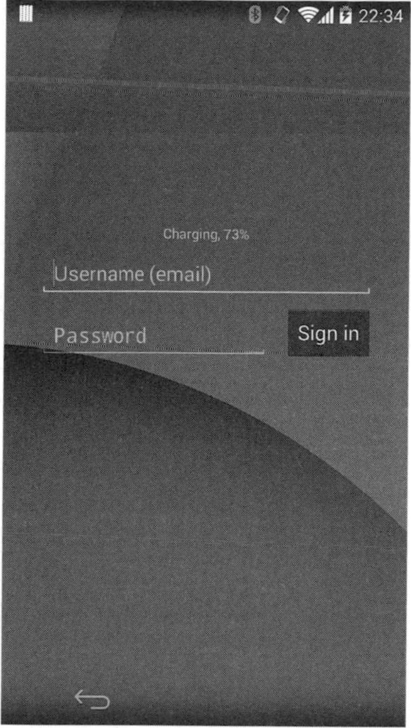

Figure 10-11: Google account unlock mode

NOTE *As of this writing, Google accounts that have been configured to require two-factor authentication cannot be used to unlock the device.*

PIN and Password Unlock

The PIN and password methods are essentially equivalent: they compare the hash of the user's input to a salted hash stored on the device and unlock it if the values match. The hash of the PIN or password is a combination of the SHA-1 and MD5 hash values of the user input, salted with a 64-bit random value. The calculated hash is stored in the */data/misc/password.key* (*/data/system/users/<user ID>/password.key* on multi-user devices) file as a hexadecimal string and may look like Listing 10-9.

```
# cat /data/system/password.key && echo
9B93A9A846FE2FC11D49220FC934445DBA277EB0AF4C9E324D84FFC0120D7BAE1041FAAC
```

Listing 10-9: Contents of the /data/misc/password.key file

The salt used for calculating the hash values was saved in the `secure` table of the system's `SettingsProvider` content provider under the *lockscreen.password_salt* key in Android versions prior to 4.2, but was moved to a dedicated database, along with other lockscreen-related metadata in order to support multiple users per device. As of Android 4.4, the database is located in */data/system/locksettings.db* and is accessed via the ILockSettings AIDL interface of the LockSettingsService.

Accessing the service requires the ACCESS_KEYGUARD_SECURE_STORAGE signature permission, which is only allowed to system applications. The *locksettings.db* database has a single table, also called locksettings, which may contain data like Listing 10-10 for a particular user (the user column contains the Android user ID).

```
sqlite> select name, user, value from locksettings where user=0;
name                            |user|value
--snip--
lockscreen.password_salt        |0   |6909501022570534487❶
--snip--
lockscreen.password_type_alternate|0   |0❷
lockscreen.password_type        |0   |131072❸
lockscreen.passwordhistory      |0   |5BFE43E89C989972EF0FA0EC00BA30F356EE7B
7C7BF8BC08DEA2E067FF6C18F8CD7134B8,EE29A531FE0903C2144F0618B08D1858473C50341A7
8DEA85D219BCD27EF184BCBC2C18C❹
```

Listing 10-10: Contents of /data/system/locksettings.db *for the owner user*

Here, the *lockscreen.password_salt* setting ❶ stores the 64-bit (represented as a Java long type) salt value, and the *lockscreen.password_type_alternate* setting ❷ contains the type of the backup (also called alternate) unlock method type (0 means none) for the current unlock method. *lockscreen.password_type* ❸ stores the currently selected password type, represented by the value of the corresponding PASSWORD_QUALITY constant defined in the DevicePolicyManager class. In this example, 131072 (0x00020000 in hexadecimal) corresponds to the PASSWORD_QUALITY_NUMERIC constant, which is the password quality provided by a numeric PIN. Finally, *lockscreen.passwordhistory* ❹ contains the password history, saved as a sequence of previous PIN or password hashes, separated by commas. The history is only saved if the history length has been set to a value greater than zero using one of the setPasswordHistoryLength() methods of the DevicePolicyManager class. When password history is available, entering a new password that is the same as any password in the history is forbidden.

The password hash can be easily calculated by concatenating the password or PIN string (*1234* for this example) with the salt value formatted as a hexadecimal string (*5fe37a926983d657* for this example) and calculating the SHA-1 and MD5 hashes of the resulting string, as shown in Listing 10-11.

```
$ SHA1=`echo -n '12345fe37a926983d657'|sha1sum|cut -d- -f1|tr '[a-z]' '[A-Z]'`❶
$ MD5=`echo -n '12345fe37a926983d657'|md5sum|cut -d- -f1|tr '[a-z]' '[A-Z]'`❷
$ echo "$SHA1$MD5"|tr -d ' '❸
9B93A9A846FE2FC11D49220FC934445DBA277EB0AF4C9E324D84FFC0120D7BAE1041FAAC
```

Listing 10-11: Calculating a PIN or password hash using sha1sum *and* md5sum

In this example the hashes are calculated using the sha1sum ❶ and md5sum ❷ commands. When concatenated ❸, the output of the two commands produces the string contained in the *password.key* file shown in Listing 10-9.

Note that while using a random hash makes it impossible to use a single precalculated table for brute-forcing the PIN or password of any device, calculating the password or hash requires a single hash invocation, so generating a targeted hash table for a particular device (assuming the salt value is also available) is still relatively cheap. Additionally, while Android calculates both the SHA-1 and MD5 hashes of the PIN or password, this provides no security value, as it is sufficient to target the shorter hash (MD5) in order to uncover the PIN or password.

The entered password is checked against the stored hash using the `LockPatternUtils.checkPassword()` method, and the hash of a user-supplied password is calculated and persisted using the one of the `saveLockPassword()` methods of that class. Calling `saveLockPassword()` updates the *password.key* file for the target (or current) user. Like *gesture.key*, this file is owned by the *system* user and has permissions 0600. In addition to updating the password hash, `saveLockPassword()` calculates the complexity of the entered password and updates the `value` column corresponding to the *lockscreen.password_type* key (❸ in Listing 10-10) in *locksettings.db* with the calculated complexity value. If password history is enabled, `saveLockPassword()` also adds the PIN or password hash to the `locksettings` table (❹ in Listing 10-11).

Recall that when the device is encrypted, the PIN or password is used to derive a KEK that encrypts the disk encryption key. Therefore, changing the PIN or password of the owner user also re-encrypts the disk encryption key by calling the `changeEncryptionPassword()` method of the system's `MountService`. (Changing the PIN or password of a secondary user does not affect the disk encryption key.)

PIN and PUK Unlock

The PIN and PUK security modes are not lockscreen unlock methods per se because they depend on the state of the device's SIM card and are only shown if the SIM card is in a locked state. A SIM card can require users to enter a preconfigured PIN code in order to unlock the card and get access to any network authentication keys stored inside, which are required to register with the mobile network and place non-emergency calls.

Because a SIM card retains its unlock state until reset, the PIN code typically must be entered only when the device first boots. If an incorrect code is entered more than three times, the SIM card locks and requires the user to enter a separate code to unlock it called the *PIN unlock key (PUK)*, or *personal unblocking code (PUC)*.

When the lockscreen is shown, Android checks the state of the SIM card, and if it's `State.PIN_REQUIRED` (defined in the `IccCardConstants` class), it shows the SIM unlock keyguard view shown in Figure 10-12. When the user enters a SIM unlock PIN, it's passed to the `supplyPinReportResult()` method of the `ITelephony` interface (implemented in the `TeleService` system application), which in turn passes it to the device's baseband processor (the device component that implements mobile network communication, also sometimes referred to as the *modem* or *radio*) via the radio interface daemon (*rild*). Finally, the baseband processor, which is directly connected to the SIM, sends the PIN to the SIM card and receives a status code in exchange. The status code is passed back to the unlock view via the same route. If the status code indicates that the SIM card accepted the PIN and no screen lock is configured, the home screen (launcher) is displayed next. If, on the other hand, a screen lock has been configured, it's shown after unlocking the SIM card, and the user must enter their credentials in order to unlock the device.

If the SIM card is locked (that is, in the `PUK_REQUIRED` state), Android shows a PUK entry screen and allows the user to set up a new PIN after they unlock the card. The PUK and new PIN are passed to the `supplyPukReportResult()` method of the `ITelephony` interface, which delivers them to the SIM card. If a screen lock is configured, it is shown when the PUK is validated and the new PIN configured.

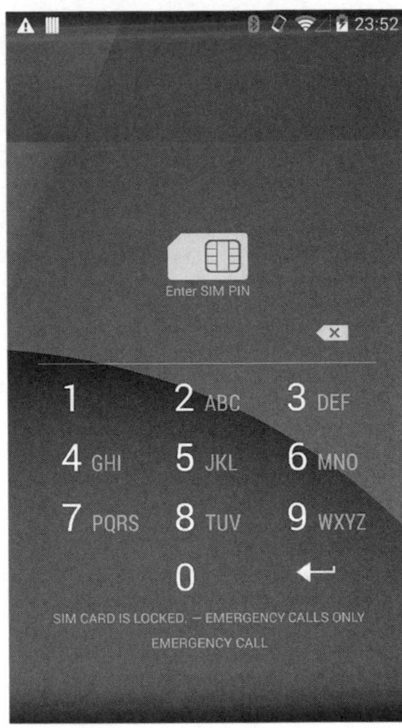

Figure 10-12: SIM unlock screen

The `Keyguard` system application monitors SIM state changes by registering for the `TelephonyIntents.ACTION_SIM_STATE_CHANGED` broadcast and shows the lockscreen if the card becomes locked or permanently disabled. Users can toggle the SIM card's PIN protection by navigating to **Settings ▸ Security ▸ Set up SIM card lock** and using the **Lock SIM card** checkbox.

Brute-Force Attack Protection

Because complex passwords can be tricky to input on a touch screen keyboard, users typically use relatively short unlock credentials, which can easily be guessed or brute-forced. Android protects against brute-force attacks executed directly on the device (online attacks) by requiring users to wait 30 seconds after each five subsequent failed authentication attempts, as shown in Figure 10-13. This technique is referred to as *rate limiting*.

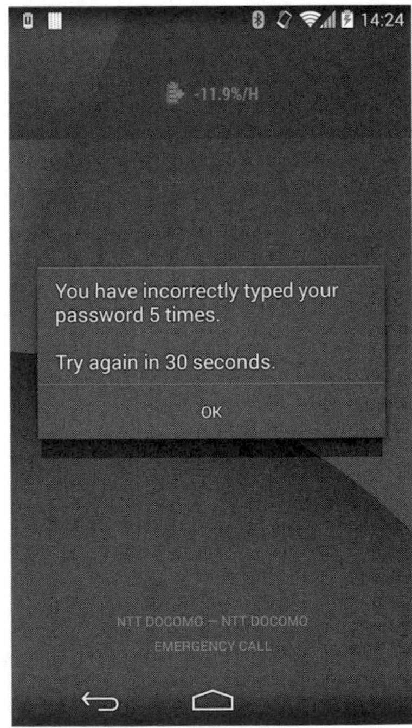

Figure 10-13: Rate limiting after five subsequent failed authentication attempts

To further deter brute-force attacks, password complexity, expiration, and history rules can be set and enforced using the `DevicePolicyManager` API, as discussed in Chapter 9. If the device stores or allows access to sensitive corporate data, device administrators can also set a threshold for the allowed failed authentication attempts using the `DevicePolicyManager.setMaximumFailedPasswordsForWipe()` method. When the threshold is reached, all user data on the device is automatically deleted, preventing attackers from gaining unauthorized access to it.

Secure USB Debugging

One reason for Android's success is the low entry barrier to application development; apps can be developed on any OS, in a high-level language, without the need to invest in developer tools or hardware (when using the Android emulator). Developing software for embedded or other dedicated devices has traditionally been difficult, because it's usually hard (or in some cases impossible) to inspect a program's internal state or otherwise interact with the device in order to debug programs.

Since its earliest versions, Android has included a powerful device interaction toolkit that allows interactive debugging and inspecting device state, called the *Android Debug Bridge (ADB)*. ADB is typically turned off on consumer devices, but can be turned on via the system UI in order to enable app development and debugging on the device. Because ADB provides privileged access to the device's filesystem and applications, it can be used to obtain unauthorized access to data. In the following sections, we'll discuss ADB's architecture, then discuss the steps recent Android versions have taken to restrict access to ADB.

ADB Overview

ADB keeps track of all devices (or emulators) connected to a host, and offers various services to its clients (command line clients, IDEs, and so on). It consists of three main components: the ADB server, the ADB daemon (*adbd*), and the default command-line client (`adb`). The ADB server runs on the host machine as a background process and decouples clients from the actual devices or emulators. It monitors device connectivity and sets their state appropriately (`CS_CONNECTED`, `CS_OFFLINE`, `CS_RECOVERY`, and so on).

The ADB daemon runs on an Android device (or emulator) and provides the actual services client use. It connects to the ADB server through USB or TCP/IP, and receives and processes commands from it. The `adb` command-line client lets you send commands to a particular device. In practice, it is implemented in the same binary as the ADB server and thus shares much of its code. Figure 10-14 shows an overview of ADB's architecture.

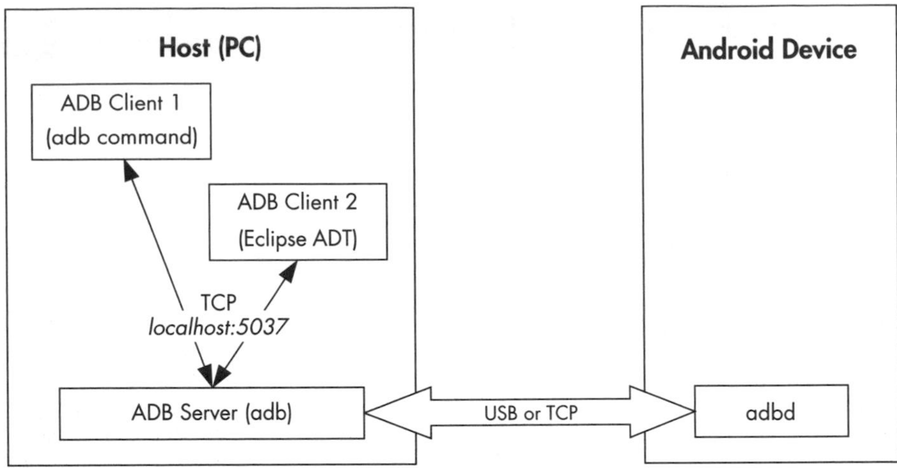

Figure 10-14: ADB architecture

NOTE *In addition to the native implementation in the* `adb` *command and the Java-based one in the Android Development Tools (ADT) Eclipse plugin, various third-party implementations of the ADB protocol are also available, including a Python client*[9] *and an ADB server implemented in JavaScript,*[10] *which can be embedded in the Chrome browser as an extension.*

The client talks to the local ADB server via TCP (typically via *localhost:5037*) using text-based commands, and receives *OK* or *FAIL* responses in return. Some commands, like enumerating devices, port forwarding, or daemon restart are handled by the local daemon, while others (like shell or log access) require a connection to the target Android device. Device access is generally accomplished by forwarding input and output streams to/from the host. The transport layer that implements this uses simple messages with a 24-byte header, which contains a command identifier, two arguments, the length and CRC32 of the optional payload that follows, and a magic value, which simply flips all bits of the command. The message structure is defined in *system/core/adb/adb.h* and is shown in Listing 10-12 for reference. Messages are in turn encapsulated in packets, which are sent over the USB or TCP link to the ADB server running on the device.

```
struct amessage {
    unsigned command;       /* command identifier constant      */
    unsigned arg0;          /* first argument                   */
    unsigned arg1;          /* second argument                  */
    unsigned data_length;   /* length of payload (0 is allowed) */
```

9. Anthony King, "PyAdb: basic ADB core for python using TCP," *https://github.com/cybojenix/PyAdb/*

10. Kenny Root, "adb-on-chrome: ADB (Android Debug Bridge) server as a Chrome extension," *https://github.com/kruton/adb-on-chrome/*

```
    unsigned data_check;     /* checksum of data payload          */
    unsigned magic;          /* command ^ 0xffffffff              */
};
```

Listing 10-12: ADB message structure

We won't discuss the ADB protocol in more detail other than to note the authentication commands added to the protocol in order to implement secure USB debugging. (For more details on ADB, see the protocol description in the *system/core/adb/protocol.txt* file in Android's source tree.)

NOTE *You can enable trace logs for all ADB services by setting the* `ADB_TRACE` *environment variable to 1 on the host and the* `persist.adb.trace_mask` *system property on the device. Selected services can be traced by setting the value of* `ADB_TRACE` *or* `persist.adb.trace_mask` *to a comma- or space-separated (columns or semi-columns as a separator are also supported) list of service tags. See* system/core/adb/adb.c *for the full list of supported tags.*

The Need for Secure ADB

If you've done any development, you know that "debugging" is usually the exact opposite of "secure." Debugging typically involves inspecting (and sometimes even changing) internal program state, dumping encrypted communication data to log files, universal root access, and other scary but necessary activities. Debugging is hard enough without having to bother with security, so why further complicate things by adding additional security layers? Android debugging, as provided by the ADB, is quite versatile and gives you almost complete control over a device when enabled. This feature is, of course, very welcome when developing or testing an application (or the OS itself), but it can also be used for other purposes.

Here's a selective list of things ADB lets you do:

- Copy files to and from the device
- Debug apps running on the device (using JWDP or `gdbserver`)
- Execute shell commands on the device
- Get the system and apps logs
- Install and remove apps

If debugging is enabled on a device, you can do all of the above and more (for example, inject touch events or input text in the UI) simply by connecting the device to a computer with a USB cable. Because ADB does not depend on the device's screen lock, you don't have to unlock the device in order to execute ADB commands, and on most devices that provide root access, connecting via ADB allows you to access and change every file, including system files and password databases. Worse, you don't actually need a computer with development tools in order to access an Android device via ADB; another Android device and a USB On-The-Go (OTG) cable are sufficient. Android tools that can extract as much data as possible from another device in a very short time are readily available.[11] If the device is rooted, such tools can extract all of your credentials, disable or brute-force the screen lock, and even log into your Google account. But even without root, anything on external storage, most notably photos, is accessible, as are your contacts and text messages.

Securing ADB

Android 4.2 was the first version to try to make ADB access harder by hiding the Developer options settings screen, requiring you to use a "secret knock" (tapping the build number seven times) in order to enable it. While not a very effective access protection method, it makes sure that most users don't accidentally enable ADB access. This is, of course, only a stop-gap measure, and as soon as you manage to turn USB debugging on, your device is once again vulnerable.

Android 4.2.2 introduced a proper solution with the so-called secure USB debugging feature. "Secure" here refers to the fact that only hosts that are explicitly authorized by the user can now connect to the *adbd* daemon on the device and execute debugging commands. Thus if someone tries to connect a device to another one via USB in order to access ADB, they must first unlock the target device and authorize access from the debug host by clicking OK in the confirmation dialog shown in Figure 10-15.

Figure 10-15: USB debugging authorization dialog

You can make your decision persistent by checking the **Always allow from this computer** checkbox and debugging will work just as before, as long as you're on the same machine.

Naturally, this secure USB debugging is only effective if you have a reasonably secure lockscreen password in place.

NOTE *On tablets with multi-user support, the confirmation dialog is only shown to the primary (owner) user.*

11. Kyle Osborn, "p2p-adb Framework," *https://github.com/kosborn/p2p-adb/*

Secure ADB Implementation

The ADB host authentication functionality is enabled by default when the *ro.adb.secure* system property is set to 1, and there is no way to disable it via the system interface. When a device connects to a host, it is initially in the `CS_UNAUTHORIZED` state and only goes into the `CS_DEVICE` state after the host has authenticated. Hosts use RSA keys in order to authenticate to the ADB daemon on the device, typically following this three-step process:

1. When a host tries to connect, the device sends an `A_AUTH` message with an argument of type `ADB_AUTH_TOKEN` that includes a 20-byte random value (read from */dev/urandom/*).
2. The host responds with an `A_AUTH` message with an argument of type `ADB_AUTH_SIGNATURE`, which includes a *SHA1withRSA* signature of the random token with one of the host's private keys.
3. The device tries to verify the received signature, and if signature verification succeeds, it responds with an `A_CNXN` packet and goes into the `CS_DEVICE` state. If verification fails, either because the signature value doesn't match, or because there is no corresponding public key to verify with, the device sends another `ADB_AUTH_TOKEN` with a new random value so that the host can try authenticating again (slowing down if the number of failures goes over a certain threshold).

Signature verification typically fails the first time you connect the device to a new host because it doesn't yet have the host's key. In that case the host sends its public key in an `A_AUTH` message with an `ADB_AUTH_RSAPUBLICKEY` argument. The device takes the MD5 hash of that key and displays it in the *Allow USB debugging confirmation* dialog shown in Figure 10-15. Since *adbd* is a native daemon, the key must be passed to the main Android OS in order for its hash to be displayed on screen. This is accomplished by simply writing the key to a local socket (also named *adbd*), which the *adbd* daemon monitors.

When you enable ADB debugging from the developer settings screen, a thread that listens to that *adbd* socket is started. When the thread receives a message starting with *PK*, it treats it as a public key, parses it, calculates the MD5 hash and displays the confirmation dialog (implemented in a dedicated activity, `UsbDebuggingActivity`, part of the SystemUI package). If you tap OK, the activity sends a simple *OK* response to *adbd*, which uses the key to verify the authentication message. If you check the Always allow from this computer checkbox, the public key is written to disk and automatically used for signature verification the next time you connect to the same host.

NOTE *As of version 4.3, Android allows you to clear all saved host authentication keys. This functionality can be triggered by selecting Settings ▸ Developer options ▸ Revoke USB debugging authorizations.*

The UsbDeviceManager class provides public methods for allowing and denying USB debugging, clearing cached authentication keys, as well as for starting and stopping the *adbd* daemon. Those methods are made available to other applications via the IUsbManager AIDL interface of the system UsbService. Calling IUsbManager methods that modify device state requires the MANAGE_USB system signature permission.

ADB Authentication Keys

Although we described the ADB authentication protocol above, we haven't said much about the actual keys used in the process: 2048-bit RSA keys generated by the local ADB server. These keys are typically stored in *$HOME/.android* (*%USERPOFILE%\.android* on Windows) as *adbkey* (private key) and *adbkey.pub* (public key). The default key directory can be overridden by setting the ANDROID_SDK_HOME environment variable. If the ADB_VENDOR_KEYS environment variable is set, the directory it points to is also searched for keys. If no keys are found in any of the above locations, a new key pair is generated and saved.

The private key file (*adbkey*), which is only stored on the host, is in standard OpenSSL PEM format. The public key file (*adbkey.pub*) contains the Base 64–encoded mincrypt-compatible representation of the public key, which is basically a serialization of mincrypt's RSAPublicKey structure (see "Enabling Verified Boot" on page 256), followed by a *user@host* user identifier, separated by space. The user identifier doesn't seem to be used as of this writing and is only meaningful on Unix-based OSes; on Windows, it is always *unknown@unknown*.

Keys are stored on the device in the */data/misc/adb/adb_keys/* file, and new authorized keys are appended to the same file as you accept them. Read-only "vendor keys" are stored in the */adb_keys* file, but it doesn't seem to exist on current Nexus devices. Public keys are in the same format as on the host, making it easy to load in libmincrypt, which *adbd* links statically. Listing 10-13 shows some sample *adb_keys*. The file is owned by the *system* user, its group is set to *shell*, and its permissions to 0640.

```
# cat data/misc/adb/adb_keys
QAAAAJs1UDFt17wyV+Y2GNGF+EgWoiPfsByfC4frNd3s64w3IGt25fKERnl7O8/A+iVPGv1W
--snip--
yZ61cFd7R6ohLFYJRPB6Dy7tISUPRpb+NF4pbQEAAQA= unknown@unknown
QAAAAKFLvP+fp1cB4Eq/6zyV+hnm1S1eV9GYd7cYe+tmwuQZFe+O4vpeow6huIN8YbBRkr7
--snip--
m7+bGd6FOhRkO82gopy553xywXU7rI/aMl6FBAEAAQA= user1@host2
```

Listing 10-13: Contents of the adb_keys *file*

Verifying the Host Key Fingerprint

While the USB debugging confirmation dialog helpfully displays a key fingerprint to let you verify that you're connected to the expected host, the adb client doesn't have a handy command to print the fingerprint of the host key. Although it may seem that there's little room for confusion (after all, there is only one cable plugged in to a single machine) when running a couple of VMs, things can get a little fuzzy. Listing 10-14 shows one way to display the host key's fingerprint in the same format used by the confirmation dialog shown in Figure 10-15 (run in *$HOME/.android* or specify the full path to the public key file).

```
$ cut -d' ' -f1 adbkey.pub|openssl base64 -A -d -a | \
openssl md5 -c|cut -d' ' -f2|tr '[a-z]' '[A-Z]'
69:D4:AC:0D:AF:6B:17:88:BA:6B:C4:BE:0C:F7:75:9A
```

Listing 10-14: Displaying the host key's fingerprint

Android Backup

Android includes a backup framework that allows application data to be backed up to Google's cloud storage and supports full backup of installed APK files, application data, and external storage files to a host machine connected via USB. While device backup is not exactly a security feature, backups allow application data to be extracted from the device, which can present a security issue.

Android Backup Overview

Android's backup framework was publicly announced in Android 2.2, but it was probably available internally earlier. The framework lets applications declare special components called *backup agents*, which are called by the system when creating a backup for an application and when restoring its data. While the backup framework did support pluggable backup transports internally, initially the only transport that was usable in practice was a proprietary one that stores application data in Google's cloud storage.

Cloud Backup

Because backups are associated with a user's Google account, when they install an application that has a backup agent on a new device, the application's data can be automatically restored if the user has registered the same Google account as the one used when the backup was created. Backup and restore is managed by the system and cannot typically be triggered or controlled by users (though developer commands that trigger cloud backup are accessible via the Android shell). By default, backups are triggered periodically, and restore only when an app is first installed on a device.

Local Backup

Android 4.0 added a new, local backup transport that lets users save backups to a file on their desktop computer as well. Local backup (also called full backup) requires ADB debugging to be enabled and authorized because backup data is streamed to the host computer using the same method that ADB (via `adb pull`) employs to transfer device files to a host.

Full backup is started by executing the `adb backup` command in a shell. This command starts a new Java process on the device, which binds to the system's `BackupManagerService` and requests a backup with the parameters specified to `adb backup`. The `BackupManagerService` in turn starts a confirmation activity like the one shown in Figure 10-16, prompting the user to authorize the backup and specify a backup encryption password if desired. If the device is already encrypted, the user must enter the device encryption password to proceed. This password will be used to encrypt the backup as well, because using a dedicated backup encryption password is not supported. The full backup process is started when the user presses the Back up my data button.

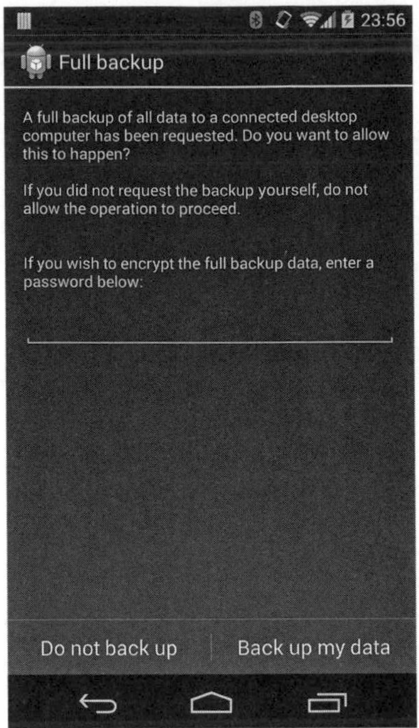

Figure 10-16: Backup confirmation dialog

Full backup calls the backup agent of each target package in order to obtain a copy of its data. If a backup agent is not defined, the `BackupManagerService` uses an internal `FullBackupAgent` class, which copies all of the package's files. Full backup honors the `allowBackup` attribute of the `<application>` tag in the package's *AndroidManifest.xml* file, and will not extract package data if `allowBackup` is set to `false`.

In addition to application data, full backup can include user-installed and system application APK files, as well as external storage contents, with some limitations: full backup doesn't back up protected (with DRM) apps, and skips some system settings such as mobile network APNs and Wi-Fi access points' connection details.

Backups are restored using the `adb restore` command. Backup restore is quite limited and doesn't allow any options to be specified, as it can only perform a full restore.

Backup File Format

Android backup files start with a few lines of text, followed by binary data. These lines are the backup header and they specify the backup format and encryption parameters (if a backup password was specified) used to create the backup. The header of an unencrypted backup is shown in Listing 10-15.

```
ANDROID BACKUP❶
1❷
1❸
none❹
```

Listing 10-15: Unencrypted backup header

The first line ❶ is the file magic (format identifier), the second ❷ is the backup format version (1 up till Android 4.4.2, 2 in later versions; version 2 denotes a change in the key derivation method, which now takes into account multibyte password characters), the third ❸ is a compression flag (1 if compressed), and the last ❹ is the encryption algorithm used (*none* or *AES-256*).

The actual backup data is a compressed and optionally encrypted tar file that includes a backup manifest file, followed by the application APK (if any), and app data (files, databases, and shared preferences). The data is compressed using the deflate algorithm and can be decompressed using OpenSSL's `zlib` command, as shown in Listing 10-16.

```
$ dd if=mybackup.ab bs=24 skip=1|openssl zlib -d > mybackup.tar
```

Listing 10-16: Uncompressing an Android backup using OpenSSL

After the backup is uncompressed, you can view its contents or extract it with the standard `tar` command, as shown in Listing 10-17.

```
$ tar tvf mybackup.tar
-rw------- 1000/1000       1019 apps/org.myapp/_manifest❶
-rw-r--r-- 1000/1000    1412208 apps/org.myapp/a/org.myapp-1.apk❷
-rw-rw---- 10091/10091      231 apps/org.myapp/f/share_history.xml❸
-rw-rw---- 10091/10091        0 apps/org.myapp/db/myapp.db-journal❹
-rw-rw---- 10091/10091     5120 apps/org.myapp/db/myapp.db
-rw-rw---- 10091/10091     1110 apps/org.myapp/sp/org.myapp_preferences.xml❺
```

Listing 10-17: Viewing the contents of an uncompressed backup using tar

Inside the tar file, app data is stored in the *apps/* directory, which contains a subdirectory for each backed-up package. Each package directory includes a *_manifest* file ❶ in its root, the APK file (if requested) in *a/* ❷, app files in *f/* ❸, databases in *db/* ❹, and shared preferences in *sp/* ❺. The manifest contains the app's package name and version code, the platform's version code, a flag indicating whether the archive contains the app APK, and the app's signing certificate.

The `BackupManagerService` uses this information when restoring an app in order to check whether it's been signed with the same certificate as the currently installed one. If the certificates don't match, it will skip installing the APK, except for system packages, which might be signed with a different (manufacturer-owned) certificate on different devices. Additionally, `BackupManagerService` expects the files to be in the order shown in Listing 10-17 and restore will fail if they are out for order. For example, if the manifest states that the backup includes an APK, the `BackupManagerService` will try to read and install the APK first, before restoring the app's files. This restore order is required because you cannot restore files for an app you don't have installed. However, `BackupManagerService` will not search for the APK in the archive, and if it is not right after the manifest, all other files will be skipped.

If the user requested external storage backup (by passing the `-shared` option to `adb backup`), there will also be a *shared/* directory in the archive, containing external storage files.

Backup Encryption

If the user supplied an encryption password when requesting the backup, the backup file is encrypted with a key derived from the password. The password is used to generate a 256-bit AES key using 10,000 rounds of PBKDF2 with a randomly generated 512-bit salt. This key is then used to encrypt another, randomly generated 256-bit AES bit master key, which is in turn used to encrypt the actual archive data in CBC mode (using the *AES/CBC/PKCS5Padding* `Cipher` transformation). A master key checksum is also calculated and saved in the backup file header. In order to generate the checksum, the generated raw master key is converted to a Java character array by casting each byte to `char`, with the result treated as a password string, and run through the PBKDF2 function to effectively generate another AES key, whose bytes are used as the checksum.

NOTE *Because an AES key is essentially a random byte sequence, the raw key usually contains several bytes that don't map to printable characters. Because PKCS#5 does not specify the actual encoding of a password string, Android's encryption checksum generation method produces implementation and version-dependent results.*

The checksum is used to verify whether the user-supplied decryption password is correct before actually decrypting the backup data. When the master key is decrypted, its checksum is calculated using the method described above and then compared to the checksum in the archive header. If the checksums don't match, the password is considered incorrect, and the restore process is aborted. Listing 10-18 shows an example backup header for an encrypted archive.

```
ANDROID BACKUP
1
1
AES-256❶
68404C30DF8CACA5FA004F49BA3A70...❷
909459ADCA2A60D7C2B117A6F91E3D...❸
10000❹
789B1A01E3B8FA759C6459AF1CF1F0FD ❺
8DC5E483D3893EC7F6AAA56B97A6C2...❻
```

Listing 10-18: Encrypted backup header

Here, *AES-256* ❶ is the backup encryption algorithm used, the next line ❷ is the user password salt as a hexadecimal string, followed by the master key checksum salt ❸, the number of PBKDF2 rounds used to derive a key ❹, and the user key IV ❺. The final line ❻ is the master key blob, which contains the archive data encryption IV, the actual master key and its checksum, all encrypted with the key derived from the user-supplied password. Listing 10-19 shows the detailed format of the master key blob.

```
byte Niv❶
byte[Niv] IV❷
byte Nmk❸
byte [Nmk] MK❹
byte Nck❺
byte [Nck] MKck❻
```

Listing 10-19: Master key blob format

The first field ❶ is the IV length, followed by the IV value ❷, the master key (MK) length ❸, and the actual master key ❹. The last two fields store the master key checksum hash length ❺, and the master key checksum hash itself ❻.

Controlling Backup Scope

Android's security model guarantees that each application runs within its own sandbox and that its files cannot be accessed by other applications or the device user, unless the application explicitly allows access. Therefore, most applications do not encrypt their data before storing it to disk. However, both legitimate users and attackers that have somehow obtained the device unlock password can easily extract applications data using Android's full backup feature. For this reason, applications that store sensitive data should either encrypt it or provide an explicit backup agent that limits exportable data in order to guarantee that sensitive data cannot be easily extracted via backup.

As mentioned in "Android Backup Overview" on page 283, if application data backup isn't needed or desirable, applications can disallow it completely by setting their `allowBackup` attribute to `false` in *AndroidManifest.xml*, as shown in Listing 10-20.

```
<?xml version="1.0" encoding="utf-8"?>
<manifest xmlns:android="http://schemas.android.com/apk/res/android"
    package="org.example.app"
    android:versionCode="1"
    android:versionName="1.0" >
    --snip--
    <application
        android:icon="@drawable/ic_launcher"
        android:label="@string/app_name"
        android:theme="@style/AppTheme"
        android:allowBackup="false">
```

```
        --snip--
    </application>
</manifest>
```

Listing 10-20: Disallowing application data backup in AndroidManifest.xml

Summary

Android employs various measures in order to protect user data and applications, and ensure the integrity of the operating system. On production devices, the bootloader is locked, and the recovery OS only allows OTA updates signed by the device manufacturer to be installed, thus ensuring that only authorized OS builds can be booted or flashed to a device. When enabled, dm-verity-based verified boot guarantees that the *system* partition is not modified by checking the hash value of each device block against a trusted hash tree, which prevents the installation of malicious programs such as rootkits on the *system* partition. Android can also encrypt the *userdata* partition, making it harder to extract applications data by directly accessing storage devices.

Android supports various screen lock methods and applies rate limiting to unsuccessful authentication attempts, thus deterring online attacks against a booted device. The type and complexity of the unlock PIN or password can be specified and enforced by device administrator applications. A device policy that wipes the device after too many unsuccessful authentication attempts is also supported. Secure USB debugging requires debug hosts to be explicitly authorized by the user and added to a whitelist, thus preventing information extraction via USB.

Finally, full device backups can be encrypted with a key derived from a user-supplied password, making it harder to access device data that has been extracted into a backup. To achieve a higher level of device security, all supported security measures should be enabled and configured accordingly.

11

NFC AND SECURE ELEMENTS

This chapter gives a brief overview of near field communication (NFC) and secure elements (SEs), and explains how they're integrated into mobile devices. While NFC has many uses, we focus on its card emulation mode, which is used to provide an interface to an SE integrated into a mobile device. Secure elements offer protected storage for private data, such as authentication keys, and provide a secure execution environment that can protect security-critical code. We'll describe which types of SEs Android supports and introduce the APIs that Android applications can use to communicate with SEs. Finally, we'll discuss host-based card emulation (HCE) and its Android implementations, and demonstrate how to implement an HCE application.

NFC Overview

NFC is a technology that allows devices that are in close proximity (usually 10 centimeters or less) to establish radio communication with each other and exchange data. NFC is not a single standard, but is based on a set of standards that define radio frequencies, communication protocols, and data exchange formats. NFC builds upon radio-frequency identification (RFID) technology and operates at the 13.56 MHz frequency, allowing various data transmission rates such as 106kbps, 212kbps, and 424kbps.

NFC communication involves two devices: an initiator and a target. In *active mode*, both the initiator and the target have their own power supplies and each can transmit a radio signal in order to communicate with the other party. In *passive mode*, the target device does not have its own power source and is activated and powered by the electromagnetic field emitted by the initiator.

When communicating in passive mode, the initiator is often called a *reader*, and the target a *tag*. The reader can be a dedicated device or be embedded in a general purpose device, such as a personal computer or a mobile phone. Tags come in various shapes and sizes and range from simple stickers with very limited amount of memory to contactless smart cards, which have an embedded CPU.

NFC devices can operate in three different modes: reader/writer (R/W), peer-to-peer (P2P), and card emulation (CE). In R/W mode, a device acts as an active initiator and can read and write data to external tags. In P2P mode, two NFC devices can actively exchange data using a bidirectional communication protocol. The CE mode allows an NFC device to emulate a tag or a contactless smart card. Android supports all three modes with some limitations. We give an overview of Android's NFC architecture and show how to use each mode in the next section.

Android NFC Support

NFC support in Android was introduced in version 2.3 and the related architecture and features remained largely unchanged until version 4.4, which introduced HCE support.

Android's NFC implementation resides in the `NfcService` system service, part of the `Nfc` system application (package `com.android.nfc`). It wraps the native libraries required to drive each supported NFC controller; implements access control, tag discovery, and dispatch; and controls card emulation. Android doesn't expose a low-level API to the functionality of `NfcService`, but instead offers an event-driven framework that allows interested applications to register for NFC events. This event-driven approach is used in all three NFC operating modes.

Reader/Writer Mode

NFC-enabled Android applications can't directly set the device in R/W mode. Instead, they declare the type of tags they're interested in, and Android's tag dispatch system selects and starts the matching application when it discovers a tag.

The tag dispatch system both uses the tag technology (discussed shortly) and parses tag contents in order to decide which application to dispatch the tag to. The tag dispatch system uses three intent actions to notify applications about the discovered tag: ACTION_NDEF_DISCOVERED, ACTION_TECH_DISCOVERED, and ACTION_TAG_DISCOVERED. The ACTION_NDEF_DISCOVERED intent has the highest priority and is sent when Android discovers a tag that is formatted using the standard NFC Data Exchange Format (NDEF)[1] and that contains a recognized data type. The ACTION_TECH_DISCOVERED intent is sent when the scanned tag does not contain NDEF data or the data format is not recognized by applications that can handle the discovered tag technology. If no applications can handle ACTION_NDEF_DISCOVERED or ACTION_TECH_DISCOVERED, the NfcService sends the generic ACTION_TAG_DISCOVERED intent. Tag dispatch events are delivered only to activities, and therefore cannot be processed in the background without user interaction.

Registering for Tag Dispatch

Applications register for NFC events using the standard intent filter system by declaring the intents that an NFC-enabled activity supports in *AndroidManifest.xml*, as shown in Listing 11-1.

```
<?xml version="1.0" encoding="utf-8"?>
<manifest xmlns:android="http://schemas.android.com/apk/res/android"
    package="com.example.nfc" ...>
    --snip--

    <uses-permission android:name="android.permission.NFC" />❶
    --snip--
    <application ...>
        <activity
            android:name=".NfcActivity"❷
            android:launchMode="singleTop" >
            <intent-filter>
                <action android:name="android.nfc.action.NDEF_DISCOVERED"/>❸
                <category android:name="android.intent.category.DEFAULT"/>
                <data android:mimeType="text/plain" />
            </intent-filter>
            <intent-filter>
                <action android:name="android.nfc.action.TECH_DISCOVERED" />❹
            </intent-filter>
            <intent-filter>
                <action android:name="android.nfc.action.TAG_DISCOVERED" />❺
            </intent-filter>

            <meta-data
                android:name="android.nfc.action.TECH_DISCOVERED"❻
                android:resource="@xml/filter_nfc" >
            </meta-data>
        </activity>
        --snip--
```

1. The NDEF format and its implementation using various tag technologies are described in the NFC Forum specification, available on its website: *http://nfc-forum.org/our-work/specifications-and-application-documents/specifications/nfc-forum-technical-specifications/*

```
    </application>
</manifest>
```

Listing 11-1: Manifest file of an NFC-enabled application

As you can see in this listing, the application first requests the `android.permission.NFC` permission ❶, which is required to access the NFC controller, and then declares an activity that handles NFC events, `NfcActivity` ❷. The activity registers three intent filters; one for each tag discovery event. The application declares that it can handle NDEF data with the *text/plain* MIME type by specifying the `mimeType` attribute of the `<data>` tag in the `NDEF_DISCOVERED` intent filter ❸. `NfcActivity` also declares that it can handle the `TECH_DISCOVERED` intent ❹, which is sent if the scanned tag uses one of the technologies specified in the associated metadata XML resource file ❻. Finally, the application requests that it be notified about all discovered NFC tags by adding the catch-all `TAG_DISCOVERED` intent filter ❺.

If more than one activity that supports the scanned tag is found, Android shows a selection dialog, allowing the user to select which activity should handle the tag. Applications already in the foreground can short-circuit this selection by calling the `NfcAdapter.enableForegroundDispatch()` method. Such an application will be given priority over all other matching applications and will automatically receive the NFC intent when it's in the foreground.

Tag Technologies

A *tag technology* is an abstract term that describes a concrete NFC tag. The tag technology is determined by the communication protocol the tag uses, its internal structure, or the features it offers. For example, a tag that uses the NFC-A protocol (based on ISO 14443-3A)[2] for communication matches the *NfcA* technology, and a tag that contains NDEF-formatted data matches the *Ndef* technology, regardless of the underlying communication protocol. (See the `TagTechnology` class reference documentation[3] for a full list of tag technologies supported by Android.)

An activity that specifies the `TECH_DISCOVERED` intent filter must provide an XML resource file that in turn specifies the concrete technologies it supports with a `<tech-list>` element. An activity is considered a match for a tag if one of the tech lists it declares is a subset of the technologies supported by the tag. Multiple tech lists can be declared in order to match different tags, as shown in Listing 11-2.

```
<?xml version="1.0" encoding="utf-8"?>
<resources>
    <tech-list>❶
        <tech>android.nfc.tech.IsoDep</tech>
```

2. Official versions of all ISO standards can be purchased on its website, *http://www.iso.org/iso/home/store/catalogue_ics.htm*. Draft versions of standards can usually be obtained from the website of the standard working group.

3. Google, *Android API Reference*, "TagTechnology," *https://developer.android.com/reference/android/nfc/tech/TagTechnology.html*

```
        <tech>android.nfc.tech.NfcA</tech>
    </tech-list>

    <tech-list>❷
        <tech>android.nfc.tech.NfcF</tech>
    </tech-list>
</resources>
```

Listing 11-2: Declaring technologies to match using tech lists

Here, the first tech list ❶ will match tags that provide a communication interface compatible with ISO 14443-4 (ISO-DEP), and which are implemented using the NFC-A technology (usually used by NXP contactless smart cards); the second tech list ❷ matches tags that use the NFC-F technology (typically Felica cards). Because both tech lists are defined independently, our example `NfcActivity` (see Listing 11-1) will be notified when either a contactless NXP smart card or a Felica card or tag is scanned.

Reading a Tag

After the tag dispatch system selects an activity to handle the scanned tag, it creates an NFC intent object and passes it to the selected activity. The activity can then use the `EXTRA_TAG` extra to obtain a `Tag` object representing the scanned tag and call its methods in order to read or write to the tag. (Tags that contain NDEF data also provide the `EXTRA_NDEF_MESSAGES` extra, which contains an array of NDEF messages parsed from the tag.)

A concrete `Tag` object representing the underlying tag technology can be obtained using the static `get()` method of the corresponding technology class, as shown in Listing 11-3. If the `Tag` object does not support the requested technology, the `get()` method returns `null`.

```
protected void onNewIntent(Intent intent) {
    setIntent(intent);

    Tag tag = intent.getParcelableExtra(NfcAdapter.EXTRA_TAG);
    IsoDep isoDep = IsoDep.get(tag);
    if (isoDep != null) {
        isoDep.connect();
        byte[] command = {...};
        byte[] response = isoDep.transceive(command);
        --snip--
    }
}
```

Listing 11-3: Obtaining a concrete `Tag` instance from the NFC intent

Using Reader Mode

In addition to the intent-based tag dispatch system, Android 4.4 adds a new method that activities can use to obtain a live `Tag` object, called reader mode. Reader mode guarantees that while the target activity is in the foreground, all other operation modes supported by the NFC controller (such as peer-to-peer and card emulation) are disabled. This mode is helpful when scanning an active NFC device, such as another Android device in host-based emulation mode, which could trigger point-to-point communication and thus take control away from the current foreground activity.

Activities can enable reader mode by calling the `enableReaderMode()` method of the `NfcAdapter` class,[4] as shown in Listing 11-4.

```
public class NfcActivity extends Activity implements NfcAdapter.ReaderCallback {
    private NfcAdapter adapter;
    --snip--
    @Override
    public void onResume() {
        super.onResume();
        if (adapter != null) {
            adapter.enableReaderMode(this, this, NfcAdapter.FLAG_READER_NFC_A❶
                    | NfcAdapter.FLAG_READER_SKIP_NDEF_CHECK, null);
        }
    }

    @Override
    public void onTagDiscovered(Tag tag) {❷
        IsoDep isoDep = IsoDep.get(tag);
        if (isoDep != null) {
             isoDep.connect();
             byte[] command = {...};
             byte[] response = isoDep.transceive(command);
             --snip--
        }
    }
    --snip--
}
```

Listing 11-4: Enabling reader mode and obtaining a Tag object using ReaderCallback

In this case, the activity enables reader mode when it comes to the foreground by calling the `enableReaderMode()` method ❶ (the activity should disable reader mode using the matching `disableReaderMode()` method when it leaves the foreground), and obtains a `Tag` instance directly (without an intermediate intent) via the `onTagDiscovered()` callback ❷. The `Tag` object is then used in the same way as in intent-based dispatch.

Peer-to-Peer Mode

Android implements a limited NFC P2P mode data exchange between devices using the proprietary NDEF push and the standard Simple NDEF Exchange Protocol (SNEP) protocols.[5] Android devices can exchange a

4. Google, *Android API Reference*, "NfcAdapter," *https://developer.android.com/reference/android/nfc/NfcAdapter.html*

5. NFC Forum, "NFC Forum Technical Specifications," *http://nfc-forum.org/our-work/specifications-and-application-documents/specifications/nfc-forum-technical-specifications/*

single NDEF message with any device that supports either of these protocols, but the P2P mode is typically used with another Android device in order to implement the so-called Android Beam feature.

In addition to NDEF messages, Android Beam allows for the transfer of larger data objects, such as photos and videos, which cannot fit in a single NDEF message by creating a temporary Bluetooth connection between devices. This process is called *NFC handover* and was added in Android 4.1.

NDEF message exchange in P2P mode is enabled by calling the `setNdefPushMessage()` or `setNdefPushMessageCallback()` methods of the `NfcAdapter` class. (See the official NFC API guide[6] for more details and sample code.)

Card Emulation Mode

As mentioned in "NFC Overview" on page 289, CE mode allows an Android device to emulate a contactless smart card or an NFC tag. In CE mode, the device receives commands over NFC, processes them, and sends replies, again over NFC. The component responsible for processing commands can be either a hardware secure element (as discussed in the next section) connected to the device's NFC controller, or an Android application running on the device (when in host-based card emulation, HCE).

In the following sections, we'll discuss secure elements in mobile devices, and the Android APIs that applications can use to communicate with SEs. We'll also describe how Android implements HCE and demonstrate how to create an application that enables card emulation.

Secure Elements

A *secure element (SE)* is a tamper-resistant smart card chip capable of running smart card applications (called *applets* or *cardlets*) with a certain level of security and isolation. A smart card is essentially a minimal computing environment on a single chip, complete with a CPU, ROM, EEPROM, RAM, and I/O port. Recent cards also include cryptographic co-processors that implement common algorithms such as AES and RSA.

Smart cards use various techniques to implement tamper resistance, making it quite hard to extract data by disassembling or analyzing the chip. Modern smart cards come pre-programmed with a multi-application OS that takes advantage of the hardware's memory protection features to ensure that each application's data is only available to itself. Application installation and (optionally) access is controlled by requiring the use of cryptographic keys for each operation.

6. Google, *Android API Guides*, "NFC Basics," *https://developer.android.com/guide/topics/connectivity/nfc/nfc.html#p2p*

The SE can be integrated in mobile devices as a Universal Integrated Circuit Card (UICC, commonly known as a *SIM card*) embedded in the handset or connected to a SD card slot. If the device supports NFC, the SE is usually connected to (or embedded into) the NFC controller, making it possible to communicate with the SE wirelessly.

Smart cards have been around since the 1970s and are now used in applications ranging from pre-paid phone calls and transit ticketing to credit cards and VPN credential storage. Because an SE installed in a mobile device has equivalent or superior capabilities to that of a smart card, it can theoretically be used for any application that physical smart cards are currently used for. Additionally, because an SE can host multiple applications, it has the potential to replace the bunch of cards people use daily with a single device. Furthermore, because the SE can be controlled by the device's OS, access to it can be restricted by requiring additional authentication (PIN, passphrase, or code signature) to enable it.

One of the main applications of SEs in mobile devices is that of emulating contactless payment cards, and the goal of enabling mobile payments has indeed been the driving force behind SE deployment. Aside from financial applications, mobile SEs could be used to emulate other contactless cards that are in wide use, such as access cards, loyalty cards, and so on.

Mobile SEs could also be used to enhance the security of apps that deal with sensitive information or algorithms: The security-critical part of the app, such as credential storage or license verification, can be implemented inside the SE in order to guarantee that it's impervious to reverse engineering and information extraction. Other apps that can benefit from being implemented in the SE are One Time Password (OTP) generators and, of course, credential storage (for shared secret keys, or private keys in a PKI).

While it's possible to implement SE-enabled apps today with standard tools and technologies, using them in practice on current commercial Android devices isn't straightforward. We'll discuss this in detail in "Android SE Execution Environment" on page 302, but let's first explore the types of SEs available on mobile devices, and the level of support they have in Android.

SE Form Factors in Mobile Devices

Figure 11-1 shows a simplified block diagram of the components of an Android device as they relate to NFC and SE support, including the embedded SE (eSE) and the UICC. We'll refer to the components in this diagram in our discussion of secure elements and host-based card emulation in the rest of this chapter.

In the following subsections, we briefly review the types of SEs available on Android devices, how they're connected to other device components, and the methods the OS uses to communicate with each type of SE.

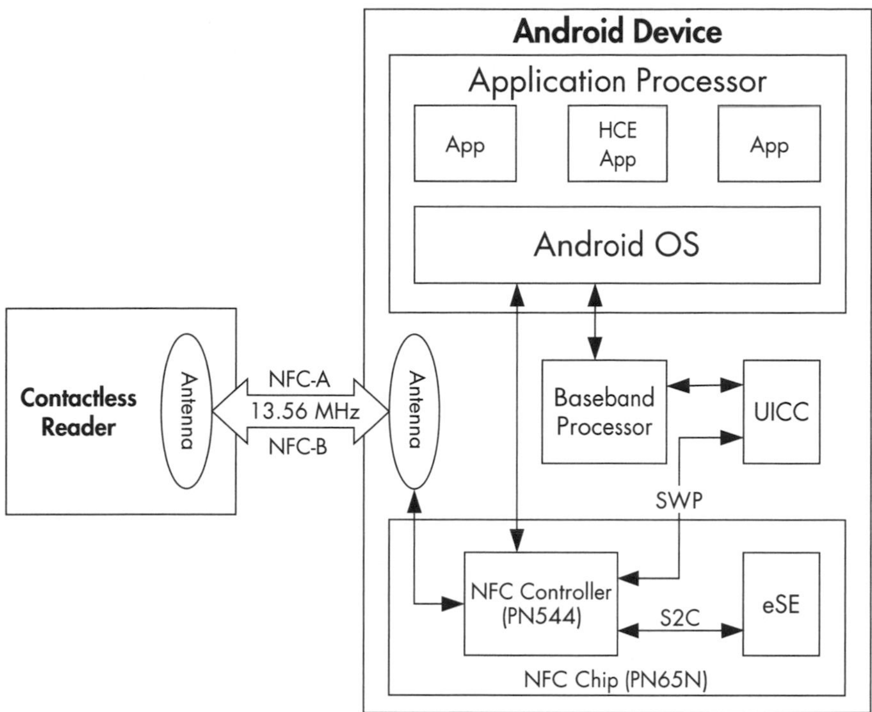

Figure 11-1: Android NFC and SE components

UICC

Most mobile devices today have some kind of UICC. Although UICCs are smart cards that can host applications, because the UICC has traditionally only been connected to the baseband processor (not the application processor that runs the main device OS), they can't be accessed directly from Android. All communication goes through the Radio Interface Layer (RIL), which is essentially a proprietary IPC interface to the baseband.

Communication with the UICC SE is carried out using extended AT commands (`AT+CCHO`, `AT+CCHC`, `AT+CGLA` as defined by 3GPP TS 27.007),[7] which the current Android telephony manager does not support. The SEEK for Android project[8] provides patches to implement the needed commands, allowing for communication with the UICC via the SmartCard API, which is a reference implementation of the SIMalliance Open Mobile API specification[9] (discussed in "Using the OpenMobile API" on page 308). However, as with most components that talk directly to the hardware in Android,

7. 3GPP, *AT command set for User Equipment (UE), http://www.3gpp.org/ftp/Specs/html-info/27007.htm*

8. "Secure Element Evaluation Kit for the Android platform," *https://code.google.com/p/seek-for-android/*

9. SIMalliance Limited, *Open Mobile API Specification v2.05, http://www.simalliance.org/en?t=/documentManager/sfdoc.file.supply&fileID=1392314878580*

the RIL consists of an open source part (*rild*), and a proprietary library (*libXXX-ril.so*). In order to support communication with the UICC secure element, support must be added both to the *rild* and to the underlying proprietary library. The choice of whether to add that support is left to hardware vendors.

As of this writing, the SmartCard API has not been integrated into mainline Android (although the AOSP source tree includes an empty *packages/apps/SmartCardService/* directory). However, Android devices from major vendors ship with an implementation of the SmartCard API, which allows communication from the UICC to third-party applications (subject to various access restrictions).

The Single Wire Protocol (SWP) offers an alternative way to use the UICC as an SE. SWP is used to connect the UICC to a NFC controller, allowing the NFC controller to expose the UICC to external readers when in card emulation mode. The NFC controllers built into recent Nexus devices (such as the Broadcom BCM20793M in the Nexus 5) support SWP, but this functionality is disabled by default. (It can be enabled by changing the configuration file of the *libnfc-brcm* library on the Nexus 5.) A standard API to switch between the UICC, the embedded SE (if available), and HCE when in card emulation mode is currently not exposed, but the "off-host" routing functionality available in Android 4.4 can theoretically route commands to the UICC (see "APDU Routing" on page 311 for details).

microSD-Based SE

Another form factor for an SE is an *Advanced Security SD card (ASSD),*[10] which is basically an SD card with an embedded SE chip. When connected to an Android device with an SD card slot, running a SEEK-patched Android version, the SE can be accessed via the SmartCard API. However, Android devices with an SD card slot are becoming the exceptions rather than the norm, so it's unlikely that ASSD Android support will make it to the mainstream. Additionally, even when available, recent Android versions treat SD cards as secondary storage devices and allow access to them only via a very high-level, restrictive API.

Embedded SE

An *embedded SE (eSE)* is not a distinct device but is usually integrated with the NFC controller and housed in the same enclosure. An example of an eSE is NXP's PN65N chip, which combines the PN544 NFC radio controller with the P5CN072 SE (part of the SmartMX series).

The first mainstream Android device to feature an embedded SE was the Nexus S, which also introduced NFC support to Android and was built using the PN65N controller. Its successors, the Galaxy Nexus and the Nexus 4, also

10. SD Association, "Advanced Security SD Card: ASSD," *https://www.sdcard.org/developers/overview/ASSD/*

came equipped with an eSE. However, recent Google-branded devices, such as the Nexus 5 and Nexus 7 (2013), have deprecated the eSE in favor of host-based card emulation and do not include an eSE.

The embedded SE is connected to the NFC controller through a SignalIn/SignalOut connection (S2C), standardized as NFC Wired Interface (NFC-WI),[11] and has three modes of operation: off, wired, and virtual. In off mode, there's no communication with the SE. In wired mode, the SE is visible to the Android OS as if it were a contactless smart card connected to the NFC reader. In virtual mode, the SE is visible to external readers as if the phone were a contactless smart card. These modes are mutually exclusive, so we can communicate with the SE either via the contactless interface (that is, from an external reader), or through the wired interface (that is, from an Android app). The next section shows how to use the wired mode to communicate with the eSE from an Android app.

Accessing the Embedded SE

As of this writing, no public Android SDK API allows communication with the embedded SE, but recent Android versions include an optional library called *nfc_extras*, which offers a stable interface to the eSE. This section demonstrates how to configure Android to allow eSE access to certain Android applications, as well as how to use the *nfc_extras* library.

Card emulation, and consequently, internal APIs for accessing the embedded SE were introduced in Android 2.3.4 (the version that introduced Google Wallet). Those APIs are hidden from SDK applications and using them required system signature permissions (`WRITE_SECURE_SETTINGS` or `NFCEE_ADMIN`) in Android 2.3.4 and subsequent 2.3.x releases, as well as in the initial Android 4.0 release (API Level 14). A signature permission is quite restrictive because it allows only parties that control the platform signature keys to distribute apps that can use the eSE.

Android 4.0.4 (API Level 15) lifted this restriction by replacing the signature permission with signing certificate whitelisting at the OS level. While this still requires modifying core OS files, and thus vendor cooperation, there is no need to sign SE applications with the vendor key, which greatly simplifies distribution. Additionally, since the whitelist is maintained in a file, it can easily be updated using an OTA to add support for more SE applications.

Granting Access to the eSE

The new whitelisting access control approach is implemented by the `NfceeAccessControl` class and enforced by the system `NfcService`. The `NfceeAccessControl` class reads the whitelist from */etc/nfcee_access.xml*, which is an XML file that stores a list of signing certificates and package names that are allowed to access the eSE. Access can be granted both to all apps

11. ECMA International, *ECMA-373: Near Field Communication Wired Interface (NFC-WI)*, *http://www.ecma-international.org/publications/files/ECMA-ST/ECMA-373.pdf*

signed by a particular certificate's private key (if no package name is specified), or to a single package (app) only. Listing 11-5 shows how the contents of the *nfcee_access.xml* file might appear:

```
<?xml version="1.0" encoding="utf-8"?>
<resources xmlns:xliff="urn:oasis:names:tc:xliff:document:1.2">
    <signer android:signature="308204a830820390a003020102020900b399...">❶
        <package android:name="com.example.nfc">❷
        </package>
    </signer>
</resources>
```

Listing 11-5: Contents of the nfcee_access.xml *file*

This configuration allows SE access to the `com.example.nfc` package ❷ if it is signed by the specified signing certificate ❶. On production devices, this file usually contains only the Google Wallet app signing certificate, thus restricting eSE access to Google Wallet.

NOTE *As of April 2014, Google Wallet is supported only on Android 4.4 and later, and uses HCE rather than the eSE.*

After an application's signing certificate has been added to *nfcee_access.xml*, no permissions other than the standard NFC permission are required to access the eSE. In addition to whitelisting the app's signing certificate, the *nfc_extras* library must be explicitly added to the app's manifest and marked as required with the `<uses-library>` tag in order to enable eSE access (because the library is optional, it's not loaded by default), as shown in Listing 11-6 at ❶.

```
<manifest xmlns:android="http://schemas.android.com/apk/res/android"
    package="com.example.nfc" ...>
    --snip--
    <uses-permission android:name="android.permission.NFC" />
    <application ...>
        --snip--
        <uses-library
            android:name="com.android.nfc_extras"❶
            android:required="true" />
    </application>
</manifest>
```

Listing 11-6: Adding the nfc_extras *library to* AndroidManifest.xml

Using the NfcExecutionEnvironment API

Android's eSE access API isn't based on a standard smart card communication API, such as JSR 177[12] or the Open Mobile API, but instead offers a very

12. Oracle, "JSR 177: Security and Trust Services API for J2METM," *https://jcp.org/en/jsr/detail?id=177*

basic communication interface, implemented in the NfcExecutionEnvironment class. The class has only three public methods, as shown in Listing 11-7.

```
public class NfcExecutionEnvironment {
    public void open() throws EeIOException {...}

    public void close() throws IOException {...}

    public byte[] transceive(byte[] in) throws IOException {...}
}
```

Listing 11-7: NfcExecutionEnvironment API

This simple interface is sufficient to communicate with the SE, but in order to use it you first need to obtain an instance of the NfcExecutionEnvironment class. An instance can be obtained from the NfcAdapterExtras class, which is in turn accessed via its static get() method, as shown in Listing 11-8.

```
NfcAdapterExtras adapterExtras =
     NfcAdapterExtras.get(NfcAdapter.getDefaultAdapter(context));❶
NfcExecutionEnvironment nfceEe =
     adapterExtras.getEmbeddedExecutionEnvironment();❷
nfcEe.open();❸
byte[] emptySelectCmd = { 0x00, (byte) 0xa4, 0x04, 0x00, 0x00 };
byte[] response = nfcEe.transceive(emptySelectCmd);❹
nfcEe.close();❺
```

Listing 11-8: Using the NfcExecutionEnvironment API

Here, we first obtain an NfcAdapterExtras instance ❶, and then call its getEmbeddedExecutionEnvironment() method in order to obtain an interface to the eSE ❷. To be able to communicate with the eSE, we first open a connection ❸, and then use the transceive() method to send a command and get a response ❹. Finally, we close the connection using the close() method ❺.

eSE-Related Broadcasts

An SE-enabled app needs to be notified of NFC events such as RF field detection, as well as of events pertaining to the eSE and the applets installed on it, such as applet selection via the NFC interface, in order to be able to change state accordingly. Because disclosure of such events to malicious applications can lead to leaking of sensitive information and denial of service attacks, access to eSE-related events must be limited to trusted applications only.

In Android, global events are implemented by using broadcasts, and applications can create and register broadcast receivers that receive the broadcasts the app is interested in. Access to eSE-related broadcasts can be controlled with standard Android signature-based permissions, but this approach has the disadvantage that only apps signed with the platform certificate can receive eSE events, thus limiting SE-enabled apps to those created by the device manufacturer or mobile network operator (MNO). To avoid this limitation, Android uses the same mechanism employed to control eSE access; namely, whitelisting application certificates, in order to control the scope of applications that can receive eSE-related broadcasts. Any application whose signing certificate (and optionally package name) is registered in *nfcee_access.xml* can receive eSE-related broadcasts by registering a receiver like the one shown in Listing 11-9.

```
<receiver android:name="com.example.nfc.SEReceiver" >
  <intent-filter>
   <action android:name="com.android.nfc_extras.action.RF_FIELD_ON_DETECTED" />❶
   <action android:name="com.android.nfc_extras.action.RF_FIELD_OFF_DETECTED" />❷
   <action android:name="com.android.nfc_extras.action.APDU_RECEIVED" />❸
   <action android:name="com.android.nfc_extras.action.AID_SELECTED" />❹
   <action android:name="com.android.nfc_extras.action.MIFARE_ACCESS_DETECTED" />❺
   <action android:name="com.android.nfc_extras.action.EMV_CARD_REMOVAL" />❻
   <action android:name="com.android.nfc.action.INTERNAL_TARGET_DESELECTED" />❼
   <action android:name="android.intent.action.MASTER_CLEAR_NOTIFICATION" />❽
  </intent-filter>
</receiver>
```

Listing 11-9: Declaring a broadcast receiver for eSE-related events in AndroidManifest.xml

As you can see, Android offers notifications for lower-level communication events, such as RF field detection ❶❷, APDU reception ❸, and applet selection ❹, as well as for higher-level events, such as MIFARE sector access ❺ and EMV card removal ❻. (APDUs are *Application Protocol Data Units*, the basic building block of smart card protocols; see "SE Communication Protocols" on page 303. The `APDU_RECIEVED` broadcast is not implemented, because in practice the NFC controller routes incoming APDUs directly to the eSE, which makes them invisible to the OS.) SE-enabled apps register for these broadcasts in order to be able to change their internal state or start a related activity when each event occurs (for example, to start a PIN entry activity when an EMV applet is selected). The `INTERNAL_TARGET_DESELECTED` broadcast ❼ is sent when card emulation is deactivated, and the `MASTER_CLEAR_NOTIFICATION` broadcast ❽ is sent when the contents of the eSE are cleared. (Pre-HCE versions of Google Wallet offered users the option to clear the eSE remotely if their device was lost or stolen.)

Android SE Execution Environment

The Android SE is essentially a smart card in a different package, so most standards and protocols originally developed for smart cards apply. Let's briefly review the most important ones.

Smart cards have traditionally been filesystem-oriented and the main role of their OS has been to handle file access and enforce access permissions. Newer cards support a virtual machine running on top of the native OS that allows for the execution of "platform independent" applications called applets, which use a well-defined runtime library to implement their functionality. While different implementations of this paradigm exist, by far the most popular one is the Java Card runtime environment (JCRE). Applets are implemented in a restricted version of the Java language and use a limited runtime library, which offers basic classes for I/O, message parsing, and cryptographic operations. While the JCRE specification[13] fully defines the applet runtime environment, it does not specify how to load, initialize, and delete applets on actual physical cards (tools are only provided for the JCRE emulator).

Because one of the main applications of smart cards are various payment services, the application loading and initialization process (often referred to as *card personalization*) needs to be controlled, and only authorized entities should be able to alter the state of the card and installed applications. Visa originally developed a specification for securely managing applets, called Open Platform, which is now maintained and developed by the GlobalPlatform (GP) organization under the name GlobalPlatform Card Specification.[14] The gist of this specification is that each GP-compliant card has a mandatory *Issuer Security Domain (ISD)* component (informally referred to as the *Card Manager*) that offers a well-defined interface for card and application life cycle management. Executing ISD operations requires authentication using cryptographic keys saved on the card, and thus only an entity that knows those keys can change the state of the card (one of `OP_READY`, `INITIALIZED`, `SECURED`, `CARD_LOCKED`, or `TERMINATED`) or manage applets. Additionally, the GP card specification defines various secure communication protocols (called Secure Channels) that offer authentication, confidentiality, and message integrity when communicating with the card.

SE Communication Protocols

As discussed in "Using the NfcExecutionEnvironment API" on page 300, Android's interface for communicating with the SE is the `byte[] transceive(byte[] command)` method of the `NfcExecutionEnvironment` class. The messages exchanged using this API are in practice APDUs, and their structure is defined in the *ISO/IEC 7816-4: Organization, security and commands for interchange* standard.[15] The reader (also known as a *Card Acceptance Device*, or *CAD*) sends command APDUs (sometimes referred to as *C-APDUs*) to the card, composed of a mandatory four-byte header with a command class (*CLA*), instruction (*INS*), and two parameters (*P1* and *P2*). This is followed by the optional command data length (*Lc*), the actual data, and finally the maximum number of response bytes expected, if any (*Le*). The card returns a response APDU (*R-APDU*) with a mandatory status word (*SW*, consisting of two bytes: *SW1* and *SW2*) and optional response data.

Historically, command APDU data has been limited to 255 bytes (total APDU length 261 bytes) and response APDU data to 256 bytes (total APDU length 258 bytes). Recent cards and readers support extended APDUs with data length up to 65536 bytes, but extended APDUs are not always usable,

13. Oracle, "Java Card Classic Platform Specification 3.0.4," *http://www.oracle.com/technetwork/java/javacard/specs-jsp-136430.html*

14. GlobalPlatform, "Card Specifications," *http://www.globalplatform.org/specificationscard.asp*

15. A summary of ISO 7816 and other smart card-related standards is available on CardWerk's website: *http://www.cardwerk.com/smartcards/smartcard_standards.aspx*

mostly for reasons of compatibility. The lower-level communication between the reader and the card is carried out by one of several transmission protocols, the most widely used of which are T=0 (byte-oriented) and T=1 (block-oriented). Both are defined in *ISO 7816-3: Cards with contacts — Electrical interface and transmission protocols*. The APDU exchange is not completely protocol-agnostic, because T=0 cannot directly send response data, but only notify the reader of the number of available bytes. Additional command APDUs (`GET RESPONSE`) need to be sent in order to retrieve the response data.

The original ISO 7816 standards were developed for contact cards, but the same APDU-based communication model is used for contactless cards as well. It's layered on top of the wireless transmission protocol defined by ISO/IEC 14443-4, which behaves much like T=1 for contact cards.

Querying the eSE Execution Environment

As discussed in "Embedded SE" on page 298, the eSE in the Galaxy Nexus is a chip from NXP's SmartMX series. It runs a Java Card–compatible operating system and comes with a GlobalPlatform-compliant ISD. The ISD is configured to require authentication for most card management operations, and the authentication keys are, naturally, not publicly available. Additionally, a number of subsequent failed authentication attempts (usually 10) will lock the ISD and make it impossible to install or remove applets, so trying to brute-force the authentication keys is not an option. However, the ISD does provide some information about itself and the runtime environment on the card without requiring authentication in order to make it possible for clients to adjust their behavior dynamically and be compatible with different cards.

Because both Java Card and GlobalPlatform define a multi-application environment, each application needs a unique identifier called the *Application Identifier (AID)*. The AID consists of a 5-byte Registered Application Provider Identifier (RID, also called a Resource Identifier) and a Proprietary Identifier eXtension (PIX), which can be up to 11 bytes long. Thus, the length of an AID can be 5 to 16 bytes long. Before being able to send commands to a particular applet, it needs to be made active, or selected, by issuing the `SELECT` (`CLA`=00, `INS`=A4) command with its AID. As all applications, the ISD is also identified by an AID, which varies between card manufacturers and GP implementations. We can find out the AID of the ISD by sending an empty `SELECT` command, which both selects the ISD and returns information about the card and the ISD configuration. An empty `SELECT` is simply a select without an AID specified, so the `SELECT` command APDU becomes `00 A4 04 00 00`. If we send this command using the `transcieve()` method of the `NfcExecutionEnvironment` class (Listing 11-8 at ❹), the returned response might look like Listing 11-10 at ❷ (❶ is the `SELECT` command).

```
--> 00A4040000❶
<-- 6F658408A000000003000000A5599F6501FF9F6E06479100783300734A06072A86488
```

```
6FC6B01600C060A2A864886FC6B0202010163090607 2A864886FC6B03640B06092A86488
6FC6B040215650B06092B8510864864020103660C060A2B060104012A026E0102 9000❷
```

Listing 11-10: Galaxy Nexus eSE's response to empty SELECT

The response includes a successful status (0x9000) and a long string of bytes. The format of this data is defined in "APDU Command Reference," Chapter 9 of the GlobalPlatform Card Specification and, as with most things in the smart card world, is in tag-length-value (TLV) format. In TLV, each unit of data is described by a unique tag, followed by its length in bytes, and finally the actual data. Most structures are recursive, so the data can host another TLV structure, which in turns wraps another, and so on. The structure shown in Listing 11-10 is called *File Control Information (FCI)* and in this case it wraps a Security Domain Management Data structure, which describes the ISD. When parsed, the FCI might look like Listing 11-11.

```
SD FCI: Security Domain FCI
   AID: a0 00 00 00 03 00 00 00❶
    RID: a0 00 00 00 03 (Visa International [US])
    PIX: 00 00 00

   Data field max length: 255
   Application prod. life cycle data: 479100783300
   Tag allocation authority (OID): globalPlatform 01
   Card management type and version (OID): globalPlatform 02020101
   Card identification scheme (OID): globalPlatform 03
   Global Platform version: 2.1.1❷
   Secure channel version: SC02 (options: 15)❸
   Card config details: 06092B8510864864020103❹
   Card/chip details: 060A2B060104012A026E0102❺
```

Listing 11-11: Parsed FCI of the ISD on the eSE in Galaxy Nexus

Here, the AID of the ISD is A0 00 00 00 03 00 00 00 ❶, the version of the GlobalPlatform implementation is 2.1.1 ❷, the supported Secure Channel protocol is SC02 ❸, and the last two fields of the structure contain some proprietary data about the card configuration (❹ and ❺). The only other GP command that doesn't require authentication is `GET DATA`, which can be used to return additional data about the ISD configuration.

UICC as a Secure Element

As discussed in "SE Form Factors in Mobile Devices" on page 296, the UICC in a mobile device can be used as a general-purpose SE when accessed using the Open Mobile API or a similar programming interface. This section gives a brief overview of UICCs and the applications they typically host, and then shows how to access the UICC via the Open Mobile API.

SIM Cards and UICCs

The predecessor of the UICC is the SIM card, and UICCs are still colloquially referred to as "SIM cards." *SIM* stands for *Subscriber Identity Module* and refers to a smart card that securely stores the subscriber identifier and the associated key used to identify and authenticate a device to a mobile network. SIMs were initially used on GSM networks and the original GSM standards were later extended to support 3G and LTE. Because SIMs are smart cards, they conform to ISO-7816 standards regarding physical characteristics and electrical interface. The first SIM cards were the same size as "regular" smart cards (Full-size, FF), but by far the most popular sizes today are Mini-SIM (2FF) and Micro-SIM (3FF), with Nano-SIM (4FF), which was introduced in 2012, also gaining market share.

Of course, not every smart card that fits in the SIM slot can be used in a mobile device, so the next question is: What makes a smart card a SIM card? Technically, it's conformance to mobile communication standards such as 3GPP TS 11.11 and certification by the SIMalliance. In practice, it is the ability to run an application that allows it to communicate with the phone (referred to as *Mobile Equipment* or *Mobile Station* in related standards) and connect to a mobile network. While the original GSM standard did not distinguish between the physical smart card and the software required to connect to the mobile network, with the introduction of 3G standards, a clear distinction has been made. The physical smart card is referred to as a *Universal Integrated Circuit Card (UICC),* and different mobile network applications that run on it have been defined: GSM, CSIM, USIM, ISIM, and so on. A UICC can host and run more than one network application (hence the name *universal*), and thus can be used to connect to different networks. While network application functionality depends on the specific mobile network, their core features are quite similar: store network parameters securely and identify to the network, as well as authenticate the user (optionally) and store user data.

UICC Applications

Let's take GSM as an example and briefly review how a network application works. For GSM, the main network parameters are network identity (International Mobile Subscriber Identity, IMSI; tied to the SIM), phone number (MSISDN, used for routing calls and changeable), and a shared network authentication key *Ki*. To connect to the network, the phone needs to authenticate and negotiate a session key. Both authentication and session keys are derived using *Ki*, which is also known to the network and looked up by IMSI. The phone sends a connection request that includes its IMSI, which the network uses to find the corresponding *Ki*. The network then uses the *Ki* to generate a challenge (*RAND*), expected challenge response (*SRES*), and session key *Kc*. When those parameters have been generated, the network sends *RAND* to the phone and the GSM application running on the SIM card comes into play: the mobile passes the *RAND* to the SIM card, which generates its own *SRES* and *Kc*. The *SRES* is sent to the network and if it matches the expected value, encrypted communication is established using the session key *Kc*.

As you can see, the security of this protocol hinges solely on the secrecy of the *Ki*. Because all operations involving the *Ki* are implemented inside the SIM card, and it never comes in direct contact with the phone or the network, the scheme is kept reasonably secure. Of course, security depends on the encryption algorithms used as well, and major weaknesses that allow intercepted GSM calls to be decrypted using off-the-shelf hardware were found in the original versions of the A5/1 stream cipher (which was initially secret).

In Android, network authentication is implemented by the baseband processor (more on this in "Accessing the UICC" below) and is never directly visible to the main OS.

UICC Application Implementation and Installation

We've seen that UICCs need to run applications; now let's see how those applications are implemented and installed. Initial smart cards were based on a filesystem model, where files (called *elementary files*, or *EF*) and directories (called *dedicated files*, or *DF*) were named with a two-byte identifier. Thus, developing "an application" involved selecting an ID for the DF that hosts the application's files (called *ADF*), and specifying the formats and names of the EFs that store data. For example, the GSM application is under the *7F20* ADF, and the USIM ADF hosts the *EF_imsi*, *EF_keys*, *EF_sms*, and other required files.

Because practically all UICCs in use today are based on Java Card technology and implement GlobalPlatform card specifications, all network applications are implemented as Java Card applets and emulate the legacy file-based structure for backward compatibility. Applets are installed according to GlobalPlatform specifications by authenticating to the ISD and issuing `LOAD` and `INSTALL` commands.

One application management feature specific to SIM cards is support for OTA updates via binary SMS. This functionality is not used by all carriers, but it allows carriers to remotely install applets on SIM cards they've issued. OTA is implemented by wrapping card commands (APDUs) in SMS T-PDUs (transport protocol data units), which the phone forwards to the UICC. In most UICCs, this is the only way to load applets on the card, even during initial personalization.

The major use case for this OTA functionality is to install and maintain SIM Toolkit (STK) applications that can interact with the handset via standard "proactive" commands (which in reality are implemented via polling), and to display menus or even open web pages and send SMS. Android supports STK with a dedicated STK system app, which is automatically disabled if the UICC card has no STK applets installed.

Accessing the UICC

As we discussed in "UICC Applications" on page 306, mobile network–related functionality in Android, including UICC access, is implemented by the baseband software. The main OS (Android) is limited in what it can do with the UICC by the features the baseband exposes. Android supports STK applications and can look up and store contacts on the SIM, so it's clear that it has internal support for communicating to the SIM. However, the Android security overview explicitly states that "low-level access to the

SIM card is not available to third-party apps."[16] How can we use the SIM card (UICC) as an SE then? Some Android builds from major vendors, most notably Samsung, provide an implementation of the SIMalliance Open Mobile API, and an open source implementation (for compatible devices) of the API is available from the SEEK for Android project. The Open Mobile API aims to provide a unified interface for accessing SEs on Android, including the UICC.

To understand how the Open Mobile API works and the cause of its limitations, let's review how access to the SIM card is implemented in Android. On Android devices, all mobile network functionality (dialing, sending SMS, and so on) is provided by the baseband processor (also referred to as *modem* or *radio*). Android applications and system services communicate with the baseband only indirectly via the Radio Interface Layer (RIL) daemon (*rild*). The *rild* in turn talks to the actual hardware by using a manufacturer-provided RIL HAL library, which wraps the proprietary interface that the baseband provides. The UICC card is typically connected only to the baseband processor (though sometimes also to the NFC controller via SWP), and thus all communication needs to go through the RIL.

While the proprietary RIL implementation can always access the UICC in order to perform network identification and authentication, as well as read and write contacts and access STK applications, support for transparent APDU exchange is not always available. As we mentioned in "UICC" on page 297, the standard way to provide this feature is to use extended AT commands such `AT+CSIM` (Generic SIM access) and `AT+CGLA` (Generic UICC Logical Channel Access), but some vendors implement APDU exchange using proprietary extensions, so support for the necessary AT commands doesn't automatically provide UICC access.

SEEK for Android implements a resource manager service (`SmartCardService`) that can connect to any supported SE (eSE, ASSD, or UICC) and extensions to the Android telephony framework that allow for transparent APDU exchange with the UICC. Because access through the RIL is hardware- and HAL-dependent, you need both a compatible device and a build that includes the `SmartCardService` and related framework extensions, such as those found in most recent Samsung Galaxy devices.

Using the OpenMobile API

The OpenMobile API is relatively small and defines classes that represent the card reader that an SE is connected to (`Reader`), a communication session with an SE (`Session`), and a basic (channel 0, as per ISO 7816-4) or logical channel with the SE (`Channel`). The `Channel` class allows applications to exchange APDUs with the SE using the `transmit()` method. The entry point to the API is the `SEService` class, which connects to the remote resource manager service (`SmartcardService`) and provides a method that returns a list

16. Google, *Android Security Overview*, "SIM Card Access," *https://source.android.com/devices/tech/security/#sim-card-access*

of Reader objects available on the device. (For more information about the OpenMobile API and the architecture of the SmartcardService, refer to the SEEK for Android Wiki.[17])

In order to be able to use the OpenMobile API, applications need to request the org.simalliance.openmobileapi.SMARTCARD permission and add the *org.simalliance.openmobileapi* extension library to their manifest as shown in Listing 11-12.

```
<manifest ...>
    --snip--
    <uses-permission android:name="org.simalliance.openmobileapi.SMARTCARD" />

    <application ...>
        <uses-library
            android:name="org.simalliance.openmobileapi"
            android:required="true" />
     --snip--
    </application>
</manifest>
```

Listing 11-12: AndroidManifest.xml *configuration required to use the OpenMobile API*

Listing 11-13 demonstrates how an application can use the OpenMobile API to connect and send a command to the first SE on the device.

```
Context context = getContext();
SEService.CallBack callback = createSeCallback();
SEService seService = new SEService(context, callback);❶
Reader[] readers = seService.getReaders();❷
Session session = readers[0].openSession();❸
Channel channel = session.openLogicalChannel(aid);❹
byte[] command = { ... };
byte[] response = channel.transmit(command);❺
```

Listing 11-13: Sending a command to the first SE using the OpenMobile API

Here, the application first creates an SEService ❶ instance, which connects to the SmartCardService asynchronously and notifies the application via the serviceConnected() method (not shown) of the SEService.CallBack interface when the connection is established. The app can then get a list of the available SE readers using the getReaders() method ❷, and then open a session to the selected reader using the openSession() method ❸. If the device does not contain an eSE (or another form of SE besides the UICC), or the SmartCardService hasn't been configured to use it, the list of readers contains a single Reader instance that represents the built-in UICC reader in the device. When the app has an open Session with the target SE, it calls the openLogicalChannel() method ❹ in order to obtain a Channel, which it then uses to send APDUs and receive responses using its transmit() method ❺.

17. *SEEK for Android*, "SmartCardAPI," *https://code.google.com/p/seek-for-android/wiki/SmartcardAPI*

Software Card Emulation

Software card emulation (also referred to as *host-based card emulation* or *HCE*) allows commands received by the NFC controller to be delivered to the application processor (main OS), and to be processed by regular Android applications, instead of by applets installed on a hardware SE. Responses are then sent back to the reader via NFC, allowing an app to act as a virtual contactless smart card.

Before being officially added to the Android API, HCE was first available as an experimental feature of the CyanogenMod Android distribution.[18] Beginning with version 9.1, CyanogenMod integrated a set of patches (developed by Doug Yeager) that unlock the HCE functionality of the popular PN544 NFC controller and provide a framework interface to HCE. In order to support HCE, two new tag technologies (`IsoPcdA` and `IsoPcdB`, representing external contactless readers based on NFC Type A and Type B technology, respectively) were added to the NFC framework. (The letters *Pcd* stand for *Proximity Coupling Device*, which is just another technical term for contactless reader.)

The `IsoPcdA` and `IsoPcdB` classes reversed the role of `Tag` objects in the Android NFC API: because the external contactless reader is presented as a "tag," "commands" you send from the phone are actually replies to the reader-initiated communication. Unlike the rest of Android's NFC stack, this architecture was not event driven and required applications to handle blocking I/O while waiting for the reader to send its next command. Android 4.4 introduced a standard, event-driven framework for developing HCE applications, which we discuss next.

Android 4.4 HCE Architecture

Unlike the R/W and P2P mode, which are only available to activities, HCE applications can work in the background and are implemented by defining a service that processes commands received from the external reader and returns responses. Such HCE services extend the `HostApduService` abstract framework class and implement its `onDeactivated()` and `processCommand()` methods. `HostApduService` itself is a very thin mediator class that enables two-way communication with the system `NfcService` by using `Messenger` objects.[19] For example, when the `NfcService` receives an APDU that needs to be routed (APDU routing is discussed in the next section) to a HCE service, it sends a `MSG_COMMAND_APDU` to `HostApduService`, which then extracts the APDU from the message and passes it to its concrete implementation by calling the `processCommand()` method. If `processCommand()` returns an APDU, `HostApduService` encapsulates it in a `MSG_RESPONSE_APDU` message and sends it to the `NfcService`, which in turn forwards it to the NFC controller. If the concrete HCE service cannot return a response APDU immediately, it

18. CyanogenMod, *http://www.cyanogenmod.org/*

19. Google, *Android API Reference*, "Messenger," *https://developer.android.com/reference/android/os/Messenger.html*

returns null and sends the response later (when it is available) by calling the sendResponseApdu(), which sends the response to the NfcService wrapped in a MSG_RESPONSE_APDU message.

APDU Routing

When the device is in card emulation mode, the NFC controller receives all APDUs coming from external readers and decides whether to send them to a physical SE (if any), or to an HCE service based on its internal APDU routing table. The routing table is AID-based and is populated using the metadata SE-enabled applications and HCE services declared in their application manifests. When the external reader sends a SELECT command that is not directly routed to the SE, the NFC controller forwards it to the NfcService, which extracts the target AID from the command and searches the routing table for a matching HCE service by calling the resolveAidPrefix() method of the RegisteredAidCache class.

If a matching service is found, NfcService binds to it and obtains a Messenger instance, which it then uses to send subsequent APDUs (wrapped in MSG_COMMAND_APDU messages, as discussed in the previous section). For this to work, the app's HCE service needs to be declared in *AndroidManifest.xml* as shown in Listing 11-14.

```
<?xml version="1.0" encoding="utf-8"?>
<manifest xmlns:android="http://schemas.android.com/apk/res/android"
    package="com.example.hce" ...>
    --snip--
    <uses-permission android:name="android.permission.NFC" />

    <application ...>
        --snip--
        <service
            android:name=".MyHostApduService"❶
            android:exported="true"
            android:permission="android.permission.BIND_NFC_SERVICE" >❷
            <intent-filter>
                <action
                    android:name="android.nfc.cardemulation.action.HOST_APDU_SERVICE" />❸
            </intent-filter>

            <meta-data
                android:name="android.nfc.cardemulation.host_apdu_service"❹
                android:resource="@xml/apduservice" />
        </service>
        --snip--
    </application>
</manifest>
```

Listing 11-14: Declaring a HCE service in AndroidManifest.xml

The application declares its HCE service ❶ as usual, using the <service> tag, but there are a few additional requirements. First, the service must be protected with the BIND_NFC_SERVICE system signature permission ❷, to guarantee that only system apps (in practice, only the NfcService) can bind to it. Next, the service needs to declare an intent filter that matches the android.nfc.cardemulation.action.HOST_APDU_SERVICE action ❸ so that it can be identified as a HCE service when scanning installed packages, and be bound to when a matching APDU is received. Finally, the service must have an XML resource metadata entry under the name *android.nfc.cardemulation.host_apdu_service* ❹, which points to an XML resource file listing the AIDs that the service can handle. The contents of this file is used to build the AID routing table, which the NFC stack consults when it receives a SELECT command.

Specifying Routing for HCE Services

For HCE applications, the XML file must include a <host-apdu-service> root element as shown in Listing 11-15.

```
<host-apdu-service
    xmlns:android="http://schemas.android.com/apk/res/android"
    android:description="@string/servicedesc"
    android:requireDeviceUnlock="false">❶
    <aid-group android:description="@string/aiddescription"❷
               android:category="other">❸
        <aid-filter android:name="A0000000010101"/>❹
    </aid-group>
</host-apdu-service>
```

Listing 11-15: HCE service AID metadata file

The <host-apdu-service> tag has a description attribute and a requireDeviceUnlock attribute ❶, which specifies whether the corresponding HCE service should be activated when the device is locked. (The device's screen must be on for NFC to work.) The root element contains one or more <aid-group> entries ❷, which each have a category attribute ❸ and contain one or more <aid-filter> ❹ tags that specify an AID in their name attribute (*A0000000010101* in this example).

An AID group defines a set of AIDs that is always handled by a particular HCE service. The NFC framework guarantees that if a single AID is handled by an HCE service, then all other AIDs in the group are also handled by the same service. If two or more HCE services define the same AID, the system shows a selection dialog letting the user choose which application should handle the incoming SELECT command. When an app is chosen, all subsequent commands are routed to it after the user confirms the selection by tapping on the dialog shown in Figure 11-2.

Each AID group is associated with a category (specified with the category attribute), which allows the system to set a default handler per category, rather than per AID. An application can check if a particular service is the default handler for a category by calling the isDefaultServiceForCategory() method of the CardEmulation class, and get the selection mode for a category by calling the getSelectionModeForCategory() method. As of this writing, only two categories are defined: CATEGORY_PAYMENT and CATEGORY_OTHER.

Android enforces a single active payment category in order to ensure that the user has explicitly selected which app should handle payment transactions. The default app for the payment category is selected in the Tap & pay screen of the system Settings app, as shown in Figure 11-3. (See the official HCE documentation[20] for more on payment applications.)

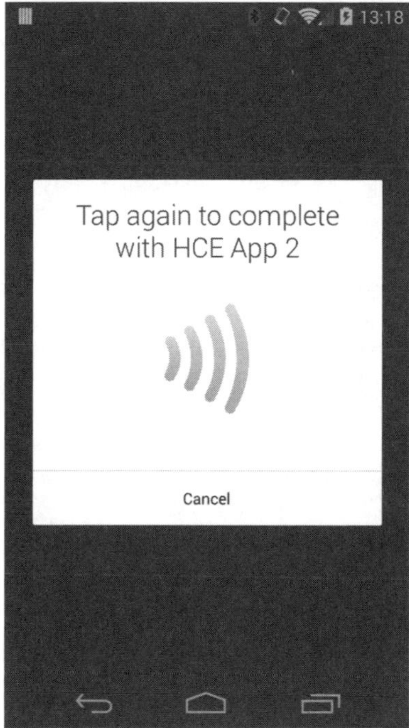

Figure 11-2: HCE application selection confirmation dialog

Figure 11-3: Selecting the default payment application in the Tap & pay screen

Specifying Routing for SE Applets

If a device supports HCE and also has a physical SE, a `SELECT` command sent by an external reader can target either an HCE service, or an applet installed on the SE. Because Android 4.4 directs all AIDs not listed in the AID routing table to the host, the AIDs of applets installed on the SE must be explicitly added to the NFC controller's routing table. This is accomplished with the same mechanism used for registering HCE services: by adding a service entry to the application's manifest, and linking it to a metadata XML file that specifies a list of AIDs that should be routed to the SE. When the route is established, command APDUs are sent directly to the SE (which processes them and returns a response via the NFC controller), so the service is used only as a marker and provides no functionality.

---

20. Google, *Host-based Card Emulation*, "Payment Applications," *https://developer.android.com/guide/topics/connectivity/nfc/hce.html#PaymentApps*

The Android SDK includes a helper service (OffHostApduService) that can be used to list AIDs that should be routed directly to the SE. This OffHostApduService class defines some useful constants, but is otherwise empty. An application can extend it and declare the resulting service component in its manifest as shown in Listing 11-16.

```
<manifest xmlns:android="http://schemas.android.com/apk/res/android"
    package="com.example.hce" ...>
    --snip--
    <uses-permission android:name="android.permission.NFC" />

    <application ... >
        --snip--
        <service android:name=".MyOffHostApduService"
                 android:exported="true"
                 android:permission="android.permission.BIND_NFC_SERVICE">
        <intent-filter>
            <action
                android:name="android.nfc.cardemulation.action.OFF_HOST_APDU_SERVICE"/>❶
        </intent-filter>
        <meta-data
            android:name="android.nfc.cardemulation.off_host_apdu_service"❷
            android:resource="@xml/apduservice"/>
    </service>
    --snip--
    </application>
</manifest>
```

Listing 11-16: Declaring an off-host APDU service in AndroidManifest.xml

The service declaration is similar to that of Listing 11-14, except that the declared intent action is *android.nfc.cardemulation.action.OFF_HOST_APDU_SERVICE* ❶ and the XML metadata name is *android.nfc.cardemulation.off_host_apdu_service* ❷. The metadata file is also slightly different, as shown in Listing 11-17.

```
<offhost-apdu-service
    xmlns:android="http://schemas.android.com/apk/res/android"
    android:description="@string/servicedesc">❶
    <aid-group android:description="@string/se_applets"
               android:category="other">❷
        <aid-filter android:name="F0000000000001"/>❸
        <aid-filter android:name="F0000000000002"/>❹
    </aid-group>
</offhost-apdu-service>
```

Listing 11-17: Off-host APDU service metadata file

As you can see, the format is the same as that of an HCE service, but the root element of the file is <offhost-apdu-service> ❶ instead of <host-apdu-service>. Another subtle difference is that <offhost-apdu-service> does not support the requireDeviceUnlock attribute, because transactions are sent directly to the SE and therefore the host cannot intervene regardless of the state of the lockscreen. The AIDs of the applets residing on the SE (❸ and ❹) are included in a <aid-group> ❷. Those AIDs are sent directly to the NFC controller, which saves them in its internal routing table in order to be able to send matching APDUs directly to the SE, without interacting with the Android OS. If the received APDU is not in the NFC controller's routing table, it forwards it to the NfcService, which sends it to the matching HCE service, or returns an error if no matches are found.

Writing an HCE Service

When the HCE service of an application has been declared in its manifest as shown in Listing 11-14, HCE functionality can be added by extending the HostApduService base class and implementing its abstract methods as shown in Listing 11-18.

```
public class MyHostApduService extends HostApduService {
    --snip--
    static final int OFFSET_CLA = 0;❶
    static final int OFFSET_INS = 1;
    static final int OFFSET_P1 = 2;
    static final int OFFSET_P2 = 3;
    --snip--
    static final short SW_SUCCESS = (short) 0x9000;❷
    static final short SW_CLA_NOT_SUPPORTED = 0x6E00;
    static final short SW_INS_NOT_SUPPORTED = 0x6D00;
    --snip--
    static final byte[] SELECT_CMD = { 0x00, (byte) 0xA4,
            0x04, 0x00, 0x06, (byte) 0xA0,
            0x00, 0x00, 0x00, 0x01, 0x01, 0x01 };❸

    static final byte MY_CLA = (byte) 0x80;❹
    static final byte INS_CMD1 = (byte) 0x01;
    static final byte INS_CMD2 = (byte) 0x02;

    boolean selected = false;

    public byte[] processCommandApdu(byte[] cmd, Bundle extras) {
        if (!selected) {
            if (Arrays.equals(cmd, SELECT_CMD)) {❺
                selected = true;

                return toBytes(SW_SUCCESS);
            }
            --snip--
        }

        if (cmd[OFFSET_CLA] != MY_CLA) {❻
            return toBytes(SW_CLA_NOT_SUPPORTED);
        }

        byte ins = cmd[OFFSET_INS];❼
        switch (ins) {
            case INS_CMD1:❽
```

```
                byte p1 = cmd[OFFSET_P1];
                byte p2 = cmd[OFFSET_P2];
                --snip--
                return toBytes(SW_SUCCESS);
            case INS_CMD2:
                --snip--
                return null;❾
            default:
                return toBytes(SW_INS_NOT_SUPPORTED);
        }
    }

    @Override
    public void onDeactivated(int reason) {
        --snip--
        selected = false;❿
    }
    --snip--
}
```

Listing 11-18: Implementing a `HostApduService`

Here, the example HCE service first declares a few constants that will be helpful when accessing APDU data ❶ and returning a standard status result ❷. The service defines the `SELECT` command that is used to activate it, including the AID ❸. The next few constants ❹ declare the instruction class (*CLA*) and instructions that the service can handle.

When the HCE service receives an APDU, it passes it to the `processCommandApdu()` method as a byte array, which the service analyzes. If the service hasn't been selected yet, the `processCommandApdu()` method checks if the APDU contains a `SELECT` command ❺, and sets the `selected` flag if it does. If the APDU contains some other command, the code checks to see if it has a class byte (*CLA*) the services supports ❻, and then extracts the instruction byte (*INS*) included in the command ❼. If the command APDU contains the `INS_CMD1` instruction ❽, the service extracts the *P1* and *P2* parameters, possibly parses the data included in the APDU (not shown), sets some internal state, and returns a success status.

If the command includes `INS_CMD2`, which in our example maps to a hypothetical operation that requires some time to process (for example, asymmetric key generation), the service starts a worker thread (not shown), and returns `null` ❾ in order not to block the main thread of the application. When the worker thread completes execution, it can return its result using the inherited `sendResponseApdu()` (defined in the parent `HostApduService` class). When another service or SE applet is selected, the system calls the `onDeactivated()` method, which should release any used resources before returning, but in our example simply sets the `selected` flag to `false` ❿.

Because an HCE service essentially parses command APDUs and returns responses, the programming model is very similar to that of Java Card applets. However, because a HCE service lives inside a regular Android application, it does not execute in a constrained environment and can take advantage of all available Android features. This makes it easy to implement complex functionality, but also impacts the security of HCE apps, as discussed next.

Security of HCE Applications

Because any Android application can declare an HCE service and receive and process APDUs, the system guarantees that a malicious application cannot inject rogue APDU commands into an HCE service by requiring the `BIND_NFC_SERVICE` system signature permission in order to bind to HCE services. Additionally, Android's sandboxing model ensures that other applications cannot access sensitive data stored by the HCE application by reading its files or calling any data access APIs it might expose without permission (assuming such APIs have been properly secured, of course).

Nevertheless, a malicious application that manages to obtain root privileges on a device (for example, by exploiting a privilege escalation vulnerability) can both inspect and inject APDUs targeted at an HCE service, and read its private data. The HCE application can take some measures to detect this situation, for example by inspecting the identity and signing certificate of the caller of its `processCommandApdu()` method, but such measures can ultimately be defeated given unconstrained access to the OS. Like all applications that store sensitive data, HCE applications should also take steps to protect stored data, such as by encrypting it on disk or by storing it in the system credential store in the case of cryptographic keys. Another way to protect both the code and data of HCE applications is to forward all received commands to a remote server, over an encrypted channel, and relay only its replies. However, because most of these measures are implemented in software, they can ultimately be disabled or bypassed by a sufficiently sophisticated malicious application with root access.

In contrast, hardware security elements offer physical tamper resistance, reduced attack surface due to their constrained functionality, and tight control over installed applets. Therefore, physical SEs are much harder to attack and provide much stronger protection of sensitive data used in typical card emulation scenarios like contactless payments, even when the default security guarantees of the host OS have been bypassed.

NOTE *For a detailed discussion of the difference in security level of card emulation applications when implemented in secure elements as opposed to in software using HCE, see the "HCE vs embedded secure element" blog post series by Cem Paya (who worked on the original eSE-backed Google Wallet implementation).*[21]

21. Cem Paya, *Random Oracle*, "HCE vs embedded secure element," parts I to VI, *http://randomoracle.wordpress.com/2014/03/08/hce-vs-embedded-secure-element-comparing-risks-part-i/*

Summary

Android supports the three NFC modes: reader/writer, point-to-point, and card emulation. In reader/writer mode, Android devices can access NFC tags, contactless cards, and NFC emulation devices, while the point-to-point mode provides simple data exchange functionality. The card emulation mode can be backed either by a physical secure element (SE) such as a UICC, one that is integrated with the NFC controller (embedded SE), or by regular Android applications since Android 4.4. Hardware security elements provide the highest security by offering physical tamper resistance and stringent control over SE application (typically implemented as Java Card applets) management. However, because the authentication keys required to install an application on an SE are typically controlled by a single entity (such as the device manufacturer or MNO), distributing SE applications can be problematic. Host-based card emulation (HCE), introduced in Android 4.4, makes it easy to develop and distribute applications that work in card emulation mode, but it relies solely on the OS to enforce security and therefore offers weaker protection of sensitive application code and data.

12

SELINUX

While previous chapters mentioned Security-Enhanced Linux (SELinux) and its Android integration, our discussion of Android's security model up until now has focused on Android's "traditional" sandbox implementation, which relies heavily on Linux's default discretionary access control (DAC). The Linux DAC is lightweight and well understood, but it has certain disadvantages, most notably the coarse granularity of DAC permissions, the potential for misconfigured programs to leak data, and the inability to apply fine-grained privilege constraints to processes that run as the root user. (While POSIX capabilities, which are implemented as an extension to the traditional DAC in Linux, offer a way to grant only certain privileges to root processes, the granularity of POSIX capabilities is fairly coarse and the granted privileges extend to all objects accessed by the process.)

Mandatory access control (MAC), as implemented by SELinux, seeks to overcome these limitations of Linux's DAC by enforcing a systemwide, more finely grained security policy that can be changed only by the system administrator, and not by unprivileged users and programs. This chapter first gives a brief overview of the architecture and concepts used in SELinux and then describes the major modifications made to SELinux in order to support Android. Finally, we give an overview of the SELinux policy that's deployed in the current version of Android.

SELinux Introduction

SELinux is a mandatory access control mechanism for the Linux kernel, implemented as a Linux security module. The Linux Security Modules (LSM) framework allows third-party access control mechanisms to be linked into the kernel and to modify the default DAC implementation. LSM is implemented as a series of security function hooks (upcalls) and related data structures that are integrated into the various modules of the Linux kernel responsible for access control.

Some of the main kernel services that have LSM hooks inserted are program execution, file and inode operations, netlink messaging, and socket operations. If no security module is installed, Linux uses its built-in DAC mechanism to regulate access to kernel objects managed by these services. If a security module is installed, Linux consults it in addition to the DAC in order to reach a final security decision when access to a kernel object is requested.

Besides providing hooks into major kernel services, the LSM framework also extends the procfs virtual filesystem (*/proc*) to include per-process and per-task (thread) security attributes, and adds support for using filesystem extended attributes as persistent security attribute storage. SELinux was the first LSM module integrated into the Linux kernel and has been officially available since version 2.6 (previous SELinux implementations were distributed as a set of patches). Since the integration of SELinux, other security modules have also been accepted into the mainline kernel, which as of this writing includes AppArmor, Smack, and TOMOYO Linux as well. These modules provide alternative MAC implementations and are based on different security models than those of SELinux.

We'll explore the SELinux security model and architecture in the next sections.

SELinux Architecture

While the SELinux architecture is quite complex, at a high level it consists of four main components: object managers (OM), an access vector cache (AVC), a security server, and a security policy, as shown in Figure 12-1.

When a subject asks to perform an action on an SELinux object (for example, when a process tries to read a file), the associated object manager queries the AVC to see if the attempted action is allowed. If the AVC contains a cached security decision for the request, the AVC returns it to the OM, which enforces the decision by allowing or denying the action (steps 1, 2, and 5 in Figure 12-1). If the cache does not contain a matching security decision, the AVC contacts the security server, which makes a security decision based on the currently loaded policy and returns it to the AVC, which caches it. The AVC in turn returns it to the OM, which ultimately enforces the decision (steps 1, 2, 3, 4, and 5 in Figure 12-1). The security server is part of the kernel, while the policy is loaded from userspace via a series of functions contained in the supporting userspace library.

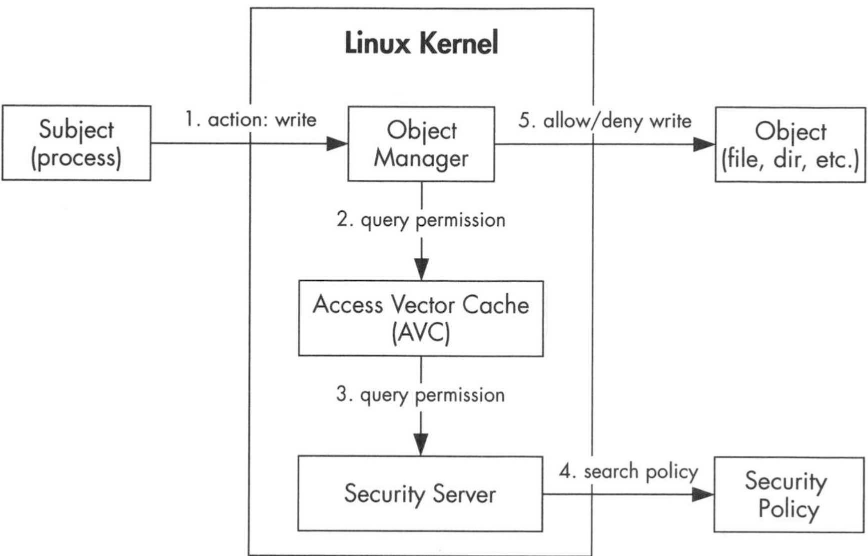

Figure 12-1: SELinux components

The OM and AVC can reside either in kernel space (when the OM is managing kernel-level objects) or userspace (when the OM is part of a so-called SELinux-aware application, which has built-in MAC support).

Mandatory Access Control

SELinux's MAC model is based on three main concepts: subjects, objects, and actions. In this model, subjects are the active actors that perform actions on objects, and the action is carried out only if the security policy allows it.

In practice, subjects are usually running processes (a process can also be an object), and objects are OS-level resources managed by the kernel, such as files and sockets. Both subjects and objects have a set of security attributes (collectively known as the *security context*, discussed in the next section), which the OS queries in order to decide whether the requested action should be allowed or not. When SELinux is enabled, subjects cannot bypass or influence policy rules; therefore, the policy is mandatory.

NOTE *The MAC policy is only consulted if the DAC allows access to a resource. If the DAC denies access (for example, based on file permissions), the denial is taken as the final security decision.*

SELinux supports two forms of MAC: *type enforcement (TE)* and *multi-level security (MLS)*. MLS is typically used to enforce different levels of access to restricted information and is not used in Android. The type enforcement implemented in SELinux requires that all subjects and objects have an associated type and SELinux uses this type to enforce the rules of its security policy.

In SELinux, a *type* is simply a string that's defined in the policy and associated with objects or subjects. Subject types reference processes or groups of processes and are also referred to as *domains*. Types referring to objects usually specify the role an object plays within the policy, such as system file, application data file, and so on. The type (or domain) is an integral part of the security context, as discussed in "Security Contexts" below.

SELinux Modes

SELinux has three modes of operation: disabled, permissive, and enforcing. When SELinux is disabled, no policy is loaded and only the default DAC security is enforced. In permissive mode, the policy is loaded and object access is checked, but access denial is only logged—not enforced. Finally, in enforcing mode, the security policy is both loaded and enforced, with violations logged.

In Android, the SELinux mode can be checked and changed with the `getenforce` and `setenforce` commands, as shown in Listing 12-1. However, the mode set with `setenforce` is not persistent and will be reset to the default mode when the device reboots.

```
# getenforce
Enforcing
# setenforce 0
# getenforce
Permissive
```

Listing 12-1: Using the `getenforce` and `setenforce` commands

Additionally, even when SELinux is in enforcing mode, the policy can specify permissive mode per domain (process) using the `permissive` statement. (See "Object Class and Permission Statements" on page 326 for an example.)

Security Contexts

In SELinux, a *security context* (also referred to as a *security label*, or just *label*) is a string with four fields delimited with colons: username, role, type, and an optional MLS security range. An SELinux username is typically associated with a group or class of users; for example, *user_u* for unprivileged users and *admin_u* for administrators.

Users can be associated with one or more roles in order to implement role-based access control, where each role is associated with one or more domain types. The type is used to group processes in a domain or to specify an object logical type.

The security range (or level) is used to implement MLS and specifies the security levels a subject is allowed to access. As of this writing, Android only uses the type field of the security context, and the user and security range are always set to *u* and *s0*. The role is set to either *r* for domains (processes) or to the built-in *object_r* role for objects.

The security context of processes can be displayed by specifying the -Z option to the ps command, as shown in Listing 12-2 (in the LABEL column).

```
# ps -Z
LABEL                          USER      PID   PPID   NAME
u:r:init:s0❶                   root      1     0      /init
u:r:kernel:s0                  root      2     0      kthreadd
u:r:kernel:s0                  root      3     2      ksoftirqd/0
--snip--
u:r:healthd:s0❷                root      175   1      /sbin/healthd
u:r:servicemanager:s0❸         system    176   1      /system/bin/
servicemanager
u:r:vold:s0❹                   root      177   1      /system/bin/vold
u:r:init:s0                    nobody    178   1      /system/bin/rmt_storage
u:r:netd:s0                    root      179   1      /system/bin/netd
u:r:debuggerd:s0               root      180   1      /system/bin/debuggerd
u:r:rild:s0                    radio     181   1      /system/bin/rild
--snip--
u:r:platform_app:s0            u0_a12    950   183    com.android.systemui
u:r:media_app:s0               u0_a5     1043  183    android.process.media
u:r:radio:s0                   radio     1141  183    com.android.phone
u:r:nfc:s0                     nfc       1163  183    com.android.nfc
u:r:untrusted_app:s0           u0_a7     1360  183    com.google.android.gms
--snip--
```

Listing 12-2: Process security contexts in Android

Similarly, the context of files can be viewed by passing the -Z to the ls command, as shown in Listing 12-3.

```
# ls -Z
drwxr-xr-x root      root              u:object_r:cgroup:s0 acct
drwxrwx--- system    cache             u:object_r:cache_file:s0 cache
-rwxr-x--- root      root              u:object_r:rootfs:s0 charger
--snip--
drwxrwx--x system    system            u:object_r:system_data_file:s0 data
-rw-r--r-- root      root              u:object_r:rootfs:s0 default.prop
drwxr-xr-x root      root              u:object_r:device:s0 dev
lrwxrwxrwx root      root              u:object_r:rootfs:s0 etc -> /system/etc
-rw-r--r-- root      root              u:object_r:rootfs:s0 file_contexts
dr-xr-x--- system    system            u:object_r:sdcard_external:s0 firmware
-rw-r----- root      root              u:object_r:rootfs:s0 fstab.hammerhead
-rwxr-x--- root      root              u:object_r:rootfs:s0 init
--snip--
```

Listing 12-3: File and directory security contexts in Android

Security Context Assignment and Persistence

We've established that all subject and objects have a security context, but how is the context assigned and persisted? For objects (which are usually associated with a file on the filesystem), the security context is persistent and is usually stored as an extended attribute in the file's metadata.

Extended attributes are not interpreted by the filesystem and can contain arbitrary data (though any such data is usually limited in size). The *ext4* filesystem, the default in most Linux distributions and current versions of Android, supports extended attributes in the form of name-value pairs, where the name is a null-terminated string. SELinux uses the *security.selinux* name to store the security context of file objects. The security context of objects can be set explicitly as part of a filesystem initialization (also called *labeling*), or be implicitly assigned when an object is created. Objects typically inherit the type label of their parent (for example, newly created files in a directory inherit the label of the directory). However, if the security policy allows, objects can receive a label that's different from that of their parent, a process referred to as *type transition*.

Like objects, subjects (processes) inherit the security context of their parent process, or they can change their context via *domain transition*, if allowed by the security policy. The policy can specify automatic domain transition as well, which automatically sets the domain of newly started processes based on the domain of their parent and the type of the executed binary. For example, because all system daemons are started by the *init* process, which has the *u:r:init:s0* security context (❶ in Listing 12-2), they would normally inherit this context, but Android's SELinux policy uses automatic domain transitions to set a dedicated domain to each daemon as needed (❷, ❸, and ❹ in Listing 12-2).

Security Policy

The SELinux security policy is used by the security server in the kernel to allow or disallow access to kernel objects at runtime. For performance reasons, the policy is typically in a binary form generated by compiling a number of policy source files. The policy source files are written in a dedicated policy language, which consists of statements and rules. *Statements* define policy entities such as types, users, and roles. *Rules* allow or deny access to objects (access vector rules); specify the type of transitions allowed (type enforcement rules); and designate how default users, roles, and types are assigned (default rules). A thorough discussion of SELinux's policy grammar is beyond the scope of this book, but the following sections will introduce some of the most widely used statements and rules.

Policy Statements

The SELinux policy language supports various types of statements, but type, attribute, and permission statements make up the bulk of a security policy. We introduce these three types of statements in the following sections.

Type and Attribute Statements

type and attribute statements declare types and their attributes, as shown in Listing 12-4.

```
attribute file_type;❶
attribute domain;❷

type system_data_file, file_type, data_file_type;❸
type untrusted_app, domain;❹
```

Listing 12-4: type and attribute statements

Here, the first ❶ and second ❷ statements declare the file_type and domain attributes, and the next statement ❸ declares the system_data_file type and associates it with the file_type and data_file_type attributes. The code at ❹ declares the untrusted_app type and associates it with the domain attribute (which marks all types used for processes).

Depending on its granularity, an SELinux policy can have dozens or even hundreds of type and attribute declarations spread across multiple source files. However, because access to all kernel objects needs to be checked against the policy at runtime, a large policy can have a negative impact on performance. The effect on performance is especially apparent when running on devices with limited computing resources, and that is why Android strives to keep its SELinux policy relatively small.

User and Role Statements

The user statement declares an SELinux user identifier, associates it with its role(s), and optionally specifies its default security level and the range of security levels that the user can access. Listing 12-5 shows the declarations of the default and only user identifier in Android.

```
user u roles { r } level s0 range s0 - mls_systemhigh;
```

Listing 12-5: Declarations of the default SELinux user identifier in Android

As you can see in Listing 12-5, the *u* user is associated with the *r* role (inside the braces), which in turn is declared using the role statement ❶ as shown in Listing 12-6.

```
role r;❶
role r types domain;❷
```

Listing 12-6: Declaration of the default SELinux role in Android

The second statement ❷ associates the *r* role with the domain attribute, which marks it as a role assigned to processes (domains).

Object Class and Permission Statements

The `permissive` statement allows a named domain to run in permissive mode (a mode that only logs MAC policy violations but doesn't actually enforce the policy, as discussed next), even if SELinux is running in enforcing mode. As we will see in "Enforcing Domains" on page 342, most domains in Android's current base policy are permissive. For example, processes in the *adbd* domain (in practice *adbd* daemon processes) run in permissive mode, as shown in Listing 12-7 ❶.

```
type adbd, domain;
permissive adbd;❶
--snip--
```

Listing 12-7: Setting a named domain to permissive mode

The `class` statement defines an SELinux object class, as shown in Listing 12-8. Object classes and their associated permissions are determined by the respective object manager implementations in the Linux kernel, and are static within a policy. Object classes are usually defined in the *security_classes* policy source file.

```
--snip--
# file-related classes
class filesystem
class file
class dir
class fd
class lnk_file
class chr_file
class blk_file
class sock_file
class fifo_file
--snip--
```

Listing 12-8: Object class declarations in the security_classes *file*

SELinux permissions (also referred to as *access vectors*) are usually defined and associated with object classes in a policy source file called *access_vectors*. Permissions can be either class-specific (defined with the `class` keyword) or inheritable by one or more object classes, in which case they're defined with the `common` keyword. Listing 12-9 shows the definition of the set of permissions common to all file objects ❶, and the association of the `dir` class (which represents directories) with all common file permissions (using the `inherits` keyword), and a set of directory-specific permissions (*add_name*, *remove_name*, and so on) ❷.

```
--snip--
common file
{
    ioctl
    read
```

```
    write
    create
    getattr
    setattr
    lock
    --snip--
}❶
--snip--
class dir
inherits file
{
    add_name
    remove_name
    reparent
    search
    rmdir
    --snip--
}❷
--snip--
```

Listing 12-9: Permission definitions in the access_vectors *file*

Type Transition Rules

Type enforcement rules and access vector rules (discussed in "Domain Transition Rules" on page 328 and "Access Vector Rules" on page 329) typically make the bulk of an SELinux policy. In turn, the most commonly used type of enforcement rule is the `type_transition` rule, which specifies when domain and type transitions are allowed. For example, the *wpa_supplicant* daemon, which manages Wi-Fi connections in Android, uses the type transition rule shown in Listing 12-10 at ❹ in order to associate the control sockets it creates in the */data/misc/wifi/* directory with the `wpa_socket` type. In the absence of this rule, the sockets would inherit the type of their parent directory: `wifi_data_file`.

```
# wpa - wpa supplicant or equivalent
type wpa, domain;
permissive wpa;❶
type wpa_exec, exec_type, file_type;

init_daemon_domain(wpa)❷
unconfined_domain(wpa)❸
type_transition wpa wifi_data_file:sock_file wpa_socket;❹
```

Listing 12-10: Type transitions in the wpa *domain (from* wpa_supplicant.te*)*

Here, `wpa`, `wifi_data_file:sock_file`, and `wpa_socket` are the source type (in this case, the domain of the *wpa_supplicant* process), the target type and class (the type and class of the object before the transition), and the type of the object after the transition, respectively.

NOTE *In order to be able to create the socket file and change its label, the* `wpa` *domain needs additional permissions on the parent directory and the socket file itself—the* `type_transition` *rule alone is not sufficient. However, because the* `wpa` *domain is both permissive* ❶ *and unconfined (granted most permissions by default)* ❸*, the transition is allowed without explicitly allowing each required permission.*

Domain Transition Rules

In Android, native system daemons like *wpa_supplicant* are started by the *init* process, and therefore inherit its security context by default. However, most daemons are associated with a dedicated domain and use domain transitions to switch their domain when started. This is typically accomplished using the `init_daemon_domain()` macro (❷ in Listing 12-10), which under the hood is implemented using the `type_transition` keyword, just like type transitions.

The binary SELinux policy build process uses the `m4` macro preprocessor[1] to expand macros before merging all source files in order to create the binary policy file. The `init_daemon_domain()` macro takes one parameter (the new domain of the process) and is defined in the *te_macros* file using two other macros: `domain_trans()` and `domain_auto_trans()`, which are used to allow transition to a new domain and to execute the transition automatically, respectively. Listing 12-11 shows the definitions of these three macros (❶, ❷, and ❸). The lines beginning with the `allow` keyword are access vector (AV) rules, which we discuss in the next section.

```
# domain_trans(olddomain, type, newdomain)
define(`domain_trans', `
allow $1 $2:file { getattr open read execute };
allow $1 $3:process transition;
allow $3 $2:file { entrypoint read execute };
allow $3 $1:process sigchld;
dontaudit $1 $3:process noatsecure;
allow $1 $3:process { siginh rlimitinh };
')❶
# domain_auto_trans(olddomain, type, newdomain)
define(`domain_auto_trans', `
domain_trans($1,$2,$3)
type_transition $1 $2:process $3;
')❷
# init_daemon_domain(domain)
define(`init_daemon_domain', `
domain_auto_trans(init, $1_exec, $1)
tmpfs_domain($1)
')❸
--snip--
```

Listing 12-11: Domain transition macros definition in the te_macros *file*

1. Free Software Foundation, Inc., "GNU M4 - GNU Project - Free Software Foundation (FSF)," *https://www.gnu.org/software/m4/*

Access Vector Rules

AV rules define what privileges processes have at runtime by specifying the set of permissions they have over their target objects. Listing 12-12 shows the general format of an AV rule.

```
rule_name source_type target_type : class perm_set;
```

Listing 12-12: Format of AV rules

The `rule_name` can be `allow`, `dontaudit`, `auditallow`, or `neverallow`. To form a rule, the `source_type` and `target_type` elements are replaced with one or more previously defined `type` or `attribute` identifiers, where `source_type` is the identifier of a subject (process), and `target_type` is the identifier of an object the process is trying to access. The `class` element is replaced with the object class of the target, and `perm_set` specifies the set of permissions that the source process has over the target object. You can specify multiple types, classes, and permissions by enclosing them in braces (`{}`). In addition, some rules support use of the wildcard (`*`) and complement (`~`) operators, which allow you to specify that all types should be included or that all types except those explicitly listed should be included, respectively.

allow Rules

The most commonly used rule is `allow`, which specifies the operations that a subject (process) of the specified source type is allowed to perform on an object of the target type and class specified in the rule. Let's take the SELinux policy for the *vold* daemon (see Listing 12-13) as an example to illustrate how to use the `allow` rule.

```
type vold, domain;
type vold_exec, exec_type, file_type;
init_daemon_domain(vold)
--snip--
allow vold sdcard_type:filesystem { mount remount unmount };❶
--snip--
allow vold self:capability { sys_ptrace kill };❷
--snip--
```

Listing 12-13: `allow` rules for the `vold` domain (from vold.te*)*

In this listing, rule ❶ allows the *vold* daemon (which runs in the `vold` domain) to mount, unmount, and remount filesystems of type `sdcard_type`. Rule ❷ allows the daemon to use the `CAP_SYS_PTRACE` (which allows `ptrace()` to be called on any process) and `CAP_KILL` (which allows signals to be sent to any process) Linux capabilities, which correspond to the permission set specified in the rule (inside the `{}`). In rule ❷, the `self` keyword means that the target domain is the same as the source, which in this case is `vold`.

auditallow Rules

The `auditallow` rule is used with `allow` to record audit events when an operation is allowed. This is useful because by default, SELinux logs only access denied events. However, `auditallow` itself doesn't grant access, and therefore a matching `allow` rule must be used in order to grant the necessary permissions.

dontaudit Rules

The `dontaudit` rule is used to suppress the auditing of denial messages when a specified event is known to be safe. For example, the rule at ❶ in Listing 12-14 specifies that no audit log be created if the *installd* daemon is denied the `CAP_SYS_ADMIN` capability. However, `dontaudit` rules can mask program errors and the use of `dontaudit` is discouraged.

```
type installd, domain;
--snip--
dontaudit installd self:capability sys_admin;❶
--snip--
```

Listing 12-14: `dontaudit` rule for the installd *domain (from* installd.te*)*

neverallow Rules

The `neverallow` rule says that the declared operation should never be allowed, even if an explicit `allow` rule that allows it exists. For example, the rule shown in Listing 12-15 forbids all domains but the `init` domain to load the SELinux policy.

```
--snip--
neverallow { domain -init } kernel:security load_policy;
```

Listing 12-15: `neverallow` rule that forbids domains other than `init` *from loading the SELinux policy (from* domain.te*)*

NOTE

This section provides only a brief overview of SELinux, focusing on the features used in Android. For a more detailed discussion of the architecture and implementation of SELinux, as well its policy language, see the SELinux Notebook.[2]

Android Implementation

As discussed in Chapters 1 and 2, Android's sandboxing security model relies heavily on the use of separate Linux UIDs for system daemons and applications. Process isolation and access control is ultimately enforced by

2. Richard Haines, *The SELinux Notebook: The Foundations*, 3rd edition, 2012, *http://www.freetechbooks.com/efiles/selinuxnotebook/The_SELinux_Notebook_The_Foundations_3rd_Edition.pdf*

the Linux kernel based on process UID and GIDs. Because SELinux is also part of the Linux kernel, SELinux is a natural candidate for hardening the Android sandboxing model using a MAC policy.

As SELinux is integrated into the mainline Linux kernel, it would seem that enabling it in Android should be a simple matter of configuring the kernel and designing an appropriate MAC policy. However, because Android introduces some unique extensions to the Linux kernel and its userspace structure is quite different from that of desktop and server Linux distributions, several changes in both kernel and userspace were needed in order to integrate and enable SELinux into Android. While the initial work required to integrate SELinux was started by Google, most of the required changes were implemented in the Security Enhancements for Android project (formally Security-Enhanced Android, or SEAndroid),[3] and were later integrated into the mainline Android source tree. The following sections survey these major changes. For a comprehensive list of changes and the rationale behind them, see the *Security Enhanced (SE) Android: Bringing Flexible MAC to Android* paper by the original authors of the SEAndroid project.[4]

Kernel Changes

Recall from earlier that SELinux is a security module that implements the various LSM hooks inserted in kernel services related to object access control. Android's Binder IPC mechanism is also implemented as a kernel driver, but because its implementation originally did not contain any LSM hooks, its runtime behavior could not be controlled by an SELinux policy. In order to add SELinux support to Binder, LSM hooks were inserted into the Binder driver, and support for the `binder` object class and related permissions was added to SELinux code.

SELinux security hooks are declared in *include/linux/security.h*, and Listing 12-16 shows the Binder-related declarations added to support Android.

```
--snip--
int security_binder_set_context_mgr(struct task_struct *mgr);❶
int security_binder_transaction(struct task_struct *from,
                                struct task_struct *  to);❷
int security_binder_transfer_binder(struct task_struct *from,
                                    struct task_struct *to);❸
int security_binder_transfer_file(struct task_struct *from,
                                  struct task_struct *to, struct file *file);❹
--snip--
```

Listing 12-16: Binder security hooks declarations in include/linux/security.h

3. Security Enhancements for Android, *https://bitbucket.org/seandroid/manifests/*

4. Craig Smalley, *Security Enhanced (SE) Android: Bringing Flexible MAC to Android, http://www.internetsociety.org/sites/default/files/02_4.pdf*

The first hook ❶ controls what process can become the binder context manager, and the second one ❷ controls the ability of a process to invoke a binder transaction. The next two functions are used to regulate who can transfer a Binder reference to another process ❸, and transfer an open file to another process ❹ using Binder.

In order to allow the SELinux policy to set restrictions for Binder, support for the `binder` object class and its permissions (`impersonate`, `call`, `set_context_mgr`, and `transfer`) was also added to the kernel, as shown in Listing 12-17.

```
--snip--
struct security_class_mapping secclass_map[] = {
    --snip--
    {"binder", {"impersonate", "call", "set_context_mgr", "transfer", NULL} },
    { NULL }
  };
```

Listing 12-17: Binder object class and permission declaration in selinux/include/classmap.h

Userspace Changes

In addition to kernel changes, a number of userspace modifications and extensions were also required in order to integrate SELinux into Android. Among these, the most important ones are support for filesystem labeling in the core C library (bionic); extensions to *init* and the core native daemons and executables; framework-level SELinux APIs; and modifications to core framework services to make them SELinux-aware. This section describes each change and how it's integrated into the Android runtime.

Libraries and Tools

Because SELinux uses extended attributes to store the security contexts of filesystem objects, wrapper functions for the system calls used to manage extended attributes (`listxattr()`, `getxattr()`, `setxattr()`, and so on) were first added to Android's C library in order to be able to get and set the security labels of files and directories.

In order to be able to take advantage of SELinux features from userspace, SEAndroid added an Android-compatible port of the *libselinux* library, as well as a set of utility commands to manage labeling, the security policy, and to switch the SELinux mode between enforcing and permissive. Like most Android command-line utilities, SELinux tools are implemented in the `toolbox` binary and are installed as symbolic links to it. Table 12-1 summarizes the added or modified command-line tools.

Table 12-1: SELinux Command-Line Utilities

Command	Description
chcon	Changes a file's security context
getenforce	Gets the current SELinux mode
getsebool	Gets policy Boolean values
id	Displays a process's security context
load_policy	Loads a policy file
ls -Z	Displays the security context of a file
ps -Z	Displays the security context of running processes
restorecon	Restores the security context of a file(s)
runcon	Runs a program in the specified security context
setenforce	Sets the enforcing mode
setsebool	Sets the value of a policy Boolean

System Initialization

As in traditional Linux systems, in Android all userspace daemons and programs are started by the *init* process, the first process the kernel starts (PID=1). However, unlike other Linux-based systems, Android's initialization scripts (*init.rc* and its variants) are not interpreted by a general-purpose shell, but by *init* itself. Each initialization script contains built-in commands that are executed by *init* as it reads the script. SEAndroid extends Android's *init* language with a number of new commands required to initialize SELinux and set the security contexts of services and files, as summarized in Table 12-2.

Table 12-2: init Built-in Commands for SELinux Support

init Built-In Command	Description
seclabel	Sets the security context of a service
restorecon	Restores the security context of a file or directory
setcon	Set the security context of the *init* process
setenforce	Sets the enforcing mode
setsebool	Sets the value of a policy Boolean

When *init* starts, it loads the SELinux policy from the */sepolicy* binary policy file, and then sets the enforcing mode based on the value of the *ro.boot.selinux* system property (which *init* sets based on the value of the *androidboot.selinux* kernel command-line parameter). When the property value is *permissive*, SELinux goes into permissive mode; when set to any other value or not set at all, the mode is set to enforcing.

Next, *init* loads and parses the *init.rc* file and executes the commands specified there. Listing 12-18 shows an excerpt of *init.rc*, focusing on the parts responsible for SELinux initialization.

```
--snip--
on early-init
    --snip--
    setcon u:r:init:s0❶
    start ueventd
--snip--
on post-fs-data
    chown system system /data
    chmod 0771 /data
    restorecon /data❷
--snip--
service ueventd /sbin/ueventd
    class core
    critical
    seclabel u:r:ueventd:s0❸
--snip--
on property:selinux.reload_policy=1❹
    restart ueventd
    restart installd
--snip--
```

Listing 12-18: SELinux initialization in init.rc

In this example, *init* sets its own security context using the `setcon` command ❶ before starting the core system daemons. Because a child process inherits the security context of its parent, *init* explicitly sets the security context of the *ueventd* daemon (the first daemon to be started) to *u:r:ueventd:s0* ❸ using the `seclabel` command. Most other native services have their domain set automatically by type transition rules defined in the policy (as in Listing 12-10). (The `seclabel` command is only used to set the security contexts of processes that start very early in the system initialization process.)

When writable filesystems are mounted, *init* uses the `restorecon` command to restore the default labels of their mount points, because a factory reset could have cleared their labels. Listing 12-18 shows the command ❷ that labels the *userdata* partition's mount point—*/data*.

Finally, because a policy reload can be triggered by setting the *selinux.reload_policy* system property to 1 ❹, *init* restarts the *ueventd* and *installd* daemons when this property is set so that the new policy can take effect.

Labeling Files

Recall that persistent SELinux objects, such as files, have a persistent security context that is typically saved in a file's extended attribute. In Android, the initial security context of all files is defined in a text file called *file_contexts*, which might look like Listing 12-19.

```
/                               u:object_r:rootfs:s0❶
/adb_keys                       u:object_r:rootfs:s0
/default.prop                   u:object_r:rootfs:s0
/fstab\..*                      u:object_r:rootfs:s0
--snip--
/dev(/.*)?                      u:object_r:device:s0❷
/dev/akm8973.*                  u:object_r:akm_device:s0
/dev/accelerometer              u:object_r:accelerometer_device:s0
--snip--
/system(/.*)?                   u:object_r:system_file:s0❸
/system/bin/ash                 u:object_r:shell_exec:s0
/system/bin/mksh                u:object_r:shell_exec:s0
--snip--
/data(/.*)?                     u:object_r:system_data_file:s0❹
/data/backup(/.*)?              u:object_r:backup_data_file:s0
/data/secure/backup(/.*)?       u:object_r:backup_data_file:s0
--snip--
```

Listing 12-19: Contents of the file_contexts *file*

As you can see, the file contains a list of paths (sometimes using wildcard characters) and their associated security contexts, each on a new line. The *file_contexts* file is consulted at various times during Android's build and bootup process. For example, because on-memory filesystems such as Android's root filesystem (mounted at */*) and the device filesystem (mounted at */dev*) are not persistent, all files are usually associated with the same security context as specified in the *genfs_contexts* file, or assigned using the `context=` mount option. In order to assign individual security contexts to specific files in such filesystems, *init* uses the `restorecon` command to look up the security context of each file in *file_contexts* (❶ for the root filesystem, and ❷ as the default for the device filesystem) and sets it accordingly. When building Android from source, the `make_ext4fs` command also consults *file_contexts* in order to set the initial contexts of files on the *system* (mounted at */system* ❸) and *userdata* partition (mounted at */data* ❹) images. The security contexts of data partitions' mount points are also restored on each boot (as shown in Listing 12-18) in order to make sure they're in a consistent state. Finally, Android's recovery OS also includes a copy of *file_contexts*, which is used to set the correct labels of files created by the recovery during system updates. This guarantees that the system remains in a securely labeled stated across updates and avoids the need for full relabeling after each update.

Labeling System Properties

Android uses global system properties that are visible to all processes for various purposes such as communicating hardware state, starting or stopping system services, triggering disk encryption, and even reloading the SELinux policy. Access to read-only system properties isn't restricted, but because changing the values of key read-write properties alters the behavior of the system, write access to these properties is restricted and allowed only to system processes running under privileged UIDs, such as *system* and *radio*. SEAndroid augments this UID-based access control by adding MAC rules that regulate write access to system properties based on the domain of the process attempting property modification. In order for this to work, system properties (which are not native SELinux objects) must be associated with security contexts. This is accomplished by listing the security contexts of properties in a *property_contexts* file, much the same way that *file_contexts* specifies the security labels of files. The file is loaded into memory by the *property_service* (part of *init*), and the resulting security context lookup table is used to determine whether a process should be allowed access to a specific property based on the security contexts of both the process (subject) and the property (object). The SELinux policy defines a new `property_service` object class, with a single permission, set, which is used to specify access rules, as shown in Listing 12-20.

```
type vold, domain;
--snip--
allow vold vold_prop:property_service set;❶
allow vold powerctl_prop:property_service set;❷
allow vold ctl_default_prop:property_service set;❸
--snip--
```

Listing 12-20: System property access rules in vold.te

In this listing, the `vold` domain is allowed to set system properties of type `vold_prop` ❶, `powerctl_prop` ❷, and `ctl_default_prop` ❸.

These types are associated with actual properties based on the property name in *property_contexts*, as shown in Listing 12-21.

```
--snip--
vold.                   u:object_r:vold_prop:s0❶
sys.powerctl            u:object_r:powerctl_prop:s0❷
ctl.                    u:object_r:ctl_default_prop:s0❸
--snip--
```

Listing 12-21: Association of property names with their security contexts in property_contexts

The effect of this policy is that *vold* can set the values of all properties whose name starts with `vold.` ❶, `sys.powerctl` ❷, or `ctl.` ❸.

Labeling Application Processes

Recall from Chapter 2 that all app processes in Android are forked from the *zygote* process in order to reduce memory usage and improve application startup time. The *system_server* process, which runs as the *system* user and hosts most system services, is also forked from *zygote*, albeit via a slightly different interface.

The *zygote* process, which runs as root, is responsible for setting each app process's DAC credentials (UID, GID, and supplementary GIDs), as well as its capabilities and resource limits. In order to support SELinux, *zygote* has been extended to check the security context of its clients (implemented in the `ZygoteConnection` class) and set the security context of each app process that it forks. The security context is determined according to the assignment rules specified in the *seapp_contexts* configuration file, according to the app's UID, its package name, a flag that marks the system server process, and an SELinux-specific string attribute called `seinfo`. The *seapp_contexts* configuration file contains security context assignment rules (one per line) that consist of input selector attributes and output attributes. In order for a rule to be matched, all input selectors should match (logical AND). Listing 12-22 shows the contents of the *seapp_contexts* file in the reference Android SELinux policy as of version 4.4.3.

NOTE *The* seapp_contexts, *like all files in the reference policy, can be found in the* external/sepolicy/ *directory of Android's source tree. See the file's comments for the full list of input selectors, the selector matching precedence rules, and outputs.*

```
isSystemServer=true domain=system❶
user=system domain=system_app type=system_data_file❷
user=bluetooth domain=bluetooth type=bluetooth_data_file
user=nfc domain=nfc type=nfc_data_file
user=radio domain=radio type=radio_data_file
user=_app domain=untrusted_app type=app_data_file levelFrom=none❸
user=_app seinfo=platform domain=platform_app type=platform_app_data_file❹
user=_app seinfo=shared domain=shared_app type=platform_app_data_file❺
user=_app seinfo=media domain=media_app type=platform_app_data_file
user=_app seinfo=release domain=release_app type=platform_app_data_file
user=_isolated domain=isolated_app❻
user=shell domain=shell type=shell_data_file
```

Listing 12-22: Contents of the seapp_contexts *file*

The first line ❶ in this listing specifies the domain of the system server (`system`), because the `isSystemServer` selector (which can be used only once) is set to `true`. Because Android uses a fixed SELinux user identifier, role and security level, the resulting security context becomes *u:r:system:s0*.

The second assignment rule ❷ matches the `user` selector against the target process's username, which is derived from its UID. If a process runs as one of the built-in Android Linux users (*system*, *radio*, *nfc*, and so on, as defined in *android_filesystem_config.h*), the associated name is used when matching the `user` selector. Isolated services are given the *_isolated* username string, and any other process is given the *_app* username string. Thus, system apps that match this selector are assigned the `system_app` domain.

The `type` attribute specifies the object type that's assigned to files owned by the target process. Because in this case the type is `system_data_file`, the security context of system files becomes *u:object_r:system_data_file:s0*.

Rule ❸ matches all apps that execute under a non-system UID and assigns their processes to the `untrusted_app` domain. The private app data directory of each untrusted app is recursively assigned the `app_data_file` object type, which results in the *u:object_r:app_data_file:s0* security context. The security context of the data directory is set by the *installd* daemon when it creates it as part of the app install process (see Chapter 3).

Rules ❹ and ❺ use the `seinfo` selector to differentiate between non-system apps and assign them to different domains: apps processes that match `seinfo=platform` are assigned the `platform_app` domain, and those matching `seinfo=shared` are assigned the `shared_app` domain. (As we'll see in the next section, an app's `seinfo` attribute is determined by its signing certificate, so in effect, rules ❹ and ❺ use each app's signing certificate as a process domain selector.)

Finally, rule ❻ assigns the `isolated_app` domain to all isolated services. (Isolated services run under a UID separate from their hosting app's UID and cannot access any system services.)

Middleware MAC

The `seinfo` attribute introduced in the previous section is part of an SEAndroid feature called *middleware MAC (MMAC)*, which is a higher-level access control scheme, separate from the kernel-level MAC (implemented in the SELinux LSM module).

The MMAC was designed to provide MAC restrictions over Android's permission model, which works at the framework level and cannot be easily mapped to the default kernel-level MAC. The original implementation includes an install-time MAC feature, which restricts the permissions that can be granted to each package based on its package name and signing certificate, regardless of a user's permission grant decision. That is, even if a user decides to grant an app all the permissions it requests, the install can still be blocked by the MMAC if the policy doesn't allow certain permissions to be granted.

SEAndroid's MMAC implementation also includes an intent MMAC feature that uses a policy to control which intents can be exchanged between applications. Another SEAndroid feature is the content provider MMAC, which defines a policy for content provider data access. However, the original SEAndroid MMAC implementation has been merged in mainline Android only partially, and the only supported feature is `seinfo` assignment based on the app signing certificate.

NOTE *As of version 4.3, Android has an experimental* intent firewall *feature that restricts what intents can be sent and received using "firewall"-style rules. This feature is similar to SEAndroid's intent MMAC but is not integrated with the SELinux implementation.*

The MMAC configuration file is called *mac_permission.xml* and resides in the */system/etc/security/* directory on the device. Listing 12-23 shows the template used to generate this file, typically stored as *external/sepolicy/mac_permission.xml* in Android's source tree.

```
<?xml version="1.0" encoding="utf-8"?>
<policy>

    <!-- Platform dev key in AOSP -->
    <signer signature="@PLATFORM" >❶
      <seinfo value="platform" />
    </signer>

    <!-- Media dev key in AOSP -->
    <signer signature="@MEDIA" >❷
      <seinfo value="media" />
    </signer>

    <!-- shared dev key in AOSP -->
    <signer signature="@SHARED" >❸
      <seinfo value="shared" />
    </signer>

    <!-- release dev key in AOSP -->
    <signer signature="@RELEASE" >❹
      <seinfo value="release" />
    </signer>

    <!-- All other keys -->
    <default>❺
      <seinfo value="default" />
    </default>

</policy>
```

Listing 12-23: Template for the mac_permission.xml *file*

Here, the *@PLATFORM* ❶, *@MEDIA* ❷, *@SHARED* ❸, and *@RELEASE* ❹ macros represent the four platform signing certificates used in Android (*platform*, *media*, *shared*, and *release*) and are replaced with their respective certificates, encoded as hexadecimal strings, when building the SELinux policy.

When scanning each installed package, the system `PackageManagerService` matches its signing certificate against the contents of the *mac_permission.xml* file and assigns the specified `seinfo` value to the package if it finds a match. If no match is found, it assigns the *default* `seinfo` value as specified by the `<default>` tag ❺.

Device Policy Files

Android's SELinux policy consists of a binary policy file and four supporting configuration files, which are used for process, app, system property, and file labeling, as well as for MMAC initialization. Table 12-3 shows where each of these files is located on a device and provides a brief description of the file's purpose and contents.

Table 12-3: Android SELinux Policy Files

Policy File	Description
/sepolicy	Binary kernel policy
/file_contexts	File security contexts, used for labeling filesystems
/property_contexts	System property security contexts
/seapp_contexts	Used to derive security contexts of app processes and files
/system/etc/security/mac_permissions.xml	Maps app signing certificates to `seinfo` values

NOTE *SELinux-enabled Android releases before version 4.4.3 supported overriding the default policy files shown in Table 12-3 with their counterparts stored in the* /data/security/current/ *and* /data/system/ *(for the MMAC configuration file) directories in order to enable online policy updates without a full OTA update. However, Android 4.4.3 removed this feature because it could create discrepancies between the security labels set on the filesystem and the labels referenced from the new policy. Policy files are now loaded only from the default, read-only locations shown in Table 12-3.*

Policy Event Logging

Access denial and access grants that have matching `auditallow` rules are logged to the kernel log buffer and can be viewed using `dmesg`, as shown in Listing 12-24.

```
# dmesg |grep 'avc:'
--snip--
<5>[18743.725707] type=1400 audit(1402061801.158:256): avc:  denied  { getattr
} for  pid=9574 comm="zygote" path="socket:[8692]" dev="sockfs" ino=8692
scontext=u:r:untrusted_app:s0 tcontext=u:r:zygote:s0 tclass=unix_stream_socket
--snip--
```

Listing 12-24: SELinux access denials logged in the kernel log buffer

Here, the audit log shows that a third-party application (source security context *u:r:untrusted_app:s0*) was denied access to the *getattr* permission on the *zygote* Unix domain socket (target context *u:r:zygote:s0*, object class `unix_stream_socket`).

Android 4.4 SELinux Policy

Android 4.2 was the first release to contain SELinux code, but SELinux was disabled at compile time in release builds. Android 4.3 enabled SELinux in all builds, but its default mode was set to permissive. Additionally, all domains were also individually set to permissive and were based on the `unconfined` domain, essentially allowing them full access (within the confines of DAC), even if the global SELinux mode was set to enforcing.

Android 4.4 was the first version to ship with SELinux in enforcing mode, and it included enforcing domains for core system daemons. This section gives an overview of Android's SELinux policy, as deployed in version 4.4, and introduces some of the major domains that make up the policy.

Policy Overview

The source code of Android's base SELinux policy is hosted in the *external/sepolicy/* directory of the Android source tree. Besides the files introduced in this chapter so far (*access_vectors*, *file_contexts*, *mac_permissions.xml*, and so on), the policy source consists mostly of type enforcement (TE) statements and rules split into multiple *.te* files, typically one for each defined domain. These files are combined to produce the binary policy file *sepolicy*, which is included in the root of the boot image as */sepolicy*.

You can examine the binary policy file using standard SELinux tools such as `seinfo`, `sesearch`, `sedispol`, and so on. For example, we can use the `seinfo` command to get a summary of the number of policy objects and rules, as shown in Listing 12-25.

```
$ seinfo sepolicy

Statistics for policy file: sepolicy
Policy Version & Type: v.26 (binary, mls)

   Classes:            84    Permissions:       249
   Sensitivities:       1    Categories:       1024
   Types:             267    Attributes:         21
   Users:               1    Roles:               2
   Booleans:            1    Cond. Expr.:         1
   Allow:            1140    Neverallow:          0
   Auditallow:          0    Dontaudit:          36
   Type_trans:        132    Type_change:         0
   Type_member:         0    Role allow:          0
   Role_trans:          0    Range_trans:         0
   Constraints:        63    Validatetrans:       0
   Initial SIDs:       27    Fs_use:             14
   Genfscon:           10    Portcon:             0
   Netifcon:            0    Nodecon:             0
   Permissives:        42    Polcap:              2
```

Listing 12-25: Querying a binary policy file using the `seinfo` command

As you can see, the policy is fairly complex: it defines 84 classes, 267 types, and 1,140 allow rules.

You can get additional information about policy objects by specifying filtering options to the `seinfo` command. For example, because all domains are associated with the `domain` attribute, the command shown in Listing 12-26 lists all domains defined in the policy.

```
$ seinfo -adomain -x sepolicy
   domain
      nfc
      platform_app
      media_app
      clatd
      netd
      sdcardd
      zygote
--snip--
```

Listing 12-26: Getting a list of all defined domains using the seinfo command

You can search for policy rules using the sesearch command. For example, all allow rules that have the zygote domain as their source can be displayed using the command shown in Listing 12-27.

```
$ sesearch --allow -s zygote -d sepolicy
Found 40 semantic av rules:
   allow zygote zygote_exec : file { read execute execute_no_trans entrypoint open } ;
   allow zygote init : process sigchld ;
   allow zygote rootfs : file { ioctl read getattr lock open } ;
   allow zygote rootfs : dir { ioctl read getattr mounton search open } ;
   allow zygote tmpfs : filesystem mount ;
   allow zygote tmpfs : dir { write create setattr mounton add_name search } ;
--snip--
```

Listing 12-27: Searching for policy rules using the sesearch commands

For details about building and customizing the SELinux policy, see the Validating Security-Enhanced Linux in Android *document.*[5]

Enforcing Domains

Even though SELinux is deployed in enforcing mode in Android 4.4, only the domains assigned to a few core daemons are currently enforcing, namely: *installd* (responsible for creating application data directories), *netd* (responsible for managing network connections and routes), *vold* (responsible for mounting external storage and secure containers), and *zygote*. All of these daemons run as root or are granted special capabilities because they need to perform administrative operations such as changing directory ownership (*installd*), manipulating packet filtering and routing rules (*netd*), mounting filesystems (*vold*), and changing process credentials (*zygote*) on behalf of other processes.

Because they have elevated privileges, these daemons have been the target of various privilege escalation exploits, which have allowed non-privileged processes to obtain root access on a device. Therefore,

5. Google, "Validating Security-Enhanced Linux in Android," *http://source.android.com/devices/tech/security/se-linux.html*

specifying a restrictive MAC policy for the domains associated with these system daemons is an important step towards strengthening Android's sandboxing security model and preventing similar exploits in the future.

Let's look at the type enforcement rules defined for the installd domain (in *instald.te*) to see how SELinux restricts what system daemons can access (see Listing 12-28).

```
type installd, domain;
type installd_exec, exec_type, file_type;

init_daemon_domain(installd)❶
relabelto_domain(installd)❷
typeattribute installd mlstrustedsubject;❸
allow installd self:capability { chown dac_override fowner fsetid setgid setuid };❹
--snip--
allow installd dalvikcache_data_file:file create_file_perms;❺
allow installd data_file_type:dir create_dir_perms;❻
allow installd data_file_type:dir { relabelfrom relabelto };❼
allow installd data_file_type:{ file_class_set } { getattr unlink };❽
allow installd apk_data_file:file r_file_perms;❾
--snip--
allow installd system_file:file x_file_perms;❿
--snip--
```

Listing 12-28: installd *type enforcement policy (from* installd.te*)*

In this listing, the *installd* daemon is first automatically transitioned to a dedicated domain (also named installd) when started ❶ using the init_daemon_domain() macro. It is then granted the relabelto permission so that it can set the security labels of the files and directories it creates ❷. Next, the domain is associated with the mlstrustedsubject attribute ❸, which allows it to bypass MLS access rules. Because *installd* needs to set the owner of the files and directories it creates to that of their owner application, it's granted the chown, dac_override, and other capabilities pertaining to file ownership ❹.

As part of the app install process, *installd* also triggers the DEX optimization process, which creates ODEX files in the */data/dalvik-cache/* directory (security context *u:object_r:dalvikcache_data_file:s0*), which is why the installer daemon is granted permission to create files in that directory ❺. Next, because *installd* creates private data directories for applications in the */data/* directory, it is given permission to create and relabel directories (❻ and ❼), as well as get the attributes and delete files ❽ under */data/* (which is associated with the data_file_type attribute). Because *installd* also needs to read downloaded APK files in order to perform DEX optimization, it's granted access to APK files stored under */data/app/* ❾, a directory associated with the apk_data_file type (security context *u:object_r:apk_data_file:s0*).

Finally, *installd* is allowed to execute system commands (security context *u:object_r:system_file:s0*) ❿ in order to start the DEX optimization process. Listing 12-28 omits a few of them, but the remaining policy rules follow the same principle: allow *installd* the least amount of privileges it needs to complete package installation. As a result, even if the daemon is compromised and a malicious program is executed under *installd*'s privileges, it would only have access to a limited number of files and directories, and would be denied any permissions not explicitly allowed by the MAC policy.

NOTE *While Android 4.4 has only four enforcing domains, as the platform evolves and the base SELinux policy is refined, eventually all domains are likely to be deployed in enforcing mode. For example, as of this writing, in the base policy in the master branch of the Android Open Source Project (AOSP), all domains are set to enforcing mode in release builds and the permissive domains are only used in development builds.*

Even if a domain is in enforcing mode, it can be allowed effectively unrestricted access if it's derived from a base domain that is granted all or most access permissions. In Android's SELinux policy, such a domain is the `unconfineddomain` domain, which we discuss next.

Unconfined Domains

Android's SELinux policy contains a base (also referred to as template) domain called `unconfineddomain`, which is allowed almost all system privileges and is used as a parent for other policy domains. As of Android 4.4, the `unconfineddomain` is defined as shown in Listing 12-29.

```
allow unconfineddomain self:capability_class_set *;❶
allow unconfineddomain kernel:security ~load_policy;❷
allow unconfineddomain kernel:system *;
allow unconfineddomain self:memprotect *;
allow unconfineddomain domain:process *;❸
allow unconfineddomain domain:fd *;
allow unconfineddomain domain:dir r_dir_perms;
allow unconfineddomain domain:lnk_file r_file_perms;
allow unconfineddomain domain:{ fifo_file file } rw_file_perms;
allow unconfineddomain domain:socket_class_set *;
allow unconfineddomain domain:ipc_class_set *;
allow unconfineddomain domain:key *;
allow unconfineddomain fs_type:filesystem *;
allow unconfineddomain {fs_type dev_type file_type}:{ dir blk_file lnk_file sock_file fifo_file
} ~relabelto;
allow unconfineddomain {fs_type dev_type file_type}:{ chr_file file } ~{entrypoint relabelto};
allow unconfineddomain node_type:node *;
allow unconfineddomain node_type:{ tcp_socket udp_socket rawip_socket } node_bind;
allow unconfineddomain netif_type:netif *;
allow unconfineddomain port_type:socket_class_set name_bind;
allow unconfineddomain port_type:{ tcp_socket dccp_socket } name_connect;
allow unconfineddomain domain:peer recv;
allow unconfineddomain domain:binder { call transfer set_context_mgr };
allow unconfineddomain property_type:property_service set;
```

Listing 12-29: unconfineddomain domain definition in Android 4.4

As you can see, the unconfineddomain domain is allowed all kernel capabilities ❶, full access to the SELinux security server ❷ (except for loading the MAC policy), all process-related permissions ❸, and so on. Other domains "inherit" the permissions of this domain via the unconfined_domain() macro, which assigns the unconfineddomain attribute to the domain passed as an argument. In Android 4.4's SELinux policy, all permissive domains are also unconfined, and thus are granted practically unrestricted access (within the limits of the DAC).

NOTE *While the unconfineddomain still exists in AOSP's master branch, it has been considerably restricted and is no longer used as an unrestricted domain, but as the base policy for system daemons and other privileged Android components. As more domains are switched to enforcing mode and their policies are fine-tuned, unconfineddomain is expected to be removed.*

App Domains

Recall that SEAndroid assigns several different domains to application processes based on their process UID or signing certificate. These application domains are assigned common permissions by inheriting the base appdomain using the app_domain() macro which, as defined in *app.te*, includes rules that allow the common operations all Android apps require. Listing 12-30 shows an excerpt from the *app.te* file.

```
--snip--
allow appdomain zygote:fd use;❶
allow appdomain zygote_tmpfs:file read;❷
--snip--
allow appdomain system:fifo_file rw_file_perms;
allow appdomain system:unix_stream_socket { read write setopt };
binder_call(appdomain, system)❸

allow appdomain surfaceflinger:unix_stream_socket { read write setopt };
binder_call(appdomain, surfaceflinger)❹

allow appdomain app_data_file:dir create_dir_perms;
allow appdomain app_data_file:notdevfile_class_set create_file_perms;❺
--snip--
```

Listing 12-30: appdomain policy excerpt (from app.te)

This policy allows the appdomain to receive and use file descriptors from *zygote* ❶; read system properties managed by *zygote* ❷; communicate with the *system_server* via pipes, local sockets, or Binder ❸; communicate with the *surfaceflinger* daemon (responsible for drawing on screen) ❹; and create files and directories in its sandbox data directory ❺. The rest of the policy defines rules that allow other required permissions, such as network access, access to downloaded files, and Binder access to core system services. Operations that apps do not typically require, such as raw block device access, kernel memory access, and SELinux domain transitions, are explicitly prohibited using neverallow rules.

Concrete app domains such as untrusted_app (which is assigned to all non-system applications according to the assignment rules in *seapp_contexts* shown in Listing 12-22) extend appdomain and add additional access rules, as required by the target application(s). Listing 12-31 shows an excerpt from *untrusted_app.te*.

```
type untrusted_app, domain;
permissive untrusted_app;❶
app_domain(untrusted_app)❷
net_domain(untrusted_app)❸
bluetooth_domain(untrusted_app)❹

allow untrusted_app tun_device:chr_file rw_file_perms;❺

allow untrusted_app sdcard_internal:dir create_dir_perms;
allow untrusted_app sdcard_internal:file create_file_perms;❻

allow untrusted_app sdcard_external:dir create_dir_perms;
allow untrusted_app sdcard_external:file create_file_perms;❼

allow untrusted_app asec_apk_file:dir { getattr };
allow untrusted_app asec_apk_file:file r_file_perms;❽
--snip--
```

Listing 12-31: untrusted_app domain policy excerpt (from untrusted_app.te*)*

In this policy file, the untrusted_app domain is set to permissive mode ❶, after which it inherits the policies of appdomain ❷, netdomain ❸, and bluetoothdomain ❹ via the respective macros. The domain is then allowed access to tunnel devices (used for VPNs) ❺, external storage (SD cards, ❻ and ❼), and encrypted application containers ❽. The rest of the rules (not shown) grant access to sockets, pseudoterminals, and a few other needed OS resources.

All other app domains (isolated_app, media_app, platform_app, release_app, and shared_app in version 4.4) also inherit from appdomain and add additional allow rules, either directly or by extending additional domains. In Android 4.4, all app domains are set to permissive mode.

NOTE *The SELinux policy in AOSP's mater branch simplifies the app domain hierarchy by removing the dedicated* media_app*,* shared_app*, and* release_app *domains and merging them into the* untrusted_app *domain. Additionally, only the* system_app *domain is unconfined.*

Summary

As of version 4.3, Android has integrated SELinux in order to reinforce the default sandbox model using the mandatory access control (MAC) available in the Linux kernel. Unlike the default discretionary access control (DAC), MAC offers a fine-grained object and permission model and a flexible security policy that cannot be overridden or changed by malicious processes (as long as the kernel itself isn't compromised).

Android 4.4 is the first version to switch SELinux to enforcing mode in release builds, but all domains other than a few highly privileged core daemons are set to permissive mode in order to maintain compatibility with existing applications. Android's base SELinux policy continues to be refined with each release, and future releases will likely switch most domains to enforcing mode and remove the supporting unconfined domain, which is currently inherited by the majority of domains associated with privileged services.

13

SYSTEM UPDATES AND ROOT ACCESS

In the preceding chapters, we introduced Android's security model and discussed how integrating SELinux into Android has reinforced it. In this chapter, we take a bit of a right turn and introduce methods that can be used to circumvent Android's security model.

In order to perform a full OS update or to restore the device to its factory state, it's necessary to escape the security sandbox and gain full access to a device, because even the most privileged Android components are not given complete access to all system partitions and storage devices. Additionally, while having full administrative (root) access at runtime is clearly against Android's security design, executing with root privileges can be useful in order to implement functionality not offered by Android, such as the addition of custom firewall rules or full (including system partitions) device backup. Indeed, the wide availability of custom Android builds (often called *ROMs*) and apps that allow users to extend or replace OS functionality using root access (commonly known as *root apps*) has been one of the reasons for Android's success.

In this chapter, we explore the design of Android's bootloader and recovery OS, and show how they can be used to replace the system software of a device. We then show how root access is implemented on engineering builds and how Android production builds can be modified to allow executing code with superuser privileges by installing a "superuser" application. Finally, we discuss how custom Android distributions implement and control root access.

Bootloader

A *bootloader* is a low-level program that is executed when a device is powered. Its main purpose is to initialize the hardware and find and start the main operating system.

As briefly discussed in Chapter 10, Android bootloaders are usually locked and only allow booting or installing an operating system image that has been signed by the device manufacturer. This is an important step in establishing a verified boot path, because it ensures that only trusted and unmodified system software can be installed on a device. However, while most users are not interested in modifying the core OS of their devices, installing a third-party Android build is a valid user choice and may even be the only way to run a recent version of Android on devices that have stopped receiving OS updates from their manufacturer. That is why most recent devices provide a way to unlock the bootloader and install third-party Android builds.

NOTE *While Android bootloaders are typically closed source, the bootloaders of most ARM devices based on Qualcomm SoCs are derived from the Little Kernel (LK) bootloader,*[1] *which is open source.*[2]

In the following sections, we'll look at how to interact with Android bootloaders and how the bootloader can be unlocked on Nexus devices. We then describe the fastboot protocol used to update devices via the bootloader.

Unlocking the Bootloader

The bootloaders of Nexus devices are unlocked by issuing the `oem unlock` command when the device is in fastboot mode (discussed in the next section). Therefore, in order to unlock a device, it must first be started in fastboot mode, either by issuing the `adb reboot bootloader` command (if the device already allows ADB access), or by pressing a special key combination while the device is booting. For example, holding down the Volume down, Volume up, and Power buttons simultaneously on a powered-down Nexus 5 interrupts the normal boot process and brings up the fastboot screen shown in Figure 13-1.

---

1. Code Aurora Forum, "(L)ittle (K)ernel based Android bootloader," *https://www.codeaurora.org/blogs/little-kernel-based-android-bootloader/*

2. Code Aurora Forum, *https://www.codeaurora.org/cgit/quic/la/kernel/lk/*

The bootloader has a simple UI that can be driven by the Volume up/down and Power buttons. It allows users to continue the boot process, restart the device in fastboot or recovery mode, and power down the device.

Connecting the device to a host machine via a USB cable allows additional commands to be sent to the device using the `fastboot` command-line tool (part of the Android SDK). Issuing the `fastboot oem unlock` command brings up the confirmation screen shown in Figure 13-2.

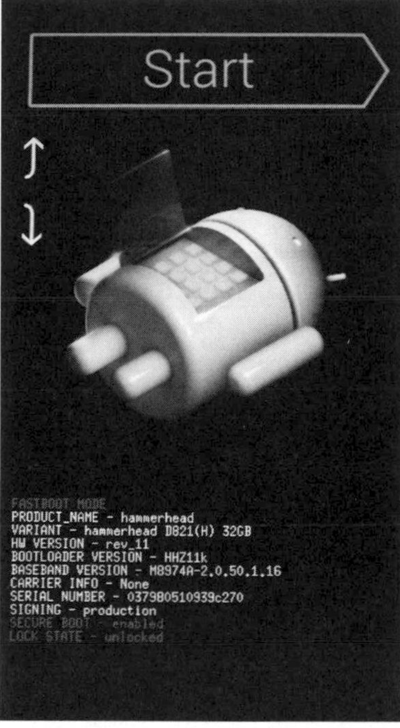

Figure 13-1: Nexus 5 bootloader screen

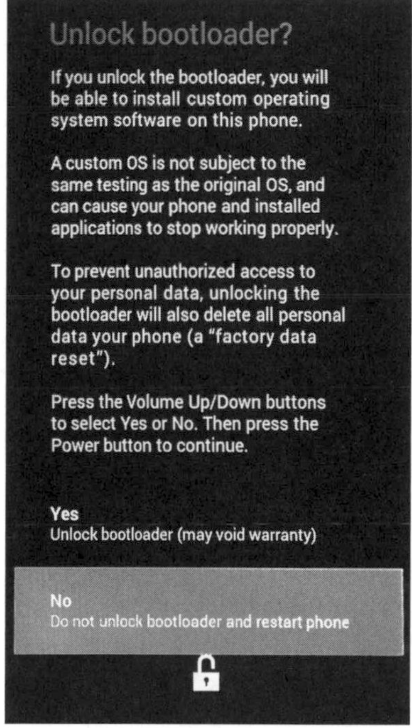

Figure 13-2: Nexus 5 bootloader unlock screen

The confirmation screen warns that unlocking the bootloader allows installation of untested third-party OS builds and clears all user data. Because a third-party OS build might not follow Android's security model and might allow unrestricted access to data, clearing all user data is an important security measure; it ensures that existing user data cannot be extracted after the bootloader is unlocked.

The bootloader can be locked again by issuing the `fastboot oem lock` command. Relocking the bootloader returns it to its original state, and loading or booting third-party OS images is no longer possible. However, besides a locked/unlocked flag, some bootloaders keep an additional, "tampered" flag that is set when the bootloader is first unlocked. This flag allows the bootloader to detect if it has ever been locked and disallow some operations or show a warning even if it is in a locked state.

Fastboot Mode

While the `fastboot` command and protocol can be used to unlock the bootloader, their original purpose was to make it easy to clear or overwrite device partitions by sending partition images to the bootloader, which are then written to the specified block device. This is particularly useful when porting Android to a new device (referred to as "device bring-up") or restoring a device to factory state using partition images provided by the device manufacturer.

Android Partition Layout

Android devices typically have several partitions, which fastboot refers to by name (rather than by the corresponding Linux device file). A list of partitions and their names can be obtained by listing the files in the *by-name/* directory corresponding to the device's SoC in */dev/block/platform/*. For example, because the Nexus 5 is based on Qualcomm SoC, which includes a Mobile Station Modem (MSM) baseband processor, the corresponding directory is called *msm_sdcc.1/* as shown in Listing 13-1 (timestamps omitted).

```
# ls -l /dev/block/platform/msm_sdcc.1/by-name
lrwxrwxrwx root      root              DDR -> /dev/block/mmcblk0p24
lrwxrwxrwx root      root              aboot -> /dev/block/mmcblk0p6❶
lrwxrwxrwx root      root              abootb -> /dev/block/mmcblk0p11
lrwxrwxrwx root      root              boot -> /dev/block/mmcblk0p19❷
lrwxrwxrwx root      root              cache -> /dev/block/mmcblk0p27❸
lrwxrwxrwx root      root              crypto -> /dev/block/mmcblk0p26
lrwxrwxrwx root      root              fsc -> /dev/block/mmcblk0p22
lrwxrwxrwx root      root              fsg -> /dev/block/mmcblk0p21
lrwxrwxrwx root      root              grow -> /dev/block/mmcblk0p29
lrwxrwxrwx root      root              imgdata -> /dev/block/mmcblk0p17
lrwxrwxrwx root      root              laf -> /dev/block/mmcblk0p18
lrwxrwxrwx root      root              metadata -> /dev/block/mmcblk0p14
lrwxrwxrwx root      root              misc -> /dev/block/mmcblk0p15❹
lrwxrwxrwx root      root              modem -> /dev/block/mmcblk0p1❺
lrwxrwxrwx root      root              modemst1 -> /dev/block/mmcblk0p12
lrwxrwxrwx root      root              modemst2 -> /dev/block/mmcblk0p13
lrwxrwxrwx root      root              pad -> /dev/block/mmcblk0p7
lrwxrwxrwx root      root              persist -> /dev/block/mmcblk0p16
lrwxrwxrwx root      root              recovery -> /dev/block/mmcblk0p20❻
lrwxrwxrwx root      root              rpm -> /dev/block/mmcblk0p3
lrwxrwxrwx root      root              rpmb -> /dev/block/mmcblk0p10
lrwxrwxrwx root      root              sbl1 -> /dev/block/mmcblk0p2❼
lrwxrwxrwx root      root              sbl1b -> /dev/block/mmcblk0p8
lrwxrwxrwx root      root              sdi -> /dev/block/mmcblk0p5
lrwxrwxrwx root      root              ssd -> /dev/block/mmcblk0p23
lrwxrwxrwx root      root              system -> /dev/block/mmcblk0p25❽
lrwxrwxrwx root      root              tz -> /dev/block/mmcblk0p4
lrwxrwxrwx root      root              tzb -> /dev/block/mmcblk0p9
lrwxrwxrwx root      root              userdata -> /dev/block/mmcblk0p28❾
```

Listing 13-1: List of partitions on a Nexus 5

As you can see, the Nexus 5 has 29 partitions, most of which store device-specific and proprietary data, such as the Android bootloader in *aboot* ❶, the baseband software in *modem* ❺, and the second stage bootloader in *sbl1* ❼. The Android OS is hosted in the *boot* ❷ partition, which stores the kernel and the *rootfs* RAM disk image, and the *system* partition ❽, which stores all other system files. User files are stored in the *userdata* partition ❾, and temporary files, such as downloaded OTA images and recovery OS commands and logs, are stored in the *cache* partition ❸. Finally, the recovery OS image resides in the *recovery* partition ❻.

The Fastboot Protocol

The fastboot protocol works over USB and is driven by the host. That is, communication is initiated by the host, which uses USB bulk transfers to send text-based commands and data to the bootloader. The USB client (bootloader) responds with a status string such as *OKAY* or *FAIL*; an information message starting with *INFO*; or *DATA*, which signifies that the bootloader is ready to accept data from the host. When all data is received, the bootloader responds with one of the *OKAY*, *FAIL*, or *INFO* messages describing the final status of the command.

Fastboot Commands

The `fastboot` command-line utility implements the fastboot protocol, and allows you to get a list of connected devices that support fastboot (using the `devices` command), obtain information about the bootloader (with the `getvar` command), reboot the device in various modes (with `continue`, `reboot`, `reboot-bootloader`), and `erase` or `format` a partition.

The `fastboot` command supports various ways to write a disk image to a partition. A single named partition can be flashed using the `flash` *`partition image-filename`* command, and multiple partition images contained in a ZIP file can be flashed at once using the `update` *`ZIP-filename`* command.

The `flashall` command automatically flashes the contents of the *boot.img*, *system.img*, and *recovery.img* files in its working directory to the *boot*, *system*, and *recovery* partitions of the device, respectively. Finally, the `flash:raw boot` *`kernel ramdisk`* command automatically creates a boot image from the specified kernel and RAM disk and flashes it to the *boot* partition. In addition to flashing partition images, `fastboot` can also be used to boot an image without writing it to the device when invoked with the `boot` *`boot-image`* or `boot` *`kernel ramdisk`* commands.

Commands that modify device partitions, such as the various `flash` variations, and commands that boot custom kernels, such as the `boot` command, are not allowed when the bootloader is locked.

Listing 13-2 shows an example fastboot session.

```
$ fastboot devices❶
004fcac161ca52c5        fastboot
$ fastboot getvar version-bootloader❷
version-bootloader: MAKOZ10o
finished. total time: 0.001s
$ fastboot getvar version-baseband❸
version-baseband: M9615A-CEFWMAZM-2.0.1700.98
finished. total time: 0.001s
$ fastboot boot custom-recovery.img❹
downloading 'boot.img'...
OKAY [  0.577s]
booting...
FAILED (remote: not supported in locked device)
finished. total time: 0.579s
```

Listing 13-2: Example fastboot session

Here, the first command ❶ lists the serial numbers of devices connected to the host, which are currently in fastboot mode. The commands at ❷ and ❸ obtain the bootloader and baseband version strings, respectively. Finally, the command at ❹ tries to boot a custom recovery image but fails because the bootloader is currently locked.

Recovery

The *recovery OS*—also called *recovery console* or simply, *recovery*—is a minimal OS that is used for tasks that cannot be executed directly from Android, such as factory reset (erasing the *userdata* partition) or applying OTA updates.

Like the bootloader's fastboot mode, the recovery OS can be started either by pressing a specific key combination while the device boots, or via ADB by using the `adb reboot recovery` command. Some bootloaders also provide a menu interface (see Figure 13-1) that can be used to start the recovery. In the following sections, we take a look at the "stock" Android recovery that ships with Nexus devices and is included in AOSP, and then introduce custom recoveries, which offer much richer functionality but require an unlocked bootloader in order to be installed or booted.

Stock Recovery

Android's stock recovery implements the minimal functionality needed to satisfy the "Updatable Software" section of the *Android Compatibility Definition Document (CDD)*, which requires that "device implementations MUST include a mechanism to replace the entirety of the system software..." and that "the update mechanism used MUST support updates without wiping user data."[3]

3. Google, *Android Compatibility Definition, https://static.googleusercontent.com/media/source.android.com/en//compatibility/android-cdd.pdf*

That said, the CDD doesn't specify the concrete update mechanism that should be used, so different approaches to system updates are possible and the stock recovery implements both OTA updates and tethered updates. For OTA updates, the main OS downloads the update file and then instructs the recovery to apply it. In the case of tethered updates, users download the update package on their PC and push it to the recovery using the `adb sideload` *`otafile.zip`* command. The actual update process for both approaches is the same; only the method of obtaining the OTA package differs.

The stock recovery has a simple menu interface (shown in Figure 13-3) that is operated using the device's hardware buttons, usually the Power button and Volume up/down. However, the menu is hidden by default and needs to be activated by pressing a dedicated key combination. On Nexus devices, the recovery menu can usually be displayed by holding down the Power and Volume down buttons simultaneously for a few seconds.

The system recovery menu has four options: *reboot*, *apply update from ADB*, *factory reset*, and *wipe cache partition*. The ***apply update from ADB*** option starts the ADB server on the device and enables the tethered update (sideload) mode. However, as you can see, there is no option for applying an OTA update because once the user chooses to apply an OTA update from the main OS (see Figure 13-4), it is applied automatically, without further user interaction. Android accomplishes this by sending control commands to the recovery, which are automatically executed when the recovery starts. (We discuss the mechanisms used to control the recovery in the next section.)

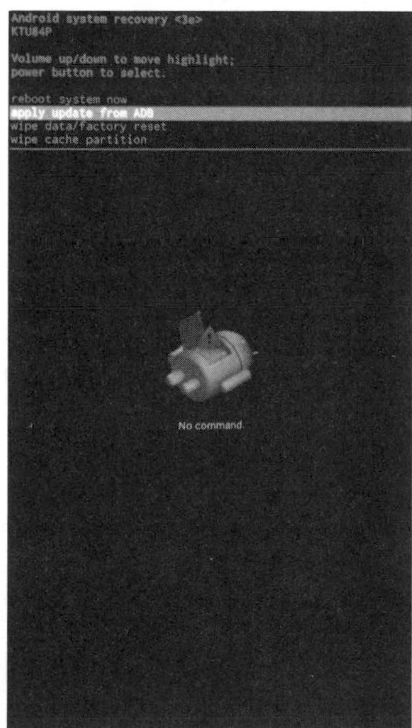

Figure 13-3: Stock recovery menu

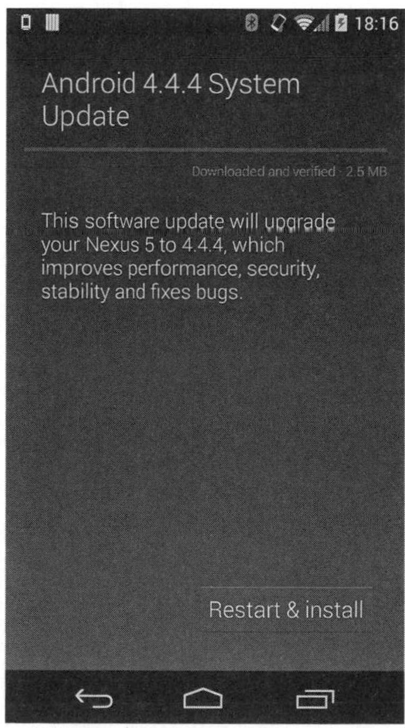

Figure 13-4: Applying a system update from the main OS

Controlling the Recovery

The main OS controls the recovery via the `android.os.RecoverySystem` API, which communicates with the recovery by writing option strings, each on a new line, to the */cache/recovery/command* file. The contents of the *command* file are read by the recovery binary (located at */sbin/recovery* in the recovery OS), which is automatically started from *init.rc* when the recovery boots. The options modify the behavior of the recovery binary and cause it to wipe the specified partition, apply an OTA update, or simply reboot. Table 13-1 shows the options supported by the stock recovery binary.

Table 13-1: Options for the Stock recovery Binary

recovery Option	Description
`--send_intent=<string>`	Save and communicate the specified intent action back to the main OS when finished
`--update_package=<OTA package path>`	Verify and install the specified OTA package
`--wipe_data`	Erase the *userdata* and *cache* partitions, then reboot
`--wipe_cache`	Erase the *cache* partition, then reboot
`--show_text`	Message to display
`--just_exit`	Exit and reboot
`--locale`	Locale to use for recovery messages and UI
`--stages`	Set the current stage of the recovery process

In order to ensure that the specified command(s) are always completed, the recovery binary copies its arguments to the bootloader control block (BCB), which is hosted on the *misc* partition (❹ in Listing 13-1). The BCB is used to communicate the current state of the recovery process to the bootloader. The format of the BCB is specified in the `bootloader_message` structure, shown in Listing 13-3.

```
struct bootloader_message {
    char command[32];❶
    char status[32];❷
    char recovery[768];❸
    char stage[32];❹
    char reserved[224];❺
};
```

Listing 13-3: BCB format structure definition

If a device is rebooted or powered down in the middle of the recovery process, the next time it is started the bootloader inspects the BCB and starts the recovery again if the BCB contains the *boot-recovery* command. If the recovery process completes successfully, the recovery binary clears the BCB before exiting (sets all bytes to zero), and on the next reboot the bootloader starts the main Android OS.

In Listing 13-3, the command at ❶ is the command to the bootloader (usually *boot-recovery*); ❷ is a status file written by the bootloader after performing a platform-specific action; ❸ contains the options for the `recovery` binary (`--update_package`, `--wipe-data`, and so on); and ❹ is a string describing the install stage of OTA packages that require multiple restarts, for example *2/3* if the installation requires three reboots. The last field ❺ is reserved and not used as of this writing.

Sideloading an OTA Package

Besides being downloaded by the main OS, an OTA package can be directly passed to the recovery from a host PC. In order to enable this update mode, the user must choose the *apply update from ADB* option from the recovery menu first. This starts a trimmed down version of the standard ADB daemon, which supports only the `sideload` command. Executing `adb sideload` *`OTA-package-file`* on the host transfers the OTA file to */tmp/update.zip* on the device and installs it (see "Applying the Update" on page 359).

OTA Signature Verification

As we learned in Chapter 3, OTA packages are code signed, with the signature applied over the whole file (unlike JAR and APK files, which include a separate signature for each file in the archive). When the OTA process is started from the main Android OS, the OTA package (ZIP file) is first verified using the `verifyPackage()` method of the `RecoverySystem` class. This method receives both the path to the OTA package and a ZIP file containing a list of X.509 certificates that are allowed to sign OTA updates as parameters. If the OTA package is signed with the private key corresponding to any of the certificates in the ZIP file, the OTA is considered valid and the system reboots into recovery in order to apply it. If no certificate ZIP file is specified, the system default, */system/etc/security/otacerts.zip*, is used.

The recovery verifies the OTA package that it is instructed to apply independently of the main OS in order to ensure that the OTA package has not been replaced before starting the recovery. The verification is performed with a set of public keys built into the recovery image. When building the recovery, these keys are extracted from the specified set of OTA signing certificates, converted to mincrypt format using the `DumpPublicKey` tool, and written to the */res/keys* file. When RSA is used as the signature algorithm, the keys are mincrypt's `RSAPublicKey` structures, serialized as C literals (as they would appear in a C source file), optionally preceded by a version identifier that specifies the hash used when signing the OTA package and the RSA key public exponent of the key. The *keys* file may look like Listing 13-4.

```
{64,0xc926ad21,{1795090719,...,3599964420},{3437017481,...,1175080310}},❶
v2 {64,0x8d5069fb,{393856717,...,2415439245},{197742251,...,1715989778}},❷
--snip--
```

Listing 13-4: Contents of the /res/keys file in the recovery OS

Here, the first line ❶ is a serialized version 1 key (implicit if a version identifier is not specified), which has a public exponent *e=3* and can be used to verify signatures created using SHA-1; the second line ❷ contains a version 2 key that has a public exponent *e=65537* and is also used with SHA-1 signatures. The currently supported signature algorithms are 2048-bit RSA with SHA-1 (key versions 1 and 2) or SHA-256 (key versions 3 and 4), and ECDSA with SHA-256 (key version 5, available in AOSP's mater branch) and 256-bit EC keys using the NIST P-256 curve.

Starting the System Update Process

If the signature of the OTA package verifies, the recovery applies the system update by executing the update command included in the OTA file. The update command is saved in the *META-INF/com/google/android/* directory of the recovery image as `update-binary` ❶, as shown in Listing 13-5.

```
.
|-- META-INF/
|   |-- CERT.RSA
|   |-- CERT.SF
|   |-- com/
|   |   |-- android/
|   |   |   |-- metadata
|   |   |   `-- otacert
|   |   `-- google/
|   |       `-- android/
|   |           |-- update-binary❶
|   |           `-- updater-script❷
|   `-- MANIFEST.MF
|-- patch/
|   |-- boot.img.p
|   `-- system/
|-- radio.img.p
|-- recovery/
|   |-- etc/
|   |   `-- install-recovery.sh
|   `-- recovery-from-boot.p
`-- system/
    |-- etc/
    |   |-- permissions/
    |   |   `-- com.google.android.ble.xml
    |   `-- security/
    |       `-- cacerts/
    |-- framework/
    `-- lib/
```

Listing 13-5: Contents of a system update OTA package

The recovery extracts `update-binary` from the OTA file to */tmp/update_binary* and starts it, passing it three parameters: the recovery API version (version 3 as of this writing); the file descriptor of a pipe that `update-binary` uses to communicate progress and messages back to the recovery; and the path to the OTA package. The *update-binary* process in turn extracts the updater script, included as *META-INF/com/google/android/updater-script* ❷ in the OTA package, and evaluates it. The updater script is written in a dedicated scripting language called *edify* (since version 1.6; previous versions used an older variant called *amend*). The edify language supports simple control structures such as `if` and `else`, and is extensible via functions, which can also act as control structures (by deciding which of their arguments to evaluate). The updater script includes a sequence of function calls that trigger the operations necessary to apply the update.

Applying the Update

The edify implementation defines and registers various functions that are used for copying, deleting, and patching files; formatting and mounting volumes; setting file permissions and SELinux labels; and more. Table 13-2 shows a summary of the most often used edify functions.

Table 13-2: Summary of Important edify Functions

Function Name	Description
`abort`	Aborts the install process with an error message.
`apply_patch`	Safely applies a binary patch. Ensures that the patched file has the expected hash value, before replacing the original. Can also patch disk partitions.
`apply_patch_check`	Checks if a file has the specified hash value.
`assert`	Checks if a condition is true.
`delete/delete_recursive`	Deletes a file/all files in a directory.
`file_getprop`	Gets a system property from the specified property file.
`format`	Formats a volume with the specified filesystem.
`getprop`	Gets a system property.
`mount`	Mounts a volume at the specified path.
`package_extract_dir`	Extracts the specified ZIP directory to a path on the filesystem.
`package_extract_file`	Extracts the specified ZIP file to a path on the filesystem or returns it as a blob.
`run_program`	Executes the specified program in a subprocess and waits for it to finish.
`set_metadata/set_metadata_recursive`	Sets the owner, group, permission bits, file capabilities, and SELinux label on file/all files in a directory.
`show_progress`	Reports back progress to the parent process.
`symlink`	Creates a symbolic link(s) to a target, deleting existing symbolic link files first.
`ui_print`	Sends a message back to the parent process.
`umount`	Unmounts a mounted volume.
`write_raw_image`	Writes a raw image to the specified disk partition.

Listing 13-6 shows the (abbreviated) contents of a typical system update edify script.

```
mount("ext4", "EMMC", "/dev/block/platform/msm_sdcc.1/by-name/system", "/system");
file_getprop("/system/build.prop", "ro.build.fingerprint") == "google/...:user/release-keys" ||
    file_getprop("/system/build.prop", "ro.build.fingerprint") == "google/...:user/release-keys" ||
    abort("Package expects build fingerprint of google/...:user/release-keys; this device has " +
    getprop("ro.build.fingerprint") + ".");
getprop("ro.product.device") == "hammerhead" ||
    abort("This package is for \"hammerhead\" devices; this is a \"" +
    getprop("ro.product.device") + "\".");❶
--snip--
apply_patch_check("/system/app/BasicDreams.apk", "f687...", "fdc5...") ||
    abort("\"/system/app/BasicDreams.apk\" has unexpected contents.");❷
set_progress(0.000063);
--snip--
apply_patch_check("EMMC:/dev/block/platform/msm_sdcc.1/by-name/boot:8835072:21...:8908800:a3...")
|| abort("\"EMMC:/dev/block/...\" has unexpected contents.");❸
--snip--
ui_print("Removing unneeded files...");
delete("/system/etc/permissions/com.google.android.ble.xml",
       --snip--
       "/system/recovery.img");❹
ui_print("Patching system files...");
apply_patch("/system/app/BasicDreams.apk", "-",
            f69d..., 32445,
            fdc5..., package_extract_file("patch/system/app/BasicDreams.apk.p"));❺
--snip--
ui_print("Patching boot image...");
apply_patch("EMMC:/dev/block/platform/msm_sdcc.1/by-name/boot:8835072:2109...:8908800:a3bd...",
            "-", a3bd..., 8908800,
            2109..., package_extract_file("patch/boot.img.p"));❻
--snip--
delete("/system/recovery-from-boot.p",
       "/system/etc/install-recovery.sh");
ui_print("Unpacking new recovery...");
package_extract_dir("recovery", "/system");❼
ui_print("Symlinks and permissions...");
set_metadata_recursive("/system", "uid", 0, "gid", 0, "dmode", 0755, "fmode", 0644,
                       "capabilities", 0x0, "selabel", "u:object_r:system_file:s0");❽
--snip--
ui_print("Patching radio...");
apply_patch("EMMC:/dev/block/platform/msm_sdcc.1/by-name/modem:43058688:7493...:46499328:52a...",
            "-", 52a5..., 46499328,
            7493..., package_extract_file("radio.img.p"));❾
--snip--
unmount("/system");❿
```

Listing 13-6: Contents of updater-script *in a full system update OTA package*

Copying and Patching Files

The updater script first mounts the *system* partition, then checks to see if the device model and its current build are what it expects ❶. This check is required because trying to install a system update over an incompatible build can leave a device in an unusable state. (This is often called a "soft brick," because it can usually be recovered by reflashing all partitions with a working build; a "hard brick" cannot be recovered.)

Because an OTA update usually does not contain complete system files, only binary patches against the previous version of each changed file (produced using `bsdiff`),[4] applying an update can succeed only if each file-to-be-patched is the same as the one used to produce the respective patch. To ensure this, the updater script checks that the hash value of each file-to-be-patched is one it expects using the `apply_patch_check` function ❷.

In addition to system files, the update process also patches partitions that don't contain a filesystem, such as the *boot* and *modem* partitions. To guarantee that patching such partitions will succeed, the updater script checks the contents of target partitions as well and aborts if they are not in the expected state ❸. When all system files and partitions have been verified, the updater script deletes unnecessary files, as well as files that will be replaced completely instead of being patched ❹. The script then goes on to patch all system files ❺ and partitions ❻. It then removes any previous recovery patches and unpacks the new recovery in */system/* ❼.

Setting File Ownership, Permissions, and Security Labels

The next step is to set the user, owner, permissions, and file capabilities of all created or patched files and directories using the `set_metadata_recursive` function ❽. As of version 4.3, Android supports SELinux (see Chapter 12), so all files must be properly labeled in order for access rules to be effective. That is why the `set_metadata_recursive` function has been extended to set the SELinux security label (the last parameter, *u:object_r:system_file:s0* in ❽) of files and directories.

Finishing the Update

Next, the updater script patches the device's baseband software ❾, which is typically stored in the *modem* partition. The final step of the script is to unmount the system partition ❿.

After the *update-binary* process exits, the recovery wipes the cache partition if it was started with the `-wipe_cache` option and copies the execution logs to */cache/recovery/* so that they are accessible from the main OS. Finally, if no errors are reported, the recovery clears the BCB and reboots into the main OS.

---

4. Colin Percival, "Binary diff/patch utility," *http://www.daemonology.net/bsdiff/*

If the update process is aborted due to an error, the recovery reports this to the user, and prompts them to reboot the device in order to try again. Because the BCB has not been cleared, the device automatically reboots in recovery mode, and the update process is started from scratch.

Updating the Recovery

If you examine the entire updater script in Listing 13-6 in detail, you'll notice that while it patches the *boot* ❻ and *modem* ❾ partitions and unpacks a patch for the *recovery* partition ❼ (which hosts the recovery OS), it does not apply the unpacked patch. This is by design. Because an update can be interrupted at any moment, the update process needs to be restarted from the same state the next time the device is powered on. If, for example, power is interrupted while writing to the *recovery* partition, updating the recovery OS would change that initial state and might leave the system in an unusable condition. Therefore, the recovery OS is updated from the main OS only when the main OS update has completed and the main OS boots successfully.

The update is triggered by the *flash_recovery* service in Android's *init.rc* file, as shown in Listing 13-7.

```
--snip--
service flash_recovery /system/etc/install-recovery.sh❶
    class main
    oneshot
--snip--
```

Listing 13-7: Definition of the flash_recovery *service in* init.rc

As you can see, this service simply starts the */system/etc/install-recovery.sh* shell script ❶. The shell script, along with a patch file for the recovery partition, is copied by the OTA updater script (❼ in Listing 13-6) if the recovery requires an update. The contents of *install-recovery.sh* might look like Listing 13-8.

```
#!/system/bin/sh
if ! applypatch -c EMMC:/dev/block/platform/msm_sdcc.1/by-name/recovery:9506816:3e90...; then❶
  log -t recovery "Installing new recovery image"
  applypatch -b /system/etc/recovery-resource.dat \
      EMMC:/dev/block/platform/msm_sdcc.1/by-name/boot:8908800:a3bd... \
      EMMC:/dev/block/platform/msm_sdcc.1/by-name/recovery \
      3e90... 9506816 a3bd...:/system/recovery-from-boot.p❷
else
  log -t recovery "Recovery image already installed"❸
fi
```

Listing 13-8: Contents of install-recovery.sh

The script uses the applypatch command to check whether the recovery OS needs to be patched by checking the hash value of the *recovery* partition ❶. If the hash of the device's *recovery* partition matches the hash of the version against which the patch was created, the script applies the patch ❷. If the recovery has already been updated or has an unknown hash, the script logs a message and exits ❸.

Custom Recoveries

A custom recovery is a recovery OS build created by a third party (not the device manufacturer). Because it is created by a third party, a custom recovery is not signed with the manufacturer's keys, and therefore a device's bootloader needs to be unlocked in order to boot or flash it. A custom recovery can be booted without installing it on the device with the `fastboot boot` *`custom-recovery.img`* command, or it may be permanently flashed using the `fastboot flash recovery` *`custom-recovery.img`* command.

A custom recovery provides advanced functionality that is typically not available in stock recoveries, such as full partition backup and restore, a root shell with a full set of device management utilities, support for mounting external USB devices, and so on. A custom recovery can also disable OTA package signature checking, which allows for installing third-party OS builds or modification, such as framework or theme customizations.

Various custom recoveries are available, but as of this writing, by far the most full-featured and actively maintained is the Team Win Recovery Project (TWRP).[5] It is based on the AOSP stock recovery and is also an open source project.[6] TWRP has a theme-able, touch screen interface that is very similar to the native Android UI. It supports encrypted partition backups, installing system updates from USB devices, and backup and restore to/from external devices, and it has an integrated file manager. The startup screen of TWRP version 2.7 is shown in Figure 13-5.

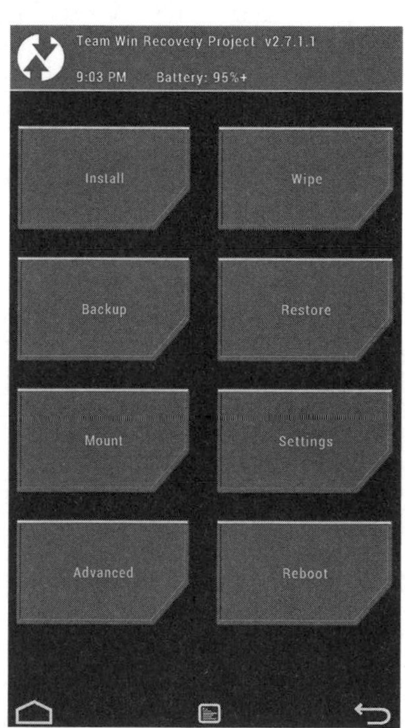

Figure 13-5: TWRP recovery startup screen

Like the stock AOSP recovery, custom recoveries can be controlled from the main OS. In addition to passing parameters via the */cache/recovery/command* file, custom recoveries usually allow some (or all) of their extended features to be triggered from the main OS. For example, TWRP supports a minimal scripting language, which

5. TeamWin, "TWRP 2.7," *http://teamw.in/project/twrp2/*

6. TeamWin, "Team Win Recovery Project (TWRP)," *https://github.com/TeamWin/Team-Win-Recovery-Project/*

describes what recovery actions should be executed upon booting the recovery. This allows Android apps to queue recovery commands via a convenient GUI interface. For example, requesting a compressed backup of the *boot*, *userdata*, and *system* partitions generates the script shown in Listing 13-9.

```
# cat /cache/recovery/openrecoveryscript
backup DSBOM 2014-12-14--01-54-59
```

Listing 13-9: TWRP backup script example

WARNING *Permanently flashing a custom recovery that has an option to ignore OTA package signatures might allow the system software of your device to be replaced and backdoored given brief physical access to the devices. Therefore, it is not recommended to flash a custom recovery on a device you use daily and which stores personal or sensitive information.*

Root Access

Android's security model applies the principle of least privilege and strives to isolate system and app processes from each other by running each process as a dedicated user. However, Android is also based on a Linux kernel, which implements a standard Unix-style DAC (unless SELinux is enabled; see Chapter 12).

One of the greatest shortcomings of this DAC security model is that a certain system user, typically called *root* (UID=0), also known as the *superuser*, is given absolute power over the system. Root can read, write, and change the permission bits of any file or directory; kill any process; mount and unmount volumes; and so on. While such unconstrained permissions are necessary for managing a traditional Linux system, having superuser access on an Android device allows one to effectively bypass Android's sandbox, and read or write the private files of any application.

Root access also allows changing the system configuration by modifying partitions that are designed to be read-only, starting or stopping system services at will, and removing or disabling core system applications. This can adversely affect the stability of a device, or even render it unusable, which is why root access is typically not allowed on production devices.

Furthermore, Android tries to limit the number of system processes that execute as root, because a programming error in any such process can open the doors to privilege escalation attacks, which could result in third-party applications gaining root access. With the deployment of SELinux in enforcing mode, processes are limited by the global security policy, and therefore compromising a root process does not necessarily grant unrestricted access to a device but could still allow access to sensitive data or allow modifying system behavior. Additionally, even a process constrained by SELinux could exploit a kernel vulnerability in order to circumvent the security policy or otherwise obtain unrestricted root access.

With all that said, root access could be very convenient for debugging or reverse engineering applications on development devices. Additionally, while allowing root access to third-party applications does compromise Android's security model, it also allows various system customizations that are typically not available on production devices to be performed.

Because one of Android's biggest selling points has always been its ease of customization, the demand for ever greater flexibility via modifying the core OS (also called *modding*), has always been high, especially during Android's early years. Besides customizing the system, having root access on an Android device allows for the implementation of applications that are not possible without modifying the framework and adding system services, such as firewalls, full device backup, network sharing, and so on.

In the following sections, we describe how root access is implemented in development (engineering) Android builds and custom Android builds (ROMs), and how it can be added to production builds. We then show how apps that require superuser access (typically called *root apps*) can request and use root privileges in order to execute processes as root.

Root Access on Engineering Builds

Android's build system can produce several build variants for a particular device that differ by the number of applications and utilities included, as well as by the values of several key system properties that modify system behavior. Some of these build variants allow root access from the Android shell, as we'll show in the following sections.

Starting ADB as Root

Commercial devices use the *user* build variant (the current build variant is set as the value of the *ro.build.type* system property), which doesn't include diagnostics and development tools, disables the ADB daemon by default, disallows debugging of applications that don't explicitly set the `debuggable` attribute to `true` in their manifests, and disallows root access via the shell. The *userdebug* build variant is very close to *user*, but it also includes some additional modules (those with the *debug* module tag), allows debugging of all apps, and enables ADB by default.

Engineering, or *eng*, builds include most available modules, allow debugging, enable ADB by default, and set the *ro.secure* system property to 0, which changes the behavior of the ADB daemon running on a device. When set to 1 (secure mode), the *adbd* process, which initially runs as root, drops all capabilities from its capability bounding set with the exception of `CAP_SETUID` and `CAP_SETGID` (which are required to implement the `run-as` utility). It then adds several supplementary GIDs that are required to access network interfaces, external storage, and system logs, and finally changes its UID and GID to `AID_SHELL` (UID=2000). On the other hand, when *ro.secure* is set to 0 (the default for engineering builds), the *adbd* daemon continues to run as root and has the full capability bounding set. Listing 13-10 shows the process IDs and capabilities for the *adbd* process on a *user* build.

```
$ getprop ro.build.type
user
$ getprop ro.secure
1
$ ps|grep adb
shell     200   1     4588   220   ffffffff 00000000 S /sbin/adbd
$ cat /proc/200/status
Name: adbd
State:      S (sleeping)
Tgid: 200
Pid:  200
Ppid: 1
TracerPid: 0
Uid:  2000  2000  2000  2000❶
Gid:  2000  2000  2000  2000❷
FDSize:     32
Groups:     1003 1004 1007 1011 1015 1028 3001 3002 3003 3006❸
--snip--
CapInh:     0000000000000000
CapPrm:     0000000000000000
CapEff:     0000000000000000
CapBnd:     fffffff0000000c0❹
--snip--
```

Listing 13-10: adbd process details on a user build

As you can see, the process's UID ❶ and GID ❷ are both set to 2000 (`AID_SHELL`), and the *adbd* process has a number of supplementary GIDs added ❸. Finally, the process's capability bounding set, which determines what capabilities child processes are allowed, is set to 0x0000000c0 (`CAP_SETUID|CAP_SETGID`) ❹. This capability setting guarantees that, on *user* builds, processes started from Android's shell are limited to the `CAP_SETUID` and `CAP_SETGID` capabilities, even if the executed binary has the SUID bit set, or its file capabilities permit additional privileges.

In contrast, on an *eng* or *userdebug* build, the ADB daemon can execute as root, as shown in Listing 13-11.

```
# getprop ro.build.type
userdebug❶
# getprop ro.secure
1❷
# ps|grep adb
root      19979 1     4656   264   ffffffff 0001fd1c S /sbin/adbd
root@maguro:/ # cat /proc/19979/status
Name: adbd
State:      S (sleeping)
Tgid: 19979
Pid:  19979
Ppid: 1
TracerPid:  0
Uid:  0     0     0     0❸
Gid:  0     0     0     0❹
FDSize:     256
```

```
Groups:❺
--snip--
CapInh:       0000000000000000
CapPrm:       ffffffffffffffff❻
CapEff:       ffffffffffffffff❼
CapBnd:       ffffffffffffffff❽
--snip--
```

Listing 13-11: adbd *process details on an* eng *build*

Here, the *adbd* process runs with UID ❸ and GID ❹ 0 (root), has no supplementary groups ❺, and has the full set of Linux capabilities (❻, ❼, and ❽). However, as you can see at ❷, the *ro.secure* system property is set to 1, which suggests that *adbd* should not be running as root.

While the ADB daemon does drop its root privileges on *userdebug* builds (as in this example, ❶), it can be manually restarted in insecure mode by issuing the `adb root` command from a host, as shown in Listing 13-12.

```
$ adb shell id
uid=2000(shell) gid=2000(shell)❶ groups=1003(graphics),1004(input),1007
(log),1009(mount),1011(adb),1015(sdcard_rw),1028(sdcard_r),3001(net_bt_
admin),3002(net_bt),3003(inet),3006(net_bw_stats) context=u:r:shell:s0
$ adb root❷
restarting adbd as root
$ adb shell ps|grep adb
root      2734  1     4644   216   ffffffff 0001fbec R /sbin/adbd❸
$ adb shell id
uid=0(root) gid=0(root) context=u:r:shell:s0❹
```

Listing 13-12: Restarting adbd *as root on* userdebug *builds*

Here, the *adbd* daemon is initially running as *shell* (UID=2000), and any shells started from the host also have UID=2000 and GID=2000 ❶. Issuing the `adb root` command ❷ (which internally sets the *service.adb.root* system property to 1) restarts the ADB daemon as root ❸, and any subsequently started shells have UID and GUID=0 ❹.

NOTE *Because this particular device has SELinux enabled, even though the UID and GID of the shell change, its security context (security label) stays the same:* u:r:shell:s0 *in both ❶ and ❹. Therefore, even after obtaining a root shell via ADB, all processes started from the shell are still bound by the permissions granted to the* shell *domain (unless allowed to transition to another domain by the MAC policy; see Chapter 12 for details). In practice, as of Android 4.4, the* shell *domain is unconfined, so when running as root, processes in this domain are allowed almost full control over the device.*

Using the su Command

On *userdebug* builds, root access can also be obtained without restarting ADB as root. This can be accomplished using the su (short for *substitute user*, also referred to as *switch user* and *superuser*) command, which is installed with the SUID bit set, thus allowing calling processes to obtain a root shell or execute a command as the specified UID (including UID=0). The default su implementation is very basic and only allows the *root* and *shell* users to use it, as shown in Listing 13-13.

```
int main(int argc, char **argv)
{
    --snip--
    myuid = getuid();
    if (myuid != AID_ROOT && myuid != AID_SHELL) {❶
        fprintf(stderr,"su: uid %d not allowed to su\n", myuid);
        return 1;
    }

    if(argc < 2) {
        uid = gid = 0;❷
    } else {
      --snip--
    }

    if(setgid(gid) || setuid(uid)) {❸
        fprintf(stderr,"su: permission denied\n");
        return 1;
    }

    --snip--

    execlp("/system/bin/sh", "sh", NULL);❹

    fprintf(stderr, "su: exec failed\n");
    return 1;
}
```

Listing 13-13: Default su *implementation for* userdebug *builds*

The main function first checks whether the calling UID is AID_ROOT (0) or AID_SHELL (2000) ❶, and exits if called by a user with a different UID. It then sets the process UID and GID to 0 (❷ and ❸), and finally starts the Android shell ❹. Any commands executed from this shell inherit its privileges by default, thus allowing superuser access to the device.

Root Access on Production Builds

As we learned in "Root Access on Engineering Builds" on page 365, commercial Android devices are usually based on the *user* build variant. This means that the ADB daemon is running as the *shell* user, and no su command is installed on the device.

This is a secure configuration, and most users should be able to achieve their device configuration and customization tasks with the tools provided by the platform, or with third-party applications such as custom launchers, keyboards, or VPN clients. However, operations that modify the look and feel or core configuration of Android are not possible, and neither is low-level access to the underlying Linux OS. Such operations can only be performed by running certain commands with root privileges, which is why many power users seek to enable root access on their devices.

Obtaining root access on an Android device is commonly known as *rooting* and can be fairly simple on devices that have an unlockable bootloader or nearly impossible on devices that don't allow bootloader unlocking and take additional measures to prevent system partition modifications. In the next sections, we describe the typical rooting process and introduce some of the most popular "superuser" apps that enable and manage root access.

Rooting by Changing the boot or system Image

On some Android devices, given an unlocked bootloader, a *user* build can easily be turned into an engineering or *userdebug* build by simply flashing a new boot image (often called a *kernel*, or *custom kernel*), which changes the values of the *ro.secure* and *ro.debuggable* system properties. Changing these properties allows the ADB daemon to execute as root and enables root access via the Android shell, as described in"Root Access on Engineering Builds" on page 365. However, most current Android *user* builds disable this behavior at compile time (by not defining the `ALLOW_ADBD_ROOT` macro) and the values of the *ro.secure* and *ro.debuggable* system properties are ignored by the *adbd* daemon.

Another way to enable root access is to unpack the system image, add a SUID `su` binary or a similar utility, and overwrite the *system* partition with the new system image. This would typically allow root access not only from the shell, but from third-party applications as well. However, several security enhancements in Android 4.3[7] and later versions disallow apps from executing SUID programs by dropping all capabilities from the bounding set of Zygote-spawned processes, and mounting the *system* partition with the `nosetuid` flag.

Additionally, on Android versions that set SELinux to enforcing mode, executing a process with root privileges does not typically change its security context, and such a process is still limited by the MAC policy. For these reasons, enabling root access on a recent Android version may not be as simple as changing a few system properties or copying a SUID binary to the device. Of course, replacing the *boot* or *system* image allows SELinux to be disabled and any security mitigation to be reverted, thus relaxing the device's security level and enabling root access. However, such a radical approach is not unlike replacing the whole OS and may prevent the device from receiving system updates from the device manufacturer. This is undesirable in most cases, and several root methods that try to coexist with the stock OS of the device have been developed.

---

7. Google, "Security Enhancements in Android 4.3," *http://source.android.com/devices/tech/security/enhancements43.html*

Rooting by Flashing an OTA Package

An OTA package can add or modify system files, without replacing the whole OS image, and is therefore a good candidate for adding root access to a device. Most popular superuser apps are distributed as a combination of an OTA package, which needs to be installed once, and a companion manager application, which can be updated online.

SuperSU

We'll use the SuperSU OTA package[8] and app[9] (developed by Jorrit "Chainfire" Jongma) to demonstrate how this approach works. SuperSU is currently the most popular superuser application and is actively maintained, keeping in step with the latest modifications to the Android platform. The SuperSU OTA package is similar in structure to a full system update package but contains only a small number of files, as shown in Listing 13-14.

```
.
|-- arm/❶
|   |-- chattr
|   |-- chattr.pie
|   `-- su
|-- common/
|   |-- 99SuperSUDaemon❷
|   |-- install-recovery.sh❸
|   `-- Superuser.apk❹
|-- META-INF/
|   |-- CERT.RSA
|   |-- CERT.SF
|   |-- com/
|   |   `-- google/
|   |       `-- android/
|   |           |-- update-binary❺
|   |           `-- updater-script❻
|   `-- MANIFEST.MF
`-- x86/❼
    |-- chattr
    |-- chattr.pie
    `-- su
```

Listing 13-14: Contents of the SuperSU OTA package

The package contains a few native binaries compiled for the ARM ❶ and x86 ❼ platforms, scripts for starting and installing the SuperSU daemon (❷ and ❸), the APK file of the management GUI application ❹, and two updater scripts (❺ and ❻) that apply the OTA package.

In order to understand how SuperSU enables root access, we need to first examine its install process. To do so, let's analyze the contents of the

8. Jorrit "Chainfire" Jongma, "CF-Root download page," *http://download.chainfire.eu/supersu/*

9. Jorrit "Chainfire" Jongma, "Google Play Apps: SuperSU," *https://play.google.com/store/apps/details?id=eu.chainfire.supersu&hl=en*

update-binary script ❺, shown in Listing 13-15. (SuperSU uses a regular shell script instead of a native binary, so updater-script is simply a placeholder.)

```
#!/sbin/sh
--snip--
ui_print "- Mounting /system, /data and rootfs"❶
mount /system
mount /data
mount -o rw,remount /system
--snip--
mount -o rw,remount /
--snip--
ui_print "- Extracting files"❷
cd /tmp
mkdir supersu
cd supersu
unzip -o "$ZIP"
--snip--
ui_print "- Placing files"
mkdir /system/bin/.ext
cp $BIN/su /system/xbin/daemonsu❸
cp $BIN/su /system/xbin/su
--snip--
cp $COM/Superuser.apk /system/app/Superuser.apk❹
cp $COM/install-recovery.sh /system/etc/install-recovery.sh❺
cp $COM/99SuperSUDaemon /system/etc/init.d/99SuperSUDaemon
echo 1 > /system/etc/.installed_su_daemon
--snip--
ui_print "- Setting permissions"
set_perm 0 0 0777 /system/bin/.ext❻
set_perm 0 0 $SUMOD /system/bin/.ext/.su
set_perm 0 0 $SUMOD /system/xbin/su
--snip--
set_perm 0 0 0755 /system/xbin/daemonsu
--snip--
ch_con /system/bin/.ext/.su❼
ch_con /system/xbin/su
--snip--
ch_con /system/xbin/daemonsu
--snip--
ui_print "- Post-installation script"
/system/xbin/su --install❽

ui_print "- Unmounting /system and /data"❾
umount /system
umount /data

ui_print "- Done !"
exit 0
```

Listing 13-15: SuperSU OTA install script

The update script first mounts the *rootfs* filesystem and the *system* and *userdata* partitions in read-write mode ❶, and then it extracts ❷ and copies the included files to their intended locations on the filesystem. The su and daemonsu native binaries ❸ are copied to */system/xbin/*, which is the usual location of extra native binaries (binaries that are not necessary for running the Android OS). The root access management application is copied to */system/app/* ❹ and is automatically installed by the package manager when the device reboots. Next, the update script copies the *install-recovery.sh* script to */system/etc/* ❺.

NOTE *As discussed in "Updating the Recovery" on page 362, this script is typically used to update the recovery image from the main OS, so you might be wondering why the SuperSU install is trying to update the recovery of the device. SuperSU uses this script to start some of its components at boot time, which we'll discuss shortly.*

The next step of the OTA package install process is to set the permissions ❻ and SELinux security labels ❼ of the installed binaries (ch_con is a shell function that calls the chcon SELinux utility and sets the *u:object_r:system_file:s0* label). Finally, the script calls the su command with the --install option ❽ in order to perform some post-install initialization, and then unmounts */system* and */data* ❾. When the script exits successfully, the recovery reboots the device into the main Android OS.

How SuperSU Is Initialized

To understand how SuperSU is initialized, let's look at the contents of the *install-recovery.sh* script (see Listing 13-16, with comments omitted), which is automatically executed by init on boot.

```
#!/system/bin/sh
/system/xbin/daemonsu --auto-daemon &❶

/system/etc/install-recovery-2.sh❷
```

Listing 13-16: Contents of SuperSU's install-recovery.sh *script*

The script first executes the daemonsu binary ❶, which starts a daemon process with root privileges. The next step executes the *install-recovery-2.sh* script ❷, which may be used to perform additional initialization, necessary for other root apps. Using a daemon in order to allow apps to execute code with root privileges is required in Android 4.3 and later, because all apps (which are forked from *zygote*) have their capability bounding set zeroed out, thus preventing them from executing privileged operations, even if they manage to start a process as root. Additionally, as of Android 4.4, SELinux is in enforcing mode, so any processes started by an application inherit its security context (typically *untrusted_app*), and therefore are subject to the same MAC restrictions as the app itself.

SuperSU gets around these security restrictions by having apps use the su binary to execute commands as root, which in turn pipes those commands via a Unix domain socket to the *daemonsu* daemon, which ultimately executes the received commands as root within the *u:r:init:s0* SELinux context. The processes in play are illustrated in Listing 13-17.

```
$ ps -Z
LABEL                       USER      PID   PPID  NAME
u:r:init:s0                 root      1     0     /init❶
--snip--
u:r:zygote:s0               root      187   1     zygote❷
--snip--
u:r:init:s0                 root      209   1     daemonsu:mount:master❸
u:r:init:s0                 root      210   209   daemonsu:master❹
--snip--
u:r:init:s0                 root      3969  210   daemonsu:10292❺
--snip--
u:r:untrusted_app:s0        u0_a292   13637 187   com.example.app❻
u:r:untrusted_app:s0        u0_a209   15256 187   eu.chainfire.supersu❼
--snip--
u:r:untrusted_app:s0        u0_a292   16831 13637 su❽
u:r:init:s0                 root      16835 3969  /system/bin/sleep❾
```

Listing 13-17: Processes started when an app requests root access via SuperSU

Here, the `com.example.app` app ❻ (whose parent process is *zygote* ❷) requests root access by passing a command to the `su` binary using its `-c` option. As you can see, the `su` process ❽ executes as the same user (*u0_a292*, UID=10292) and in the same SELinux domain (*untrusted_app*) as the requesting app. However, the process ❾ of the command the app requested to be executed as root (`sleep` in this example) indeed executes as root in the *init* SELinux domain (security context *u:r:init:s0*). If we trace its parent PID (PPID, in the fourth column), we find that the *sleep* process is started by the *daemonsu:10292* process ❺, which is a *daemonsu* instance dedicated to our example app (with UID=10292). The *daemonsu:10292* process ❺ inherits its *init* SELinux domain from the *daemonsu:master* instance ❹, which is in turn started by the first *daemonsu* instance ❸. This is the instance started via the *install-recovery.sh* script (see Listing 13-16), and it runs within the domain of its parent—the *init* process ❶ (PID=1).

The *eu.chainfire.supersu* process ❼ belongs to the SuperSU management application, which shows the root access grant dialog shown in Figure 13-6.

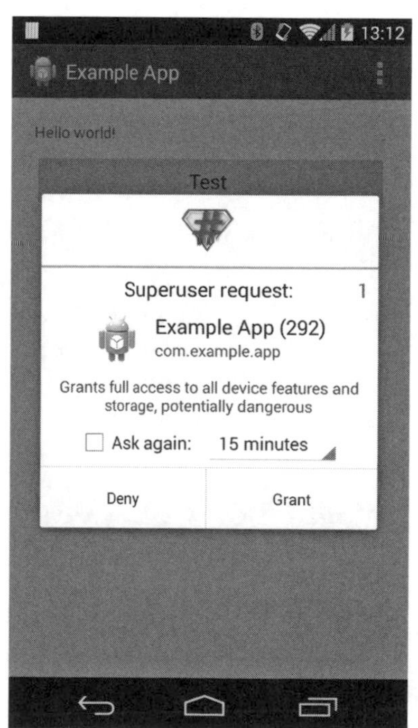

Figure 13-6: SuperSU root access request grant dialog

Superuser access can be granted one time only, for a certain period of time, or permanently. SuperSU keeps an internal whitelist of apps that have been granted root access and does not show the grant dialog if the requesting app is already in the whitelist.

NOTE *SuperSU has a companion library,* libsuperuser,[10] *which makes it easier to write root apps by providing Java wrappers for the different patterns of calling the* su *binary. The author of SuperSU also provides a comprehensive guide to writing root apps called* How-To SU.[11]

Root Access on Custom ROMs

Custom ROMs that provide root access don't have to go through *install-recovery.sh* in order to start their superuser daemon (equivalent to SuperSU's *daemonsu*) because they can customize the startup process at will. For example, the popular CyanogenMod open source Android distribution starts its *su* daemon from *init.superuser.rc*, as shown in Listing 13-18.

```
service su_daemon /system/xbin/su --daemon❶
    oneshot

on property:persist.sys.root_access=0❷
    stop su_daemon

on property:persist.sys.root_access=2❸
    stop su_daemon

on property:persist.sys.root_access=1❹
    start su_daemon

on property:persist.sys.root_access=3❺
    start su_daemon
```

Listing 13-18: Startup script for the su *daemon in CyanogenMod*

This *init* script defines the *su_daemon* service ❶, which can be started or stopped by changing the value of the *persist.sys.root_access* persistent system property (❷ through ❺). The value of this property also determines whether root access should be granted only to apps, ADB shells, or both. Root access is disabled by default and can be configured via CyanogenMod's Development options, as shown in Figure 13-7.

WARNING *While SuperSU and custom ROMs that allow root access take certain measures to regulate what apps are allowed to execute commands as root (usually by adding them to a whitelist), an implementation flaw could allow apps to bypass these measures and obtain root access without user confirmation. Therefore, root access should be disabled on everyday-use devices and used only when necessary for development or debugging.*

10. Jorrit "Chainfire" Jongma, libsuperuser, *https://github.com/Chainfire/libsuperuser/*

11. Jorrit "Chainfire" Jongma, "How-To SU Guidelines for problem-free su usage," *http://su.chainfire.eu/*

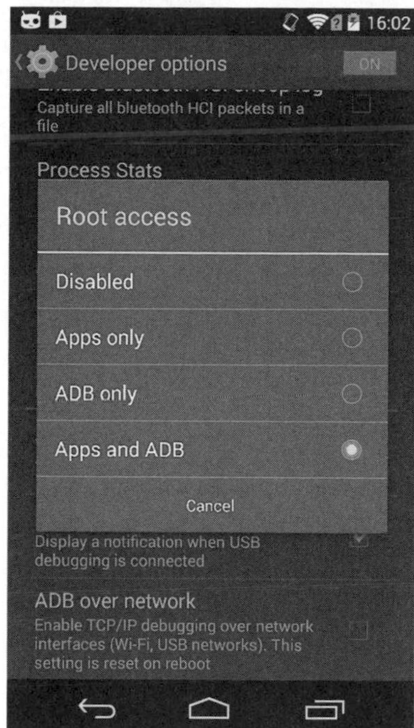

Figure 13-7: CyanogenMod root access options

Rooting via Exploits

On production devices that don't have an unlockable bootloader, root access can be obtained by exploiting a privilege escalation vulnerability, which allows an app or shell process to start a root shell (also called *soft root*) and modify the system. The exploits are typically packaged into "one-click" apps or scripts, which try to persist root access by installing a su binary or modifying system configuration. For example, the so-called towelroot exploit (which is distributed as an Android app) takes advantage of a vulnerability in the Linux kernel (CVE-2014-3153) to obtain root access and installs SuperSU in order to persist it. (Root access can also be persisted by overwriting the *recovery* partition with a custom recovery, thus allowing the installation of arbitrary software, including superuser applications. However, some devices have additional protections that prevent modifications to the *boot*, *system*, and *recovery* partitions, so permanent root access might not be possible.)

NOTE *See Chapter 3 of the* Android Hacker's Handbook *(Wiley, 2014) for a detailed description of the major privilege-escalation vulnerabilities that have been used to obtain root access in various Android versions. Chapter 12 of the same book introduces the main exploit-mitigation techniques that have been implemented in Android in order to prevent privilege-escalation attacks and generally harden the system.*

Summary

In order to allow for updating the system software or returning a device to its factory state, Android devices allow unrestricted, low-level access to their storage via the bootloader. The bootloader typically implements a management protocol, usually fastboot, that allows for transferring and flashing partition images from a host machine. Bootloaders on production devices are usually locked and allow flashing only of signed images. However, most bootloaders can be unlocked, thus allowing flashing images from third parties.

Android uses a dedicated partition to store a second, minimal OS, called a recovery, which is used to apply OTA update packages or clear all data on the device. Like bootloaders, recoveries on production devices typically allow applying only those OTA packages signed by the device manufacturer. If the bootloader is unlocked, a custom recovery, which allows installing updates signed by third parties or completely forgoes signature verification, can be booted or permanently installed.

Engineering or debug builds of Android allow root access via the Android shell, but root access is typically disabled on production devices. Root access on such devices can be enabled by installing a third-party OTA package that includes a "superuser" daemon and a companion application that allow controlled root access to applications. Third-party Android builds (ROMs) typically allow root access out of the box, although it can also be disabled via the system settings interface.

INDEX

B

C

E

F

G

H

I

J

K

N

Q

R

S

T

U

V

W

X

Z

Android Security Internals is set in New Baskerville, Futura, TheSansMono Condensed, and Dogma. The book was printed and bound by Lake Book Manufacturing in Melrose Park, Illinois. The paper is 60# Husky Opaque Offset Smooth, which is certified by the Sustainable Forestry Initiative (SFI).

The book uses a layflat binding, in which the pages are bound together with a cold-set, flexible glue and the first and last pages of the resulting book block are attached to the cover. The cover is not actually glued to the book's spine, and when open, the book lies flat and the spine doesn't crack.